Micah Laaker

DISCARD

SAMS
SAMS
Teach Yourself
SVG
in 24 Hours

SAMS

201 West 103rd St., Indianapolis, Indiana, 46290 USA

Sams Teach Yourself SVG in 24 Hours
Copyright © 2002 by Sams Publishing

International Standard Book Number: 0-672-32290-0

Library of Congress Catalog Card Number: 2001092347

Printed in the United States of America

First Printing: February 2002

04   03   02   4   3   2   1

Trademarks

Warning and Disclaimer

ACQUISITIONS EDITORS
Patricia Barnes
Betsy Brown

DEVELOPMENT EDITORS
Heather Goodell
Jill Hayden

MANAGING EDITOR
Charlotte Clapp

PRODUCTION EDITOR
Theodore Young, Jr.
(Publication Services, Inc.)

COPY EDITOR
Michael Kopp
(Publication Services, Inc.)

INDEXER
Richard Bronson
(Publication Services, Inc.)

PROOFREADER
Phil Hamer
(Publication Services, Inc.)

TECHNICAL EDITORS
Andrew Watt
Tobias Reif

TEAM COORDINATOR
Amy Patton

MEDIA DEVELOPER
Dan Scherf

INTERIOR DESIGNER
Gary Adair

COVER DESIGNER
Aren Howell

PAGE LAYOUT
Jennifer Faaborg
Michael Tarleton
Jim Torbit
Jessica Vonasch
(Publication Services, Inc.)

Contents at a Glance

Contents

About the Author

MICAH LAAKER is an award-winning graphic designer and illustrator in New York. In addition to writing, he is focused on finding effective communications solutions across multiple media.

Micah was instrumental in the founding and operations of the research & development department at Iguana Studios, a leading New York–based creative development firm. With Iguana's resources and Adobe Systems, Inc.'s support, he coordinated the development of the first commercial SVG project: the redesign of BattleBots.com.

Supplementing this development, Micah has authored and published a series of documents detailing practical applications of Scalable Vector Graphics, guest-lectured university classes and community groups concerning online vector graphic technologies, and created SVGnow.com, which he now operates.

Micah has won numerous awards for both creative and Web development, including the 2001 Industrial Design Society of America's Industrial Design Excellence Gold Award and a 2000 London International Advertising Award. He has lectured on new media topics and has served repeatedly as a judge for the annual New York Festivals Award committee. His corporate and entertainment clients have included Disney Channel, Sprint PCS, Lockheed Martin, and Adobe Systems.

Micah can be reached online at www.laaker.com and micah@laaker.com.

Dedication

This book is dedicated to both my close and my extended family, especially the Rev. Dr. Damon, Mary, and Amanda Laaker; Sarah and Tom Emery; Aaron Steckelberg, and Carrie Patton. Their love, strength, and support ensured that I saw this project (and all before it) through till the end, and they have never once wavered in supporting my every effort.

To truly express my gratitude for such a blessing is impossible. As one attempt, though, all of the author's proceeds from the book after taxes are being donated to the Rev. Dr. Damon and Mary Laaker Scholarship Fund.

Acknowledgments

This very book would never have been possible without the following factors:

- Close friends that have provided a much-needed alternative to thinking about technology and are ever a creative inspiration.

- The management and development team at Iguana Studios, a former NY-based Web development firm, that enthusiastically supported our research & development efforts.

- Andrew Watt and Tobias Rief, the technical editors of this book. These gentlemen worked unbelievably hard to ensure that what you are about to read is correct, useful, and informative. Their knowledge of SVG is tremendous, and anyone interested in SVG should not hesitate to visit their sites. Andrew operates both www.svgspider.com and www.xmml.com, and Tobias operates www.pinkjuice.com/svg/.

- Michael Morrison, Jim Moore, and Ben Strawbridge, who contributed their expertise to explain how JavaScript can be used to enhance SVG.

- The SVG team at Adobe (especially Andrew Watanabe, Michael Bierman, and Steve Snell), who have patiently answered our questions, thoughtfully listened to our feedback, and tirelessly worked to make SVG a very real phenomenon in the present.

- Jay Vidheecharoen of Red Eye Type (www.redeyetype.com), who so generously offered some of his exceptional custom typefaces to be made freely available to the SVG development community.

- The team at Sams Publishing, including Pat Barnes, Betsy Brown, Jennifer Kost-Barker, Jill Hayden, and Heather Goodell, who had both the foresight to see the value in such a book and the determination to help it see the light of day.

- And finally, the readers of Laaker.com, who truly make writing a joyful process.

Tell Us What You Think!

As the reader of this book, *you* are our most important critic and commentator. We value your opinion and want to know what we're doing right, what we could do better, what areas you'd like to see us publish in, and any other words of wisdom you're willing to pass our way.

You can e-mail or write me directly to let me know what you did or didn't like about this book—as well as what we can do to make our books stronger.

Please note that I cannot help you with technical problems related to the topic of this book, and that, due to the high volume of mail I receive, I might not be able to reply to every message.

When you write, please be sure to include this book's title and author as well as your name and phone or fax number. I will carefully review your comments and share them with the author and editors who worked on the book.

E-mail: webdev@samspublishing.com

Mail: Mark Taber
            Associate Publisher
            Sams Publishing
            201 West 103rd Street
            Indianapolis, IN 46290 USA

Introduction

SVG is not an application. There are no "quick keys" or drop-down menus, and it doesn't come neatly packaged with a tutorial at your local computer store. Rather, SVG is a markup language that has thus far existed with only a technical "recommendation" that outlines the functions of all its code—the W3C's *Scalable Vector Graphics (SVG) 1.0 Specification.*

Though that document is of a tremendous value to any developer using the technology (and hopefully this means you in 24 hours), it provides little practical instruction to the beginner.

That's where this book comes into play.

Who Should Read This Book

This book assumes that you are reading this with little knowledge of SVG before beginning. As such, this book will provide you with conceptual overviews of the technology, step-by-step instruction, and, most importantly, practical application of the technology. It also will assuredly provide you with strong selling points on the technology.

Your comfort with this technology, and many of its related concepts, will be greatly increased if you have already produced Web content. If you understand HTML, you will have a basic knowledge of how a markup language works; as SVG is also a markup language, the structure of SVG will seem familiar. Knowledge of XML will surely be helpful, as SVG is an XML language and consequently follows the structure and syntax of this technology. Other technologies, such as SMIL, JavaScript, and CSS, are used in various ways to define SVG content, and any experience with them may help you create more advanced graphics. Aside from JavaScript, this book will provide you with enough information about these technologies to create SVG artwork. To advance your understanding, you may consider investigating these technologies after you finish this book. SVG's ability to work easily with other technologies is one of its many strong points.

Lastly, SVG is a language for defining graphics. Though SVG has a technical side, its purpose is to define visual appearance. Your experience with design theory and your ability to translate ideas into visual expression will directly impact your ability to create impressive visual graphics (in SVG or otherwise) on your own. However, if you do not have such inclinations, you needn't put this book down; visual examples are already defined and illustrated, allowing you to learn the technical aspects of the technology without having to come up with your own artwork for each lesson. Furthermore, this book will define how to accomplish certain visual effects common to WYSIWYG graphics tools (such as Adobe Illustrator, Corel Draw, and so on). These effects are illustrated in this book's figures, in case you are unfamiliar with their appearance and vocabulary.

How This Book Is Organized

This book is organized into 24 chapters; each chapter contains a series of lessons that were created to take roughly one hour to read and complete. Nearly every hour's lessons relate in some form to your construction of a completed piece that will be the culmination of this book. With the knowledge that each lesson works towards a larger goal, you will hopefully remain motivated towards completing the example.

The book is organized into a series of parts:

- SVG Fundamentals—Understanding the syntax, structure, and basic elements of the technology is the first step to using SVG. This section will explain the environment and rules, as well as basic drawing commands.

- Manipulating SVG—Although the previous section explains how to create code and shapes, this section explains how to affect their appearance. Applying fills, strokes, and filters, as well as symbols, you will begin to see your artwork take shape.

- Bringing SVG to Life—SVG is more than flat, non-moving imagery. This section will teach you the basics of animation and interaction (such as buttons and rollovers).

- Text and Typography—SVG's ability to control the appearance and manipulation of letterforms separates this technology from most of its peers. These chapters will cover font, size, alignment, and style application, as well as font creation.

- Using JavaScript to Unleash SVG—SVG, though an amazing technology, cannot accomplish every imaginable interaction and animation. These chapters will provide a series of examples that illustrate SVG's ability to utilize JavaScript enhancements in its code.

- SVG Mastery—This final group of chapters covers more complex concepts that will enhance your ability to create SVG: organization, optimization, WYSIWYG SVG creation, SVG resources, and common problems. This section also contains the book's complete example, with its code detailed line-by-line.

The 24 hours are followed by an appendix, which provides you with further reference material. Once finished with all the hours' examples, you will not only have an impressive-looking example of the technology, but you also will have become truly knowledgeable in the fundamental concepts and application of SVG.

As many of the concepts and lessons of this book are dependent on information from previous chapters, you are strongly encouraged to read this book in the order the chapters are arranged. If you are looking for a fast track to learning the basic concepts, you can skip to Hour 4, "Document Layout," and work through Hour 17, "Typefaces." The chapters preceding Hour 4 detail the requirements of the technology, and the chapters following Hour 17 discuss more advanced concepts detailing how to enhance your code and content.

Though this book cannot serve as the one-and-definitive guide to the technology, it *will* serve as a strong introduction to the technology. By following all the examples in their order, you will significantly reduce your need to look elsewhere for any questions that may arise, as you will likely find their answers in a previous chapter.

This book will not teach you everything about SVG, but it will teach you everything you need to know to get started developing SVG.

With that said, it's time to start learning. On to Hour 1, "Getting Started with SVG."

PART I
SVG Fundamentals

Hour

Hour 1

Getting Started with SVG

SVG is an acronym for *Scalable Vector Graphics*, a language created by the World Wide Web Consortium (W3C) to handle vector graphic display and animation in XML. Because of its development in the W3C, SVG is an open, standards-based solution for vector graphics.

SVG is an entirely text-based language; its functions and content are never hidden from authors or users. As such, SVG is editable in text editors, just like HTML, and its source code is easily viewable. Even better, element tags are often in plain English; for instance, a circle is described in code as `<circle/>`.

Because SVG is a vector graphic technology, it is resolution independent. This means your content does not visually suffer when scaled to extremely large sizes(or even smaller sizes). Also due to its vector nature, SVG files can be quite small in file size when designed with the technology's strengths in mind. A considerable amount of vector imagery can be stored using a fraction of the disk space required for a comparable high-quality raster (pixel-based) image. To further reduce file size, SVG supports GZIP compression, an industry standard for file compression. (You can learn more about GZIP compression independently at `http://www.gzip.org/`.) Once you have finished coding an SVG file, you can GZIP the document, allowing even smaller file sizes. Any conformant SVG viewer will be able to display the more compact SVG format (known as SVGZ).

SVG gives developers an amazing level of control over screen appearance compared with other Web and onscreen technologies. Supporting alpha channel transparency, smooth gradients, anti-aliased selectable text, and Photoshop-like effects, SVG was designed from the ground up to answer the design community's needs for an interactive graphics technology. Furthermore, SVG supports animation, interactivity, control over raster imagery, and pixel-precise layouts, allowing SVG to compete against existing, formidable Web technologies.

SVG works hand-in-hand with other technologies. Developed by the W3C, SVG was guaranteed thoughtful consideration toward interoperability with other Web technologies. SVG can exist on its own, be nested within an XML document from within another XML namespace, be referenced from HTML, utilize JavaScript and CSS, display JPEGs, and much, much more.

In this hour, you will learn the following:

- Advantages and disadvantages of using SVG
- What SVG offers designers and developers

Advantages of Using SVG

SVG offers designers and developers alike an amazing level of control for both the appearance and function of their graphics.

- **Easy editing**

  SVG files are easily editable, allowing quick access and precise control over the presentation of imagery. Unlike SWF binaries (the file format for Macromedia's Flash), SVG exists as raw, editable code. This basic nature of SVG has two distinct advantages:

  1. **SVG is compatible with other technologies.**

     SVG works together with SMIL (Synchronized Multimedia Integration Language), CSS, JavaScript, and other technologies. This ability allows SVG to leverage these technologies to its own advantage, using the best features of other suites to enhance its own product. For instance, rather than forcing developers to learn a whole new method of defining object style, SVG can utilize CSS. This not only extends SVG's capabilities, but also reduces the learning curve developers face when exploring this new technology.

2. **Editable code decreases the impact a software package's limitations may have on development.**
   Anyone who has used a WYSIWYG HTML editor is well aware of the limitations a particular software implementation may impose on development. By retaining an editable, easy-to-read format, SVG can be finessed by a developer regardless of the origination of the file—whether from a software export or from a fellow developer.

- **Searchable content**
  Because the graphics are code-based, SVG content is fully searchable. As opposed to other graphic formats where your textual content is embedded in a binary file, or converted into a graphical representation of text, SVG content is housed within the code (just like HTML), allowing a deep search through your graphic's contents. For instance, you could search for "18th Street," and be taken to that specific location on an SVG map.

- **Localization**
  Because content is defined by text, imagery and text can be converted to different languages more efficiently than with other technologies. For instance, one graphic file can serve as a visual template for English, German, and French versions of the same graphic!

- **Global styling**
  Graphical style can be applied and changed globally, allowing an entire suite of graphics, or even a Web site, to be visually altered simply by changing one file.

- **Open standard**
  Additional support and functionality can be easily added by harnessing XML's DTD (document type definition) and namespace technology. For instance, with certain SVG viewers you can add audio and graphing features by incorporating other technologies via an SML namespace reference. (It is important to note that either the viewer or accompanying plug-ins must be able to handle the additional features, as the SVG viewers will likely handle only SVG rendering.)

- **Bitmap effects on vectors**
  You can apply real-time Photoshop-like effects to your SVG artwork using filter effects. SVG has a series of highly customizable filters that can be applied to both vector and raster content on the display side. This allows you to have preset filters applied to dynamic content as it is passed to the SVG file. Thus, you can apply a drop shadow effect on dynamic text without having to convert that text into a raster image (such as a GIF).

- **Data handling**
  SVG and other open standard formats can be used to create dynamic graphics. This can be an advantage when other options, such as Flash Generator, are financially out of reach. Being an XML subset, SVG also offers the advantage of being truly designed for data handling.

- **Rich typographic control**
  SVG allows you to use your actual fonts. Without requiring additional plug-ins to utilize typefaces not on the viewer's computer, SVG allows designers to use high-quality, professional fonts. With a variety of methods for encoding the typeface, developers can choose whether to embed the entire typeface (to allow for dynamic content's possibilities) or just specific character outlines (to reduce file size).

- **WYSIWYG**
  SVG allows for true "What You See Is What You Get" display. Designers can ascertain their document's display by embedding original typefaces and setting precise pixel values for their content. Even better, SVG allows designers to set certain attributes, such as machine fonts, as variable to allow for faster file downloads.

- **Debugger**
  Unlike HTML and other formats, SVG has a "zero tolerance" policy for code conformance: if your SVG code is incorrect, it will display only up to the point of error. To help developers sort through their large files, many SVG viewers (such as the Adobe SVG Viewer) will pinpoint the line and column number of an erring SVG statement within the code.

Disadvantages of Using SVG

So, with all these advantages, what could possibly be deterring SVG from becoming the *de facto* display language of the Web? Several issues have hampered SVG's adoption, but most are due to the fact that SVG was only recently adopted as a "recommendation" from the W3C. This classification gives the technology a seal of approval, legitimizing it in the development community.

The second largest drawback to the adoption of SVG surely lies in its lack of native viewing support. Currently, the only way regular Web users interact with SVG is through the aid of a plug-in. Ideally, SVG will be supported natively in consumer browsers, such as Netscape and Internet Explorer. As any Web developer knows, plug-in dependency is not a desirable solution: witness the long and arduous road developers faced when trying to develop Flash content for the masses.

1

SVG has already made major inroads, considering its lack of final candidacy until recently. Adobe Systems, Inc., the maker of Photoshop, Illustrator, Premiere, and After Effects (the design industry's most popular tool suite), has been active in the support and adoption of SVG. They have released the most easily available SVG viewer (appropriately dubbed the Adobe SVG Viewer) on the market free of charge, as well as provided the plug-in as a default install with all of their recent software packages. Adobe has also secured a distribution deal with Real Network's RealPlayer to include the SVG Viewer within existing RealPlayer viewers.

The Mozilla Project (the open source movement behind the construction of the latest Netscape browsers) is also at work getting builds of their browser to support SVG display. "Croczilla" is another effort to bring SVG to the Mozilla project, with working versions of the browser for the Mac, PC, and Linux. Other browsers are working on full SVG implementation; X-Smiles, a Java-based, platform-independent XML browser, has already shown native support for the technology.

The push for full support is far from over, and you can actually be an active part of the success of SVG's adoption. This book's companion Web site, www.svgnow.com, contains contact information for browser and software vendors. By contacting these developers and voicing your support for a technology that eases your project development significantly, not only will SVG be guaranteed to see the light of day in the commercial world, but it also may see that day sooner than expected.

What Spurred the Development of SVG?

SVG was created by the W3C's SVG Working Group, a body of the industry's top developers focused on creating a viable vector display language for the Web. The impetus for the group began with several software developers proposing competing vector graphic standards for the web. The W3C brought together a team of leading graphics software developers to unite them in one effort and began defining the requirements of a vector graphics markup language.

Thus, progression began on SVG as an open, vector-based graphic display standard. The first public draft of SVG was released in February 1999.

Following the same process as for their other technologies, such as HTML, XML, and PNG, the W3C has submitted SVG to a rigorous battery of tests, as well as allowing extensive feedback from developers in the field.

As the Working Group progressed on SVG, several large technology providers saw that SVG offered amazing possibilities when used in conjunction with existing XML-oriented products. Sun, HP, and Adobe have all put extensive work into seeing that SVG reaches the mainstream. Their efforts, although benefiting developers tremendously, also extend the value of their products and offerings by providing a level of display previously unavailable to their products' XML-formatted content.

Alongside the corporate push was an intense developer effort. Congregating in Yahoo!'s group forums, this development community grew month after month. The group, still alive and active today, focused largely on sharing ideas and theories on how to execute challenging concepts in the then-fledgling technology. Representing a variety of interests and skill levels, the group has housed debates ranging from how to increase SVG's popularity to the ethics of code-based design. Several developers have created tutorials and resource sites, while others have worked hard at answering specific questions posed by other members.

Information about the group, as well as the ability to join, is available at http://groups.yahoo.com/group/svg-developers.

As you can see, SVG has had a relatively short childhood. At the time of this book's going to press, several more companies have announced support for SVG, including Quark and Corel. Smaller, nimbler organizations are also producing a series of tools for SVG developers that have an amazing level of control and options. By the time you read this paragraph, you will have an amazing breadth of tools available for a wide range of needs, whether they are simply exporting SVG artwork, editing existing artwork, animating motion, applying effects, or linking SVG to other technologies. (For a list of tools available, you can check Chapeter 24, "References," as well as the companion site: www.svgnow.com.)

What Does SVG Offer Designers?

SVG offers creative professionals a chance to truly control the visual appearance of content onscreen and on the Web. It affords this control while still allowing the best attributes of online technology (scalability, dynamic generation, and so on) to seep through.

Designers have full control over the presentation of their imagery. Using transparency, gradients, typographic controls, filter effects, and more, the designer is able to execute designs for the Web that once were possible only within the realms of print and CD-ROMs.

Furthermore, SVG is supported by Adobe, creator of the bulk of the creative professional's toolkit. By leveraging familiar tools, the designer is able to create SVG content quickly and easily. Lastly, via style sheets, pixel-precise placement, and SVG's modular code, designers are able to finesse their SVG content until it appears as desired.

What Does SVG Offer Developers?

SVG's syntax and structuring make it a familiar environment for most developers. Being an application of XML, and similar in concept and syntax to HTML, SVG hardly seems foreign to anyone who has ever written code for the Web.

Consisting largely of text, SVG allows for an incredible array of authoring and editing options. Whether through a plain text editor (for example, Notepad or SimpleText), a code editor (for example, HomeSite and BBEdit), an XML editor (for example, XML Spy), or even a WYSIWYG editor (for example, GoLive), SVG can be authored in whatever environment with which a developer is most comfortable.

In fact, because SVG is nothing more than text, SVG authoring is platform agnostic. You can author an SVG file on a 286 PC, a Mac Plus, or even a Palm Pilot. Anywhere you can write and save a text file, you can author SVG.

How Does SVG Compare with Flash?

Macromedia's Flash has long dominated vector graphics display on the Web; as such, developers are curious as to how SVG compares with this technology. Both SVG and Flash offer small file sizes and were created to deliver vector graphics online. Both feature a wide array of features designers seek, including alpha channel transparency, typographic support, and animation. Both are currently dependent on plug-ins to view their content, and both can handle dynamic content.

But the similarities tend to end once you look under the hood of the two technologies. Cost is one of the biggest differences between SVG and Flash. Although both technologies offer free viewers and abilities for dynamic graphics to consumers, Flash requires a $50,000 Flash Generator license to produce large-scale dynamic content; SVG allows for a number of packages (such as PHP, XSLT, and ASP) that can range anywhere in price from free to expensive. SVG offers developers the opportunity to use the technologies they are familiar with and can afford while allowing the ability to create complex, large-scale dynamic content.

Typography is also very different. Macromedia allows developers to embed typefaces within their Flash files, ensuring that everyone sees the same font, regardless of whether it is on the viewer's computer or not. SVG also allows developers to embed typeface information, but in a much different manner. In SVG, a typeface can be exported into an external file, allowing multiple SVG documents to reference one SVG font file. The difference in file size can be tremendous, as the same font is loaded only once for several documents. With Flash's method, users must download the same font each time for each document. Also, in many instances, Flash embeds typographic information as a series of paths and outlines, whereas SVG applies typographic handling to the original text. This separation ensures that your text is both searchable and selectable.

SVG stands apart from Flash in terms of filter effects. Whereas Flash does not have the capability to support them, SVG facilitates Photoshop-like effects on its vector content. Drop shadows and blurs can be applied to vector artwork, text, and raster images alike within SVG. Even more, SVG allows for easy animation of these effects, such as the ability to animate the angle of a drop shadow to change over time.

As mentioned repeatedly, SVG is a text-based language. Flash SWF files, on the other hand, are self-contained binary files that are not directly editable. Whereas Flash relies on a master Flash file (known as an FLA file) that can be exported as an executable SWF file, an SVG file is both the master file and the executable file.

Lastly, SVG truly shines in terms of its expandability. Although Macromedia has opened the SWF format to allow other developers to create SWF files, they have not allowed other developers the opportunity to freely add functionality to the format. SVG is an open format by its very nature, allowing anyone to add functionality if need be.

For instance, whereas Flash supports MP3 audio natively, SVG is strictly a "graphic" language; it has no audio support. However, recognizing developers' desires for synchronizing audio with their graphics, Adobe created an extension to SVG that allows MP3 playback. SVG's extensible nature allows this sort of innovation to occur without the need to alter the original specification, letting developers bring their ideas to market much more quickly.

Despite its similarities to (and, in some cases, improvements on) Flash's feature set, SVG should *not* be viewed as a "Flash killer," as some would brand it. Support for SVG display is still in its early stages (being handled only by a handful of viewers), and animation and interaction performance are not yet comparable to Flash. SVG stands a larger chance for widespread adoption if designers and developers are mindful of display limitations at present, as end users may wrongly conclude that sluggish animation playback is the result of SVG technology itself rather than SVG viewers.

Flash also has a significant lead in viewer install base. With Flash functionality of some sort available to 96% of Web browsers in the United States, SVG faces a substantial challenge. With the inclusion of SVG support in XML browsers, however, this gap becomes far more manageable.

What Does SVG Offer You?

SVG affords its practitioners an endless list of possibilities. SVG can be used to create both simple, scalable illustrations and complex, feature-rich topography maps. It can beautify daily financial data and handle gorgeous animations. It can be used to help walk a user through an assembly diagram, can serve as an easily updateable navigation bar, or can even be used as the core technology of an entire Web site.

Aside from the advantages of the technology listed above, SVG can offer you, as a developer, the ability to save both time and money. The following list details some of the ways SVG benefits developers:

- **Save money**

  SVG can be used to save money on the production of a dynamic content site that requires an impressive visual interface. The technology itself is free and so are many of the tools and technologies required to author and accentuate it. Although you certainly can purchase and implement expensive technologies to interact with SVG, the beauty of an open standard like SVG is that you are not forced to do so.

  From a management perspective, the very nature of using open-standard XML technologies greatly increases the likelihood of finding talent to complete your project. Many developers are already well familiar with XML and XSLT, and thus their learning curve to adopt SVG, as well as to implement complementary technologies, is greatly reduced. In all probability, you already have a team capable of executing a top-notch SVG site within your company right now.

- **Save time**

  SVG can be used to save time on a site that requires frequent changes to the appearance of its content. Almost all visuals in SVG are rendered according to style sheets, and anyone familiar with CSS knows how easy it can be to change the look of an entire site with some quick changes to a style sheet. Rather than having to re-export and recode an entire site when visual changes are made, in many instances you will be able to update one style sheet and watch your graphics change instantly.

  SVG can be used to decrease initial project development time, as well, by allowing developers and designers to work simultaneously. As visual elements can be created alongside functionality, both teams can work in unison. Developers can code functional elements and intensive animation with placeholder elements, and, as SVG content is no more than code, swap out the placeholders with actual graphic content upon the design team's completion of work. Although getting production teams to become comfortable with this situation may take some customization time, the savings in the long term can be tremendous. (You'll learn more in Hour 20.)

- **Save headaches**

  While SVG is relatively new to the scene, you are certainly not alone in your curiosity or need for the technology. Thriving user groups have emerged around the technology, and several software developers have begun creating and modifying tools to assist in SVG development.

  Although SVG has not reached the critical mass that HTML or flash has, it has attracted a group of people who are very passionate about the technology and willing to share ideas. Such a community is, in and of itself, one of the most useful assets of the technology; if you find yourself stumped with a basic problem or a far-fetched idea in regard to the technology, you will certainly find someone more than willing to help you through your challenge.

  As a reader of this book, you are certainly among an emerging wave of newcomers to this technology. Just remember, you are not riding this wave alone, and many of your fellow developers understand the need to assist newcomers like yourself.

- **Save confusion**

  SVG can be used to create just about anything onscreen that depends on visual formatting. Just as important as knowing what SVG offers you, though, is knowing what it does not offer you. SVG is not a three-dimensional graphic language like VRML. It can give the illusion of three dimensions, as can Flash and other 2D graphics technologies, but it does not directly deal with a third dimension of space. SVG is not appropriate for creating raster or photographic images, although it can reference raster images in its files. Lastly, SVG is not in and of itself a dynamic content generation tool. Similar to Flash Generator template files, SVG acts only as the presentation layer to dynamic content. The dynamic content still needs to come from somewhere, whether a database or an XML document, and it needs to be passed to SVG using an additional technology (such as XSLT or ASP).

SVG Needs You!

Just as the United States Army's World War II recruitment posters suggested that Uncle Sam needed your support, SVG *also* needs you! As mentioned earlier, SVG's future is dependent on two critical factors:

- Developer support
- Implementations

More than anything else, SVG needs practical use and advocacy. The more developers use SVG and see its strengths, the more browser and software vendors will need to support them. After you complete this book and have a firm understanding of how to use SVG today, the author's hope is for you to continue active development with SVG. If enough useful and amazing SVG solutions begin entering the market, a demand for a quick and easy ability to view SVG will become a driving force.

As with most decisions in today's world, the acceptance of SVG is being evaluated using economic factors. Are enough developers using the technology to warrant inclusion in our product? Are enough sites using SVG to warrant native support in our browser? These are questions currently being asked by corporations and software developers, and the answers are largely dependent on how active developers become in pushing for SVG's full adoption.

Lastly, these corporations and software developers don't always have a man with an ear to the street. Most companies don't actively investigate what technologies are coming ahead; they wait until the clamor of their customers becomes more annoying than the work to implement their request. You can do just that, though. After finishing this book, send a couple letters to your favorite software developer (Microsoft included) and request support for SVG *natively* in their products. To help you out, there is a letter already written for you online at `http://www.svgnow.com`, as well as contact information for many important software developers.

What Will You Get out of This Book?

This book will focus on providing practical information to help you develop SVG content. You will walk through a series of fundamental concepts and aspects of SVG development by completing lessons in each hour. Each of the lessons in this book will work toward creating one final product: an SVG "news center." The news center graphic (see Figure 1.1) will contain the bulk of the examples in this book, and will provide more advanced readers with several opportunities to modify and add to the learned code.

FIGURE 1.1

This news center graphic will be the result of many of the exercises given in this book.

Readers of this book will walk away with a variety of knowledge. At the very least, each reader will have a strong concept of

- Document setup
- Basic drawing commands
- Application of visual styles
- Symbols
- Filter effects
- Transformations
- Animation and interaction
- Typography
- Incorporating outside imagery

Later sections of the book detail how to create dynamic SVG graphics, as well as how to use JavaScript and other technologies in conjunction with SVG. Each hour also has a series of exercises that allow readers to pursue more advanced material, if they wish.

All readers will walk away with a sense of confidence in the technology, an ability to apply it, and an idea of what it can be applied to. The book's final example will serve as an impressive culmination of the various concepts and will also allow further exploration on the reader's part.

Summary

SVG is an amazing, practical solution for vector artwork both on the Web and on the screen. Using little more than text, SVG defines static, animated, and dynamic graphics and works hand-in-hand with other open standards technologies.

To provide you with a solid understanding of SVG, its vocabulary, and its nuances, the first several hours will cover the specifics of the technology, devoid of the example to be built. Starting in Hour 5, after having established a solid foundation, you will begin to build this example. The book ends with a series of resources that provide curious readers with further information, as well as some technology comparison charts and other useful reference charts. Lastly, this book's companion Web site (www.svgnow.com), maintained by the author, will be updated as frequently as possible to provide current information about SVG and links to tools, tips, and more.

That said, it's time to dive into the foundation of the technology.

Q&A

Q Who is the W3C?

A The W3C, the World Wide Web Consortium, is a group dedicated to defining the standards on the Internet experience. They have provided the recommendations for standards such as HTML, PNG, XML, and much more. You can learn more about them at `http://www.w3.org/`.

Q Why SVG? Can't Flash do everything I need already?

A Although Flash and SVG may both be vector graphics technologies, each has its own strengths and weaknesses. Many developers are looking for a technology that is easily expandable (meaning they can add additional functionality without paying royalties to a patent-holder), is compatible with XML and other technologies (allowing for data to be quickly shared or reformatted without a lot of development effort), allows concurrent development (both designers and developers can work side-by-side during an SVG project), and is inexpensive (the technology is free and does not require any expensive authoring tools for entry)—and SVG fits this bill. Flash, on the other hand, is still well suited for animation and has a large plug-in install base.

Workshop

The Workshop is designed to help you anticipate possible questions, review what you've learned, and begin learning how to put your knowledge into practice.

Quiz

1. What do the letters in SVG stand for?
2. What existing technology is SVG based on?
3. What common compression scheme is used for SVGZ, the compressed form of SVG?
4. True or false: SVG and Flash are both designed for creating photographic imagery.
5. What group of industry experts developed the SVG specification?

Answers

1. SVG is an acronym for Scalable Vector Graphics.
2. SVG is an XML technology, adhering to all of XML's syntax and structuring requirements.
3. SVGZ uses GZIP compression technology to result in fully functional lightweight files.

4. False. Both Flash and SVG are vector graphics technologies, specialized for the display of flat, graphic imagery.

5. SVG was developed by the W3C, the World Wide Web Consortium.

Exercises

1. Consider photocopying the illustration (Figure 1.1) of the news center graphic to be built in this book. Alternatively, visit www.svgnow.com and print out a copy of the illustration.

   By having a physical copy of the graphic, you'll be able to see the big picture of what you're building, as well as understand the reason for certain coordinate locations (all to be explained later in this book).

2. Visit http://www.w3.org/tr/svg/ and read chapter 2 (2.5 pages) of the SVG specification for further details on the big picture view of SVG. SVG's relation to other standards, the intent of the specification, and other topics are covered.

3. Visit http://www.adobe.com/svg/ and peruse several examples in their Gallery section. Seeing all the complex possibilities the technology can accomplish, such as the interactive employee finder and the drawing application, may spark your imagination for uses of SVG.

Hour 2

SVG's Foundation

As SVG is an XML vocabulary, it is important that you review XML before diving into SVG. XML, like SVG, was developed by the W3C. XML was created to provide developers with a common means for structuring data apart from its display. While similar in appearance to HTML (in the sense that it uses a bracketed tag system), XML is quite different from other markup languages.

In this hour, you will learn

- XML syntax
- Use of elements and attributes
- SVG document structure

Syntax

In most markup languages, tags relate to specific functions; for instance, the `table` tag specifically instructs a browser to draw its contents within a table. In XML, tags only label data. Function, such as presentation and appearance, is handled via another technology, such as an XSL or SVG processor. For instance, if you created a sample XML document for the news center graphic defining the weather in Philadelphia, you would create a series of tags describing the type of content it contained. As XML is used to store content, you are able to name your tags according to your needs rather than according to a markup language's preset names. Thus, one possible example of the Philadelphia weather document would be the following:

```
<?xml version="1.0" ?>
<weatherinfo>
        <city>Philadelphia</city>
        <forecast>sunny</forecast>
        <high>75°</high>
        <low>62°</low>
</weatherinfo>
```

It is important to note, however, that you could give those tags any other name, as well. The tag names in the previous example were chosen because they clearly described their contained content. But for all practical purposes, you could create the same document with nonsensical tag names, as in the following:

```
<?xml version="1.0" ?>
<things>
        <dog>Philadelphia</dog>
        <cat>sunny</cat>
        <bird>75°</bird>
        <fish>62°</fish>
   </things>
```

As you can see, those tag names made no sense in relationship to their content and would make much less sense to any other developer that may have to work with your file. In XML, tag names (officially known as "element type names") can be made at will, although whether they can be interpreted by developers or a parser is another matter entirely. In this way, XML separates its content from how it is displayed, as the tags surrounding the content need have no bearing on how the content will be presented.

The flexibility of separating content and its structure from a display markup allows the same content to be styled in different manners for different applications, such as a PC Web browser or a cellular phone screen. In the case of the weather forecast, the information could be displayed as text on a Palm Pilot screen or as a dynamic Flash graphic, depending on the presentation layer the developer prefers.

Content stored in XML requires other technologies to handle its display. XSL (in conjunction with an XSL parser) and SVG, both XML technologies, can be used to handle the display of this data. Other technologies, such as CSS (Cascading Style Sheets), can also be used. It is merely important to remember that XML does not determine the way data looks but rather how it is filed away; another technology suited to the issues of displaying content is used to present XML data.

As SVG is an application of XML, the rules that hold true for XML's syntax hold true for SVG. The three most basic rules of XML and SVG syntax (to ensure well-formed documents) are as follows:

1. All tags are case sensitive. (That is, if you designate `<aa>` as an element, `<aA>` would refer to a different element.

2. All tags must be closed. (That is, tags must follow one of the two conventions: `<tag>...</tag>` or `<tag/>`.

3. All attribute values must be contained in quotations.

As you are likely well aware, HTML is known for its tolerance for tag variation. This reality makes for an abrupt adjustment to SVG, which has a "zero tolerance" ordinance for such variation. Whereas HTML allows both upper- and lowercase characters to define its element names (such as accepting both `<p>` and `<P>` to signify a paragraph break), SVG allows no such flexibility. All SVG tags are case sensitive.

HTML is also noted for its acceptance of both `<p>...</p>` and just plain old `<p>` to create paragraph breaks. Within SVG, however, only the first example would be structured properly, as the first example closes the `<p>` element. In some instances, where a tag exists on its own (such as an independent `<animate ...>` tag), a "close" notation can be added within the tag, creating a result like `<animate .../>`.

Aside from keeping an XML or SVG document well formed, these documents should be *valid*. One way to make a document valid XML is to have it adhere to a *DTD (Document Type Definition)*. A DTD outlines the structure and grammar of a document. Thus, to make either of the Philadelphia weather examples valid, a corresponding DTD would need to be created, explicitly stating that "high" (or "bird") is an acceptable tag name. (You'll learn more about DTDs later in this chapter.)

As you move into learning the structure of an SVG file, you will need to review two important terms that you will encounter throughout this book and in other SVG resources. These two definitions refer to the syntax of an SVG tag (and an HTML and XML tag, for that matter). The two terms are as follows:

- Element—The element type name can be thought of as the tag name. It determines how the tag will function and consists of one empty (also known as "closed") tag or two enclosing tags (a start tag and an end tag).

- Attribute—"Attribute" describes an element by giving further information. The attribute specifications consist of an attribute name and an attribute value.

FIGURE 2.1

Diagram showing the relationship of the element, attribute name, and attribute value to each other within a sample SVG tag.

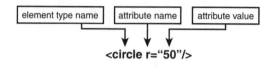

Figure 2.1 shows how the element, attribute name, and attribute value work together:

You should make note of two very common occurrences that you will encounter repeatedly throughout this book. The first, the id attribute, properly names an SVG element, whereas the second, the comment, allows the developer the means of adding comments just about anywhere in the document.

The id attribute names the element it describes; in many ways, it acts as an element's "label." The syntax is quite simple:

```
id="ValueName",
```

where *ValueName* is any text you insert. id attribute values conform to XML's naming convention. Any id value can contain only alphanumerical characters, underscores, periods, and hyphens; no spaces or special characters are allowed, though. It is important to note, however, that id attribute values cannot start with a period, hyphen, or number.

What is the importance of the id attribute? By naming your elements, you can add plain English descriptions to your code, making it easier to scan your document to find a specific object. Also, many interactive SVG functions need an id value to know what to apply their function to. Without the id attribute and its associated values, SVG documents would be pretty static. As you begin dealing with a large amount of objects in your documents, these plain-English labels will make finding and editing your content infinitely easier.

Also adding to the ease of reviewing your code is the comment. Comments are not SVG elements, despite the fact that they reside between tags. They allow you to write, in plain English (with spaces and some punctuation), descriptive notes detailing any code that may need further explanation.

A comment is created by inserting your comments in between the following tags: <!--
and -->. These tags can be placed almost anywhere within your SVG document, but a comment may not reside within another comment, nor within a closed tag. For instance, you can insert <!-- The following group animates the sun illustration. -->
before a group of animations to clarify their function or to help another developer understand the purpose of your code, but you cannot insert the comment within the actual animate element.

Anything within the comment's tags will not be displayed by an SVG Viewer. Instead of creating or modifying a display, a comment serves the function of revealing information to the developer. In Hour 5, you'll also learn an added benefit of the comment—disabling code.

Structure

The structure of an SVG document will seem very familiar to anyone who has looked at an HTML file before. The analogy works far better when referring to XHTML, as you saw when the previous section noted SVG's strict interpretation of code. Far from complex, the structure of SVG code is but a series of elements, some of which enclose other data.

In every SVG file, the content is enclosed with the svg element's tags: <svg>...</svg>. This is sometimes referred to as the document, or root, element. All your SVG content must appear between these two tags. The only data that should appear outside of these two tags will be XML data defining the document type and nature.

Thus, one of the simplest SVG documents that you can create is composed of:

```
<svg>
   <title>My first SVG file!</title>
</svg>
```

Obviously, this document results in a blank screen, as the SVG file contains no visual information. Fortunately, this book provides you with much more useful examples of SVG than a blank document. As such, you'll need to understand what types of information you'll be including in our SVG documents.

Although no formal classifications exist, SVG content generally consists of elements belonging to one of six categories:

- Document data (namespace definitions, XML header info, stylesheets, and so on)
- Annotations (descriptions, comments, and so on)
- Reference material (definitions, symbols, and so on)
- Graphic content (shapes, paths, and so on)
- Manipulation data (animation, transforms, masking, and so on)
- Text

Each element in the following code is labeled in order to better illustrate these categories. Don't worry; all the code will be explained later in the book. For now, simply observe how SVG looks as code, and see some of the differences between the types of elements an SVG file is comprised of.

FIGURE 2.2

*This diagram shows
the six different types
of information used
in an SVG document.*

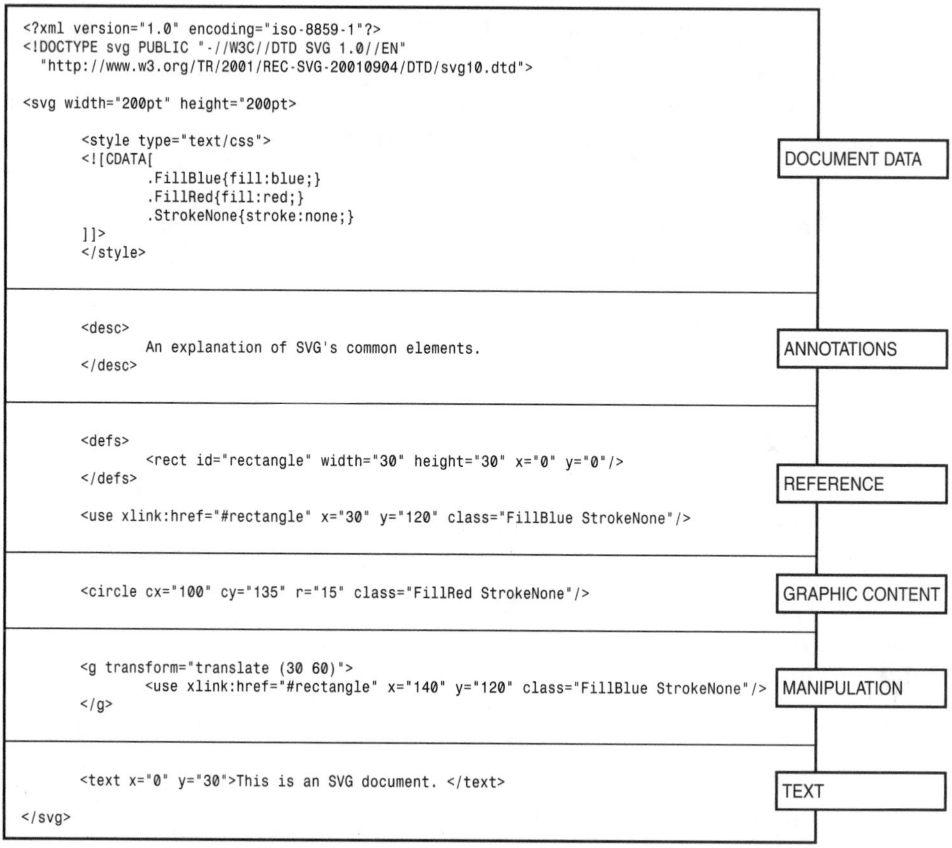

```
<?xml version="1.0" encoding="iso-8859-1"?>
<!DOCTYPE svg PUBLIC "-//W3C//DTD SVG 1.0//EN"
  "http://www.w3.org/TR/2001/REC-SVG-20010904/DTD/svg10.dtd">

<svg width="200pt" height="200pt">

        <style type="text/css">
        <![CDATA[
                .FillBlue{fill:blue;}
                .FillRed{fill:red;}
                .StrokeNone{stroke:none;}
        ]]>
        </style>


        <desc>
                An explanation of SVG's common elements.
        </desc>


        <defs>
                <rect id="rectangle" width="30" height="30" x="0" y="0"/>
        </defs>

        <use xlink:href="#rectangle" x="30" y="120" class="FillBlue StrokeNone"/>


        <circle cx="100" cy="135" r="15" class="FillRed StrokeNone"/>


        <g transform="translate (30 60)">
                <use xlink:href="#rectangle" x="140" y="120" class="FillBlue StrokeNone"/>
        </g>


        <text x="0" y="30">This is an SVG document. </text>
</svg>
```

DOCUMENT DATA

ANNOTATIONS

REFERENCE

GRAPHIC CONTENT

MANIPULATION

TEXT

In Figure 2.2 the first two lines in the "document data" category are common to some
XML documents, defining the subsequent code as belonging to a specific XML language
and referencing a DTD.

It is important to note that the `<?xml version...>` and `<!DOCTYPE...>` elements at the
top of the file are used to determine whether the following SVG code is valid. The first
line explains that this document is a piece of XML data, whereas the second line provides a link to the W3C's SVG DTD (document type definition).

A DTD allows XML code to describe its content for verification whenever the document is parsed; as such, SVG requires its own DTD. The SVG DTD is used to validate the SVG document by checking items such as the structure, the elements, and their attributes (and corresponding values). In most cases, you will want to link to the W3C's DTD. However, if you are adding custom tags, or integrating your SVG document with another XML file, you will want to point to your custom XML namespace. This will allow you to define custom structures for your XML and SVG data.

Creating a custom DTD or namespace, however, isn't quite subject matter for a beginner's introduction to SVG. Suffice things to say that should you encounter a need to extend the functionality of your SVG content through an extension, you will likely use the DTD and/or namespace that a vendor provides to facilitate their SVG extension. Otherwise, your best bet is to stick with the SVG DTD.

Rendering Order

SVG files are *rendered* (or displayed) from bottom to top, meaning the first chunk of code found in the SVG document appears first on the screen (and thus below subsequent artwork), the next chunk appears above the first, and so on.

FIGURE 2.3

Visualize the ordering of SVG content. Content that appears on top (top layer) on the screen (the dark grey box) is found at the bottom (or end) of the SVG document's code. As a general rule, think of display ordering as the opposite of code ordering.

For instance, to create the example in Figure 2.3, the element for the light gray box would need to appear first in the SVG file's code, followed by the gray box element, and finally with the dark gray box element.

Unlike graphic content (such as the example above) and text, manipulation data, annotations, and reference material can appear anywhere within the SVG document without affecting the drawing order. Their display is determined by the ordering of either the content they reference (in the case of manipulation data) or the reference used (in the case of reference material).

An exception to this rule is that a comment cannot reside within another comment.

Summary

Proper syntax and structure are critical for creating an SVG document that can be displayed correctly. Remembering to close all your tags, use the proper case, and quote your attribute values will help reduce the amount of errors you'll inevitably face when beginning to learn SVG. Paying attention to the ordering of your code can also explain mysterious disappearances of your artwork, as display order is hinged on code order. Lastly, be sure to include the XML declaration and DTD information. Although many viewers can display your document without this information, this approach is short sighted. Some viewers allow this, but some don't, and future viewers may not be so forgiving; code once correctly and you won't need to revise all your documents down the road.

Q&A

Q HTML allows both all-caps and lowercase tag names. Why doesn't SVG?

A SVG is a subset of XML. XML tags are case sensitive, as developers may define two separate meanings for a tag with different letter cases.

Q Do I have to use the W3C's DTD? Can I use someone else's? Can I write my own?

A You are in no way limited to using the W3C's SVG DTD. The W3C DTD is obviously the purest DTD available but may not have some additions that you need for your unique application. If you do not wish to depend on a connection to the W3C site, you can download the DTD and use it locally (whether on your site or your machine); just make sure you change the URL of the DTD to match your new location.

Q Do I need to use an `id` attribute on every element?

A You do not need to use an `id` attribute on every element you create in SVG. However, keep in mind that an `id` attribute not only allows animation and interactive controls to access an object, but it also helps other developers understand your code. By using the `id` attribute, you provide yourself and others a glimpse into the function of every line of code you author. Keep in mind that what may make sense today may not seem so apparent tomorrow; code accordingly.

Workshop

The Workshop is designed to help you anticipate possible questions, review what you've learned, and begin learning how to put your knowledge into practice.

Quiz

1. DTD is an acronym for which XML term?
2. True or False: "Rendering order" refers to the sequence of objects being drawn onscreen.
3. Name the three possible components of an SVG tag.
4. Why would you want to use a DTD with your SVG document?
5. True or False: SVG tags are not case-sensitive.

Answers

1. DTD is an acronym for Document Type Definition.
2. True. Rendering order is the term used to describe the order in which objects are drawn onscreen. The last element in the document that defines visible artwork is the last object drawn, and thus it appears on the very top of the rendered SVG file.
3. The three possible components of an SVG tag are the element type name, the attribute name, and the attribute value. Not all tags contain attributes (and thus do not contain attribute values), but all tags certainly contain an element type name (such as `svg`).

4. A DTD allows your SVG viewer to ensure the document is valid.

5. False. SVG tags are case-sensitive, as they adhere to the grammar of XML, wherein all tags are case-sensitive.

Exercises

1. Visit www.svgnow.com, this book's companion site, and check out the SVG Gallery. Look over the code of some of the examples there, and observe the strict adherence to syntax and structure. Pay attention to the case of all the tags, the quoting of all values, the clear identification of each element, the display order of the artwork, and the consistent naming structure. If you're feeling brave, download some of the examples to your computer and try changing the names of the tags to uppercase or deleting quotation marks around values; observe the error that is displayed in your browser's display bar.

2. Learn more about XML at the W3Schools site. They have several introductions to XML, DTDs, XSL, and other XML technologies. For newcomers to XML, this site's quick examples can bring you up to speed with the latest in data-handling technologies. If nothing else, be sure to explore the section *Introduction to XML* under the Learn XML link on the home page, as this tutorial explains the concepts of XML clearly. The W3Schools site can be found at http://www.w3schools.com/.

HOUR 3

Viewing SVG

Now that you've seen the different elements of SVG, you're probably excited to see what this stuff looks like in the real world. Before viewing your SVG files, though, you will need to know the realities of viewing SVG content today.

This chapter will address a variety of issues regarding how you view SVG, such as:

- How to view SVG content
- What types of SVG viewers are on the market
- What MIME types your Web server should use to host your SVG documents
- How to embed an SVG document within an HTML document

Although this chapter will not cover every possible method of viewing SVG content, it will review the most common, and hint at some of the soon-to-be exciting, methods available.

Understanding Limitations

The means of viewing SVG content is often through using a browser accompanied by a viewer plug-in. Although this obviously extends the potential audience for viewing your content, plug-in viewing (of any content, SVG or otherwise) does not offer the same experience as native viewing. Each plug-in has its limitations, and, as you will see from examples in this book and from your own experience, they may limit the possibilities of what your SVG content can do.

For instance, many of the viewers in distribution over the past two years have supported only a portion of the W3C specification. This was due, in large part, to the state of flux of the specification, as well as to the need for timeliness in releasing a product for developers' use. This does mean, however, that what works in one viewer may not work in another.

Although this is usually not a news flash for anyone who has dealt with computer technology over the past several years, and more specifically Web technology, it is important to note. Before releasing SVG on a wide scale, you will want to test your content against the various viewers available. As of this writing, there is no one viewer that offers 100% support for the entire W3C recommendation.

Aside from feature support, there are also issues of performance. The Adobe SVG Viewer is noticeably sluggish when dealing with animations (especially animations involving filters), and also ties up the bulk of your computer's processing cycles. Do not let these current issues deter your development, though. Later hours in this book will talk about optimizing your code so that you can circumvent many difficulties inherent in today's viewers. Also, today's viewers are just that—today's viewers. With enough development, more viewers will continue to be released until complete specification support and optimal performance are reached. Your efforts, therefore, have a significant impact on how well your SVG content is viewed in both the present and future.

What Environments Can View SVG?

If this technology is so amazing, you'll want to see what it looks like, right? Thankfully, SVG isn't vaporware, and you're able to view SVG documents in a variety of ways. SVG content can currently be viewed in a variety of Web browsers, as well as in some alternative environments.

Browsers

The most common environment (as of publication) in which you will encounter SVG is your Web browser. Some XML browsers, such as X-Smiles (http://www.xsmiles.org/), actually have native support for SVG in the browser, meaning you need not do anything to view SVG files; they will automatically appear in the browser window.

Sadly, that doesn't hold true for just about any other browser out there, much less for any well-known and well-used browser. Both Microsoft Internet Explorer and Netscape Navigator allow the viewing of SVG content through the Adobe SVG Viewer, a third-party browser plug-in. Adobe has been one of the biggest corporate promoters of SVG, and they have been working hard to get the public to be able to see and work with SVG. Their plug-in works with Internet Explorer and Netscape Navigator versions 4 and above on both the Macintosh and PC platforms.

Like Flash and other plug-ins, the SVG Viewer can be enhanced in certain ways by using JavaScript. Sadly, unlike its PC counterpart, Internet Explorer on the Macintosh does not allow plug-ins to communicate with the browser, and vice versa, via JavaScript. Although the bulk of SVG development does not require JavaScript, you may find certain tasks easier to accomplish using JavaScript. This issue, which has been quite problematic for Flash developers as well, limits the ability of the Adobe SVG Viewer to work with such enhancements. Accordingly, any non-native SVG scripting will not perform as expected. Although version 3 of the plug-in has its own built-in JavaScript interpreter, Macintosh IE users will still encounter difficulties viewing such enhanced SVG content. The bulk of the examples in this book will not require JavaScript for proper execution, except where noted.

Requiring an installation similar to Flash and other common plug-ins, the Adobe SVG Viewer is generally the quickest method for users to get access to SVG display. However, the Adobe plug-in is not the only means on the market of viewing SVG in a browser. Several others have emerged and may increase in popularity over time.

IBM's alphaWorks division has produced SVGView, a Java-based SVG viewer that works on the Windows platform. The viewer uses Java2D and XML Parser (another alphaWorks product) to display SVG graphics. Also available is CSIRO's (Australia's Commonwealth Scientific Industrial Research Organisation) SVG Toolkit. This software package is also a Java implementation and, as such, requires a Java applet to be called from the browser in order to function (or to be run as a Java application). The knowledge requirements of SVG View and SVG Toolkit, as well as their limited support for the specification, are an impediment to most people's utilization of these tools. However, both are alternative solutions should you be looking for display on Windows machines in a Java environment.

Last but not least is the Apache XML Project's Batik software. Batik offers developers an array of SVG functionality in one product. Functioning as viewer, generator, and converter of SVG, Batik provides another Java-based solution. Experienced developers can use Batik to pull data from an XML file, create an SVG file, and then convert the file to another format if the person accessing the file does not have SVG-viewing abilities. Similar to SVG View and SVG Toolkit, Batik is not for the novice, nor does it support animation or scripting in its 1.1 release. Before venturing off into the much more complex realms of these three alternative viewers, you should strongly consider completing this book (and thus the basics of SVG).

All the examples in this book have been tested against the Adobe SVG Viewer (Version 3.0), as this viewer is the most predominant and easily accessible means of seeing SVG on most people's machines. Because of this, and because of the ease of installation, this book will assume you have the plug-in installed to view and test these examples. It is important to note, however, that the Adobe SVG Viewer is not the be-all, end-all viewer. The Viewer accommodates a very large portion of the W3C SVG specification, albeit not all of the specification, and some results (especially performance) can be buggy. Ideally, as mentioned before, SVG will be rendered by the browsers themselves.

To download the Adobe SVG Viewer, visit http://www.adobe.com/svg/. The download option is prominently featured at the top of the page. Be certain to download the most recent version of the plug-in. Further installation instructions are on the Adobe Web site.

Other Environments

Fortunately (for its chances of success), SVG isn't tied to the Web browser. Applications for SVG are popping up in various places already. The two emerging areas for viewing SVG content are handheld devices and interactive TV.

CSIRO, the company that makes the SVG Toolkit, which was mentioned before, has also released a viewer for PocketPC handheld devices. Built as an ActiveX control, the Pocket SVG Viewer is able to display a variety of SVG graphics on a wide variety of popular handheld devices.

BitFlash, on the other hand, has developed an SVG viewer for an array of small-screen devices. Their viewer is actually a part of the larger BitFlash Mobility Suite (BMS), a series of technologies for converting and delivering a wide number of graphic and data formats into SVG content for display in the viewer, and the BitFlash Mobile Messaging Suite 2.1. Both Palm and PocketPC handhelds are supported, as well as a number of cellular phones and RIM Blackberry devices. The viewer is currently available only to developers building solutions using the BMS.

Also on the horizon is support for SVG in interactive television set-top boxes. Nokia's Media Terminal harnesses the Linux development of Mozilla (the open source version of Netscape's commercial browser) and offers support for using SVG as a graphics format for the terminal. As this box has yet to hit the United States, it will be hard to tell how popular SVG will become in handling the graphical display of content for interactive television.

Implementation

Knowing that there are several viewers for displaying content in SVG, we now need to learn how to get our SVG content to these viewers. If you have the Adobe SVG Viewer installed, you can open an SVG file directly in the browser to see it in action. However, at the present time, the bulk of any commercial development will require your SVG content to reside within the framework of an HTML page.

To include SVG content just as you would any other image within an HTML page, you will need to use the embed element. Although technically not a W3C-approved method for including SVG content, the embed element offers the only sure method for having your SVG image appear in SVG Viewer–supported browsers. The simplest way to include your SVG content is as follows, where *filepath* refers to the directory location of the SVG file in relation to the HTML file and *filename* refers to the name of your document:

```
<html>
    <head>
    <title>Embedding SVG</title>
    </head>
    <body bgcolor="white">
    <embed src="filepath/filename.svg" />
    </body>
</html>
```

You are able to further define the embed element by naming the graphic (the attribute value graphic_name), giving it precise dimensions (the attribute values x and y, where each attribute is defined by a number of pixels), labeling the image type (which should always be image/svg+xml), and providing an URL for the Viewer download.

```
<embed src="filepath/filename.svg" name="graphic_name"
       width="x" height="y" type="image/svg+xml"
pluginspage="http://www.adobe.com/svg/viewer/install/" />
```

Including the pluginspage property will help accommodate users who do not yet have the plug-in installed. Rather than being faced with a confusing "plug-in not found" message, their browser will direct them to the most current SVG Viewer download page.

For many of the examples in this book, you are likely to view the SVG documents locally (off your hard drive, as opposed to a Web server). However, by the end of this book, you'll hopefully be creating awesome examples of SVG to show the world. In that case, you might need to know a couple of items about the configuration of your Web server.

It is important to note the MIME types your Web server will need to have configured to display SVG properly. *MIME types* tell your server, and subsequently the viewer's browser, how different types of content are handled. As every server and platform is a bit different, the method for adding these MIME types will vary. If you are unsure, please check the support of your hosting provider. The proper settings for your server are as follows:

Extension: .svg

MIME type: image/svg+xml

Extension: .svgz

MIME type: image/svg+xml

You'll notice that we added an extension with the name svgz in this last setting. SVGZ is the compressed format for SVG, which you will cover in Hour 21, "Using Adobe Illustrator to Create Artwork." Although you will not need to configure MIME types to complete the exercises in this book (as you can work with these examples on your own computer, without the need for a Web server), you should be aware of these settings before deploying your content online. In many cases, you will not have permission to add or modify MIME types on your server, but your server's administrator may be willing to make the appropriate changes.

To view all the examples in this book, create the following document (named "index.html"), which will embed all the work you'll be creating throughout the remaining hours. Just be sure to replace *filepath/filename.svg* with the directory path and name of the SVG file you save.

LISTING 3.1 SVG Can Be Contained within an HTML Document Using the embed Element

```
01: <html>
02:        </head>
03:            <title>Embedding SVG</title>
04:        </head>
05:        <body bgcolor="white">
06:            <embed src="filepath/filename.svg" name="SVG News Center"
07:                    width="500" height="300" type="image/svg"
08:                    pluginspage="http://www.adobe.com/svg/viewer/install/"/>
09:        </body>
10: </html>
11: + svg
```

By viewing all your examples within this HTML framework, you'll be seeing your code just as anyone else would. As will be mentioned several times throughout this book, it is easier to code correctly the first time than it is to come back later and clean everything up.

Summary

Full support for properly displaying SVG content may still be a ways off, but this has not prevented other software vendors and Web developers (yourself included) from pushing for SVG support in their products. There are, nonetheless, a variety of viewers available for developers and the public-at-large. Whether they're using an XML browser, a plug-in addition to existing browsers, a handheld computer's viewer, or even next-generation devices, those interested in engaging new content are able to easily view SVG files today. Understanding how to set up your server and code your files to ensure they display properly takes a small amount of time up front but ensures your audience has the easiest possible means to view your content.

In the next chapter, you will begin to create an SVG document to learn about document layout, coordinate systems, size, and position. Such basic information will provide a framework as you build all future SVG documents.

Q&A

Q I'm having troubles installing the Adobe SVG Viewer. What can I do?

A Although Adobe has worked pretty hard to make their viewer work for just about everyone, you may still encounter some difficulties getting the plug-in installed. If so, be sure to visit `http://www.adobe.com/svg/viewer/install/main.html`, where they've posted a variety of documentation on their viewer.

Q This chapter mentioned that no one viewer supports the entire SVG recommendation at present. What features does the Adobe SVG Viewer not support in their latest release?

A Visit `http://www.adobe.com/svg/indepth/releasenotes.html`, where you can find a series of PDF files documenting the various supported and unsupported features in the Adobe SVG Viewer.

Workshop

The Workshop is designed to help you anticipate possible questions, review what you've learned, and begin learning how to put your knowledge into practice.

Quiz

1. True or False: Netscape Communicator and Internet Explorer can both view SVG content without the help of a plug-in.

2. What is the acronym used to describe SVG's compressed file format?

3. Which element is used to insert an SVG file into an HTML document?

4. How many viewers currently support every feature in the SVG specification?

5. True or False: SVG can only be viewed within Web browsers.

Answers

1. False. Neither Netscape Navigator nor Microsoft Internet Explorer can view SVG content natively without a plug-in. Both browsers require an extension of some sort to view SVG content, and most extensions/plug-ins require version 4 and above browsers.

2. SVGZ is the shorthand acronym for SVG documents reduced in size with GZIP compression.

3. The `embed` element is used to call an SVG file into an HTML document

4. Currently, there are no SVG viewers that support every feature in the SVG specification.

5. False. SVG can only be viewed with an SVG viewer, which can exist as a stand-alone application or an extension of another application (such as a browser plug-in).

Exercises

1. Visit `www.svgnow.com/` and check out some of the many examples. If you don't already have the Adobe SVG Viewer installed, notice how the page automatically redirects you to the Adobe site to download the plug-in right away. This is the same code you learned about at the end of this hour.

2. Download the Adobe SVG Viewer (`http://www.adobe.com/svg/viewer/install/main.html`), and install it on your computer. After installing the plug-in, visit the SVG in Action section (`http://www.adobe.com/svg/demos/main.html`) to see some amazing examples of SVG at work.

3. If you're really adventurous and have an Apache Web server, try installing the Batik package. Although not covered in this book, experimenting with Batik's various abilities to publish SVG content will reveal a wealth of opportunities with SVG. More information on Batik can be found at `http://xml.apache.org/batik/index.html`.

HOUR 4

Document Layout

Having just learned how to view your SVG content, you are now ready to begin creating SVG. Before diving right into drawing SVG content, though, you will need to learn the basics of SVG document construction.

Although SVG document layout and construction is a bit unique, it shares some similarities with both HTML and traditional graphics applications (two very dissimilar environments). To help familiarize you with how SVG documents are created, you will be introduced to the following during this hour:

- SVG's coordinate system
- Units of measurement
- The purpose and use of the `viewBox`
- Creating a resizable document

With these lessons, you'll have the information needed for when you begin drawing shapes and artwork in the next chapters.

Understanding SVG Document System

The svg element can have several attributes that will affect the way your SVG file is displayed. To best illustrate how an SVG document works and how these attributes affect display, think in terms of a common, identifiable object, such as a bulletin board. The bulletin board will symbolize the SVG document you'll begin to create.

Before you can begin defining the content of an SVG file, you'll need to define the size of the SVG document. Thus, the most common attributes of the svg element are width and height. These attributes will define the width and height of the SVG file's display, known as the *viewport*. You can think of the width and height as defining the size of the bulletin board you'll be posting other objects to later.

width and height can be specified in numerical units, and SVG documents can use a number of measurement units to define positioning and dimensions. The default unit of measurement in SVG is the "user space value," but SVG is also open to a variety of alternate units.

A *user space value* is an abstract unit in what the recommendation describes as the *user space*, the coordinate environment of the document before it is parsed to match the requirements of the display. These units are intentionally left abstract so that an SVG document can be translated easily into different "spaces," such as a computer screen, a cell phone display, or a piece of paper. On the computer screen, this unit translates into a pixel, as that is the default unit of a computer screen. In another environment, however, the user unit may be three times as large as a computer screen's pixel.

If no measurement unit is specified with a numerical value (for attributes such as width and height), an SVG viewer will assume this value to be in user space values. In the case of this book's examples, as you are testing them within an Internet browser on a computer, any non-specified values will be interpreted as pixels.

You are also able define measurements by points, picas, millimeters, centimeters, inches, and percentages.

Table 4.1 shows each of these available units, their SVG nomenclature, and their value in pixels (the default unit of measurement). This table is taken from the W3C specification at http://www.w3.org/TR/SVG/coords.html#Units.

TABLE 4.1   Units in SVG Can Be Specified in a Variety of Popular Formats

Unit Name	SVG Identifier	Unit Conversion to Pixels
Pixel	px	1
Point	pt	1.25
Pica	pc	15
Millimeter	mm	3.543307
Centimeters	cm	35.43307
Inches	in	90

You can also use percentages to define the width and height of the document. If you are defining your attributes with percentages, note that the percentages are based on the height and width values of their containing element. In the case of artwork, its percentages will be based on the size of the SVG document or its containing element; in the case of the svg element, it will be based on the size of the browser window.

To demonstrate this, try the example shown in Listing 4.1. In this example, the document will display at various sizes, according to the browser's width and height.

LISTING 4.1   An SVG Document's Width and Height Can Be Set As Percentages Relative to Their Containing Environment (Such As a Browser Window)

```
01: <?xml version="1.0" standalone="no"?>
02: <!DOCTYPE svg PUBLIC "-//W3C//DTD SVG 1.0//EN"
03:    "http://www.w3.org/TR/2001/REC-SVG-20010904/DTD/svg10.dtd">
04:
05: <svg width="90%" height="50%">
06:        <title>Percentages</title>
07: </svg>
```

When the shape of the browser window changes, the display of the SVG document will change in proportion to these new values.

SVG's coordinate system is rather unique and quite important to note. SVG is a two-dimensional graphic display language, and thus all of its measurement units reflect off a dual axis. Just as in high school geometry, the x axis represents horizontal activity, and the y axis represents vertical activity. To represent coordinates, you use (x,y) notation.

The intersection of the axes creates the (0,0) point, and this point is generally the upper left corner of your viewport. The x units increase positively as you move to the right of the y axis and increase negatively as you move to the left. Similarly, y units increase positively as you move down from the x axis and increase negatively as you move up.

4

Be certain to note SVG's handling of the direction of the y axis, as y units traditionally increase positively as you move *up* from the x axis in mathematics.

The following example illustrates how the coordinate system works in SVG. The gradient reflects the orientation of the top left corner of any SVG file, whereas the directional
arrows show the positive escalation of x and y values.

FIGURE 4.1

*SVG's coordinate sys-
tem relates all objects
to a (0,0) point on a
grid similar to this.
Thus, an SVG docu-
ment shows only the
lower right qudrant
upon its initial load.
Positive* x *and* y *values
are obtained by moving
to the right and bottom
of this (0,0) point,
which is the SVG docu-
ment's top left corner.*

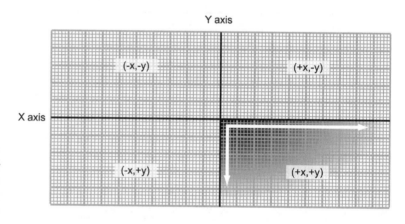

Not only does the top left corner of the SVG document adhere to this coordinate system,
but all SVG content does also. When establishing the x and y coordinates (as well as
height and width dimensions) of any shape or path, the same rules of positive and negative value escalation hold true. These x and y coordinates are generally always in reference to the top left (0,0) coordinate.

This holds true except when a transformation (see Hour 14, "Transforms") is applied to
an object or group; at that point, a unique coordinate system is established for the applied
object. The (0,0) point for the affected object/group is offset according to the transformation values applied.

Using the `viewBox`

You saw earlier how an SVG document is similar to a bulletin board. Taking this analogy
a step further, suppose you have five separate notes pinned in different locations on the
bulletin board. However, rather than letting your audience see the entire bulletin board at
one time, you decide they should see only one of the notes on the board. To achieve this
sort of "peephole" view, the svg element uses an attribute called the `viewBox`.

As mentioned earlier, the top left corner of the SVG document is the (0,0) point. The `viewBox` honors the coordinates of a file's content but adjusts the display to match its coordinates. To do this, the `viewBox` has four values, each separated by a comma or a space. The first two values specify the x and y coordinates from the SVG file that will now serve as the display's (0,0) point. The final two values specify the width and height of the content (and subsequently the scale of the content).

Thus, the `viewBox` has the following syntax:

`viewBox="X1 Y1 A B"`

where

- *X1* specifies the horizontal offset from the SVG's leftmost edge.
- *Y1* specifies the vertical offset from the SVG's topmost edge.
- *A* specifies the width of the `viewBox` in user units (unless described otherwise).
- *B* specifies the height of the `viewBox` in user units (unless described otherwise).

Each of these has a default value of `0`, meaning that no changing of the SVG document's viewport will occur unless defined otherwise. If no `viewBox` attribute is present in the `svg` element, a value of `0` is assumed for each of the four values. To better visualize the effect the `viewBox` can have on a document, refer to Figure 4.2.

4

- In all four examples, the black rectangle represents the SVG document's size (200 pixels wide by 100 pixels tall, as defined in the `svg` element).
- In example A, no changes are made to the scale of the content or the positioning of the viewport, as all values are set to `0`.
- The first two values in example B shift the viewport 20 pixels to the right and 20 pixels down but do not scale the content due to the last two values being `0`.
- Example C scales 100 pixels of width to the document's 200-pixel width and 50 pixels of height to the document's 100-pixel height. Although it is apparent that the artwork was scaled, it is important to note that the coordinate system was scaled as well. By doing so, one pixel in the SVG document will be represented as 4 pixels (2 pixels wide by 2 pixels high) in the viewer's display.
- Lastly, by customizing all the values for the `viewBox`, example D shows both the viewport being shifted and the content being scaled.

FIGURE 4.2

Four different possibil-
ities for your SVG doc-
ument's display using
the viewBox.

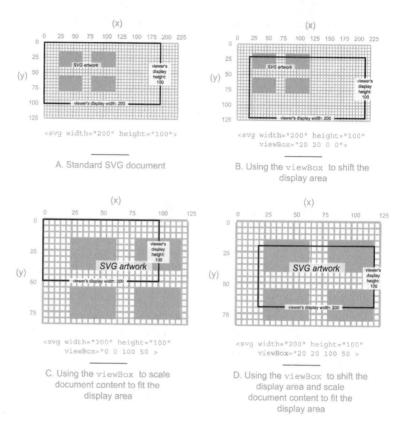

To learn the viewBox functionality, you'll need to create a simple SVG document with a basic shape in order to get an idea of how the display is altered. A document with nothing more than a circle will serve your purpose for comparing different viewBox attribute values. (Although you haven't seen any explanation of circles (or any other basic shapes) yet, don't worry; you'll learn all about how to create these shapes and more in the next hour.)

Figure 4.3 shows such a circle, created in Listing 4.2. Using Listing 4.1 as a guide, you will need to modify the svg element's width and height values to create a 100-pixel by 100-pixel document (line 5 in Listing 4.2). Line 7 then creates the circle. The result of this code, when viewed in a browser, will appear similar to Figure 4.3.

LISTING 4.2   Simple SVG Document with a Circle

```
01: <?xml version="1.0" standalone="no"?>
02: <!DOCTYPE svg PUBLIC "-//W3C//DTD SVG 1.0//EN"
03:    "http://www.w3.org/TR/2001/REC-SVG-20010904/DTD/svg10.dtd">
04:
05: <svg width="100" height="100">
06:
07: <circle cx="50" cy="50" r="30"/>
08:
09: </svg>
```

FIGURE 4.3

Simple SVG document with no viewBox *attribute (the default).*

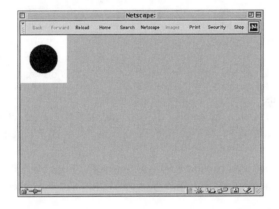

Now, to use the viewBox to move your display, add the viewBox attribute to your svg element (see line 5 in Listing 4.3 below). The viewBox attribute should be added to the svg element with a value of 20 20, thus offsetting the view of your artwork by 20 units along both the x and the y axes. Figure 4.4 shows the result: your circle now appears touching the left and top edges of the display.

LISTING 4.3   Simple SVG Document with a Circle Offset 20 Pixels Using the viewBox Attribute

```
01: <?xml version="1.0" standalone="no"?>
02: <!DOCTYPE svg PUBLIC "-//W3C//DTD SVG 1.0//EN"
03:    "http://www.w3.org/TR/2001/REC-SVG-20010904/DTD/svg10.dtd">
04:
05: <svg width="100" height="100" viewBox="20 20">
06:
07: <circle cx="50" cy="50" r="30"/>
08:
09: </svg>
```

4

FIGURE 4.4

Simple SVG document with viewBox *values that shift the document's viewport.*

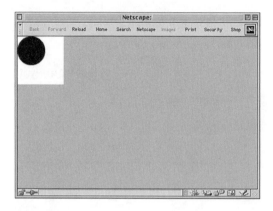

In other words, when you give the viewBox attribute two positive values on line 5, your visible area shifts to the right and down. By giving the viewBox values of 20 20, your peephole moved 20 pixels over to the right and 20 pixels down, as you saw in Figure 4.4.

With the previous example, you moved the display with the first two values for the viewBox. Now, to stretch the display to focus more on the circle, change your viewBox attribute values to 0 0 60 60 (see line 5 in Listing 4.4). By changing these two final values of the viewBox attribute, you are equating 60 pixels from the document's original coordinate space with an actual 100-pixel dimension. Figure 4.5 shows the result of such a code change—a cropped circle focusing on the left and top edges.

LISTING 4.4   Adjusting the viewBox Attribute's Final Values Stretches the Display to Focus More on the Circle

```
01: <?xml version="1.0" standalone="no"?>
02: <!DOCTYPE svg PUBLIC "-//W3C//DTD SVG 1.0//EN"
03:    "http://www.w3.org/TR/2001/REC-SVG-20010904/DTD/svg10.dtd">
04:
05: <svg width="100" height="100" viewBox="0 0 60 60">
06:
07: <circle cx="50" cy="50" r="30"/>
08:
09: </svg>
```

Figure 4.5
Simple SVG document with viewBox *values that scale content to draw more attention to the circle.*

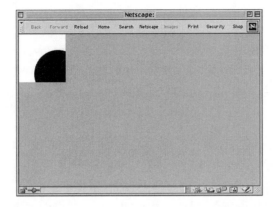

The two final values in line 5's viewBox attribute determine the scale of the content compared with the actual size of the document. In this example, you equated 60 pixels from the document's original coordinate space with the document's actual 100-pixel width and height.

It is important to note that although the viewBox changes the (0,0) point for the screen display and its scale, it does not affect the actual content's coordinate system. Rather, it simply pans (and/or stretches) the content to its coordinates.

Creating a Resizable Document

In certain instances, it may be desirable to create an SVG file that can stretch to fill your browser's screen. As SVG is made of vector graphics, your images will scale quite beautifully in most instances (unless you've embedded raster images, which will be covered in Hour 11, "Images").

To create scaling content, you will need to do two things:

1. Modify your SVG document data
2. Modify your HTML embed element data

In order to specify the method in which your content will scale, you must include the preserveAspectRatio attribute in your svg element. This attribute determines how your content distorts in accordance with the shape of the viewBox. There are dozens of possible values for this attribute, each offering developers the choice of how their content's aspect ratio (the proportional relationship between the width and height) is scaled and/or cropped in relation to the viewBox. (As the possible values are so numerous, consider checking the specification, http://www.w3.org/TR/SVG/ coords.html#PreserveAspectRatioAttribute, should you be so inclined.)

If the preserveAspectRatio attribute is not included in the svg element, an SVG viewer will assume it should scale all content so that the width and height scale relative to each other. However, if the preserveAspectRatio attribute is included with a value of none, your document's content will scale so that the height and width of your content are relative to the height and width of your document (and not in relation to each other).

To illustrate this possibility, first create a document with a rectangle and a text snippet (lines 6 and 8 in Listing 4.5). (Again, don't worry; you'll cover basic shapes next hour and text in Hour 16, "Formatting.") In order for this content to stretch according to the dimensions of its eventual container (the browser window) you must include the preserveAspectRatio attribute (with a value of none) within the svg element (line 4). The SVG document's dimensions will then change according to the size of the browser window once you have modified your HTML file in the next step.

LISTING 4.5   Editing the svg Element to Allow the SVG Content to Scale According to the Document's Dimensions

```
01: <?xml version="1.0" standalone="no"?>
02: <!DOCTYPE svg PUBLIC "-//W3C//DTD SVG 1.0//EN"
            "http://www.w3.org/TR/2001/REC-SVG-20010904/DTD/svg10.dtd">
03:
04: <svg viewBox="0 0 500 300" preserveAspectRatio="none" >
05:
06:         <rect x="20" y="20" width="90%" height="75%" />
07:
08:         <text x="40" y="280">Stretch your boundaries to the max.</text>
09:
10: </svg>
```

Next, modify your HTML (Listing 4.6). Replace the embed element's dimension values you normally would use to hard code the width and height of the SVG file with percentages (line 5). Change the name of the SVG document to reflect the file name you are using, and then load the HTML in your browser.

LISTING 4.6   Modifying the Dimensions of Your HTML's Embed Element to Accommodate Percentage-Based Values Allows Your SVG to Stretch to the Dimensions of the Browser Window

```
01: <html>
02:
03:         <body bgcolor="grey">
04:
05:                 <embed src="document_name.svg" width="100%" height="100%"/>
06:
07:         </body>
08:
09: </html>
```

By modifying these two chunks of code, your SVG files will stretch to fill the browser window (minus the browser's default margins between content and browser frame). Notice how even text is stretched to fit these new dimensions. Although this is an interesting and sometimes useful trick, the remaining examples in this book will all be set to fixed sizes.

 Be sure to set your HTML file's embed element's height and width attribute values back to their original dimension settings when you've finished this experiment. If you do not, your examples in the next several hours will distort according to the browser's dimensions.

Summary

SVG allows for a variety of units of measurement, letting you code your documents according to your preferences. Although defaulting to user units (which equate to pixels on the computer screen) unless otherwise specified, SVG allows for variable dimensions for both object and document dimensions. By using percentages, your SVG content can scale in proportion to its container (most often the Web browser).

The viewBox attribute modifies how content is displayed within the SVG document's dimensions. viewBox can be used to alter the location of the top leftmost corner of the content's display, scale the content to match the dimension's of the display, or both.

Knowing the fundamentals of SVG document layout, you're now ready to begin drawing. Hour 5 will introduce you to the basic shapes, lines, and paths you can create in SVG.

Q&A

Q Do I need to include a `viewBox` attribute on every `svg` element?

A No. The `viewBox` is a special attribute used when you specifically need to distort the viewport of your content. In most cases, you will never need to deal with a `viewBox` attribute. Keep in mind, however, that most SVG WYSIWYG editors (such as Adobe Illustrator) will export a `viewBox` setting that does nothing to your viewport. Unless you need to edit those settings to distort your viewport, you can just delete this attribute and its values.

Q When using percentages, do both `width` and `height` need to be percentage-based?

A No. Just as you can specify varying units for the `width` and `height` attributes (such as `<rect width="50px" height="3in"/>`), you can specify only one dimension as a percentage (such as `<rect width="50%" height="3in"/>`).

Workshop

The Workshop is designed to help you anticipate possible questions, review what you've learned, and begin learning how to put your knowledge into practice.

Quiz

1. What is SVG's default unit of measurement?

2. Aside from precise units, `width` and `height` attributes can also accept which kind of values?

3. True or False: When there is no `preserveAspectRatio` attribute, the proportions of the SVG are preserved when it is resized.

4. To which element does the `viewBox` attribute belong?

5. What is the purpose of the `viewBox` attribute?

Answers

1. SVG's default unit of measurement is known as a "user space value." This value is equivalent to the screen pixel, unless modified by a transformation.

2. SVG can use percentages to define the width and height dimensions of an object.

3. **True.** The default value of the `preserveAspectRatio` attribute (the one used if no `preserveAspectRatio` attribute is used) ensures that the proportions of the SVG are preserved when it is resized.

4. The `viewBox` attribute belongs to the `svg` element, but its results affect all of the document's displayed artwork.

5. The `viewBox` attribute determines what area of the document's content gets displayed within the document's dimensions. Content may appear to be offset, stretched or cropped depending on the values applied.

Exercises

1. Using the last example in this hour as a guide, modify the SVG document (and the associated HTML) by specifying the height but giving it variable width.

2. SVG doesn't demand an adherence to one unit of measurement. Try changing the height and width of your document by giving each variable a different unit of measurement. For instance, use inches for the width, and centimeters for the height.

3. For the adventurous, check out the SVG specifications section on the `preserveAspectRatio` attribute at `http://www.w3.org/TR/SVG/coords.html#PreserveAspectRatioAttribute`. Try the various alternate values in place of the `none` value to see how your content is positioned and scaled.

4

Hour 5

SVG's Shape Toolbox

Now that you're familiar with how an SVG document is set up and structured, you are ready to move on to more exciting challenges. Vector graphics are generally made from a variety of shapes. Unlike raster imagery, such as a photograph, vector artwork is composed of a series of strokes (lines) and fills that define geometric shapes, such as rectangles, ellipses, and freeform paths.

Before you can learn to "paint" your artwork (with fills and strokes), you must learn how to draw the shapes that define the borders for such painting. In this chapter, you will learn how to create the following shapes:

- rectangles
- circles and ellipses
- polygons, polylines, and lines
- freeform paths

After learning how to *draw* each of these shapes, and after understanding their common and unique notations, you'll be ready to face the challenge of determining how they *look* in the next hour.

Basic Shapes

Drawing shapes in SVG can be quite simple. Whereas most designers use their drawing program's shape tools to eyeball the dimensions and placement of the shapes they draw, SVG demands precision from the start. You will never need to guess whether some piece of your artwork is aligned with another, as the mathematical coordinates you use to define every piece of artwork will answer such a question. Although entering exact values for every element may seem a bit demanding of the designer at first, you will quickly come to appreciate the opportunities this precision affords.

In some ways, it is more fitting to think of drawing in SVG with words than with a paintbrush. To help ease this "verbal drawing," the authors of the specification created a series of SVG elements that literally interpreted their own described shapes. By using the `rect`, `circle`, `ellipse`, and `line` elements, you will get exactly the described object.

Two other available drawing elements are the `polyline` and `polygon` elements. Whereas the `line` element defines only a straight line with two points, the `polyline` element defines a sequence of straight lines. The `polygon` element is much the same, except that it is used for defining a multi-lined element that is closed.

Rectangles

The rectangle is likely the most common object you will draw, and drawing such a box is made possible using the `rect` element. The `rect` element has four easy-to-understand attributes that define its position and size:

```
x
y
width
height
```

The x and y attributes define the coordinates of the starting corner of the rectangle, whereas width describes the horizontal measurement (moving right of the x coordinate if a positive value) and height describes the vertical measurement (moving south of the y coordinate if a positive value).

Using the news center graphic referred to at the end of Hour 1, you can begin using the `rect` element to build this graphic. To illustrate how the `rect` element operates, begin by creating the initial outline of the news center, as shown in Listing 5.1. Using the 500-pixel width and 300-pixel height document dimensions shown in previous figures, start the `rect` element 10 pixels from the document's edge to provide a comfortable margin around the piece.

LISTING 5.1 Drawing the Outline of the Content Area for the News Center Graphic

```
01: <?xml version="1.0" standalone="no"?>
02: <!DOCTYPE svg PUBLIC "-//W3C//DTD SVG 1.0//EN"
03:    "http://www.w3.org/TR/2001/REC-SVG-20010904/DTD/svg10.dtd">
04:
05: <svg  width="500" height="300" >
06:
07:        <rect id="Outline" x="10" y="10" width="480" height="280"/>
08:
09: </svg>
```

FIGURE 5.1

A simple rectangle that will serve as the outline of the book's news center example.

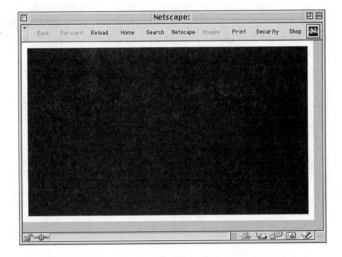

You'll notice several things in the code you just created:

1. In line 5, you created a 500-pixel wide by 300-pixel tall SVG document.

> As mentioned last chapter, any unit that is not specified is actually a "user space value." For the simplicity of the explanations in this book, the assumption is that you will be viewing these examples within an Internet browser on your computer, and thus the term "pixels" is used. If you do not, then the values may be interpreted in a unit of measurement standard to that device.

2. In line 7, you've created a 480-pixel wide by 280-pixel tall rectangle that has an even 10 pixels between the rectangle's edge and the document's edge.

5

3. Also in line 7, you've used an id attribute (which you learned about in Hour 3) within the rect element to name the particular use of this rectangle. While naming elements may seem meaningless in such a small example, it's a good habit to get into.

When you open the above document in your browser, you will notice that a giant black 480 × 280 rectangle appears, as shown in Figure 5.1. Without any style definitions applied, all elements will appear with a black fill and without a stroke (or outline). As you will be covering style in the next hour, you need not worry about the large rectangle's current appearance.

Now that you've taken the first step in creating the news center, you'll proceed in Listing 5.2 to create the remaining major rectangles used in the file. Notice that each item should be labeled with its own unique id attribute. As none of the rectangles have any specified style information, they will all appear as black boxes; as you created the document's outline previously, none of the rectangles you create next will be discernible over the top of the large "Outline" rectangle.

LISTING 5.2 Adding Major Rectangles to the News Center Graphic Code

```
01: <?xml version="1.0" standalone="no"?>
02: <!DOCTYPE svg PUBLIC "-//W3C//DTD SVG 1.0//EN"
03:    "http://www.w3.org/TR/2001/REC-SVG-20010904/DTD/svg10.dtd">
04:
05: <svg  width="500" height="300">
06:
07:        <rect id="Background" x="0" y="0" width="500" height="300"/>
08:
09:        <rect id="BkgdSun" x="10" y="45" width="200" height="245"/>
10:
11:        <rect id="Outline" x="10" y="10" width="480" height="280"/>
12:
13:        <rect id="BarTitle" x="10" y="10" width="480" height="35"/>
14:
15:        <rect id="BarStatistics" x="10" y="245" width="200" height="45"/>
16:
17: </svg>
```

In this example, you have created a series of black rectangles, one on top of the other, but you have no way to discern which is which. Before moving to circles, there is a convenient trick that can help you hide objects from view.

As you learned in Hour 2, "SVG's Foundation," any content, whether plain English or SVG code, enclosed with comment tags will not be interpreted, and thus not displayed. (Remember, though, that a comment may not reside within another comment or within a tag.) Thus, to make sure the rectangles you just created appear properly, you can "hide" all but one by placing them inside the comment tags. Before hiding any objects, you should begin by creating a sample document. For example, the code in Listing 5.3 shows a valid use of the comment in lines 17, 18, and 19.

LISTING 5.3   Proper Use of the Comment

```
01: <?xml version="1.0" standalone="no"?>
02: <!DOCTYPE svg PUBLIC "-//W3C//DTD SVG 1.0//EN"
03:    "http://www.w3.org/TR/2001/REC-SVG-20010904/DTD/svg10.dtd">
04:
05: <svg  width="500" height="300">
06:
07:        <rect id="Background" x="0" y="0" width="500" height="300"/>
08:
09:        <rect id="BkgdSun" x="10" y="45" width="200" height="245"/>
10:
11:        <rect id="Outline" x="10" y="10" width="480" height="280"/>
12:
13:        <rect id="BarTitle" x="10" y="10" width="480" height="35"/>
14:
15:        <rect id="BarStatistics" x="10" y="245" width="200" height="45"/>
16:
17:        <!--
18:               This is a comment field.
19:        -->
20: </svg>
```

As the code in Listing 5.2 appears in your browser, you'll notice that you still can't see any of the new rectangles, as they simply appear as black rectangles on top of one large black rectangle. To solve this issue, you can use the comment tags to surround each of the rectangle elements that you want to prevent from displaying. By containing several of the `rect` elements within the comment field, you will be able to see the one remaining rectangle's placement when viewed with an SVG viewer.

Listing 5.4 shows such a use of the comment tags. On line 7, the comment bracket opens and contains all but one of the rectangles by the time it closes on line 17. Line 19's rectangle is the only one that will appear as a viewer parses the SVG document (shown in Figure 5.2), as it remains outside of the comment's tags.

LISTING 5.4   Using the Comment to Prevent Elements from Displaying

```
01: <?xml version="1.0" standalone="no"?>
02: <!DOCTYPE svg PUBLIC "-//W3C//DTD SVG 1.0//EN"
03:    "http://www.w3.org/TR/2001/REC-SVG-20010904/DTD/svg10.dtd">
04:
05: <svg  width="500" height="300">
06:
```

continues

LISTING 5.4   Continued

```
07:        <!--
08:
09:                <rect id="Background" x="0" y="0" width="500" height="300"/>
10:
11:                <rect id="BkgdSun" x="10" y="45" width="200" height="245"/>
12:
13:                <rect id="Outline" x="10" y="10" width="480" height="280"/>
14:
15:                <rect id="BarTitle" x="10" y="10" width="480" height="35"/>
16:
17:        -->
18:
19:        <rect id="BarStatistics" x="10" y="245" width="200" height="45"/>
20:
21: </svg>
```

FIGURE 5.2

By enclosing all the rect *elements except one within a comment, only the rectangle in the lower left corner with the* id *value of "BarStatistics" is visible.*

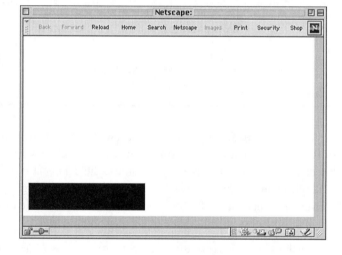

In this way, comments serve two purposes for developers: 1) to insert notes in plain English to describe neighboring content's purpose or 2) to disable code, preventing the comments' content from rendering and functioning (as in the case of an animation or interaction), thus allowing for selective development and testing.

Circles

Arguably as commonly used as rectangles, circles are incredibly easy to create. The circle element has three frequent attributes, unlike rectangle's four. To define a circle, you need to know only the center point coordinates and the radius. The attribute names are as follows:

cx center point coordinate
cy center point coordinate
r   radius

To keep your examples in terms of the news center graphic you'll be creating throughout this book, begin using the `circle` element to draw the sun in the weather illustration. In line 7 of Listing 5.5, you'll see the `circle` element with its three attributes. The cx and cy attributes are positioning the circle's center point in accordance with the news center graphic, whereas the r attribute sizes the circle's radius according to the sun's width. Figure 5.3 shows the result of this code.

LISTING 5.5   Creating a Circle

```
01: <?xml version="1.0" standalone="no"?>
02: <!DOCTYPE svg PUBLIC "-//W3C//DTD SVG 1.0//EN"
03:    "http://www.w3.org/TR/2001/REC-SVG-20010904/DTD/svg10.dtd">
04:
05: <svg  width="500" height="300">
06:
07:        <circle id="Sun" cx="105" cy="160" r="56"/>
08:
09: </svg>
```

FIGURE 5.3

A simple circle serves as the foundation for the sun illustration in the news center's weather graphic.

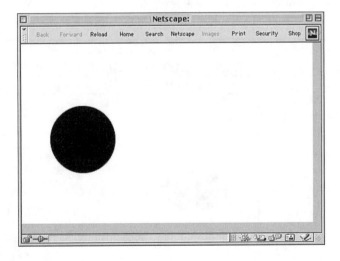

5

With only three important attributes to remember, the `circle` element provides a quick and easy method of drawing circular objects.

Ellipses

Similar to the `circle` element, the `ellipse` element creates an oval, whether circular or oblong in nature. The syntax for the `ellipse` element has four attributes:

cx center point coordinate
cy center point coordinate
rx horizontal radius
ry vertical radius

To illustrate the `ellipse` element, take the same coordinates you used to create the center point of the `circle` in the last exercise. As the `ellipse` has two radiuses (one horizontal, one vertical), you'll need to provide two separate values. In line 9 of Listing 5.6, the value for the horizontal radius is made greater than the value for the vertical radius to show the difference in appearance between the ellipse and the circle. Figure 5.4 shows the wide ellipse in the circle's former location.

LISTING 5.6   Creating an Ellipse

```
01: <?xml version="1.0" standalone="no"?>
02: <!DOCTYPE svg PUBLIC "-//W3C//DTD SVG 1.0//EN"
03:    "http://www.w3.org/TR/2001/REC-SVG-20010904/DTD/svg10.dtd">
04:
05: <svg  width="500" height="300">
06:
07: <ellipse cx="105" cy="160" rx="56" ry="35"/>
08:
09: </svg>
```

FIGURE 5.4

An ellipse uses syntax similar to the circle, except that it allows for different radiuses for the height and width.

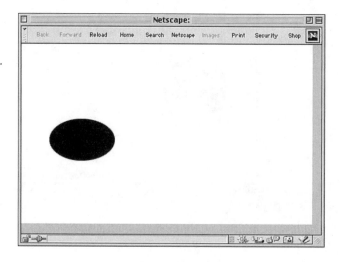

The `ellipse` element can easily make circles as well. By making the `rx` and `ry` values the same, the resulting ellipse is a perfect circle.

Lines

The `line` element is also a very simple shape to create. There are only four attributes for this element: `x1`, `x2`, `y1`, and `y2`. `x1` and `y1` represent the initial x,y coordinates of the line, whereas `x2` and `y2` represent the end coordinates. Listing 5.7 shows the simplicity of the `line` element and is displayed in Figure 5.5. You'll need to include a `style` property in the `line` element, as shown in line 7, otherwise the line will render invisible in some viewers. (Don't worry; you'll learn all about how to apply style in the next hour.)

LISTING 5.7   Creating a Line

```
01: <?xml version="1.0" standalone="no"?>
02: <!DOCTYPE svg PUBLIC "-//W3C//DTD SVG 1.0//EN"
03:    "http://www.w3.org/TR/2001/REC-SVG-20010904/DTD/svg10.dtd">
04:
05: <svg  width="500" height="300">
06:
07: <line x1="105" y1="160" x2="410" y2="100" style="stroke:black;"/>
08:
09: </svg>
```

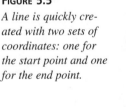

FIGURE 5.5

A line is quickly created with two sets of coordinates: one for the start point and one for the end point.

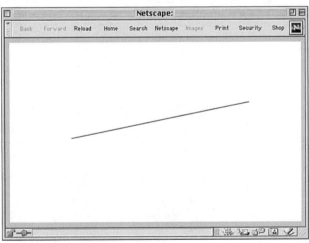

Drawing a line is a simple process. Know your four points (2 for the start point and 2 for the end point) and you've got all you need to define this element.

Polylines and Polygons

polyline and polygon elements are very similar; their differences lie only in whether the produced shape is closed. To draw using these elements, you'll need a different set of notations than that used for the previous shapes. Whereas with the rect element, you defined beginning 'x' and 'y' coordinates followed by width and height attributes, you will now use only (x,y) coordinates to define the points of a polyline or polygon.

The syntax for both polyline and polygon elements is the same. To describe a polyline or a polygon, you must add a points attribute. The value for the points attribute is a list of coordinate pairs (two coordinates separated by a comma) separated by whitespace (such as a space or a line break). Lines are drawn sequentially, connecting the coordinates in the order they are listed, starting with the first point and continuing to the last. In the case of the polygon, a line will connect the last point listed and the first, effectively "closing" the artwork.

To help distinguish the subtle differences between the polyline and polygon elements, you can create a lightning bolt for the news center's weather example by using each element. The bolt is commonly rendered with only eleven points to define its jagged edges. To understand the coordinates you'll be using (whether in the bolt illustration or otherwise), it often helps to draw the illustration on graph paper. By using this ruled and numbered grid, plotting precise coordinates becomes quite simple. (To assist you, a reproducible grid has been included in Hour 24, "References.") To represent the bolt, draw out Figure 5.6:

FIGURE 5.6

Define your artwork on a grid to determine the coordinates it will require. In this case, a lightning bolt can be simplified to eleven necessary coordinates.

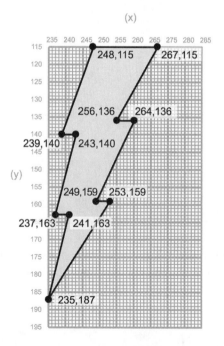

Using these eleven coordinates, you would then create the document, as shown in Listing 5.8. Note that the points for the bolt are listed in the value of the `points` attribute. Each (x,y) coordinate is separated by whitespace. To see whether the object is closed or not, you will need to add two brief style properties to your artwork (shown on line 8). The lightning bolt is shown in Figure 5.7.

LISTING 5.8   Figure 5.7's Lighting Bolt Drawn with the `polyline` Element

```
01:   <?xml version="1.0" standalone="no"?>
02:   <!DOCTYPE svg PUBLIC "-//W3C//DTD SVG 1.0//EN"
03:     "http://www.w3.org/TR/2001/REC-SVG-20010904/DTD/svg10.dtd">
04:
05:   <svg  width="500" height="300">
06:
07:
08:       <polyline style="stroke:black; fill:yellow;"
09:             points="248,115
10:                     239,140 243,140
11:                     237,163 241,163
12:                     235,187
13:                     253,159 249,159
14:                     261,136 256,136
15:                     267,115" />
16:   </svg>
```

FIGURE 5.7

A lightning bolt is drawn using the `polyline` *element.*

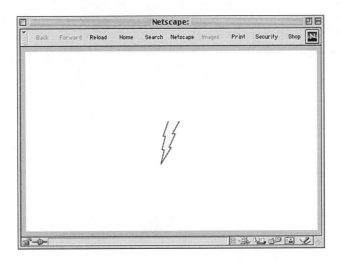

5

The result is a beautiful, yellow lightning bolt with no top. Technically, you could create a twelfth point to close the bolt; however, the polygon element will do the same trick with the existing coordinates. By replacing the polyline element with the polygon element, as shown in Listing 5.9 (line 8), the bolt will have an outline around its entire perimeter (Figure 5.8).

LISTING 5.9   Figure 5.8's Lighting Bolt Drawn with the polygon Element

```
01:  <?xml version="1.0" standalone="no"?>
02:  <!DOCTYPE svg PUBLIC "-//W3C//DTD SVG 1.0//EN"
03:    "http://www.w3.org/TR/2001/REC-SVG-20010904/DTD/svg10.dtd">
04:
05:  <svg  width="500" height="300">
06:
07:
08:      <polygon style="stroke:black; fill:yellow;"
09:            points="248,115
10:                239,140 243,140
11:                237,163 241,163
12:                235,187
13:                253,159 249,159
14:                261,136 256,136
15:                267,115" />
16:  </svg>
```

FIGURE 5.8

A lightning bolt gains its top, defining line using the polygon *element.*

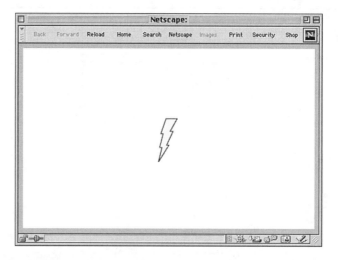

By simply using the polygon element, the same coordinates result in a solid, closed shape. Although saving one coordinate pair's worth of information may not seem to be worth the hassle, remember that the simpler your files are constructed, the simpler they are to manage. The importance of this will manifest itself later in this book, as we compound several items together.

Paths

The path element is similar to the polyline and polygon elements in the sense that it is used to draw continuous lines. Using the basic shapes you've read about thus far is really not much different than describing the objects in the path format, other than that their required information set is far simpler. In other words, drawing with basic shape elements is much easier than defining every simple shape as a series of coordinates and directional notations by using the path element. However, the path element allows you to draw anything the basic shapes allow, plus much more.

A path need not be comprised of straight lines, as polyline and polygon are forced to be. As curves are supported with the path element, more information than coordinates is required, making path considerably more complex than previous shapes.

If you are familiar with Bézier curves and illustration programs then you will have a leg up in this area, as paths operate under similar concepts in those applications. For every curve rendered, four coordinates are required: two coordinates for the beginning and end of the line and two coordinates for defining the arc of the curve. To illustrate this concept, take a look at Figure 5.9.

FIGURE 5.9

Four coordinates are required to define any curve.

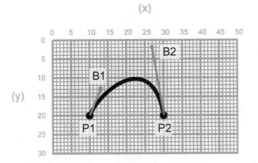

In Figure 5.9, the two points of the line are represented as 'P1' and 'P2,' whereas the two coordinates defining the degree of the arc are 'B1' and 'B2.' In illustration programs, the lines you see above (extending from the line points to the arc points) are dubbed "arc handles." They do not visibly appear in the final illustration, but rather help designers visualize how their curves are being created. To change the degree and direction of the arc between these two points, you simply need to change the location of the 'B1' and 'B2' points, as shown in Figure 5.10.

FIGURE 5.10

To adjust the arc of a curve, simply modify the "arc handle" coordinates.

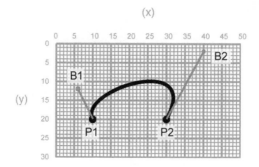

As you can see, the complexity of information required to define a line has significantly increased. Thankfully, the news center illustration you will be creating throughout this book does not require extensive `path` illustrations. To illustrate the use of the `path` element, you will create the raindrops for the thunderstorm illustration in the weather graphic. The raindrop serves as a good example, as it contains both straight and curved lines.

The `path` element requires significantly different notation than our other elements. Rather than a `points` attribute, as you saw in the `polyline` and `polygon` elements, `path` uses the `d` attribute to define the list of coordinates and directions that describe the displayed line. As you're describing arc and curve data, you'll need to include additional commands with your coordinates.

The syntax for the `d` attribute may seem a bit complex at first glance. The values associated with the `d` attribute are a series of coordinates and "path commands." These values always start with M (which signifies the starting of a path) and are followed by an x,y coordinate (which defines the starting point of the path). What follows next depends on what kind of path you are trying to draw (whether straight or curved) and how complex it is. Although there are several path commands available to accomplish these tasks, the most common commands are presented in Table 5.1.

TABLE 5.1 Common `path` Commands

Command	Meaning	Description
M	Moveto	Used to start a path. For example, *"<path d="M x1,y1..."/>*
L	Lineto	The L command draws a straight line from the previous coordinates to the coordinates following the command. For example, *"<path d="M x1,y1 L x2,y2 "/>*

continues

TABLE 5.1   Continued

Command	Meaning	Description
C	Curveto	Used to draw a curve. Followed by three coordinates, the C command requires a total of four coordinates to define a curve. It takes the coordinate previous to its location ("P1" in Figure 5.9) as its starting point, establishes the first following coordinate as the first arc handle ("B1"), the second coordinate as the second arc handle ("B2"), and the third coordinate as the end point of the curve. For example, "*<path d="M x1,y1 C x2,y2 x3,y3 x4,y4 "/>*
z	Closepath	The Z command closes off a path, similar to the way the poly-gon element closed our lightning bolt illustration. For example, "*<path d="M x1,y1 L x2,y2 x3,y3 Z"/>*

path commands use capitalized letters to refer to absolute coordinates, meaning that x1,y1 and x2,y2 refer to specific points on our SVG document's grid. However, if you use lower case letters instead, the path element will think of the coordinates following the lowercase command as relative. In other words, x2,y2's position would not be plotted in relation to the document's 0,0 position, but rather from the position of x1,y1.

To demonstrate the difference between absolute and relative coordinates in path commands, you should observe the difference between the examples shown in Figure 5.11. Both examples draw the same line, but you will notice that the coordinates listed in the example to the right (except for the start point of the path) don't match the document's coordinates. That's because the coordinates are relative to the first coordinates. The coordinates given in the left example are absolute, meaning that they refer to specific coordinates within the SVG document's coordinate system. The first arc handle's coordinates are listed as 12,0, meaning that the arc handle's position is 12 pixels to the right and 0 pixels down from the previous coordinates' location.

5

FIGURE 5.11

Compare the manner in which absolute (left) and relative (right) path commands draw the same line.

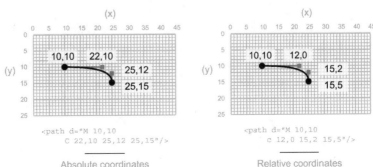

Absolute coordinates   Relative coordinates

Absolute and relative coordinate systems each have their own advantages. Absolute coordinates are oftentimes easier to plot initially but require lots of mental math to move the object around. You either need to recalculate every coordinate in the path or use a transformation on the entire path (covered in Hour 14, "Transforms"). Relative coordinates, on the other hand, are easier to move around the page. You need only edit the first coordinate in the path, and the subsequent coordinates follow.

To further explore the path element and its complexities, creating the raindrop from the news center's thunderstorm weather graphic will provide a solid example. Before you begin coding, however, you will need to plan the coordinates of the drop. Similar to the way the lightning bolt was plotted earlier in this hour, you will need to draw the raindrop out on your graph paper (Figure 5.12).

FIGURE 5.12

The raindrop to be drawn in SVG, overlaying a grid in order to demonstrate the coordinates required to draw such a path.

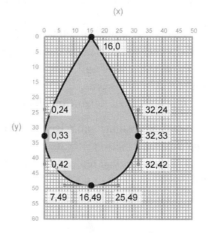

You'll notice that the top of the raindrop does not have "arc handles" that define the curve's arc. They have been intentionally left off to create the sharp point; thus, the handles share the same coordinates as the point itself (effectively eliminating any curvature).

To create the raindrop for the thunderstorm illustration, you will need to take the coordinates displayed in Figure 5.11 and use them in conjunction with the path commands from Table 5.1, mentioned earlier in the hour. By combining these two chunks of information, you can create the illustration in SVG (shown in Figure 5.13), similar to the code shown in Listing 5.10.

LISTING 5.10 Using Absolute Points in the `path` Element to Create a Raindrop Illustration

```
01: <?xml version="1.0" standalone="no"?>
02: <!DOCTYPE svg PUBLIC "-//W3C//DTD SVG 1.0//EN"
03:    "http://www.w3.org/TR/2001/REC-SVG-20010904/DTD/svg10.dtd">
04:
05: <svg  width="500" height="300">
06:
07:         <path d="M16,0
08:                 C 16,0 0,24 0,33
09:                 C 0,42 7,49 16,49.
10:                 C 25,49 32,42 32,33
11:                 C 32,24 16,0 16,0" />
12:
13: </svg>
```

FIGURE 5.13

Using the coordinates determined in Figure 5.12, you can draw this raindrop illustration quickly in SVG using the path *element.*

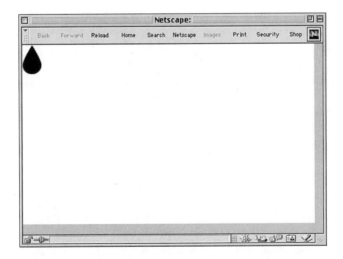

If you look at line 7 in this code, you will see that the path begins at the coordinates 16,0. (Thinking back to the diagram in Figure 5.10, these coordinates are similar to "P1.") As line 8 begins with a capital C, you know two things: 1) you will be defining a curve and 2) the coordinate system is absolute.

The last coordinates on line 8 describe the next point on the path, and the cycle begins again, with the C command designating the next two coordinate pairs as arc handle points and the remaining coordinate pair as the next path point.

5

If you wanted to move this raindrop illustration out of the corner of the document, you'd have to recalculate every coordinate to accommodate for the shifted x and y positions. As you can imagine, there are probably things you'd rather be doing in the middle of a coding project than a series of calculations. To accommodate developers who want the ability to easily move their paths around their documents, the relative path commands were defined.

As shown back in Figure 5.11, relative paths look the same as absolute paths; only their coordinates and notation are different. To assist in creating a relative path example using the same raindrop, you'll need to plot the points in terms of their relationship to other points. Compare Figure 5.12, which shows the absolute system's coordinates, with Figure 5.14, which shows the relative system's coordinates.

FIGURE 5.14

The same raindrop as Figure 5.12 but plotted with relative coordinates. Notice how only the topmost coordinate pair is in accordance with the document's coordinates. The remaining coordinate pairs are relative to their previous path command.

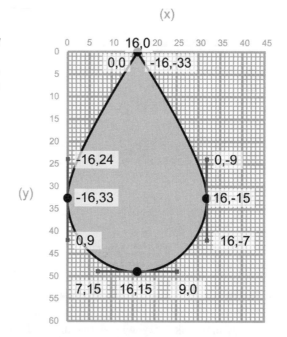

Only the topmost coordinates adhere to the document's coordinate system. Moving in a counter-clockwise direction, the next three coordinate pairs (`0,0` `-16,24` `-16,33`) are relative to the topmost. The next three coordinate pairs (`0,9` `7,15` `16,15`) are relative to the point immediately previous to it (`-16,33`). Such coordinates produce the beginning code for the `path` element:

```
<path d="M 16,0
  c 0,0 -16,24 -16,33
  c 0,9 7,15 16,15
  ../>
```

This structure mimics the absolute path command's syntax; the first coordinate pair (immediately after the start command: M) represents a point on the path, the two pairs immediately following the path command (c, in this case) represent arc handles, and the third and final pair represents the next point on the path. The cycle continues again, this time with the coordinates relating to the previous coordinate. Translating all the plotted coordinates to the appropriate path command translates into the code shown in Listing 5.11.

LISTING 5.11   Using Relative Points in the path Element to Create a Raindrop Illustration

```
01: <?xml version="1.0" standalone="no"?>
02: <!DOCTYPE svg PUBLIC "-//W3C//DTD SVG 1.0//EN"
03: "http://www.w3.org/TR/2001/REC-SVG-20010904/DTD/svg10.dtd">
04:
05: <svg  width="500" height="300">
06:
07:        <path d="M16,0
08:                c 0,0 -16,24 -16,33
09:                c 0,9 7,15 16,15
10:                c 9,0 16,-7 16,-15
11:                c 0,-9 -16,-33 -16,-33"/>
12:
13: </svg>
```

The benefit of relative path values is the ease of moving your path around the document. For instance, changing the initial start point of the path (16,0) to a more central point (250,140) simply moves the entire artwork (see Figure 5.15). If you apply the same change to the code in Listing 5.10, the top point of the raindrop will be stretched to the document's center point, but the remainder of the image will retain its original place.

5

FIGURE 5.15

Using the relative coordinates determined in Figure 5.14, you can draw a raindrop that can easily be repositioned.

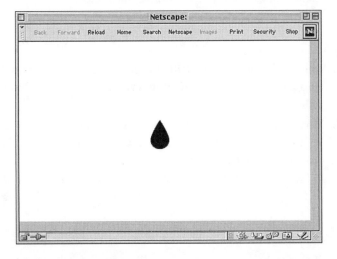

On a small scale, such as that of a raindrop, drawing with paths doesn't seem so tough. As your path illustration becomes more complex, however, mastering path commands becomes essential.

 Programs such as Adobe Illustrator and Jasc WebDraw allow for their artwork to be exported as SVG files. Thus, by using one of these tools (or any of the others that are available), you can significantly reduce the amount of time required to draw complex paths in the code by hand.

Summary

When possible, you will want to draw your objects using the basic shapes—rectangle, circle, and ellipse—covered in this hour. Paths, used to define other shapes, can contain hundreds of coordinates and path commands. Their textual information does not leave many clues as to their visual interpretation, whereas basic shapes use element names that are easy to visualize.

On the other hand, the world is all the more exciting of a place because it doesn't confine every object to the rules of a rectangle, ellipse, or line. As such, you will encounter incredibly complex illustrations that are only possible using paths. What's more, you can describe your paths using absolute or relative coordinates, allowing you some flexibility in how to describe your shapes. Whichever method you prefer (whether basic shapes or paths), you will need to have a solid grasp on both, as you will invariably need their services to tackle certain drawings.

Now that you've examined basic SVG drawing functionalities, the next hour will be spent learning how to apply style information to them.

Q&A

Q I'm not interested in plotting the coordinates for every point in my design. How can I design my content in a traditional fashion but end up with SVG code?

A Most designers will cringe at the thought of only being able to design in code. WYSIWYG SVG editors do exist, allowing you to draw and arrange your designs onscreen before exporting or saving the documents into an SVG format. For a list of the available WYSIWYG tools, please see Hour 24, "References."

Q **I understand how to draw shapes in SVG, but how can I create more subtle, paint-like effects instead of harsh lines?**

A SVG is composed of vector graphics, which are, by their very nature, geometrical. Thus, you cannot "paint" with soft edges in the same fashion you could using PhotoShop or another raster imagery program. You can, however, apply filter effects (see Hour 10) to your geometric shapes to create raster-like effects.

Workshop

The Workshop is designed to help you anticipate possible questions, review what you've learned, and begin learning how to put your knowledge into practice.

Quiz

1. What element is used to create a box shape?

2. What two attributes does the `circle` element need to define its center point?

3. True or False: The `polyline` element automatically completes its paths?

4. What does the `M` path command stand for?

5. How do path commands differentiate between absolute and relative coordinates?

Answers

1. The `rect` element is used to describe any rectangular shape, including squares.

2. The `cx` and `cy` attributes are used to define the center point of a circle.

3. False. The `polygon` element automatically closes its path, while the `polyline` element does not.

4. The `M` path command is short for `moveto`, the command that signifies the start of a line.

5. Uppercase path commands are used to describe absolute coordinates, whereas their lowercase alternatives are used for relative coordinates.

Exercises

1. Having learned how to draw circles and ellipses, try creating a puffy cloud. By clustering a series of these shapes together, you can create an object that looks like a silhouette of a cloud. In the next hour, you'll learn how to fill that silhouette with white (or any other color). (If you find your illustration looking like a blob, you can sneak a peek at Listing 8.1 in Hour 8.)

5

2. If you own Adobe Illustrator or Jasc WebDraw, try creating some simple illustrations and then export/save the files in SVG format. Open the SVG export in a text editor and observe how those programs deal with the drawing of objects. For instance, Illustrator converts all shapes (whether rectangles, circles, or freeform paths) into path data, as opposed to WebDraw, which exports some basic shapes as their SVG element counterparts.

3. Refer to Hour 24 for a reproducible grid. Make several copies of this grid and begin plotting paths and their arc handles. By visualizing your data before coding, you can reduce the anxiety of not knowing what coordinates and path commands are necessary to execute your illustration.

4. Play with the code in Listing 5.10, changing the absolute path command C to the relative path command c. Save your file, load it within your browser, and observe the bizarre effects. Understanding the radical difference between the two coordinate systems will help you troubleshoot issues you may encounter with paths later.

PART II

Manipulating SVG

Hour

Hour **6**

Styling SVG

Leaving shapes as their default solid black objects is rarely the designer's intent. To solve this issue, you will need to apply *style* to your elements. Style allows a developer to add a variety of display properties to an element, thus massaging its default appearance to look as the designer intended.

In this hour, you will learn the following:

- The syntax and application of the `style` attribute
- How to create a style sheet
- The difference between internal and external style sheets
- How to organize your style sheet

By the time you finish this chapter, you will be able to move towards applying fills and strokes to your artwork (Hour 7). However, without the ability to apply style to your creation, any such beautifications would become much more difficult.

The `style` Attribute

The application of style to elements is not a very complicated process, and there are a variety of ways to handle such applications. SVG offers developers four methods of applying style to elements:

- XML presentation attributes
- Inline CSS property declarations
- Internal CSS style sheet references
- External CSS style sheet references

Developers can apply style directly to objects (using the first two methods listed) or they can use a style sheet (be it internal or external). Direct application of style allows for the quickest method to test the results of style application, whereas style sheets allow for cleaner, more organized documents.

This hour will focus on the three CSS methods of applying style to SVG elements for three reasons:

- Most Web developers are already quite familiar with CSS.
- The XML presentation attributes method produces excessive code, as styles cannot be consolidated.
- Most SVG WYSIWYG editors produce code based on one of the three CSS methods.

Because of these reasons, the CSS methods will provide you with the most flexible and widely used conventions of applying style in SVG.

Inline CSS Property Declarations

The first of the three CSS methods, inline CSS property declarations, can be considered the "quick and dirty" process of applying style to an element. To apply this method, you add a `style` attribute to an element, along with its desired attribute values. For instance, in the lightning bolt example you created previously (Listing 5.8), you applied a stroke and a fill to the object to demonstrate the difference between the `polyline` and `polygon` elements. This was done by inserting the following snippet in the `polygon` element:

```
style="stroke:black; fill:yellow;".
```

As you can see from the example, nomenclature for `style` attributes is quite simple. Each attribute value consists of a style "declaration": a style "property" (`stroke` in the previous example) and a style "value" (`black` in the same example) separated by a colon. If more than one attribute value is desired, they are separated with a semicolon.

Keep in mind, a style property must be one of the allowed property names (Hour 7, "Painting," covers the most commonly used properties, `fill` and `stroke`, whereas the W3C recommendation's appendix contains the complete list of possible properties), and the style value must be an accepted value for its associated property.

> As style cannot be applied without style declarations, this hour will use a select few `fill` and `stroke` properties to illustrate the style concept. Detailed instruction in these properties (and others) will be covered in Hour 7, "Painting."

In the last hour's lightning bolt example (Listing 5.8), you created a `polyline` element with a yellow fill and a black stroke. In that case, the bolt had all its style information spelled out with its `style` attribute. However, if you duplicated the bolt with the same style information dozens of times for your image, you would see `style="stroke:black; fill:yellow;"` as many times as you saw the `polyline` element. Obviously, this would create unnecessarily large and bloated files.

To resolve this matter, you can do two things: 1) create a CSS style sheet to decrease the amount of information needed to apply style to objects and 2) utilize groups to more effectively apply style. Such a solution will bring you into the realm of the second CSS style application—internal CSS style sheet references.

Before detailing the process to create and use a style sheet, however, an explanation of the technology is in order. A style sheet is a collection of style rules. Style sheets are created to store a series of rules and to allow a developer to reference these rules within her code.

To allow referencing, a style rule is composed of two items: a *selector* and a style declaration block. A selector is the label used to reference a particular style declaration, whereas a declaration block consists of a style declaration (which was described earlier this hour) between curly brackets: { }. You can also store multiple declarations within a declaration block by separating them with semicolons.

Selectors can be either an element name or a unique name of your choice. In the instance of a unique name, you must insert a period before the selector in your rule. This period designates the selector as a "class" selector (which can be thought of a a style rule's `id` value) rather than an element name. As a rule, a selector's name (whether an element name or a class name) consists only of alphanumerical characters and can contain no spaces, periods, or other special characters. If you were to create a rule for your style sheet using an element name, the syntax would be as follows:

```
element{styleproperty:stylevalue;}
```

6

If, on the other hand, you were to create a rule for your style sheet using a unique selector name, the syntax would be as follows:

```
.selector{styleproperty:stylevalue;}
```

A style sheet (whether internal or external) can then contain a series of rules, allowing you to store a myriad of style information.

Using a style sheet then can be quite simple; it is merely a matter of linking your style sheet to your document (whether through internal placement or an external link) and applying one of its rules to an element using the `class` property.

Style sheets can reside in two locations—either within the SVG document or in an external file. When you are creating a style sheet in an SVG document, it must be located within a surrounding `style` element. To clarify the syntax of your styles, you will need to add a `type` attribute to the `style` element; give `type` an attribute value of `text/css` to designate the syntax as CSS. As a result, your internal style element will appear as follows:

```
<style type="text/css"> … </style>
```

As CSS syntax is quite different from XML and SVG syntax, an SVG viewer might immediately kick back a "well-formed" error if it tried to parse your CSS content within an *internal* style sheet. To prevent this from happening, you will need to use XML's CDATA sections. A parser ignores any content that resides within a CDATA section. Thus, by enclosing your internal style sheet within `<![CDATA[` and `]]>` (CDATA's syntax), you will keep its content as readable CSS information.

Creating a Style Sheet

With an understanding of what a style sheet is fresh in your memory, you can actually begin the process of making one for your SVG content. You can start by creating an internal CSS style sheet.

To make sense of all this style information, you can modify the raindrop example from last hour, shown in Figure 6.1. Using Listing 5.10 as a foundation, you'll need to insert a `style` element into your new document (line 6 in Listing 6.1). Within this element, you will need to insert a CDATA section (line 7), which alerts the SVG viewer not to parse its contents.

Now it's time to create a rule. First take the two style declarations used to create the appearance of a yellow fill and a black stroke to create a declaration block on line 8. Then create a selector name, such as style1, to label this block. Lastly, use the class attribute (instead of the style property, as Listing 5.8 showed) to associate your new style with the path element on line 12.

LISTING 6.1   Using a Style Sheet to Define an Object's Style

```
01: <?xml version="1.0" standalone="no"?>
02: <!DOCTYPE svg PUBLIC "-//W3C//DTD SVG 1.0//EN"
             "http://www.w3.org/TR/2001/REC-SVG-20010904/DTD/svg10.dtd">
03:
04: <svg  width="500" height="300">
05:
06:     <style type="text/css">
07:             <![CDATA[
08:                     .style1 {stroke:black; fill:yellow;}
09:             ]]>
10:     </style>
11:
12:     <path class="style1"
                d="M250,140
                c 0,0 -16,24 -16,33
                c 0,9 7,15 16,15
                c 9,0 16,-7 16,-15
                c 0,-9 -16,-33 -16,-33"/>
13:
14: </svg>
```

FIGURE 6.1

An internal style sheet can provide the information to paint this raindrop.

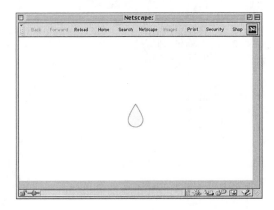

6

Your style sheet now contains all your style information for the raindrop. Now, to demonstrate the efficiency of CSS style sheet application, you can create two more raindrops, each using the same class.

First, take Listing 6.1 and duplicate (via a copy and paste) the raindrop path twice. As you were working with relative path coordinates, you can change the first coordinates of the first drop (line 12 in Listing 6.2) and the last drop (line 16) by 100 horizontal pixels. Subsequently, that path's coordinates will follow the lead of their first coordinate, creating three evenly spaced drops in a straight horizontal line (see Figure 6.2).

As you duplicated the original drop, the two new drops will already have the class="style1" code applied. Now, load this new document in your browser, and you should see results similar to Figure 6.2.

LISTING 6.2   Using a Style Sheet to Define an Object's Style

```
01: <?xml version="1.0" standalone="no"?>
02: <!DOCTYPE svg PUBLIC "-//W3C//DTD SVG 1.0//EN"
            "http://www.w3.org/TR/2001/REC-SVG-20010904/DTD/svg10.dtd">
03:
04: <svg  width="500" height="300">
05:
06:         <style type="text/css">
07:                 <![CDATA[
08:                         .style1 {stroke:black; fill:yellow;}
09:                 ]]>
10:         </style>
11:
12:         <path class="style1"
                 d="M150,140
                 c 0,0 -16,24 -16,33
                 c 0,9 7,15 16,15
                 c 9,0 16,-7 16,-15
                 c 0,-9 -16,-33 -16,-33"/>
13:
14:         <path class="style1"
                 d="M250,140
                 c 0,0 -16,24 -16,33
                 c 0,9 7,15 16,15
                 c 9,0 16,-7 16,-15
                 c 0,-9 -16,-33 -16,-33"/>
15:
16:         <path class="style1"
                 d="M350,140
                 c 0,0 -16,24 -16,33
                 c 0,9 7,15 16,15
                 c 9,0 16,-7 16,-15
                 c 0,-9 -16,-33 -16,-33"/>
17:
18: </svg>
```

FIGURE 6.2

An internal style sheet can provide the same information to paint several pieces of art-work.

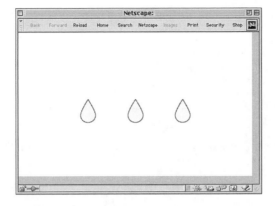

Now you've successfully created a style sheet and figured out how to apply one of its classes to your artwork. Your next step will be to create multiple classes.

In Listing 6.2, you added two new raindrops to your document. If you decided that you wanted to change the appearance of these two new drops, giving one a black stroke and no designated fill and another a yellow fill but no black stroke, you would need to create two new classes.

To do so, duplicate the style1 rule twice and rename the two resulting rules' selectors style2 and style3 respectively. Listing 6.3 shows these two new rules on lines 9 and 10. Make each style unique by deleting the fill:yellow; declaration from the style2 class and the stroke:black; declaration from the style3 class. Finally, apply style2 to the second drop (line 16) and style3 to the third drop (line 18). When you're done, your results should look like Figure 6.3.

LISTING 6.3   Using a Style Sheet to Define Several Different Objects' Style

```
01: <?xml version="1.0" standalone="no"?>
02: <!DOCTYPE svg PUBLIC "-//W3C//DTD SVG 1.0//EN"
             "http://www.w3.org/TR/2001/REC-SVG-20010904/DTD/svg10.dtd">
03:
04: <svg  width="500" height="300">
05:
06:        <style type="text/css">
07:                <![CDATA[
08:                        .style1 {stroke:black; fill:yellow;}
09:                        .style2 {stroke:black;}
10:                        .style3 {fill:yellow;}
11:                ]]>
12:        </style>
13:
```

6

continues

LISTING 6.3   Continued

```
14:        <path class="style1"
                d="M150,140
                c 0,0 -16,24 -16,33
                c 0,9 7,15 16,15
                c 9,0 16,-7 16,-15
                c 0,-9 -16,-33 -16,-33"/>
15:
16:        <path class="style2"
                d="M250,140
                c 0,0 -16,24 -16,33
                c 0,9 7,15 16,15
                c 9,0 16,-7 16,-15
                c 0,-9 -16,-33 -16,-33"/>
17:
18:        <path class="style3"
                d="M350,140
                c 0,0 -16,24 -16,33
                c 0,9 7,15 16,15
                c 9,0 16,-7 16,-15
                c 0,-9 -16,-33 -16,-33"/>
19:
20: </svg>
```

FIGURE 6.3
*Each raindrop is using
a unique class to
define its appearance.*

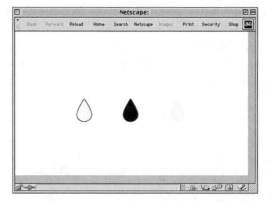

Although this method accomplishes the goal of creating three differently styled objects, you've ended up duplicating your style declarations several times. Rather than defining your rules with multiple style declarations, you can instead give each declaration its own rule, allowing you the flexibility to change an object's appearance without first creating a new rule.

By naming each style declaration, you can free yourself to make class combinations on the artwork's element rather than inside the style sheet. As an example, consider an instance where you want to change the color of an object in your artwork. First, you must find the object you wish to modify. Once found, you see which selector name is being referenced, and then you must double back to your style sheet to modify the appropriate rules.

Instead of darting back and forth between two locations in your code (or in some cases between two documents, should you be using an external style sheet), you can simply replace one selector name with another if you have a unique selector name for each declaration (several fills, in this instance). By keeping the groupings of an object's style on the object level, rather than on the style sheet level, you are afforded a greater control over your artwork, allowing you to quickly edit it.

Try this out by creating a new document based on Listing 6.3. First, delete the style1 class, and then apply both style2 and style3 to the first raindrop. To apply more than one class to an object, separate class attribute values with a space (see line 14 of Listing 6.4).

LISTING 6.4   Associating Only One Declaration with Each Selector

```
01: <?xml version="1.0" standalone="no"?>
02: <!DOCTYPE svg PUBLIC "-//W3C//DTD SVG 1.0//EN"
03:    "http://www.w3.org/TR/2001/REC-SVG-20010904/DTD/svg10.dtd">
04:
05: <svg  width="500" height="300">
06:
07: <style type="text/css">
08:        <![CDATA[
09:                .style2{stroke:black;}
10:                .style3{fill:yellow;}
11:        ]]>
12: </style>
13:
14:        <path class="style2 style3"
15:                d="M150,140
16:                c 0,0 -16,24 -16,33
17:                c 0,9 7,15 16,15
18:                c 9,0 16,-7 16,-15
19:                c 0,-9 -16,-33 -16,-33"/>
20:
21:        <path class="style2"
22:                d="M250,140
23:                c 0,0 -16,24 -16,33
24:                c 0,9 7,15 16,15
25:                c 9,0 16,-7 16,-15
26:                c 0,-9 -16,-33 -16,-33"/>
```

6

continues

LISTING 6.4 Continued

```
27:
28:            <path class="style3"
29:                   d="M350,140
30:                   c 0,0 -16,24 -16,33
31:                   c 0,9 7,15 16,15
32:                   c 9,0 16,-7 16,-15
33:                   c 0,-9 -16,-33 -16,-33"/>
34:
35: </svg>
```

Though the code may have changed, the result of your experiment here will look exactly the same as Figure 6.3. On a small level such as this three raindrop example, you may not see any value in naming each style declaration. The results, however, begin to manifest themselves once you start dealing with very long and complicated SVG documents.

Labeling Your Style Sheet's Rules

For simplicity's sake, the three rules you just dealt with were arbitrarily named to represent each style declaration: style1, style2, and style3, respectively. However, should you hand this SVG file to a fellow developer, these three names would seem rather meaningless. Not only would they rightfully appear to be a random naming scheme, but the names could also cause confusion in large-scale coding projects. For instance, if the developer knew she wanted to make a circle yellow, she would have no choice but to refer to the style sheet to see what class accomplished this task.

There is a simpler way, though. Naming a class's selector according to its purposes gives a development team a common language to work with. By creating a unified and descriptive class-naming system, developers (yourself included) will be able to quickly determine the name of their desired class.

For instance, rather than naming your first selector style2, use a name that reflects the actual style declaration, such as StrokeBlack. In Listing 6.5, style2 and style3 (lines 9 and 10) have been renamed to more closely reflect their respective declarations' functions.

Listing 6.5   Name Selectors to Mirror Their Declarations' Functions

```
01: <?xml version="1.0" standalone="no"?>
02: <!DOCTYPE svg PUBLIC "-//W3C//DTD SVG 1.0//EN"
03:    "http://www.w3.org/TR/2001/REC-SVG-20010904/DTD/svg10.dtd">
04:
05: <svg  width="500" height="300">
06:
07: <style type="text/css">
08:        <![CDATA[
09:                .StrokeBlack{stroke:black;}
10:                .FillYellow{fill:yellow;}
11:        ]]>
12: </style>
13:
14:        <path class="StrokeBlack FillYellow"
15:                d="M150,140
16:                c 0,0 -16,24 -16,33
17:                c 0,9 7,15 16,15
18:                c 9,0 16,-7 16,-15
19:                c 0,-9 -16,-33 -16,-33"/>
20:
21:        <path class="StrokeBlack"
22:                d="M250,140
23:                c 0,0 -16,24 -16,33
24:                c 0,9 7,15 16,15
25:                c 9,0 16,-7 16,-15
26:                c 0,-9 -16,-33 -16,-33"/>
27:
28:        <path class="FillYellow"
29:                d="M350,140
30:                c 0,0 -16,24 -16,33
31:                c 0,9 7,15 16,15
32:                c 9,0 16,-7 16,-15
33:                c 0,-9 -16,-33 -16,-33"/>
34:
35: </svg>
```

6

Again, this listing will appear the same as Figure 6.3. However, when another developer examines this code, she will be able to quickly identify the function of the class being applied without needing to look up the selector in the style sheet. Should you follow a naming convention such as this and your style sheet be two pages long with 50 fills and 50 strokes, the same developer would be able to guess (with a high probability at success) at the selector name of a red fill: FillRed. When faced with large documents of code and an impending deadline, such naming conventions can be a lifesaver for your development team.

Be certain to be consistent in naming conventions. If you name one class StrokeGreen and another class BlueStroke, you will destroy the usefulness of your system. If done inconsistently, a developer will be forced to look up every selector name, as a naming convention (such as <propertyName><propertyValue>) is not being followed.

Grouping Styles

Applying style to a grouping of objects, rather than individual elements, is also very effective for reducing the number of applications of the class attribute in your files. Similar to how most design programs handle groupings, SVG allows developers the ability to associate elements together using the g element.

The group element itself generally does not affect the display of its enclosed content. However, when a style or transformation (you'll learn about this in Hour 14, "Transforms") is applied to the group, the enclosed content is affected according to such an application. In the case of the raindrops, if you want every raindrop to appear the same, you can apply one class to a group surrounding all three objects by moving your class attribute there.

In Listing 6.6, such a change has been made (using Listing 6.5 as a starting point). First, a group is wrapped around all three raindrops, starting on line 14 and ending on line 22. The class attribute is removed from each of the raindrops and placed within the g element.

LISTING 6.6   Applying Style to a Group

```
01: <?xml version="1.0" standalone="no"?>
02: <!DOCTYPE svg PUBLIC "-//W3C//DTD SVG 1.0//EN"
03:    "http://www.w3.org/TR/2001/REC-SVG-20010904/DTD/svg10.dtd">
04:
05: <svg  width="500" height="300">
06:
07: <style type="text/css">
08:        <![CDATA[
09:                .StrokeBlack{stroke:black;}
10:                .FillYellow{fill:yellow;}
11:        ]]>
12: </style>
13:
14:        <g class="StrokeBlack FillYellow">
15:
16:                <path    d="M150,140
                                c 0,0 -16,24 -16,33
```

continues

LISTING 6.6   Continued

```
                              c 0,9 7,15 16,15
                              c 9,0 16,-7 16,-15
                              c 0,-9 -16,-33 -16,-33"/>
17:
18:               <path   d="M250,140
                              c 0,0 -16,24 -16,33
                              c 0,9 7,15 16,15
                              c 9,0 16,-7 16,-15
                              c 0,-9 -16,-33 -16,-33"/>
19:
20:               <path d="M350,140
                              c 0,0 -16,24 -16,33
                              c 0,9 7,15 16,15
                              c 9,0 16,-7 16,-15
                              c 0,-9 -16,-33 -16,-33"/>
21:
22:          </g>
23:
24: </svg>
```

The result of such a change will appear visually no different than Figure 6.3. Moving the class application to one central area, however, eliminates the need to duplicate every instance of the class attribute for similar objects.

By the same token, you can apply a class to a group while still applying a class to a grouped element. It's important to note that in the case of two conflicting style commands (such as two fill commands), the style command closest to the element will be honored. In Listing 6.6, although the raindrops' group is told to fill the objects with yellow (shown via the class value on line 15), the middle raindrop itself is designated to fill itself with orange (via its class attribute on line 19). Thus the middle raindrop will appear in orange.

LISTING 6.7   Style Application Hierarchy

```
01: <?xml version="1.0" standalone="no"?>
02: <!DOCTYPE svg PUBLIC "-//W3C//DTD SVG 1.0//EN"
03:    "http://www.w3.org/TR/2001/REC-SVG-20010904/DTD/svg10.dtd">
04:
05: <svg  width="500" height="300">
06:
07: <style type="text/css">
08:        <![CDATA[
09:              .StrokeBlack{stroke:black;}
10:              .FillYellow{fill:yellow;}
```

continues

6

LISTING 6.7 Continued

```
11:                    .FillOrange{fill:orange;}
12:        ]]>
13: </style>
14:
15:        <g class="StrokeBlack FillYellow">
16:
17:                 <path   d="M150,140
                            c 0,0 -16,24 -16,33
                            c 0,9 7,15 16,15
                            c 9,0 16,-7 16,-15
                            c 0,-9 -16,-33 -16,-33"/>
18:
19:                 <path class="FillOrange"
                    d="M250,140
                            c 0,0 -16,24 -16,33
                            c 0,9 7,15 16,15
                            c 9,0 16,-7 16,-15
                            c 0,-9 -16,-33 -16,-33"/>
20:
21:                 <path   d="M350,140
                            c 0,0 -16,24 -16,33
                            c 0,9 7,15 16,15
                            c 9,0 16,-7 16,-15
                            c 0,-9 -16,-33 -16,-33"/>
22:
23:        </g>
24:
25: </svg>
```

The class closest to this middle rain drop determined the fill (orange). The same rule holds true no matter how nested your content may be. For instance, take the example of three rectangles following:

```
01: <g class="FillBlue">
02:        <g class="FillRed">
03:                 <rect id="Box1" class="FillGreen".../>
04:                 <rect id="Box2".../>
05:        </g>
06:        <rect id="Box3".../>
07: </g>
```

Assuming that the selector names match an appropriate style declaration in a style sheet (not shown), the Box1 rectangle (line 3) will be filled green, the Box2 rectangle (line 4) will be filled red, and the Box3 rectangle (line 6) will be filled blue.

In each case, the class attribute closest to the element determines the fill. Thus, line 3's Box1 has its own class attribute, which determines that it will be filled green. Line 4's Box2 does not have a class attribute; it is, however, closer in hierarchy to line 2 than line 1 (as it is a child of line 2's element) and thus accepts line 2's style application of a red fill. Line 6's Box3 also has no class attribute, but, being a child of line 1's group, it accepts line 1's style application of a blue fill.

Organizing Your Style Sheet

Organization of your style sheet is critical to both efficient coding and collaborative environments. Oftentimes, your SVG file will contain dozens (if not hundreds) of selectors. Because of this, it becomes very difficult to quickly scan over a list of selectors that do not clearly define what their style declarations accomplish or are not grouped according to accomplishment.

In collaborative development environments, where multiple developers and designers are working with the same SVG file (or a group thereof), having style sheets clearly labeled and organized can severely decrease the number of duplicate styles.

For instance, if you had a style sheet with ten rules that represented different fill colors, four classes that represented four stroke colors, and two rules that determined an object's visibility, you would need to group these classes according to their function.

In Listing 6.8, all four stroke color rules are positioned together within the style sheet on lines 9 through 12. The fill rules are together on lines 14 through 23, and two display rules are positioned on lines 25 and 26.

LISTING 6.8 Grouping Style Classes

```
01: <?xml version="1.0" standalone="no"?>
02: <!DOCTYPE svg PUBLIC "-//W3C//DTD SVG 1.0//EN"
03:    "http://www.w3.org/TR/2001/REC-SVG-20010904/DTD/svg10.dtd">
04:
05: <svg  width="500" height="300">
06:
07: <style type="text/css">
08:      <![CDATA[
09:             .StrokeGreen{stroke:green;}
10:             .StrokeYellow{stroke:yellow;}
11:             .StrokePurple{stroke:purple;}
12:             .StrokeOrange{stroke:orange;}
13:
14:             .FillGreen{fill:green;}
15:             .FillYellow{fill:yellow;}
```

6

continues

LISTING 6.8 Continued

```
16:                    .FillPurple{fill:purple;}
17:                    .FillOrange{fill:orange;}
18:                    .FillBlue{fill:blue;}
19:                    .FillPink{fill:pink;}
20:                    .FillBrown{fill:brown;}
21:                    .FillRed{fill:red;}
22:                    .FillBlack{fill:black;}
23:                    .FillWhite{fill:white;}
24:
25:                    .DisplayInline{display:inline;}
26:                    .DisplayNone{display:none;}
27:        ]]>
28: </style>
29:
30:        <path class="StrokeGreen FillYellow DisplayInline"
                    d="M150,140
                    c 0,0 -16,24 -16,33
                    c 0,9 7,15 16,15
                    c 9,0 16,-7 16,-15
                    c 0,-9 -16,-33 -16,-33"/>
31:
32:        <path class="StrokeGreen DisplayNone"
                    d="M250,140
                    c 0,0 -16,24 -16,33
                    c 0,9 7,15 16,15
                    c 9,0 16,-7 16,-15
                    c 0,-9 -16,-33 -16,-33"/>
33:
34: </svg>
```

Note the new style commands that were added in lines 25 and 26: `display:inline` and `display:none`. In Hour 5, you learned how to prevent some of your elements from displaying by commenting them out of your code. Using the `display` property, however, allows you a much more efficient method of enabling or disabling the rendering of your elements.

Storing and Accessing Style Sheets

In many cases, you will be designing multiple SVG files that all use the same style sheet information. Rather than duplicating your style sheet information in each SVG file, you can use the third CSS style sheet option: referencing your external CSS style sheet. To try this out, create a file named `style.css` in the same directory as your `index.html` and SVG files. Then, copy the style sheet information (just the rules, not the CDATA and `style` elements) from the previous example and paste it into this new document. When you are finished, the "style.css" document will appear just as Listing 6.9.

LISTING 6.9   Creating an External Style Sheet

```
01:        .StrokeGreen{stroke:green;}
02:        .StrokeYellow{stroke:yellow;}
03:        .StrokePurple{stroke:purple;}
04:        .StrokeOrange{stroke:orange;}
05:
06:        .FillGreen{fill:green;}
07:        .FillYellow{fill:yellow;}
08:        .FillPurple{fill:purple;}
09:        .FillOrange{fill:orange;}
10:        .FillBlue{fill:blue;}
11:        .FillPink{fill:pink;}
12:        .FillBrown{fill:brown;}
13:        .FillRed{fill:red;}
14:        .FillBlack{fill:black;}
15:        .FillWhite{fill:white;}
16:
17:        .DisplayInline{display:inline;}
18:        .DisplayNone{display:none;}
```

Now you will need your SVG document to be able to reference this external style sheet.
Linking your SVG file to this external style sheet is quite easy. First, using Listing 6.6 as
a starting point, remove the style element and its contents (lines 7 through 12). Then,
add the line `<?xml-stylesheet href="style.css" type="text/css"?>` to the document header information (see line 2 in Listing 6.10).

> Should you have moved the style.css file outside of the directory where
> you've been saving your SVG and HTML files, you could set the directory path
> information accordingly. In such a case, keep in mind that the href attribute
> for this element operates in a similar manner to HTML's href attribute.

LISTING 6.10   Referencing an External Style Sheet

```
01: <?xml version="1.0" standalone="no"?>
02: <?xml-stylesheet href="style.css" type="text/css"?>
03: <!DOCTYPE svg PUBLIC "-//W3C//DTD SVG 1.0//EN"
04:   "http://www.w3.org/TR/2001/REC-SVG-20010904/DTD/svg10.dtd">
05:
06: <svg  width="500" height="300">
07:
08:        <g class="StrokeGreen FillYellow DisplayInline">
09:
```

6

continues

LISTING 6.10   Continued

```
10:                     <path   d="M150,140
                                 c 0,0 -16,24 -16,33
                                 c 0,9 7,15 16,15
                                 c 9,0 16,-7 16,-15
                                 c 0,-9 -16,-33 -16,-33"/>
11:
12:                     <path   d="M250,140
                                 c 0,0 -16,24 -16,33
                                 c 0,9 7,15 16,15
                                 c 9,0 16,-7 16,-15
                                 c 0,-9 -16,-33 -16,-33"/>
13:
14:                     <path   d="M350,140
                                 c 0,0 -16,24 -16,33
                                 c 0,9 7,15 16,15
                                 c 9,0 16,-7 16,-15
                                 c 0,-9 -16,-33 -16,-33"/>
15:
16:         </g>
17:
18: </svg>
```

For convenience's sake, you'll continue to keep your style sheet within your document for the remainder of this book's examples (minus the final example). You can place your style element (and its subsequent style sheet content) in a variety of places in your document but not within other artwork elements (such as the rect, circle, and so on). As a general rule of thumb, you should keep your style sheet at either the top or bottom of your document, away from your content code, to make it easy to find for other developers.

The examples in the remainder of this book will keep the style sheets at the top of the files, making things easier when you edit your code (as their position will be familiar).

Summary

Although there are several methods for applying style, using CSS offers newcomers an easy-to-understand avenue to shaping the appearance of SVG content. To maximize the efficiency of style sheets, though, you need to name and order its contents according to a standardized system. By doing so, you can edit your large documents more quickly, and so can other developers on your project.

With the ability to create style sheets, you are now ready to start applying visual information on the shapes you learned to create in the previous hour. Hour 7, "Painting," will take you on a step-by-step lesson through color, strokes, fills, gradients and transparencies. With these effects, you will be able to replicate the painting capabilities of most drawing programs.

Q&A

Q **This chapter has suggested creating a class for every style declaration. This would seem to create a long style sheet to accommodate every possible declaration. Are other methods possible?**

A Certainly. The author has made this suggestion based on his experience developing SVG with a team of developers. Other methods are possible and equally beneficial (if not more, in some cases), and you are encouraged to code your style sheets in a fashion that best suits your team and work environment. In some cases, grouping several declarations into one class can be quite helpful. For instance, if you were to create a class labeled "errormsg" to style text that appeared whenever a user did something wrong, you could place several declarations inside to create your effect: a red fill, 24-point underlined text, Arial Bold typeface, and so on. Whatever you choose, try out competing methods and see what works best for you.

Q **I would like to learn more about CSS. What resources are available?**

A You can read the W3C's CSS2 recommendation online at `http://www.w3.org/TR/REC-CSS2`. The W3Schools' site also features a tutorial at `http://www.w3schools.com/css/default.asp`.

Workshop

The Workshop is designed to help you anticipate possible questions, review what you've learned, and begin learning how to put your knowledge into practice.

Quiz

1. What is the term used to describe a CSS class's label?
2. Describe the components of a style declaration.
3. Style sheets are contained within what element?
4. What is the function of a CDATA section?
5. What does the author recommend naming class selectors according to?

Answers

1. A selector is the label used to reference a CSS class.
2. A style declaration is composed of a style property (such as stroke) and a style value (such as green) separated by a colon.
3. An internal style sheet is contained within a CDATA section, which is contained within a style element.

6

4. CDATA sections are used to prevent their contained content from being parsed as SVG by an SVG viewer. Nonetheless, CDATA's content must adhere to the XML syntax rules for the element. For more information on CDATA, see the W3School's example: `http://www.w3schools.com/xml/xml_cdata.asp`.

5. Naming selectors according to their declaration's function allows other developers the ability to discern the function of a class without needing to reference the style sheet.

Exercises

1. Check out the W3C SVG recommendation and read chapter 6.4 about using XML presentation attributes to define style application. If you feel daring, revisit Listing 6.1 and apply the selected styles already in use via the XML method.

2. Review the possible style properties in the recommendation's Appendix N. Although Hour 7, "Painting," will discuss fills and strokes, there are a variety of other properties that can be applied to your artwork that won't be covered in this book.

HOUR 7

Painting

Drawing your artwork's containers (its shapes and forms) is only part of a designer's challenge. Tied to this challenge is what goes in and around the containers you've drawn. In SVG, the method of applying visual information to a shape is called "painting." In this hour, you will execute five common painting attributes used in designers' palettes (visualized in Figure 7.1):

- Fills
- Strokes
- Transparency
- Gradients
- Patterns

With these five methods of applying visual information to your artwork's shapes, your content can begin to take form. Before diving into the process of these methods, however, you will need to learn how SVG handles color information (a key component to nearly all of these methods).

FIGURE 7.1

Comparing the different painting attributes available in SVG.

Fills   Strokes   Transparency   Gradients   Patterns

Working with Color

SVG's color handling is similar to HTML; many of the same terms and properties are shared between the two markup languages. Developers can designate color values through several methods. Two of the most common methods are: 1) using a color's name or 2) using a color's RGB hexadecimal value.

In the previous examples, you've used the first method by designating a color by its name. It's important to note, however, that not just any color name will work. A set of color keywords has been defined by the W3C and is viewable in the appendix of this book.

Color keywords are great for quick designation of a color. However, they are often not the precise color that a designer is looking for. Hexadecimal notation of color offers a greater number of possibilities for defining an RGB color than the keyword method.

As nearly all designers and developers who have created images for the Web are already familiar with hexadecimal notation, this book will not attempt to provide a tutorial on the subject. Still, a cursory overview of the notation is in order to serve as an explanation of how this book will refer to color values.

For those unfamiliar with hexadecimal notation, a quick refresher course should help. Color on a monitor is defined by mixing three color channels: red, green, and blue (known as "RGB"). Each channel has 256 levels, allowing for a total of 16,777,216 possible colors. Traditionally, screen colors were represented as three values, based on the level value of each channel. For instance, to create a solid blue hue, you would define the color as (0r, 0g, 255b).

To offer an alternative to defining color using this nine number structure, the hexadecimal system was adopted.

Each channel's 3-digit level value can be condensed to two characters, using the numbers 0 through 9 and the letters A through F. By combining two of these characters, you can represent any channel value. The combination of characters to equal a 3-digit value is based upon a mathematical calculation.

Most designers do not think in terms of RGB values, much less in terms of the hexadecimal notation of such values. Rather, they use their design program's color "pickers," a palette or interface that allows a color to be created by adjusting its levels of red, green, and blue. In many cases, though, the same program can display the determined color's value in hexadecimal notation (a select set of colors defined with this notation—216 colors to be precise—is sometimes referred to as "Web-safe" colors) by changing a setting in the color picker.

Adobe PhotoShop and Illustrator, Macromedia FreeHand, Corel Draw, Jasc WebDraw, and many other image creation programs have such an ability. If you do not own one of these tools, you can still find a color's hexadecimal notation through one of these many methods:

- Apple's Macintosh operating system has a system-wide color picker (available in almost any Mac program that allows you to select colors) with an "HTML Picker." Once accessed, you can hold the "option" key to convert your cursor into an "eyedropper" capable of capturing any color on screen. After clicking on a color with the eyedropper, the HTML Picker will display its hexadecimal value in a form field that you can copy and paste into your code.

- You can use Kresch.com's Java RGB Color Tester tool free-of-charge online at `http://kresch.com/resources/javacolor.htm`. This Java applet is an incredibly useful tool for those without a design program, as it visually adjusts the color of the applet according to three sliders (red, green and blue). Both the traditional RGB values and hexadecimal values are displayed as you adjust the sliders.

- A limited list of colors, their RGB values, their RGB hexadecimal notation, and their color "keywords" are listed in the appendix of this book.

- Lastly, you can visit this book's companion site, `www.svgnow.com`. You will be able to find up-to-date links to free hexadecimal notation converters for several operating systems at the site.

Again, SVG can accept a variety of ways to specify a color. If you are trying to quickly apply a color and don't know the hexadecimal value, you can simply use an accepted color name. Most likely, however, if you are an experienced Web developer, you will use the hexadecimal notation for describing a color's RGB value. Thus, the remainder of this book will use hexadecimal notation for defining RGB color values.

Applying a Fill

Fills can be applied to an object using a style declaration. The structure of the declaration is `fill:color-value` (where `color-value` is replaced by a color keyword or a hexadecimal value).

7

You can also specify that an object have no fill to avoid having the object painted with its default black fill. As you saw in Hour 5, an unstyled object is assumed to be filled with black. To counter this automatic fill, you will need to give the desired object a style of `fill:none`.

To demonstrate the use of hexadecimal values and the `fill` command, follow Listing 7.1 to begin to create your first weather graphic scene for the news center example first introduced in Hour 1: the sunny sky. First, use the rectangle you created in Listing 5.2 on line 9 to serve as the weather graphic's "sky" (shown on line 13); follow the rectangle with the circle first created in Listing 5.5 to represent the sun (shown on line 15).

Next, create your style sheet (lines 6 through 11) with two classes: one to describe a blue fill via the hexadecimal notation of #99CCFF (shown on line 8) and another to describe a yellow fill via the hexadecimal notation of #FFFF00 (shown on line 9). Finally, apply these classes to their appropriate objects (lines 13 and 15). The resulting graphic is shown in Figure 7.2.

LISTING 7.1   Creating an Illustration of the Sun in the Sky

```
01: <?xml version="1.0" standalone="no"?>
02: <!DOCTYPE svg PUBLIC "-//W3C//DTD SVG 1.0//EN
         "http://www.w3.org/TR/2001/REC-SVG-20010904/DTD/svg10.dtd">
03:
04: <svg  width="500" height="300">
05:
06:        <style type="text/css">
07:                <![CDATA[
08:                        .Fill99CCFF{fill:#99CCFF;}
09:                        .FillFFFF00{fill:#FFFF00;}
10:                ]]>
11:        </style>
12:
13:        <rect id="Sky" x="10" y="45" width="200" height="245" class="Fill99CCFF"/>
14:
15:        <circle id="Sun" cx="105" cy="160" r="56" class="FillFFFF00"/>
16:
17: </svg>
```

FIGURE 7.2

Creating an illustration of the sun in the sky.

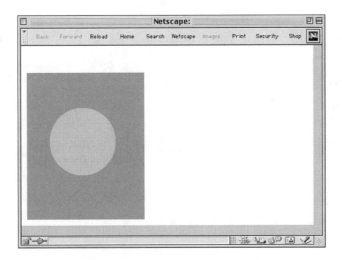

Note how the style sheet class names reflect the color value terminology in lines 8 and 9. As mentioned before, the "#" symbol was intentionally left out of the selector because CSS does not support certain characters in class names. Rather than attempting to determine whether a character is valid or not according to CSS, you can simplify your task by only using upper- and lowercase letters and the numbers 0 through 9.

Applying a Stroke

Adding a stroke to an object is almost as simple as adding a fill. Instead of the single declaration that fills operate on, strokes require two commands to clearly specify their purpose. The first declaration, stroke, is used to describe the color of the stroke. The second declaration, stroke-width, describes the width of the stroke.

To use the two, you need to add the commands using the following syntax: stroke:*stroke-color* and stroke-width:*x*. In this example, *stroke-color* is replaced with a color keyword or hexadecimal value, and *x* is replaced with a numerical value (including decimal numbers, such as "2.35").

To demonstrate the application of stroke, follow Listing 7.2 to begin adding the rectangular framework you first created in Hour 5 (in Listing 5.2) to the weather graphic scene in Listing 7.1. Lines 19 and 21 show the circle and rectangle from your previous example, each with the same class applied. Lines 23 and 24 introduce two elliptical shapes to represent the puffy white clouds you'll be creating later in this book.

The rectangle on line 26 (labeled as BarStatistics) defines the space where the weather temperatures will later be displayed. Line 28 creates a group to contain the graphic's

7

framework outline—the box surrounding the entire graphic (line 29) and the box that will eventually surround the graphic's title (line 30).

Finally, you will need to create the style sheet for the document (lines 6 through 17) and apply the classes to appropriate objects.

In this case, four new fills were added: 1) a gray fill (line 8) for the BarStatistics rectangle (line 26), 2) an orange fill (line 9) for the graphic's BarTitle rectangle (line 30), 3) a white fill (line 12) for the elliptical clouds on lines 23 and 24, and 4) a lack of a fill (line 13) for the Outline rectangle (line 29) so that the content behind it can appear through its edges.

To finalize the style sheet, you will need to add two stroke rules. The first, shown on line 14, describes a black stroke (via the hexadecimal notation of #000000). The second, on line 15, describes a width of 1.

 Remember, if no unit of measurement, such as px or in, is specified (as in this and other examples), this value is interpreted in "unit space values." As you are likely viewing these examples within an Internet browser on your computer screen, the user space value will be equivalent to a pixel. Thus, in this example, stroke-width:1 will describe a stroke with a 1-pixel width.

Both of these stroke styles are to be applied on line 28, the GraphicFramework group consisting of the Outline and BarTitle rectangles. The resulting graphic is shown in Figure 7.3.

LISTING 7.2 Applying Stroke Information to Your Artwork

```
01: <?xml version="1.0" standalone="no"?>
02: <!DOCTYPE svg PUBLIC "-//W3C//DTD SVG 1.0//EN
            "http://www.w3.org/TR/2001/REC-SVG-20010904/DTD/svg10.dtd">
03:
04: <svg  width="500" height="300">
05:
06:         <style type="text/css">
07:                 <![CDATA[
08:                         .Fill333333{fill:#333333;}
09:                         .FillC66A10{fill:#C66A10;}
10:                         .Fill99CCFF{fill:#99CCFF;}
11:                         .FillFFFF00{fill:#FFFF00;}
12:                         .FillFFFFFF{fill:#FFFFFF;}
13:                         .FillNone{fill:none;}
14:                         .Stroke000000{stroke:#000000;}
```

continues

LISTING 7.2   Continued

```
15:                          .StrokeWidth1{stroke-width:1;}
16:            ]]>
17:        </style>
18:
19:        <rect id="Sky" x="10" y="45" width="200" height="245"
                    class="Fill99CCFF"/>
20:
21:        <circle id="Sun" cx="105" cy="160" r="56" class="FillFFFF00"/>
22:
23:        <ellipse cx="25" cy="100" rx="50" ry="25" id="Cloud1"
                    class="FillFFFFFF"/>
24:        <ellipse cx="180" cy="235" rx="50" ry="25" id="Cloud2"
                    class="FillFFFFFF"/>
25:
26:        <rect id="BarStatistics" x="10" y="245" width="200" height="45"
                    class="Fill333333 StrokeNone"/>
27:
28:        <g id="GraphicFramework" class="StrokeWidth1 Stroke000000">
29:                <rect id="Outline" x="10" y="10" width="480" height="280"
                        class="FillNone"/>
30:                <rect id="BarTitle" x="10" y="10" width="480" height="35"
                        class="FillC66A10"/>
31:        </g>
32:
33: </svg>
```

FIGURE 7.3

Applying stroke information to your artwork.

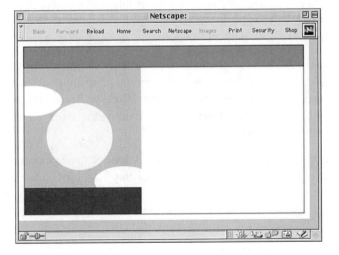

7

Similar to the `fill` style property's ability to apply no fill, the `stroke` style property can designate an object to have no stroke. In such a case, you need only apply the declaration `stroke:none`; you do not need to add a `stroke-width` declaration to an object with a `stroke:none` declaration applied.

Setting Transparency

Changing the transparency of an object is a common need for designers. For the uninitiated, transparency in the design realm refers to how opaque an object is, or how much light is allowed to show through.

For a simple explanation, imagine a thick white sheet of paper. Undisturbed, you will not be able to see another piece of colored paper underneath. The white sheet is 100% opaque. However, if you add grease to the white sheet, you'll slowly begin to see the color underneath, albeit as a feathered, blurry image. The grease has taken away some of the opacity of the white sheet. As you add more grease to the top paper, it finally becomes completely see-through, or 0% opaque, and the paper below is completely revealed in the areas the grease has soaked.

Achieving a transparent effect in SVG also is possible by taking away the opacity of an object, but instead of grease, you use the opacity style declaration.

The syntax for transparency is `opacity:1`, where 1 equals 100% opaque (not see-through) and 0 equals 0% opaque (completely see-through). A value above 1 is interpreted as 1, and a value below 0 is interpreted as 0. Thus, to attain varying levels of opacity, you simply define your value as a decimal point (`0.25`, for instance).

In some cases, SVG takes advantage of several `opacity` declarations to get the job done. If you are looking to change the transparency of an entire object (both strokes and fills), the `opacity` declaration will do just fine. However, if you are looking to change only the opacity of the fill of an object, you would use `fill-opacity`, whereas a stroke is modified with `stroke-opacity`.

You can experiment with the results of all three of these commands by modifying the "BarStatistics" rectangle (line 26 in Listing 7.2). First, create a new style class (line 8 in Listing 7.3) to modify the `fill-opacity` of the object to 25% of its original value. Then, apply this class to the `BarStatistics` rectangle on line 29. Figure 7.4 shows the resulting appearance.

LISTING 7.3   Adjusting the Transparency of the Statistics Bar

```
01: <?xml version="1.0" standalone="no"?>
02: <!DOCTYPE svg PUBLIC "-//W3C//DTD SVG 1.0//EN
            "http://www.w3.org/TR/2001/REC-SVG-20010904/DTD/svg10.dtd">
03:
04: <svg  width="500" height="300">
05:
06:      <style type="text/css">
07:              <![CDATA[
08:                      .FillOpacityPoint25{fill-opacity:0.25;}
09:                      .Fill333333{fill:#333333;}
10:                      .FillC66A10{fill:#C66A10;}
11:                      .Fill99CCFF{fill:#99CCFF;}
12:                      .FillFFFF00{fill:#FFFF00;}
13:                      .FillFFFFFF{fill:#FFFFFF;}
14:                      .FillNone{fill:none;}
17:                      .Stroke000000{stroke:#000000;}
18:                      .StrokeWidth1{stroke-width:1;}
19:              ]]>
20:      </style>
21:
22:      <rect id="Sky" x="10" y="45" width="200" height="245"
                class="Fill99CCFF"/>
23:
24:      <circle id="Sun" cx="105" cy="160" r="56" class="FillFFFF00"/>
25:
26:      <ellipse cx="25" cy="100" rx="50" ry="25" id="Cloud1"
                class="FillFFFFFF"/>
27:      <ellipse cx="180" cy="235" rx="50" ry="25" id="Cloud2"
                class="FillFFFFFF"/>
28:
29:      <rect id="BarStatistics" x="10" y="245" width="200" height="45"
                class="Fill333333 StrokeNone FillOpacityPoint25"/>
30:
31:      <g id="GraphicFramework" class="StrokeWidth1 Stroke000000">
32:              <rect id="Outline" x="10" y="10" width="480" height="280"
                        class="FillNone"/>
33:              <rect id="BarTitle" x="10" y="10" width="480" height="35"
                        class="FillC66A10"/>
34:      </g>
35:
36: </svg>
```

7

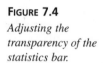

FIGURE 7.4

Adjusting the transparency of the statistics bar.

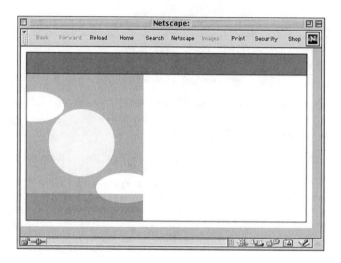

Observe how a transparent object's color *appears* to change according to how much it reveals of the object below. (In reality, the color never changes; rather, what changes is how much of that color is revealed.)

Creating Gradients

Gradients create smooth blends between two distinct colors. One of the most over-used graphic effects since the origination of desktop publishing, gradients have been extensively and poorly used in attempts to mimic the shadings evident in shadows and dimensions in the natural world.

Gradients do have some beneficial uses, however. When used to create subtle shading within a non-realistic element, gradients can produce desirable effects.

Gradients come in two flavors: *linear* and *radial*. Linear gradients transition colors across a straight path, whereas radial gradients transition colors between an outer circle and an inner circle (see Figure 7.5). To create a gradient, you need two items: an element that defines the gradient and a style rule that applies the gradient to the object.

FIGURE 7.5

Two types of gradients: linear (left) and radial (right).

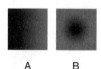

A   B

Linear Gradients

In the case of the linear blend, the `linearGradient` element defines a gradient according to the direction of a line. This element contains attributes similar to the `line` element. `x1` and `y1` define the start point of the line, and `x2` and `y2` define the end point of the line. Thus, the element uses the following syntax: `<linearGradient x1="A" x2="B" y1="C" y2="D">…</linearGradient>`, where A, B, C, and D represent values defining the coordinates of the gradient's directional line (known as the "gradient vector").

Inside of the `linearGradient` element is a series of `stop` child elements. Each `stop` element contains two important components: an `offset` attribute and a `stop-color` style rule. The `offset` attribute determines the point on the gradient line at which a color is defined. This value is in relation to the start and stop points defined previously. Often, you will see the `offset` attribute listed as a percentage, although pixel values are also accepted. Thus, if a percentage is used, it is in relation to the length of the line defined in the `linearGradient` element. The `stop-color` style rule defines the color value at that stop element's point.

To create a gradient then, you will need at least two `stop` elements within your `linearGradient` element. The syntax for your stop elements will then appear as follows, where *E* and *F* represent points along the directional line (usually noted in percentages) and *color-name* defines a color:

```
<linearGradient x1="A" y1="B" x2="C" y2="D">
        <stop offset="E" style="stop-color:color-name"/>
        <stop offset="F" style="stop-color:color-name"/>
</linearGradient>
```

Just as with the `stroke` and `fill` declarations, the `stop-color` declaration can accept any color notation that SVG allows (including the common hexadecimal notation and color keywords).

To apply a gradient to an object, you'll need to add a gradient style rule. The style rule used for applying gradients is `fill:url(#BlendID)`, where *BlendID* is the value of the gradient's `id` attribute.

The gradient can take advantage of the `gradientUnits` attribute to interpret the line data from the `x1`, `y1` and `x2`, `y2` coordinates. The attribute has two possible values: `objectBoundingBox` and `userSpaceOnUse`.

The `objectBoundingBox` value tells the gradient to base the coordinates on the object's bounding box. In other words, the (x1,y2) coordinates are calculated against the top left-most corner of the object, rather than the top left-most corner of the SVG document.

7

The userSpaceOnUse value tells the gradient to consider the line coordinates relative to the user coordinate system (generally the document's coordinate system, unless a transformation has been applied to the gradient beforehand). Thus, the (x1,y2) coordinates are usually calculated against the document's (0,0) point.

To demonstrate the linear gradient in action, you'll create a simple box with a white-to-black gradient fill, as shown in Listing 7.4:

1. First, create the gradient on line 14, naming it BlendLinear and drawing the gradient's path from 50,0 to 150,0 according to the SVG document's coordinate system.

2. Then, set two stops (lines 16 and 17): white at 0% (the 50,0 point) and black at 100% (the 150,0 point).

3. Lastly, create a class (line 8) that fills an object with the gradient, and then apply the class to your square (line 20).

LISTING 7.4   Creating a Linear Gradient

```
01: <?xml version="1.0" standalone="no"?>
02: <!DOCTYPE svg PUBLIC "-//W3C//DTD SVG 1.0//EN
            "http://www.w3.org/TR/2001/REC-SVG-20010904/DTD/svg10.dtd">
03:
04: <svg  width="500" height="300">
05:
06: <style type="text/css">
07:         <![CDATA[
08:                 .FillBlendLinear{fill:url(#BlendLinear);}
09:                 .Stroke000000{stroke:#000000;}
10:                 .StrokeWidth1{stroke-width:1;}
11:         ]]>
12: </style>
13:
14: <linearGradient id="BlendLinear" gradientUnits="userSpaceOnUse"
15:         x1="50" y1="0" x2="150" y2="0">
16:                 <stop offset="0%" style="stop-color:#FFFFFF"/>
17:                 <stop offset="100%" style="stop-color:#000000"/>
18: </linearGradient>
19:
20: <rect class="FillBlendLinear StrokeWidth1 Stroke000000"
            x="50" y="50" width="100" height="100"/>
21:
22: </svg>
```

Figure 7.6 shows the results of the added code.

FIGURE 7.6

Linear gradients can be used to create the blend apparent in this rectangle's fill.

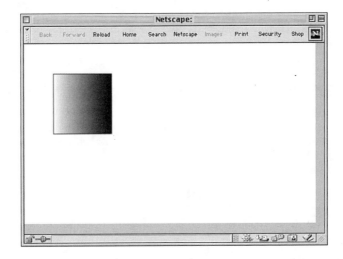

Gradients can have multiple colors and stop points. You can add multiple stop elements to create a blend that spans several colors. Each stop element will then blend towards the color on either side of it. For instance, subtle metal effects are possible by blending across several light shades of gray.

To experiment with this possibility, you can alter your previous code (Listing 7.4) to include additional stop points, as in Listing 7.5. First, copy the two stop elements and paste between them, resulting in a total of four stop elements within your linearGradient element (lines 16 through 19 in Listing 7.5). Then, change the color values of each stop to a gray, and modify the two interior stop elements (lines 17 and 18) so that their offset value is somewhere between 0 and 100%. Figure 7.7 shows the result: a rectangle filled with various shades of gray, suggesting the appearance of a metal cylinder.

LISTING 7.5   Adding Multiple Stops and Colors to a Gradient

```
01: <?xml version="1.0" standalone="no"?>
02: <!DOCTYPE svg PUBLIC "-//W3C//DTD SVG 1.0//EN
            "http://www.w3.org/TR/2001/REC-SVG-20010904/DTD/svg10.dtd">
03:
04: <svg  width="500" height="300">
05:
06: <style type="text/css">
07:        <![CDATA[
08:                .FillBlendLinear{fill:url(#BlendLinear);}
09:                .Stroke000000{stroke:#000000;}
10:                .StrokeWidth1{stroke-width:1;}
```

continues

7

LISTING 7.5   Continued

```
11:          ]]>
12: </style>
13:
14: <linearGradient id="BlendLinear" gradientUnits="userSpaceOnUse"
15:         x1="50" y1="0" x2="150" y2="0">
16:                 <stop offset="0%" style="stop-color:#666666"/>
17:                 <stop offset="35%" style="stop-color:#999999"/>
18:                 <stop offset="80%" style="stop-color:#333333"/>
19:                 <stop offset="100%" style="stop-color:#666666"/>
20: </linearGradient>
21:
22: <rect class="FillBlendLinear StrokeWidth1 Stroke000000"
              x="50" y="50" width="100" height="100"/>
23:
24: </svg>
```

FIGURE 7.7

Linear gradients with multiple stops can create multiple blends within one object.

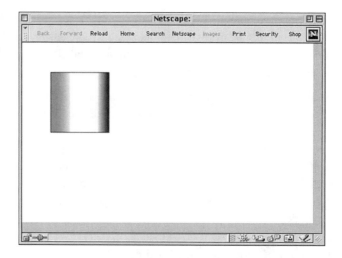

Gradients need not go only from left to right; they can angle as well. By altering your line coordinates, you can change the direction of a gradient. Using Listing 7.5 as a starting point, you can alter your gradient by a 45° angle. Simply change the values in line 15 to reflect a line going from the lower left-hand corner of your square to the top right corner, as shown in Listing 7.6. Figure 7.8 shows the resulting angled gradient.

LISTING 7.6 Changing the Gradient Vector Alters the Angle of the Gradient's Display

```
01: <?xml version="1.0" standalone="no"?>
02: <!DOCTYPE svg PUBLIC "-//W3C//DTD SVG 1.0//EN
          "http://www.w3.org/TR/2001/REC-SVG-20010904/DTD/svg10.dtd">
03:
04: <svg  width="500" height="300">
05:
06: <style type="text/css">
07:      <![CDATA[
08:             .FillBlendLinear{fill:url(#BlendLinear);}
09:             .Stroke000000{stroke:#000000;}
10:             .StrokeWidth1{stroke-width:1;}
11:      ]]>
12: </style>
13:
14: <linearGradient id="BlendLinear" gradientUnits="userSpaceOnUse"
15:      x1="5" y1="95" x2="95" y2="5">
16:             <stop offset="0%" style="stop-color:#FF0000"/>
17:             <stop offset="35%" style="stop-color:#FFFFFF"/>
18:             <stop offset="80%" style="stop-color:#FFFFCC"/>
19:             <stop offset="100%" style="stop-color:#000000"/>
20: </linearGradient>
21:
22: <rect class="FillBlendLinear StrokeWidth1 Stroke000000"
23:          x="50" y="50" width="100" height="100"/>
24: </svg>
```

FIGURE 7.8

A linear gradient can be displayed on an angle by altering its directional line.

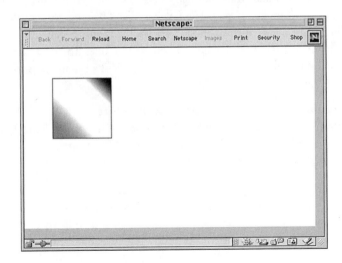

7

You can also leave off the line coordinates, at which point the gradient start point will be the left edge of the object, and the gradient will increase as it moves rightwards. To do so, you'll also need to remove the gradientUnits property. Thus, instead of `<linearGradient x1="A" x2="B" y1="C" y2="D">…</linearGradient>`, you can define your simplified gradient as `<linearGradient>…</linearGradient>`.

Radial Gradients

In the case of the radial blend, the radialGradient element contains attributes similar to the circle element. cx and cy define the circle, and r defines the radius of said circle. There are two additional properties that can be used to offset the circle's center: fx and fy. (As with the linearGradient element's directional attributes, all of these attributes can be left out.) The stop element functions just as it did for the linearGradient element.

To illustrate the radial blend, you'll create a glowing center for the news center graphic's sun in Listing 7.7. Using Listing 7.1 as a base, add a radialGradient element (line 15 in Listing 7.7). To determine how the cx and cy values will be interpreted, you will need to add a gradientUnits attribute.

In the last example, you used the value userSpaceOnUse, resulting in values that related to the document's coordinate system. In this case, use objectBoundingBox so that the other attribute's values are in relation to the coordinates of the object to which the gradient will be applied.

The cx and cy values (both defined as 50%) determine that the gradient will start in the middle of the applied object. The r value (also 50%) determines that the gradient will extend to the edges of its applied circle (as the radius of any circle is 50% of its actual dimensions). Two stop elements are created on lines 16 and 17, each defining a shade of yellow at their respective point along the gradient's radius (moving outward from the center point).

Lastly, the gradient is given an id value of GradientSunCenter (line 15). This value is then referenced when you create a style rule (on line 8) filling an object with that specific gradient. The rule is then applied to the circle on line 14, completing your document. Figure 7.9 shows the resulting image: a "glowing" sun.

LISTING 7.7 Creating a Radial Gradient

```
01: <?xml version="1.0" standalone="no"?>
02: <!DOCTYPE svg PUBLIC "-//W3C//DTD SVG 1.0//EN
            "http://www.w3.org/TR/2001/REC-SVG-20010904/DTD/svg10.dtd">
03:
04: <svg  width="500" height="300">
05:
06:      <style type="text/css">
07:              <![CDATA[
08:                     .GradientSun{fill:url(#GradientSunCenter);}
09:                     .Fill99CCFF{fill:#99CCFF;}
10:              ]]>
11:      </style>
12:
13:      <rect id="Sky" x="10" y="45" width="200" height="245"
                  class="Fill99CCFF"/>
14:      <circle id="Sun" cx="105" cy="160" r="56" class="GradientSun"/>
15:      <radialGradient id="GradientSunCenter" cx="50%" cy="50%" r="50%"
                  gradientUnits="objectBoundingBox">
16:              <stop offset="50%" style="stop-color:#FFFFCC"/>
17:              <stop offset="85%" style="stop-color:#FFFF00"/>
18:      </radialGradient>
19:
20: </svg>
```

FIGURE 7.9

A radial gradient can be used to create a glowing effect.

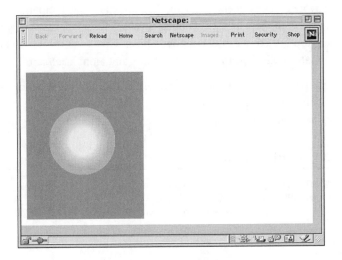

Lastly, note how even though the gradient elements existed within the SVG file, they did not display unless applied through the style command. You can store your gradient elements inside many elements, including svg and g elements, as well as definition and symbol elements (see Hour 8, "Symbols").

Creating Patterns

The pattern element allows you to define a graphic element (or group of elements) as a repeatable pattern. Rather than duplicating the element multiple times, the pattern element reduces the number of code lines needed to perform the same task. The savings are two-fold:

- Your file is easier to manage and peruse
- Your file size is dramatically reduced

Using a pattern requires a pattern element surrounding the content to be tiled. This element has several characteristics that define how the tiled content will be displayed. The x and y attributes determine the top left-most position of the first tiled object within the object using the tile. The width and height properties define the respective distances between the top left-most edge of the first tiled object and its neighboring objects.

To apply the pattern, add the style rule fill:url(#PatternID), where PatternID is the name of the pattern's id value.

To try out the pattern element, you can take a break from the news center example. Instead, using Listing 7.8 as a guide, create a large rectangle in your SVG document (line 17).

Next, create a pattern element (line 13), and name the element with the id attribute. Then, give both the x and y attributes a value of 0 so that the object to be tiled starts in the very top-left corner of the applied object. Give both the width and height attributes a value of 25 so the object is repeated equidistant along each axis.

With the pattern element created, you will need to define its tiling content: a 10-by-10, blue-filled square (described on line 14). Line 8 shows the style rule needed to apply the pattern to the rectangle you created (line 17). Figure 7.10 shows the result.

LISTING 7.8   Creating a Pattern Fill

```
01: <?xml version="1.0" standalone="no"?>
02: <!DOCTYPE svg PUBLIC "-//W3C//DTD SVG 1.0//EN
            "http://www.w3.org/TR/2001/REC-SVG-20010904/DTD/svg10.dtd">
03:
04: <svg  width="500" height="300">
05:
06: <style type="text/css">
07:        <![CDATA[
08:                .FillBoxPattern{fill:url(#BoxPattern);}
09:                .Fill99CCFF{fill:#99CCFF;}
10:        ]]>
```

continues

LISTING 7.8   Continued

```
11:  </style>
12:
13:        <pattern id="BoxPattern" x="0" y="0" width="25" height="25"
                  patternUnits="userSpaceOnUse">
14:                <rect x="0" y="0" width="10" height="10" class="Fill99CCFF"/>
15:        </pattern>
16:
17:        <rect id="BoxPatternBox" class="FillBoxPattern"
                  x="0" y="0" width="500" height="300"/>
18:
19:  </svg>
```

FIGURE 7.10

A repeating object can be made using the pattern *element.*

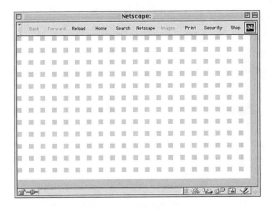

Summary

By providing a framework for fills and strokes, SVG can match the output of other traditional design tools. Offering more complex features like transparency, gradients, and patterns allows it to compete head-on with other sophisticated formats. As SVG provides designers with a complete palette of possibilities, there is little that can be rendered in other applications that cannot be rendered in SVG.

With your newfound ability to paint objects, the next hour will teach you how to create and use symbols. Symbols have become popular in other design programs and technologies thanks to Flash, and the W3C was sure to include such a useful component in SVG.

7

Q&A

Q I would like to learn more about hexadecimal notation. What resources are available?

A Several online resources exist regarding hexadecimal notation and its use for describing RGB color values. WebMonkey has an article explaining hexadecimal notation at `http://hotwired.lycos.com/webmonkey/97/17/index2a.html`, and HTMLGoodies has an introduction to hexadecimal notation at `http://www.htmlgoodies.com/tutors/colorexp.html`.

Q Can the `pattern` element stagger the offset of its tiling content, similar to a diagonal grid?

A Although the element itself does not facilitate this, you can achieve this effect. Rather than enclosing only one object within the `pattern` element, enclose two. The two objects to be repeated should then, somewhat obviously, be arranged diagonally. Adjust the `width` and `height` of the `pattern` element to match the spacing of the two objects, and your desired effect is accomplished.

Workshop

Quiz

1. What style properties are used to adjust the transparency of an object?
2. True or False: The `stroke-weight` style declaration is used to determine the thickness of a stroke.
3. Describe the two types of gradients possible in SVG.
4. Which element is used to repeat an object's display at a set offset within another object?
5. True or False: SVG can accept hexadecimal notation to describe color values.

Answers

1. The `opacity`, `fill-opacity`, and `stroke-opacity` style properties are used to adjust the transparency of an object. The first of the three, `opacity`, adjusts both fill and stroke opacities simultaneously.
2. False. The `stroke-width` declaration is used to determine the thickness of a stroke.
3. Two types of gradients exist in SVG: linear and gradient. Linear gradients follow a straight directional path (known as a gradient vector), whereas radial gradients blend colors along the radius of a circle.

4. The `pattern` element is used to create a repeatable object inside another object. When applied, it acts just like a color fill, tiling its contents across the dimensions of the object.

5. True. SVG can accept many methods of describing a color, including both color keywords and hexadecimal notation of RGB values.

Exercises

1. Flex your mastery of patterns and gradients by creating a pattern containing a series of gradated objects. Copy lines 8 and 14 through 22 of Listing 7.6 and paste the lines into their appropriate location in Listing 7.8 (line 8 belongs in the style sheet, whereas the remaining lines can replace the blue square on line 14).

2. Observe the interesting effects you can create by layering a series of semi-transparent objects over each other. Make sure each object has a different fill and that none of the objects share the same coordinates and dimensions.

3. Apply transparency to a gradient. Place the gradient over an object with a pattern fill, and adjust this object's transparency as well.

7

HOUR 8

Symbols

One of the most useful features in SVG is the ability to establish an object (or group of objects) as a symbolic group. By doing so, this "symbol" can be referenced multiple times throughout the document.

For example, say you were creating a bulleted list of ten items that would need to be updated for every season. For lack of a better example, say you wanted a pumpkin for your Halloween bullet. Rather than drawing one pumpkin and duplicating it nine times (creating a lot of additional code), you can create the bullet graphic once and store it within a reference library. Now your pumpkin exists abstractly and can be referenced with a small line of code ten times to create your list. Even better, when you decide to change the pumpkin to a pilgrim's hat for your Thanksgiving list, you simply change the symbol in your definition to reflect the new artwork. Voila! Instantly, you will now have ten pilgrim's hats instead of ten pumpkins.

By keeping your commonly used graphics in your SVG document separated from the remaining graphical content, you are able to make sweeping changes to the appearance of your file far more quickly than by any other means.

This hour will introduce you to the following of concepts:

- What a symbol is
- How to create a symbol
- Referencing a symbol
- Using symbols efficiently

When you are finished with this chapter, you will be able to use artwork you have created as reusable objects within your documents. You may find, in fact, that your artwork can be redrawn more efficiently by using symbols in place of unique objects.

Creating Symbols and Definitions

As far as most Web developers are concerned, symbols came onto the scene when Flash was introduced. By saving an object into Flash's symbol library, the same item could be used over and over again with very little impact on file size.

Obviously, in the case of Web graphics, smaller is generally better, as many users still access the Web through dial-up modems. Thus, a technology that intelligently recycles its content becomes a popular tool in the online world.

SVG's use of symbols offers the same value that Flash does: 1) graphics become smaller to download as more of their visual components are replicated using symbols, and 2) graphics become easier to modify when their content comprises symbols.

With such benefits, why not make everything a symbol? For starters, if an object does not appear more than once, making it a symbol *increases* the amount of your code. As you go through this chapter, you will see that every instance (the term used to describe the application of a symbol within the content of the document) requires a reference element. When an object appears more than once, each reference element will likely be smaller in size than the actual artwork it represents; when the object appears only once, adding a reference only adds to the file size.

Second, if an object appears only once, making it a symbol can produce confusing results for a developer. Symbols are kept apart from the content area inside an SVG document. When several instances of the symbol occur, the efficiency of the coding and file size justify the inconvenience of looking elsewhere to understand the content being referenced. If only one instance exists, most developers will scratch their heads trying to understand why you made a "one-trick pony" a symbol.

The application of symbols is even easier than the concept and the rationale. To create a symbol, you need two items:

- The artwork or item to be referenced, contained within a definitions library
- A reference element

Artwork to be used as a symbol can be stored within either a defs or a symbol element. For a symbol to be referenced, however, it must have been named with the id attribute (first introduced in Hour 2). Once named, the symbol can be referenced with the use element. The use element can have a variety of attributes added to it, such as x and y to determine the symbol's placement on the page, but the most important attribute references the symbol. This attribute uses the syntax xlink:href=#symbolName, where symbolName is the name of the symbol to be referenced.

An SVG viewer will never render any content placed within a defs or symbol element. Such content will appear only when referenced by the use element.

To illustrate the symbol concept, follow Listing 8.1 to store your cloud illustrations (from the news center weather graphic example begun in Hour 1) in the defs element. First, begin by copying the code from Listing 7.1 and pasting it into a new document. This will provide you with a basic illustration of the sun and sky.

Next, create a defs element (line 15 in Listing 8.1) to store your cloud symbol in. In Listing 7.2, you began by using ellipses in place of the actual cloud artwork. If you were successful with the first exercise at the end of Hour 5, however, you likely produced art similar to lines 17 through 22. To make this a usable symbol, group the artwork (lines 16 and 23) and provide an id attribute value to name the symbol (Cloud will do just fine).

Add a use element (line 27) to reference the new Cloud symbol, and position the instance of the symbol with the x and y attributes. Add a style rule (line 9) for a white fill, and apply the class to the use element. Once positioned and stylized, copy this element and paste it on the line below (line 28) to create the second cloud; be sure to modify the x and y attribute values so that the two instances aren't overlapping.

By keeping the actual Cloud symbol devoid of style information, you can use the same artwork for both the "Sunny" and "Rainy" illustrations. (You will be building the rainy illustration later.) With these changes in place, your resulting graphic will look like Figure 8.1.

LISTING 8.1 Storing the Cloud Illustration As a Symbol

```
01: <?xml version="1.0" standalone="no"?>
02: <!DOCTYPE svg PUBLIC "-//W3C//DTD SVG 1.0//EN"
03:   "http://www.w3.org/TR/2001/REC-SVG-20010904/DTD/svg10.dtd">
04:
```

continues

LISTING 8.1   Continued

```
05: <svg width="500" height="300">
06:
07:      <style type="text/css">
08:              <![CDATA[
09:                      .FillFFFFFF{fill:#FFFFFF;}
10:                      .Fill99CCFF{fill:#99CCFF;}
11:                      .FillFFFF00{fill:#FFFF00;}
12:              ]]>
13:      </style>
14:
15:      <defs>
16:              <g id="Cloud">
17:                      <circle cx="24" cy="36" r="15"/>
18:                      <circle cx="41" cy="26" r="17"/>
19:                      <circle cx="90" cy="40" r="13"/>
20:                      <circle cx="105" cy="31" r="13"/>
21:                      <ellipse cx="75" cy="20" rx="27" ry="20"/>
22:                      <ellipse cx="56" cy="50" rx="25" ry="18"/>
23:              </g>
24:      </defs>
25:
26:      <rect id="Sky" x="10" y="45" width="200" height="245" class="Fill99CCFF"/>
27:      <use id="SunCloud1" xlink:href="#Cloud" x="-20" y="20" class="FillFFFFFF"/>
28:      <use id="SunCloud2" xlink:href="#Cloud" x="150" y="210" class="FillFFFFFF"/>
29:      <circle id="Sun" cx="105" cy="160" r="56" class="FillFFFF00"/>
30:
31: </svg>
```

FIGURE 8.1

Using symbols to reference the cloud illustrations.

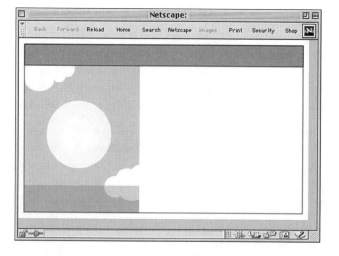

As you develop the news center further throughout the book, you'll notice that the same symbol is used to create the thunderstorm clouds. By the end of the example, you will have saved 28 lines of code simply by using the symbol concept for your cloud illustrations.

To further maximize your coding efficiency, symbols can be made up of other symbols. By reusing symbols within each other, grouping one with another and then creating a new symbol with this content, you can create complex but easy to change graphics.

To attempt this symbol-within-a-symbol effect, take a break from the news center example and picture a pegboard with alternating white and red pegs in its holes. Creating such an image will require code (Listing 8.2) that builds up from the lowest common denominator.

First, create a symbol based on a circle named peg (line 7 in Listing 8.2); this will serve as the shape for all the pegs on the board, regardless of color. To distinguish the pegs by color, use the use element to create two new symbols, pegRed and pegWhite, that reference the original peg symbol for shape; then apply paint information (lines 8 and 9).

Next, create two more symbols (lines 10 and 16) to define pegboard columns that start with red and white pegs respectively. Each column symbol should contain references to the colored peg symbols with appropriate coordinate information for placement. This ends your symbol creation. Finally, create six references to the column symbols with coordinate information to correctly arrange their positions (lines 24–29). When you're finished, your symbol-within-a-symbol example will render similar to Figure 8.2.

LISTING 8.2   Using Symbols within Symbols

```
01: <?xml version="1.0" standalone="no"?>
02: <!DOCTYPE svg PUBLIC "-//W3C//DTD SVG 20010904//EN"
            "http://www.w3.org/TR/2001/REC-SVG-20010904/DTD/svg10.dtd">
03:
04: .<svg  width="500" height="300">
05:
06:     <defs>
07:             <circle id="peg" r="15"/>
08:             <use id="pegRed" xlink:href="#peg" style="fill:red; stroke:black;"/>
09:             <use id="pegWhite" xlink:href="#peg" style="fill:white;
                    stroke:black;"/>
10:             <g id="columnRed">
11:                 <use xlink:href="#pegRed" x="100" y="50"/>
12:                 <use xlink:href="#pegWhite" x="100" y="100"/>
13:                 <use xlink:href="#pegRed" x="100" y="150"/>
14:                 <use xlink:href="#pegWhite" x="100" y="200"/>
15:             </g>
16:             <g id="columnWhite">
```

continues

LISTING 8.2   Continued

```
17:                                <use xlink:href="#pegWhite" x="150" y="50"/>
18:                                <use xlink:href="#pegRed" x="150" y="100"/>
19:                                <use xlink:href="#pegWhite" x="150" y="150"/>
20:                                <use xlink:href="#pegRed" x="150" y="200"/>
21:                    </g>
22:            </defs>
23:
24:            <use xlink:href="#columnRed" x="0" y="0"/>
25:            <use xlink:href="#columnWhite" x="0" y="0"/>
26:            <use xlink:href="#columnRed" x="100" y="0"/>
27:            <use xlink:href="#columnWhite" x="100" y="0"/>
28:            <use xlink:href="#columnRed" x="200" y="0"/>
29:            <use xlink:href="#columnWhite" x="200" y="0"/>
30:
31: </svg>
```

FIGURE 8.2

Creating a pegboard illustration to demonstrate symbol-within-symbol creation.

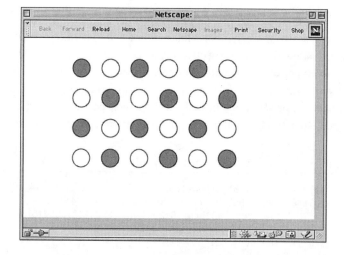

By containing symbols within symbols, you can maximize the use of your objects. In this example, one circle became a multi-colored pegboard. However, due to its modular creation, the same pegboard could become a checkerboard in seconds simply by swapping out the circle with a rectangle, as shown in line 7 of Listing 8.3. Results are shown in Figure 8.3.

LISTING 8.3   Demonstrating the Efficiency of Symbols within Symbols

```
01: <?xml version="1.0" standalone="no"?>
02: <!DOCTYPE svg PUBLIC "-//W3C//DTD SVG 20010904//EN"
            "http://www.w3.org/TR/2001/REC-SVG-20010904/DTD/svg10.dtd">
```

continues

LISTING 8.3 Continued

```
03:
04: .<svg  width="500" height="300">
05:
06:      <defs>
07:              <rect id="peg" width="50" height="50"/>
08:              <use id="pegRed" xlink:href="#peg" style="fill:red;
                        stroke:black;"/>
09:              <use id="pegWhite" xlink:href="#peg" style="fill:white;
                        stroke:black;"/>
10:              <g id="columnRed">
11:                      <use xlink:href="#pegRed" x="100" y="50"/>
12:                      <use xlink:href="#pegWhite" x="100" y="100"/>
13:                      <use xlink:href="#pegRed" x="100" y="150"/>
14:                      <use xlink:href="#pegWhite" x="100" y="200"/>
15:              </g>
16:              <g id="columnWhite">
17:                      <use xlink:href="#pegWhite" x="150" y="50"/>
18:                      <use xlink:href="#pegRed" x="150" y="100"/>
19:                      <use xlink:href="#pegWhite" x="150" y="150"/>
20:                      <use xlink:href="#pegRed" x="150" y="200"/>
21:              </g>
22:      </defs>
23:
24:      <use xlink:href="#columnRed" x="0" y="0"/>
25:      <use xlink:href="#columnWhite" x="0" y="0"/>
26:      <use xlink:href="#columnRed" x="100" y="0"/>
27:      <use xlink:href="#columnWhite" x="100" y="0"/>
28:      <use xlink:href="#columnRed" x="200" y="0"/>
29:      <use xlink:href="#columnWhite" x="200" y="0"/>
30:
31: </svg>
```

FIGURE 8.3

Similar code to Listing 8.2 suddenly produces a checkerboard image.

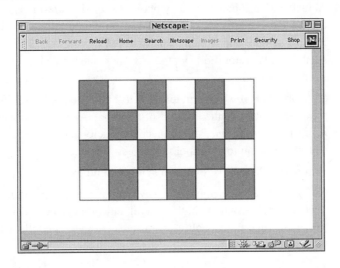

By using this efficient method to design your documents, you will be able to make sweeping changes to your imagery with the replacement of one object. Although more code was used to create this checkerboard/pegboard than if you drew each element by hand, the rule of "less is more" can often be overruled by "efficiency is the key." By intelligently planning your artwork to use symbols when possible or practical, you can significantly reduce the amount of effort necessary to modify the work later.

Summary

Symbols are a Web developer's dream come true; rather than forcing an end-user to download the same information multiple times, symbols allow for an efficient duplication of objects with far less impact on overall file size. Also, by keeping style and location information separate from the symbol, the same piece of artwork can appear very different throughout your document. Lastly, by using symbols within symbols, your coding efficiency is multiplied.

The flexibility that symbols offer developers is tremendous; one piece of art can be used multiple times and in multiple appearances. Symbols, however, aren't the only impressive feature SVG has to offer. The next hour will introduce you to the concept of masking and clipping objects. A technique familiar to most designers, these two methods of selectively revealing artwork can be useful for "cleaning up rough edges."

Q&A

Q I am familiar with Flash's symbol library. How does SVG's concept of a symbol differ from Flash's?

A Actually, SVG's handling of symbols is very similar to Flash's. Conceptually, the two handle symbols the same. In Flash, an item is stored in a library by converting it into a symbol and is then visually stored in a separate library palette. In SVG, a symbol is also removed from the artwork content by placing it within a defs or symbol element.

SVG offers an advantage in terms of its ability to apply considerable amounts of style information to the instance of a symbol. Although Flash allows certain adjustments to be made to a symbol (such as opacity and overall color), SVG can pass any style rule on to a symbol via the use element.

Q Can a use element reference a symbol in an external file?

A No. Sadly, the use element can only reference material within the same document. Such a feature would be highly useful, however. You can consider writing the W3C to suggest such functionality, as this technology will continued to be improved upon as time goes on.

Workshop

The Workshop is designed to help you anticipate possible questions, review what you've learned, and begin learning how to put your knowledge into practice.

Quiz

1. True or False: Symbols allow you to reuse the same piece of artwork multiple times in one document.

2. Which element is used to store a series of symbols and other referential items?

3. For an object to be referenced as a symbol by the use element, what attribute must it have defined?

4. True or False: The use element cannot accept the style attribute.

5. True or False: Symbols can reside within other symbols.

Answers

1. True. A symbol can be referenced indefinitely within a document, creating as many duplicates of the symbol as there are references for it in the document.

2. The defs element is used to harbor symbols and other content to be referenced in an SVG document.

3. The use element requires an symbol to be named via the id attribute so that its xlink:href attribute can specify a specific item.

4. False. SVG symbols can accept radically different appearances because their referencing agent (the use element) can accept additional visual information through the style attribute.

5. True. Yet another powerful aspect of the SVG symbol is its ability to use other symbols within itself. By using a symbol within a symbol (within a symbol, and so on), you can create a very modular design that is easy to update quickly.

Exercise

In last hour's exercises, you created a pattern containing a series of gradated objects and applied it to an object. Now, take that object, make it a symbol, and reference it several times in your document. Alter one of the gradient's colors and watch your efficiency at work.

HOUR 9

Masking and Clipping

In the design world, masking can refer to a variety of concepts. Generally, in most drawing tools, "masking" is similar in concept to a keyhole—a mask is a shape that reveals content below through its *inner* shape but prevents the same content from appearing *outside* its shape.

However, in SVG, "masking" refers to something more akin to a photo-imaging program's definition of it. In an SVG "mask," the amount of content revealed beneath the mask is based on the color value of the pixels in the mask. In other words, as the color value across the mask changes, so too changes the visibility of the image masked.

To handle the "keyhole" concept, SVG uses "clipping paths." These objects can range in complexity from a simple rectangle to a complex series of unique paths. Clipping paths do not have the smooth transitions and blending that masking allows; instead, clipping paths are hard edged. Either content shows through (in the case of the inner area of the clipping path data) or it doesn't (in the case of any area outside of the path).

To introduce you to both of these methods, this hour will teach you the following:

- What clipping and masking are
- How to create a mask
- How alpha channels and artwork affect a mask
- How to create a clipping path

With these concepts, you will be capable of quickly performing some amazing modifications to your artwork without actually altering the existing artwork.

Masking

Masking relies on the following three components to operate:

- The mask style property
- The mask element
- The mask content, which determines the level of opacity

The mask style declaration consists of mask:url(#MaskID), where MaskID is most often the value of the mask's id attribute.

The mask element is most similar to the rect element, as it uses the x, y, width, and height attributes to define its maximum boundaries. Within the mask element is the mask content. This content is used to resolve what amount of artwork below the mask is visible and in what locations.

As mentioned earlier this hour, a mask uses the values of its content's colors (the objects within the mask element) to determine what artwork peeks through and what does not. This mask content is interpreted as an alpha channel. Colors that are dark in value prevent artwork from displaying, whereas lighter values (those closest to white) allow the masked content to show through. To help remember which values do what, use this mnemonic device: black means blank, white means sight.

To help cement this new information, you'll need to create a demonstration of the mask element. In the case of the following example (Listing 9.1), you'll mask the existing news center graphic with a multi-stop gradient. The results, though odd-looking, show how the varying values in the blend allow different amounts of the background artwork to show through.

To create the example, you will first need to copy the code from Listing 8.1 and paste it into a new document. (Listing 8.1 was the first use of the Cloud symbol.) Next, you will need to create a gradient that will serve as your mask (line 27). This gradient will make a mask that slowly fades from transparent to solid and back to transparent.

To accomplish this effect, your gradient will need the following four stops:

- The first stop (on line 28), which is transparent (`stop-color:black`), will need to start at the left edge of the document (`offset="0%"`). Remember: as the `linearGradient` element you just created does not have any directional coordinates, any percentage-based `offset` values will be in relation to the document's width.

- The second stop (line 29), which is solid (`stop-color:white`), will start further into the document (`offset="30%"`).

- The third stop (line 30), which is also solid (`stop-color:white`), will continue solid opacity through 45% of the width of the document (`offset="45%"`).

- The final stop (line 31) is transparent (`stop-color:black`) and ends the gradient at 55% of the document's width (`offset="55%"`).

You may be wondering, "Why bother creating two solid stops in the middle of the gradient?" The third stop will ensure that the masked content appears completely between this and the second stop. If only one solid stop existed, only one pixel would have 100% solid display of the masked content. In that case, either side of this pixel would be gradating towards transparency, resulting in a more ghost-like image.

With the gradient now created, you will need to create a `mask` element (line 33) and label it `MaskArt` by using an `id` attribute. As the gradient you created earlier can't exist by itself, you will need to make a rectangle the size of the document with the gradient applied to it (line 34). This gradient-filled rectangle now serves as an effective mask ready to be applied to artwork.

As neither the gradient nor the mask render without being referenced and applied to an object, you should place them within the `defs` element (line 18) already holding your `Cloud` symbol. To show the effect the gradient mask will have on your artwork, you should create a red-filled rectangle the size of the document (line 39).

Lastly, you'll need to create a class (named `FillMask`) to apply the mask (line 9) and then actually apply it to your artwork (from the Listing 8.1 code). As your artwork consists of more than one object, you can more easily apply the mask by first grouping the artwork and then applying the `FillMask` class to the surrounding group (line 41).

With this last step complete, your document should render similar to Figure 9.1. As the left and right edges of the mask were rendered transparent, the red rectangle should be appearing through the artwork in those areas. (Please note: the grayscale figures in this book cannot accurately depict the subtle transitions you will see on your computer screen.)

LISTING 9.1   Masking the News Center Graphic

```
01: <?xml version="1.0" standalone="no"?>
02: <!DOCTYPE svg PUBLIC "-//W3C//DTD SVG 20010904//EN"
03:    "http://www.w3.org/TR/2001/REC-SVG-20010904/DTD/svg10.dtd">
04:
05: <svg  width="500" height="300">
06:
07:        <style type="text/css">
08:                <![CDATA[
09:                        .FillMask{mask:url(#MaskArt);}
10:                        .FillMaskBlend{fill:url(#MaskBlend);}
11:                        .FillCC0000{fill:#CC0000;}
12:                        .Fill99CCFF{fill:#99CCFF;}
13:                        .FillFFFF00{fill:#FFFF00;}
14:                        .FillFFFFFF{fill:#FFFFFF;}
15:                ]]>
16:        </style>
17:
18:        <defs>
19:                <g id="Cloud1">
20:                        <circle cx="24" cy="36" r="15"/>
21:                        <circle cx="41" cy="26" r="17"/>
22:                        <circle cx="90" cy="40" r="13"/>
23:                        <circle cx="105" cy="31" r="13"/>
24:                        <ellipse cx="75" cy="20" rx="27" ry="20"/>
25:                        <ellipse cx="56" cy="50" rx="25" ry="18"/>
26:                </g>
27:                <linearGradient id="MaskBlend">
28:                  <stop offset="0%" style="stop-color:black"/>
29:                  <stop offset="30%" style="stop-color:white"/>
30:                  <stop offset="45%" style="stop-color:white"/>
31:                  <stop offset="55%" style="stop-color:black"/>
32:                </linearGradient>
33:                <mask id="MaskArt">
34:                  <rect x="0" y="0" width="500" height="300"
                          class="FillMaskBlend" />
35:                </mask>
36:        </defs>
38:
39:        <rect x="0" y="0" width="500" height="300" class="FillCC0000"/>
40:
41:        <g id="Sunny" class="FillMask">
42:                <rect id="Sky" x="10" y="45" width="200" height="245"
                          class="Fill99CCFF"/>
43:                <use id="SunCloud1" xlink:href="#Cloud1" x="-20" y="80"
                          class="FillFFFFFF"/>
44:                <use id="SunCloud2" xlink:href="#Cloud1" x="150" y="200"
                          class="FillFFFFFF"/>
45:                <circle id="Sun" cx="105" cy="160" r="56" class="FillFFFF00"/>
46:        </g>
47:
48: </svg>
```

FIGURE 9.1

Using a gradient as a mask, the sunny sky artwork gradually becomes transparent on its left and right edges to the object beneath it.

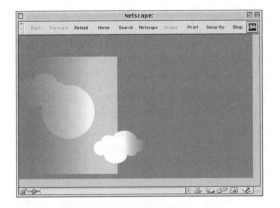

The resulting artwork, shown in Figure 9.1, appears to be semi-transparent and wrapped around a drum. This effect is due to the nature of using a gradient for your mask. By using different objects instead of the linear gradient, such as a blurred circle, your effect would look much different. In reality, however, the mask would operate the same. Simply wrap any object (or group of objects) that you want to serve as a mask within the mask element and then apply the mask to your artwork; it's that easy.

Clipping

To let content appear only through a specific shape, you'll need to take advantage of clipping paths. In Hour 7, you learned to fill a container with a pattern. Clipping paths are similar in concept, minus the repeating tiles.

Clipping paths require two components:

- A clipPath element
- A clip-path style property

The clipPath element contains the graphics that will serve as the content for the "keyhole" shape. This graphic content resides between <clipPath> and </clipPath> tags. Naming your clipPath element will allow it to be applied to other objects.

The style declaration used to apply a clipping path consists of clip-path:url(#*ClipID*), where "*ClipID*" is most often the name of the clipping path's id value. Applying this style declaration to other objects will allow only that part of their content that resides within the boundaries of the clipping path's graphic to show through.

To demonstrate clipping paths, you can crop the clouds from your news center graphic so that they do not extend past the width of the blue-sky background. First, copy the code from Listing 9.1 and paste it into a new document. Then, remove the gradient, mask, and the first two style classes (and their subsequent references).

With this clean new document, create a `clipPath` element within the `defs` element and name it `WeatherCrop` using the `id` attribute (line 26 in Listing 9.2). As you will not want your clouds to extend past the edges of the blue rectangle (labeled `Sky`), you will need to copy this rectangle (line 34) and paste it within the `clipPath` element (line 27).

With your clipping path created, you will need to create a new style class to apply the path to your artwork. Line 9 shows the new class pointing to the clipping path you made minutes ago named `WeatherCrop`. Now, apply the style rule to your artwork by styling the group surrounding your artwork (line 33). Figure 9.2 shows the result: the clouds no longer extend past the boundary of the blue sky.

LISTING 9.2 Cropping Illustrations of Clouds to Appear within the Weather Graphic's Defined Area

```
01: <?xml version="1.0" standalone="no"?>
02: <!DOCTYPE svg PUBLIC "-//W3C//DTD SVG 1.0//EN"
03:    "http://www.w3.org/TR/2001/REC-SVG-20010904/DTD/svg10.dtd">
04:
05: <svg width="500" height="300">
06:
07:       <style type="text/css">
08:              <![CDATA[
09:                     .WeatherCropBox{clip-path:url(#WeatherCrop);}
10:                     .FillCC0000{fill:#CC0000;}
11:                     .Fill99CCFF{fill:#99CCFF;}
12:                     .FillFFFF00{fill:#FFFF00;}
13:                     .FillFFFFFF{fill:#FFFFFF;}
14:              ]]>
15:       </style>
16:
17:       <defs>
18:              <g id="Cloud">
19:                     <circle cx="24" cy="36" r="15"/>
20:                     <circle cx="41" cy="26" r="17"/>
21:                     <circle cx="90" cy="40" r="13"/>
22:                     <circle cx="105" cy="31" r="13"/>
23:                     <ellipse cx="75" cy="20" rx="27" ry="20"/>
24:                     <ellipse cx="56" cy="50" rx="25" ry="18"/>
25:              </g>
26:              <clipPath id="WeatherCrop">
27:                     <rect id="WeatherBox" x="10" y="45" width="200"
                                height="245"/>
28:              </clipPath>
29:       </defs>
30:
31:       <rect x="0" y="0" width="500" height="300" class="FillCC0000"/>
32:
33:       <g id="Sunny" class="WeatherCropBox">
```

continues

LISTING 9.2   Continued

```
34:                    <rect id="Sky" x="10" y="45" width="200" height="245"
35:                            class="Fill99CCFF"/>
36:                    <use id="SunCloud1" xlink:href="#Cloud" x="-20" y="80"
37:                            class="FillFFFFFF"/>
38:                    <use id="SunCloud2" xlink:href="#Cloud" x="150" y="200"
39:                            class="FillFFFFFF"/>
40:                    <circle id="Sun" cx="105" cy="160" r="56"
                            class="FillFFFF00"/>
41:            </g>
42:
43: </svg>
```

FIGURE 9.2

*Using a clipping path,
the clouds are confined
to the shape of the sky.
Note how the left edge
of the cloud at left and
the right edge of the
cloud at right are
cut off.*

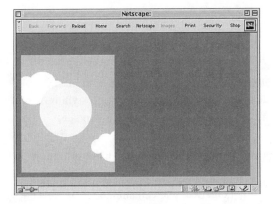

Having laid the artwork over the dark background (line 42) from the previous example, you can see that the clouds do not extend past the boundaries of the clipping path. Clipping paths can prove to be quite useful when you have more information than you want to show in one particular area.

By cropping your content using the shapes described within the clipPath element, you can save considerable time by not retooling your artwork to fit another shape. For instance, compare the amount of time needed to apply a clipping path to the amount of time required to plot path data (instead of circles and ellipses) so that the side edges of your clouds are straight and aligned with the rectangle's edges. In such cases, clipping paths prove their use by reducing your coding time.

Summary

Masking and clipping paths each provide a means of selectively revealing content. By using the mask element, you can create subtle blends between masked content and non-masked content. The clipPath element, on the other hand, provides a method of cropping content according to the definition of its enclosed path. The use of either depends solely on the effect you're trying to accomplish; when you need to hide particular elements of your artwork, you can assess which option will serve you best.

With masking and clipping fresh in your mind, you'll move into one of the most challenging and exciting aspects of SVG: filter effects. The next hour will introduce you to filter effects, how to apply them, how to combine them, and more.

Q&A

Q How does SVG's concept of masking and clipping differ from Flash's?

A Flash actually uses a mask to accomplish both masking and clipping. Rather than using two distinct methods, Flash's cropping style is determined by whether the mask is solid or transparent. If the mask's content is 100% opaque, the mask can serve the purpose of a clipping path.

Q Aside from the examples in this hour, what else can a mask or clipping path be used for?

A If you want to get creative, you can animate a mask or clipping path to produce an effect similar to the gun barrel view in the introduction to James Bond movies. Hour 15, "Animation," will introduce you to the basics of animating objects. Rather than animating artwork, however, you could animate a mask or clipping path to move your "keyhole" without moving its contents. Conversely, you could animate your content within the mask or clipping path, creating a window to another world of sorts. This book's final example will illustrate such a possibility by having the clouds animate across the sky within their clipping path.

Q Do masks and clipping paths need to be continuous shapes?

A Absolutely not. You could, for instance, have your clipping path comprise the pegboard artwork you created in Listing 8.2, revealing content through its series of "portholes." Both the mask and the clipPath elements serve as containers for any number of other elements, allowing multiple distinct shapes to define their content.

Workshop

The Workshop is designed to help you anticipate possible questions, review what you've learned, and begin learning how to put your knowledge into practice.

Quiz

1. To crop artwork, which element would you use?
2. True or False: The `mask` element renders its contents as an alpha channel.
3. How are clipping paths and masks applied to objects?
4. To create a mask that shows a progression between an object's fill and the background, what object would you contain in your mask?
5. What components are required to create a clipping path?

Answers

1. The `clipPath` element is used to crop content by revealing it only *within* the clipping path's described content area.
2. True. Content inside a `mask` element is interpreted as an alpha channel. This channel then determines how content is revealed through it.
3. A style rule is used to apply a clipping path or mask to content. In both cases, the syntax `fill:url(#idValue)` is used on the content to reference the mask or clipping path.
4. By using a linear or radial gradient within your mask, you can show a measured progression between the object and the artwork below it.
5. To create a clipping path, you will need the following:
    a. a `clipPath` element
    b. artwork within the `clipPath` element
    c. artwork to apply to the clipping path
    d. a style rule on the artwork to reference the clipping path

Exercises

1. Alter the masking example in this hour so that it includes several more gradient stops. Continue by adding other elements (such as solid rectangles and circles) within the mask in order to create a more complex alpha channel for your artwork.
2. Place artwork behind both your `clipPath` and `mask` examples. Observe the differences between the ways in which content appears behind them.

HOUR 10

Using Filters

Filters are one of the major differentiators between SVG and other Web graphic technologies. Filters allow developers to add effects that were once relegated to the domain of raster images (such as GIFs, JPEGs, and TIFFs). Effects like drop shadows, Gaussian blurs, and noise could only be attempted in vector graphics by attempting to manually create the effects themselves (such as placing a semi-transparent rectangle behind an object to fake a drop shadow), whereas raster programs allowed quick application of effects to objects.

SVG, however, allows you to apply filter effects to your artwork without physically affecting the original artwork. This means that a symbol can be used *without* effects in one section and *with* effects in another.

This hour will focus on the wide world of filter effects and will specifically address the following:

- What filter effects are
- How to apply filter effects
- Using the following effects:
  - Blur
  - Offset
  - Merge
  - Texture
- How to combine filter effects
- Creating new filter effects

Filter effects are likely the most amazing visual alterations possible using SVG, and their possibilities are numerous. Accordingly, there are more effects and combinations to discuss than would be possible within a 24-hour learning period. Thus, this chapter focuses on several common effects, as well as the premise behind filter effects in general, to provide you with enough information should you decide to learn the other effects.

Understanding Filters

Filter effects are created by using one or a number of "filter primitives." Filter primitives are generally simple filter executions, such as blurring or blending objects. When combined, they are able to create incredibly complex filter effects. Even better, they can be mixed and matched to create unique filter effects (more on this later in this hour).

The possible filter primitives are detailed in Table 10.1.

TABLE 10.1 Filter Primitives

Filter Name	Filter Function
FeBlend	Content can visually merge with content below.
FeFlood	Content is filled with color.
FeColorMatrix	Similar to Photoshop's Hue/Saturation/Balance tool, content's colors and alpha channels are modified according to matrix mathematics.
feComponentTransfer	Similar to Photoshop's Contrast/Brightness tool, content's colors and alpha channels are modified according to matrix mathematics.

continues

TABLE 10.1 Continued

Filter Name	Filter Function
feComposite	Content is visually blended with other content.
feConvolveMatrix	Content's edges are modified according to matrix mathematics, creating bevels, embossing, blurring, and so forth.
feDiffuseLighting	Content is lit according to alpha channel values.
feDisplacementMap	Content is moved according to mathematics based on RGB color values.
feGaussianBlur	Content appears to be blurred and fuzzy.
feImage	Content calls upon external image files.
feMerge	Content can be duplicated in any number of instances, allowing different effects (from other primitives) to be applied to each instance.
feMorphology	Content is modified by adding or subtracting weight from the edges of the content (thus fattening or slimming the shape of the content).
feOffset	Content has its position shifted.
feSpecularLighting	Content appears to have a light source above.
feSpotLight	Light source with a defined source point.
fePointLight	Light source with a defined source point and defined target point.
feDistantLight	Light source determined by angles.
feTile	Content is filled with tiled objects, similar to the pattern fill.
feTurbulence	Content is filled with randomized patterns of dots and/or colors, similar to Photoshop noise filters.

10

In this book, you will only learn the usage of five of these primitives (feMerge, feGaussianBlur, feTurbulence, feComposite and feOffset), as their usage leads to a general understanding of the other primitives.

Before diving into how to use the various primitives, however, you'll need to understand their limitations. Filter effects in SVG are similar to sprinkles on donuts. When applied in small doses, they compliment the original nicely; when applied profusely, they overwhelm the original.

In the case of SVG, applying too many filters may bog down your viewer (and subsequently your computer's CPU) when trying to draw these effects onscreen. The larger the object with an applied filter, the more system resources required to render it. Performance can be so hindered at times by filter effects that a user's browser may crash or movement onscreen will appear jerky.

That said, filters shouldn't necessarily be avoided. They should, however, be used intelligently. As you experiment with filter usage, be certain to repeatedly ask yourself the following questions:

- Have I tested this file on an older, slower machine to measure performance? (Your audience will likely not have the same configuration and machine as you. If you do not have an older machine to test your work on, try and visit a library or university computer lab to measure the performance of your graphic.)

- If animated, does my graphic play back with comparable quality to Flash and other motion graphics technologies?

If you find yourself unable to resolve these issues, be prepared to assess the necessity of keeping the filter effect. In many cases, having a graphic that displays and performs well (and according to the expectations of users based on their familiarity with other technologies) is preferable to a graphic that looks awesome until it flounders around the screen. Rarely are users more interested in technical achievement than accessibility.

So, with your cold shower of reality now taken, let's look into how to make these filter effects work.

Using Filters

At the most basic level, filters are created by inserting various filter primitives inside a `filter` element. For example, most filters will start like this example:

```
<filter id="FilterID">
<!-- Filter primitives go here -->
</filter>
```

The filter primitives that reside within this element are structured similarly and in some cases house other filter primitives. Filters can be applied to objects using the style declaration `filter:url(#FilterID)`, where `FilterID` is the value of the filter's `id` attribute.

Filter primitives, despite their different functions, have a common vocabulary in many of their attributes. The `x`, `y`, `width`, and `height` attributes are means of specifically specifying an area wherein the filter effect should be applied. For instance, if you were applying a blur to a circle but only wanted to blur half the circle, you would specify the `width` and `height` to equal only half the circle's size.

Using the `feGaussianBlur` filter primitive as an example, you could add these attributes to define the coordinate space wherein the blur could be applied, as in the following:

```
<filter id="Blur">
   <feGaussianBlur x="0" y="0" width="500" height="300"/>
</filter>
```

Two other common attributes for filter primitives are `in` and `result`. `result` names the output of any filter primitive, allowing a subsequent primitive to use the output from the original primitive to build upon, rather than the original image. (Think of `result` as the `id` attribute for filter primitives.)

> Filters render in the same manner as SVG files, top to bottom. Thus, if you do not name your primitive's result, providing specific access to a particular effect, each primitive will build upon the previous primitive's output.

10

The `in` attribute is a bit more complicated. This attribute tells a filter primitive from which source to draw the information for which to generate the effect. As a default, each primitive assumes it should be applied to its designated graphic; the corresponding attribute value is known as `SourceGraphic`. Similar to `SourceGraphic` is `SourceAlpha`, which tells the primitive to draw only from the alpha channel of the designated artwork.

On the other hand, the `in` attribute can draw from `BackgroundImage` and `BackgroundAlpha`. `BackgroundImage` allows information to be drawn from all elements visible below the `SourceGraphic`. `BackgroundAlpha` relies on the alpha channel for the same information. Remember that the `in` attribute allows primitives to draw upon this imagery to determine how its effects will be rendered, but does not actually affect the background imagery.

For anyone unfamiliar with alpha channels in graphics, this concept may be a bit difficult to grasp. Figure 10.1 shows the difference between `SourceGraphic`, `SourceAlpha`, `BackgroundImage`, and `BackgroundAlpha` through the use of a graphic example. In this figure, the star in the original graphic (on the left) has been selected to have a filter effect applied to its artwork.

FIGURE 10.1

Filter primitives can be directed to work with different parts of a chosen artwork based upon the value of the in *attribute.*

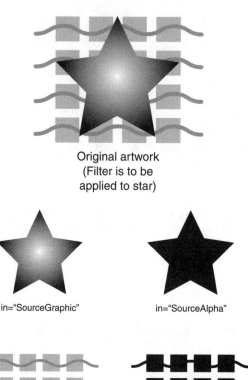

Original artwork
(Filter is to be
applied to star)

in="SourceGraphic"   in="SourceAlpha"

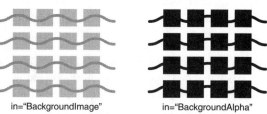

in="BackgroundImage"   in="BackgroundAlpha"

To show how the in and result attributes are applied to a filter primitive, consider the feGaussianBlur filter primitive example used earlier. You could add the in and result attributes to determine what aspect of the artwork is being used to generate the effect and the name of the resulting artwork:

```
<filter id="Blur">
   <feGaussianBlur x="0" y="0" width="500" height="300" in="SourceAlpha"
         result="BigBlur"/>
</filter>
```

In some cases, such as when creating an emboss effect, you will need your filter to access the both the artwork selected and the artwork outside of the applied object to blend the effect. (Remember: filter effects only modify an object(s) with a fill style declaration referencing such effects.) To allow the effect to interact with the object's background, apply the style property enable-background with the value new to the group containing both the modified artwork and the background imagery. In many cases, it makes most sense to apply this style rule to a group surrounding your entire document's content.

In the code snippet following, by surrounding the background imagery and the affected imagery with the enable-background-styled group, the emboss filter will successfully render by extruding the circle from the pattern-filled rectangle.

```
<defs>
        <filter id="emboss">
            ...
        </filter>
        <pattern id="patternfill">
            ...
        </pattern>
</defs>
<g id="Artwork" style="enable-background:new">
    <rect id="BackgroundArt" style="fill:url(#patternfill);"/>
    <circle id="FilterArt" style="filter:url(#emboss);"/>
</g>
```

Blurring Images with `feGaussianBlur`

Blurring an object has a variety of uses. Perhaps you are trying to distort a group of objects so that a remaining object draws more attention. Perhaps you are trying to create a drop shadow. Or maybe you just don't want harsh, graphic shapes and lines in a certain instance. In any case, the blur effect is designed to make objects look "cloudy."

The feGaussianBlur primitive uses one primary attribute—stdDeviation. (As loaded as this attribute name is, it's only short for "standard deviation.") This attribute's value determines the degree of the blur; the higher the number, the more the object is blurred. Thus, your code for a feGaussianBlur will generally appear as follows, where x represents a value defining the extent of the blur:

```
<filter id="Blur">
   <feGaussianBlur in="SourceGraphic" stdDeviation="x"/>
</filter>
```

To illustrate the blurring effect, start with Listing 8.1: a simplified version of the sun and clouds from our weather graphic. To create your first filter, you'll apply a blur to these clouds. First copy the code of Listing 8.1 and paste into a new document (Listing 10.1).

Next, you will need to create the blur filter within the defs element. In line 17, a filter has been created with the name "Blur." In line 18, the feGaussianBlur primitive has been inserted; it has been directed to blur the object to which it has been applied (in="sourceGraphic") a level of three times (stdDeviation="3"). Remember, the value you choose for the stdDeviation attribute determines the amount of blur; a value of 3 provides a mild blur, whereas a value of 20 makes the original shape hard to discern.

Line 9 contains the style rule used to apply the Blur filter to an object, and lines 31 and 32 have the filter applied to the cloud symbols. Figure 10.2 shows the result—clouds that appear fluffy behind the yellow sun.

LISTING 10.1   Creating a Blur

```
01: <?xml version="1.0" standalone="no"?>
02: <!DOCTYPE svg PUBLIC "-//W3C//DTD SVG 1.0//EN"
03:    "http://www.w3.org/TR/2001/REC-SVG-20010904/DTD/svg10.dtd">
04:
05: <svg width="500" height="300">
06:
07:        <style type="text/css">
08:               <![CDATA[
09:                        .FilterBlur{filter:url(#Blur);}
10:                        .FillFFFFFF{fill:#FFFFFF;}
11:                        .Fill99CCFF{fill:#99CCFF;}
12:                        .FillFFFF00{fill:#FFFF00;}
13:               ]]>
14:        </style>
15:
16:        <defs>
17:               <filter id="Blur">
18:                        <feGaussianBlur in="SourceGraphic" stdDeviation="3"/>
19:               </filter>
20:               <g id="Cloud">
21:                        <circle cx="24" cy="36" r="15"/>
22:                        <circle cx="41" cy="26" r="17"/>
23:                        <circle cx="90" cy="40" r="13"/>
24:                        <circle cx="105" cy="31" r="13"/>
25:                        <ellipse cx="75" cy="20" rx="27" ry="20"/>
26:                        <ellipse cx="56" cy="50" rx="25" ry="18"/>
27:               </g>
28:        </defs>
29:
30:        <rect id="Sky" x="10" y="45" width="200" height="245"
                  class="Fill99CCFF"/>
31:        <use id="SunCloud1" xlink:href="#Cloud" x="-20" y="80"
                  class="FillFFFFFF FilterBlur"/>
32:        <use id="SunCloud2" xlink:href="#Cloud" x="150" y="150"
                  class="FillFFFFFF FilterBlur"/>
33:        <circle id="Sun" cx="105" cy="160" r="56" class="FillFFFF00"/>
34:
35: </svg>
```

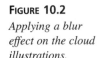

Figure 10.2

Applying a blur effect on the cloud illustrations.

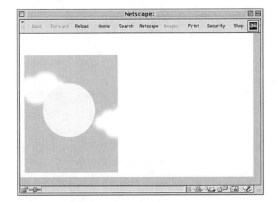

As Figure 10.2 shows, the blur you applied to the clouds is consistent in its distortion around all edges of the clouds. You may, however, wish to create a blur that distorts more according to one axis than the other, creating the impression of a motion blur.

Motion blurs can be created by adding a second value to the `stdDeviation`'s attribute value list. If only one value is given, the value is applied to both the x and y axes of the object. However, when two numbers (separated by spaces or commas) are inserted (one greater than the other), the visual suggestion of motion is created, as one axis will have a stronger blur than the other.

To see the result of a motion blur, modify Listing 10.1 by changing the `stdDeviation` value to `10 1` (note line 18 in Listing 10.2). This will result in making your clouds appear to be moving in a horizontal direction, as the largest value (`10`) describes the x axis distortion. Figure 10.3 shows the product of such a change; the clouds appear to be moving across the sky.

LISTING 10.2   Creating a Motion Blur

```
01: <?xml version="1.0" standalone="no"?>
02: <!DOCTYPE svg PUBLIC "-//W3C//DTD SVG 1.0//EN"
03:    "http://www.w3.org/TR/2001/REC-SVG-20010904/DTD/svg10.dtd">
04:
05: <svg width="500" height="300">
06:
07:        <style type="text/css">
08:                <![CDATA[
09:                        .FilterBlur{filter:url(#Blur);}
10:                        .FillFFFFFF{fill:#FFFFFF;}
11:                        .Fill99CCFF{fill:#99CCFF;}
12:                        .FillFFFF00{fill:#FFFF00;}
13:                ]]>
```

continues

LISTING **10.2**   Continued

```
14:        </style>
15:
16:        <defs>
17:                <filter id="Blur">
18:                        <feGaussianBlur in="SourceGraphic" stdDeviation="10 1"/>
19:                </filter>
20:                <g id="Cloud">
21:                        <circle cx="24" cy="36" r="15"/>
22:                        <circle cx="41" cy="26" r="17"/>
23:                        <circle cx="90" cy="40" r="13"/>
24:                        <circle cx="105" cy="31" r="13"/>
25:                        <ellipse cx="75" cy="20" rx="27" ry="20"/>
26:                        <ellipse cx="56" cy="50" rx="25" ry="18"/>
27:                </g>
28:        </defs>
29:
30:        <rect id="Sky" x="10" y="45" width="200" height="245"
                class="Fill99CCFF"/>
31:        <use id="SunCloud1" xlink:href="#Cloud" x="-20" y="80"
                class="FillFFFFFF FilterBlur"/>
32:        <use id="SunCloud2" xlink:href="#Cloud" x="150" y="150"
                class="FillFFFFFF FilterBlur"/>
33:        <circle id="Sun" cx="105" cy="160" r="56" class="FillFFFF00"/>
34:
35: </svg>
```

FIGURE **10.3**

*Creating a motion blur
effect on the cloud
illustrations.*

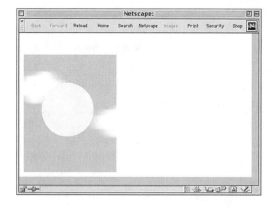

Moving Objects with `feOffset`

One of the most popular effects in a designer's palette today is the drop shadow. A drop shadow is often the result of several different operations combined together. The following steps describe how to create a drop shadow:

1. The object to be shadowed must be cloned based upon its alpha channel, creating a duplicate of the object behind itself.

2. A blur is applied to this duplicate object.

3. The blurred duplicate is moved a small distance from the original object to create the illusion of depth.

If you have used Photoshop or other design tools that automatically create drop shadow effects, you are likely familiar with the offset concept. Offsetting is the term used to move an object, as in step 3 of the drop shadow operation process.

A shadow is only as effective as it is visible. Thus, by distancing the shadow (which in some cases is the same size and shape as the original) from the original artwork, the shadow becomes an effective means of defining a three-dimensional space in a two-dimensional environment. The further the shadow is offset, the further the apparent distance between object and shadow.

One of SVG's filter primitives, `feOffset`, can be used to perform the function needed in the drop shadow's third operation. The primitive does nothing more than alter the positioning coordinates of its applied artwork. Thus, used on its own, `feOffset` will not create a drop shadow any more than applying `feGaussianBlur` would; used in conjunction, however, these primitives can accomplish impressive results.

`feOffset` uses two attributes, `dx` and `dy`, to specify the distance on the x and y axes from the original location. The values for these two attributes are numerical units of measurement. Thus, a filter such as

```
<filter id="Shift2inches">
  <feOffset in="SourceGraphic" dx="2in" dy="2in"/>
</filter>
```

would be used to move an object 2 inches to the right and 2 inches down.

To demonstrate `feOffset`, you can move the sun object down 35 pixels on each axis, as shown in Listing 10.3. In line 17, a filter has been created with the name `"Offset"`. In line 18, the `feOffset` primitive has been inserted; it has been directed to move the object to which it has been applied 35 units to the right (`dx="35"`) and 35 units down (`dy="35"`). Line 9 creates a style rule that can be used to apply the filter to an object, and line 33 has the filter applied to the sun circle.

LISTING 10.3   Using the `Offset` Filter

```
01: <?xml version="1.0" standalone="no"?>
02: <!DOCTYPE svg PUBLIC "-//W3C//DTD SVG 1.0//EN"
03:   "http://www.w3.org/TR/2001/REC-SVG-20010904/DTD/svg10.dtd">
04:
05: <svg width="500" height="300">
06:
07:      <style type="text/css">
08:            <![CDATA[
09:                    .FilterOffset{filter:url(#Offset);}
10:                    .FillFFFFFF{fill:#FFFFFF;}
11:                    .Fill99CCFF{fill:#99CCFF;}
12:                    .FillFFFF00{fill:#FFFF00;}
13:            ]]>
14:      </style>
15:
16:      <defs>
17:            <filter id="Offset">
18:                    <feOffset dx="35" dy="35"/>
19:            </filter>
20:            <g id="Cloud">
21:                    <circle cx="24" cy="36" r="15"/>
22:                    <circle cx="41" cy="26" r="17"/>
23:                    <circle cx="90" cy="40" r="13"/>
24:                    <circle cx="105" cy="31" r="13"/>
25:                    <ellipse cx="75" cy="20" rx="27" ry="20"/>
26:                    <ellipse cx="56" cy="50" rx="25" ry="18"/>
27:            </g>
28:      </defs>
29:
30:      <rect id="Sky" x="10" y="45" width="200" height="245" class="Fill99CCFF"/>
31:      <use id="SunCloud1" xlink:href="#Cloud" x="-20" y="80" class="FillFFFFFF"/>
32:      <use id="SunCloud2" xlink:href="#Cloud" x="150" y="150" class="FillFFFFFF"/>
33:      <circle id="SunnySun" cx="105" cy="160" r="56" class="FillFFFF00 FilterOffset"/>
34:
35: </svg>
```

FIGURE 10.4

Using an offset effect to move the sun illustration.

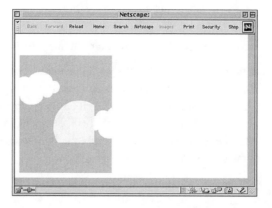

Though the circle representing the sun was moved over and down, it also now appears cropped on its right and bottom. To reveal the offset element completely, you will need to add the `filterUnits` attribute to the `filter` element. The `filterUnits` attribute determines the viewport system for the object to which the filter element is being applied and can affect the result of all filter primitives, not just `feOffset`.

This attribute has two possible values: `userSpaceOnUse` and `objectBoundingBox`. `objectBoundingBox` is the default value and gives the viewport a boundary of the object's original edges. This boundary is defined as a rectangle drawn to the furthest edge of each side of the object (see Box A in Figure 10.4).

`userSpaceOnUse` is the alternate value, defining the viewport's boundary as the coordinate system the object existed in before the filter was applied. Thus, in most cases, the boundary is defined as the document's original viewport dimensions (not to be confused with the object's viewport). As with the `objectBoundingBox` value, the boundary is defined as a rectangle drawn to the furthest edge of each side of the space (see Box B in Figure 10.5).

10

FIGURE 10.5

Comparing the different viewport areas of the two `filterUnits` *values.*

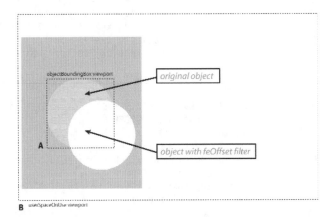

To change your code in Listing 10.3 to accommodate for a completely revealed sun after its offset, you will thus need to add the `filterUnits` attribute. This attribute, with the appropriate value of `userSpaceOnUse`, is added to the filter element in line 17 of Listing 10.4. As shown in Figure 10.5's Box B, this will move the viewport to reveal the offset circle entirely. The modified code will result in a display similar to Figure 10.6: a complete circle, uncropped, offset by 35 pixels to the right and bottom.

LISTING 10.4 Modifying the `Offset` Filter to Correctly Show the Sun

```
01: <?xml version="1.0" standalone="no"?>
02: <!DOCTYPE svg PUBLIC "-//W3C//DTD SVG 1.0//EN"
03:    "http://www.w3.org/TR/2001/REC-SVG-20010904/DTD/svg10.dtd">
04:
```

continues

LISTING 10.4   Continued

```
05: <svg width="500" height="300">
06:
07:         <style type="text/css">
08:                 <![CDATA[
09:                         .FilterOffset{filter:url(#Offset);}
10:                         .FillFFFFFF{fill:#FFFFFF;}
11:                         .Fill99CCFF{fill:#99CCFF;}
12:                         .FillFFFF00{fill:#FFFF00;}
13:                 ]]>
14:         </style>
15:
16:         <defs>
17:                 <filter id="Offset" filterUnits="userSpaceOnUse">
18:                         <feOffset dx="35" dy="35"/>
19:                 </filter>
20:                 <g id="Cloud">
21:                         <circle cx="24" cy="36" r="15"/>
22:                         <circle cx="41" cy="26" r="17"/>
23:                         <circle cx="90" cy="40" r="13"/>
24:                         <circle cx="105" cy="31" r="13"/>
25:                         <ellipse cx="75" cy="20" rx="27" ry="20"/>
26:                         <ellipse cx="56" cy="50" rx="25" ry="18"/>
27:                 </g>
28:         </defs>
29:
30:         <rect id="Sky" x="10" y="45" width="200" height="245"
                class="Fill99CCFF"/>
31:         <use id="SunCloud1" xlink:href="#Cloud" x="-20" y="80"
                class="FillFFFFFF"/>
32:         <use id="SunCloud2" xlink:href="#Cloud" x="150" y="150"
                class="FillFFFFFF"/>
33:         <circle id="SunnySun" cx="105" cy="160" r="56" class="FillFFFF00
                FilterOffset"/>
34:
35: </svg>
```

FIGURE 10.6

Using the
userSpaceOnUse *value*
for the filterUnits
attribute, the entire
circle appears cor-
rectly after its offset
filter is applied.

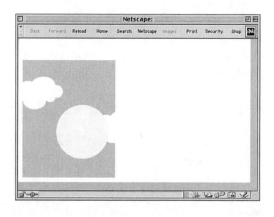

As the steps showed earlier in this section, a drop shadow requires several independent operations to take place. Although the `feOffset` primitive performs a very basic function, its value takes shape when used in combination with other primitives. The next section will teach you how to do just that.

Merging Filter Primitives with `feMerge`

Now that you're able to blur and move an object, you're almost able to create a drop shadow filter. All that is left is to find a method of combining these primitives into one filter and performing the first step in the drop shadow operation (mentioned at the beginning of the last section). As said repeatedly in this book, any way to reduce the amount of code needed should be taken. In the case of the drop shadow filter, you'll need to have a shadow of the same shape as the main object offset blurred behind the main object.

Though you can certainly apply these effects on another instance of the desired object, you will end up with unnecessarily duplicated code. Instead, use `feMerge`. `feMerge` allows an object to be loaded several times with different effects, all within one filter element. If you wanted to apply a drop shadow to the sun in the news center graphic, you could use `feMerge` to load a copy of the sun (with the blur and offset primitives applied) underneath another copy of the sun (with no primitives applied).

`feMerge` does not apply any special effect to content; rather, it arranges instances for display (that can subsequently have effects applied from other primitives). Using a series of sub-primitives named `feMergeNode`, you can determine the order and subject of `feMerge`'s arrangement. Each `feMergeNode` element needs only the `in` property. `in` can take advantage of the results of another primitive's execution (defined by a primitive's `result` attribute) or any of the standard input values.

For instance, a common `feMerge` element (with appropriate `feMergeNode` elements) will appear as follows:

```
<feMerge>
   <feMergeNode in="filterID1"/>
   <feMergeNode in="filterID2"/>
</feMerge>
```

In this example, the two `in` values would be replaced with the `result` values of two other filter primitives.

Visual hierarchy is based on SVG's display order, so the first `feMergeNode` element will render in back, whereas the last element will render up front. To see `feMerge` in action, you can consolidate all your `offset` and `blur` primitives within one `filter` element and apply them using the `feMerge` primitive on a copy of the news center graphic's sun. As you will be combining several lessons within one example, you will be taking more steps than with previous examples.

First, copy the code from Listing 10.4 and paste it into a new file (shown following as Listing 10.5). As the filter you will be creating will be more than just an offset, rename the id value to DropShadow (line 17) and modify the style rule (line 9) so that it references the newly named filter.

Next, on the line before the feOffset primitive, create an feGaussianBlur element within the DropShadow filter element with a stdDeviation value of 10 to provide a very fuzzy edge to the blur (line 18). As you do not want your drop shadow to be yellow (and thus indistinguishable from the sun itself), define its in value as SourceAlpha. The alpha channel of any artwork is black in areas of 100% opacity, and thus the SourceAlpha value will represent a black circle with the same shape as the original yellow circle. Finish this element by providing a result value (shadow) for the element so that the next primitive can utilize the operation's product.

With the feGaussianBlur element complete, you can now modify the feOffset element (line 19). Rather than offsetting the original artwork with the SourceImage in value from Listing 10.4, populate this value with shadow, the result of the feGaussianBlur primitive. (Remember, the in attribute accepts not only the four keywords demonstrated in Figure 10.1 but also values from previous primitives' result values.) You can also name the feOffset element's result value shadow, as result values are interpreted sequentially. Because the feOffset primitive's result value follows (and depends upon) the feGaussianBlur primitive's result value, it will only overwrite the shadow value after processing the result of the combination.

With a shadow value in memory now that defines a black-filled, blurred, and offset version of the sun's shape, you are ready to merge this artwork with the original sun artwork. To complete the document, add an feMerge element (line 20) below the feOffset element.

Within this element, insert two feMergeNode elements to reference the drop shadow artwork as well as the original artwork. As the drop shadow should appear behind the sun, its artwork needs to be the first feMergeNode reference (line 21). To reference this artwork, you will need to specify the in value as shadow (which will reference the last instance of the value). For the second and final feMergeNode element to reference the original artwork, its in value should be specified as SourceImage (line 22).

As you changed the style references at the beginning of this example, your drop shadow document should now be complete. Figure 10.7 shows the resulting image—a sun with a drop shadow against the sky.

LISTING 10.5   Creating a Drop Shadow Effect

```
01: <?xml version="1.0" standalone="no"?>
02: <!DOCTYPE svg PUBLIC "-//W3C//DTD SVG 1.0//EN"
03:   "http://www.w3.org/TR/2001/REC-SVG-20010904/DTD/svg10.dtd">
04:
05: <svg width="500" height="300">
06:
07:      <style type="text/css">
08:            <![CDATA[
09:                  .FilterDropShadow{filter:url(#DropShadow);}
10:                  .FillFFFFFF{fill:#FFFFFF;}
11:                  .Fill99CCFF{fill:#99CCFF;}
12:                  .FillFFFF00{fill:#FFFF00;}
13:            ]]>
14:      </style>
15:
16:      <defs>
17:            <filter id="DropShadow" filterUnits="userSpaceOnUse">
18:                  <feGaussianBlur in="SourceAlpha" stdDeviation="10"
                           result="shadow"/>
19:                  <feOffset dx="10" dy="10" in="shadow"
                           result="shadow"/>
20:                  <feMerge>
21:                        <feMergeNode in="shadow"/>
22:                        <feMergeNode in="SourceGraphic"/>
23:                  </feMerge>
24:            </filter>
25:            <g id="Cloud">
26:                  <circle cx="24" cy="36" r="15"/>
27:                  <circle cx="41" cy="26" r="17"/>
28:                  <circle cx="90" cy="40" r="13"/>
29:                  <circle cx="105" cy="31" r="13"/>
30:                  <ellipse cx="75" cy="20" rx="27" ry="20"/>
31:                  <ellipse cx="56" cy="50" rx="25" ry="18"/>
32:            </g>
33:      </defs>
34:
35:      <rect id="Sky" x="10" y="45" width="200" height="245"
                  class="Fill99CCFF"/>
36:      <use id="SunCloud1" xlink:href="#Cloud" x="-20" y="80"
                  class="FillFFFFFF"/>
37:      <use id="SunCloud2" xlink:href="#Cloud" x="150" y="150"
                  class="FillFFFFFF"/>
38:      <circle id="Sun" cx="105" cy="160" r="56" class="FillFFFF00
                  FilterDropShadow"/>
39:
40: </svg>
```

10

FIGURE 10.7

Using the feMerge *primitive, you can combine several primitives together, creating a more complex filter effect, such as this drop shadow.*

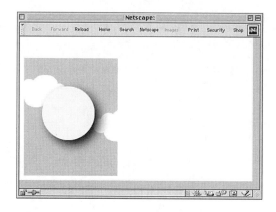

By naming the result of each filter effect shadow, you can add effects one by one to the same value. You can, however, name the result of each effect differently. In such cases, the appropriate in value would need to be modified to match the previous effect's result.

Creating Textures with feTurbulence

Creating noise, marble, or cloud effects across an image requires using the feTurbulence primitive. feTurbulence creates a texture-like pattern on an object using a variety of custom properties.

Somewhat oddly, feTurbulence has two different functions (specified by the type attribute): turbulence and noise. The turbulence value creates soft, bubble-like patterns that appear as prismatic clouds, whereas fractalNoise creates a randomized dot texture, similar to gravel or snow being tossed across the image.

feTurbulence has three major attributes to determine the result of the effect: type, numOctaves, and baseFrequency. type allows you to choose between the noise and turbulence options, using the respective values fractalNoise and turbulence. baseFrequency accepts a numerical value to designate the amount of noise or turbulence to apply, whereas numOctaves uses a number to determine the amount of variance from the baseFrequency value (the greater the number, the greater the variance).

An example of the feTurbulence element's syntax would appear as follows:

```
<filter id="NoiseMaker">
        <feTurbulence type="fractalNoise" baseFrequency="17" numOctaves="3"/>
</filter>
```

The easiest way to see how the feTurbulence element (with its several attributes) really works is to repeatedly alter its attributes' values, increasing one value while decreasing the other. As a starting point, you can apply a noise filter to one cloud and turbulence to another cloud in the news center illustration. (Again, to really learn this primitive, you'll want to alter the values to see the possibilities these two options allow.)

First, copy the code of Listing 10.1 and paste it into a new document (Listing 10.6). Add a `filterUnits` attribute to the `filter` element, and supply the attribute with an `ObjectBoundingBox` value. (Don't worry if this doesn't make sense at the moment. The reason for this break from the previously used `userSpaceOnUse` value will be described after this example.)

Replace the `feGaussianBlur` element with a `feTurbulence` element (line 19), and designate the `type` attribute to `fractalNoise`. Add the `baseFrequency` and `numOctaves` attributes, and provide each with test values.

As you will be creating two separate effects, duplicate this first `filter` element by copying the original and pasting the second below the original. Alter the copy of the filter (lines 23 through 26) so that this filter uses `turbulence` instead of `fractalNoise` as the `type` attribute value (line 25). You can supply a new set of test values for the `baseFrequency` and `numOctaves` attributes.

Lastly, change the names of each filter via their `id` values to correspond to their function (lines 18 and 23). Duplicate the style rule that applied the blur filter and then make the according changes to the style rules so that they reference the correct filter (lines 9 and 10). Likewise, rename the class selectors to be in accordance with the function of their rules, and apply them to the cloud artwork (lines 40 and 42).

With those changes, you have created your first `feTurbulence` filters. Figure 10.8 shows the resulting textures within the confines of the clouds' bounding boxes.

LISTING 10.6 Applying Turbulence Effects to the Clouds

```
01: <?xml version="1.0" standalone="no"?>
02: <!DOCTYPE svg PUBLIC "-//W3C//DTD SVG 1.0//EN"
03:    "http://www.w3.org/TR/2001/REC-SVG-20010904/DTD/svg10.dtd">
04:
05: <svg width="500" height="300">
06:
07:      <style type="text/css">
08:              <![CDATA[
09:                      .FilterNoise{filter:url(#Noise);}
10:                      .FilterTurbulence{filter:url(#Turbulence);}
11:                      .FillFFFFFF{fill:#FFFFFF;}
12:                      .Fill99CCFF{fill:#99CCFF;}
13:                      .FillFFFF00{fill:#FFFF00;}
14:              ]]>
15:      </style>
```

continues

LISTING 10.6   Continued

```
16:
17:        <defs>
18:            <filter id="Noise" filterUnits="objectBoundingBox">
19:                <feTurbulence result="NoiseArtwork"
20:                    type="fractalNoise" baseFrequency="0.8"
                        numOctaves="14"/>
21:            </filter>
22:
23:            <filter id="Turbulence" filterUnits="objectBoundingBox">
24:                <feTurbulence result="TurbulenceArtwork"
25:                    type="turbulence" baseFrequency="0.1"
                        numOctaves="4"/>
26:            </filter>
27:
28:            <g id="Cloud">
29:                <circle cx="24" cy="36" r="15"/>
30:                <circle cx="41" cy="26" r="17"/>
31:                <circle cx="90" cy="40" r="13"/>
32:                <circle cx="105" cy="31" r="13"/>
33:                <ellipse cx="75" cy="20" rx="27" ry="20"/>
34:                <ellipse cx="56" cy="50" rx="25" ry="18"/>
35:            </g>
36:        </defs>
37:
38:        <rect id="Sky" x="10" y="45" width="200" height="245"
                class="Fill99CCFF"/>
39:        <use id="SunCloud1" xlink:href="#Cloud" x="-20" y="80"
40:                class="FilterNoise"/>
41:        <use id="SunCloud2" xlink:href="#Cloud" x="150" y="150"
42:                class="FilterTurbulence"/>
43:        <circle id="Sun" class="FillFFFF00" cx="105" cy="160" r="56"/>
44:
45: </svg>
```

FIGURE 10.8

Applying turbulence effects to the cloud illustrations.

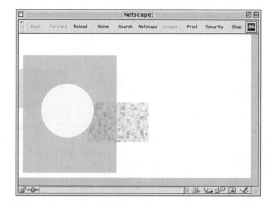

You'll note in this example that the clouds were, somewhat surprisingly, changed from puffy ovals into big rectangular boxes. This is due to the way the feTurbulence primitive draws its effects; unlike most other primitives, feTurbulence does not use the in attribute. Thus, its resulting effects do not confine themselves to the shape of the artwork to which they are applied.

Instead, feTurbulence draws its effects across the entire screen by default (the userSpaceOnUse value for the filterUnits attribute), basically ignoring the data of the object it is being applied to (other than for its filterUnits value). By changing the filterUnits value, you confined the feTurbulence filters' results within their applied artworks' bounding boxes, allowing you to see the results of each effect while still seeing the remaining artwork.

feTurbulence can be tamed, however, to fit within a certain shape (not just rectangles); in the next example, you'll do just that by learning how to use the feComposite primitive to merge your artwork with your filter.

10

Taming feTurbulence Effects' Display with feComposite

In the case of some primitives, effects may apply themselves across the bounding box of the entire object (such as you saw with feTurbulence). In most cases, this will not be a desirable effect; you will want your effects to take the shape of the objects they are applied to. Thus, you'll need to use a primitive such as feComposite to merge certain filter effects with the shape of the original object.

At a common level of usage, feComposite's syntax is simple, as shown in the following:

```
<feComposite in="id1" in2="id2" operator="value"/>.
```

As feComposite involves the compositing of two sets of content, it needs the capabilities for two inputs, hence the addition of the in2 attribute. How these two sets of content are composited is determined by the operator attribute.

The feComposite primitive uses the operator attribute to determine its function, allowing the following values: over, in, out, atop, xor, and arithmetic. The over, in, out, atop, and xor values' functions are in accordance with popular image compositing functions, but their functions are listed in Table 10.2 nonetheless.

TABLE 10.2   operator Values

Operator Value	Operator Function
over	over, the default value, simply places the object from the in attribute over the object from the in2 attribute.
in	The in value fills the shape of the object from the in2 attribute with the content of the in attribute.
out	The out value punches the shape of the object from the in2 attribute out of the content from the in attribute.
atop	The atop value fills the shape of the content from the in2 attribute with the addition of the contents from both in and in2 attributes.
xor	The xor value places the contents of the in attribute over the contents of the in2 attribute, merging the two sets of content together at their intersections.
arithmetic	The arithmetic value uses a formula to determine how to composite the content from both attributes together.

Reviewing this table, the logical choice for getting filter effects to conform to the shape of the artwork to which they are applied would be the in value. In the task at hand (combining the feTurbulence effects with the cloud illustrations), you will need to designate the alpha channel of the artwork (SourceAlpha) as the in attribute's value to define the shape to which the resulting effect should confine itself, and the turbulence effect (named via the result value in the feTurbulence primitive) as the in2 attribute's value to define the content to be confined.

As a result, your syntax for the feComposite element, which should be placed within the same filter element as the primitive it is working with, would look similar to the following:

```
<feComposite in="SourceAlpha" in2="TurbulenceArtwork" operator="in"/>
```

The order of which item is represented in in and in2 is important. Your results will change depending on input ordering, as the in attribute is drawn before the in2 attribute.

To see this example in action, copy the code from Listing 10.6 and paste into a new document (Listing 10.7). Keep the result attribute for each feTurbulence element (lines 19 and 24). This allows the future feComposite element to reference the results of the feTurbulence operations.

Within each filter element, insert an feComposite element after the feTurbulence element (lines 21 and 26). For both, designate the operator attribute value to in and the in2 attribute value to SourceAlpha. This will allow the shape of the clouds' alpha channels to be filled with the content referenced next in the in attribute values.

Complete the document by supplying the feComposite elements' in attributes with the result values from the respective feTurbulence elements. The result, clouds each filled with different types of textures, is shown in Figure 10.9.

LISTING 10.7 Using the feComposite Primitive to Have the Turbulence Effects Conform to the Shape of the Clouds

```
01: <?xml version="1.0" standalone="no"?>
02: <!DOCTYPE svg PUBLIC "-//W3C//DTD SVG 1.0//EN"
03:   "http://www.w3.org/TR/2001/REC-SVG-20010904/DTD/svg10.dtd">
04:
05: <svg width="500" height="300">
06:
07:     <style type="text/css">
08:         <![CDATA[
09:                 .FilterNoise{filter:url(#Noise);}
10:                 .FilterTurbulence{filter:url(#Turbulence);}
11:                 .FillFFFFFF{fill:#FFFFFF;}
12:                 .Fill99CCFF{fill:#99CCFF;}
13:                 .FillFFFF00{fill:#FFFF00;}
14:         ]]>
15:     </style>
16:
17:     <defs>
18:         <filter id="Noise" filterUnits="objectBoundingBox">
19:             <feTurbulence result="NoiseArtwork"
20:                 type="fractalNoise" baseFrequency="0.8"
                        numOctaves="14"/>
21:             <feComposite in="NoiseArtwork" in2="SourceAlpha"
                    operator="in"/>
22:         </filter>
23:         <filter id="Turbulence" filterUnits="objectBoundingBox">
24:             <feTurbulence result="TurbulenceArtwork"
25:                 type="turbulence" baseFrequency="0.1"
                        numOctaves="4"/>
26:             <feComposite in="TurbulenceArtwork" in2="SourceAlpha"
27:                 operator="in"/>
28:         </filter>
29:         <g id="Cloud">
30:             <circle cx="24" cy="36" r="15"/>
31:             <circle cx="41" cy="26" r="17"/>
32:             <circle cx="90" cy="40" r="13"/>
33:             <circle cx="105" cy="31" r="13"/>
34:             <ellipse cx="75" cy="20" rx="27" ry="20"/>
35:             <ellipse cx="56" cy="50" rx="25" ry="18"/>
36:         </g>
37:     </defs>
38:
39:     <rect id="Sky" x="10" y="45" width="200" height="245"
            class="Fill99CCFF"/>
```

continues

10

LISTING 10.7   Continued

```
40:        <use id="SunCloud1" xlink:href="#Cloud" x="-20" y="80"
41:            class="FilterNoise"/>
42:        <use id="SunCloud2" xlink:href="#Cloud" x="150" y="150"
43:            class="FilterTurbulence"/>
44:        <circle id="Sun" class="FillFFFF00" cx="105" cy="160" r="56"/>
45:
46: </svg>
```

FIGURE 10.9

Compositing the turbu-lence effects with the shapes of the cloud illustrations.

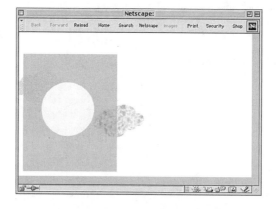

By simply adding the feComposite primitive in lines 21 and 26, you are able to reign in the oddball display of the feTurbulence primitives.

Creating New Filters

Making your own filter is as easy as experimenting with a combination of primitives. Nonetheless, filter primitives are often based on complex mathematics, and may seem prohibitive to beginners. Don't get overwhelmed; rather, play around with the values and possibilities with each primitive (and combinations thereof). The worst that could happen is that your display isn't as you'd hoped!

Important tips to remember, though, while assembling custom filters are:

1. Make sure your in values correspond to the correct result values.

2. Are you using the correct filterUnits value? Switch between userSpaceOnUse and objectBoundingBox to see which viewport is most appropriate for your effect.

3. In some cases, your primitive's in value should reference the alpha channel instead of the actual object. Be sure to switch between SourceAlpha and SourceGraphic, as well as BackgroundAlpha and BackgroundGraphic.

With a little investigation on your part, you'll find some amazing Photoshop-like effects available for your vector images. For further filter examples (such as blends and embossing), check the appendix and this book's Web site.

Summary

Filter effects, created by using a single filter primitive (or group thereof), have the ability to add a visual dimension to flat, vector artwork. Even better, they free the designer as the effects are applied to their respective content by the SVG viewer; if you wish to modify the shape of an object with a drop shadow effect applied, the drop shadow will adjust itself to match the new shape. Also, with over two dozen filter primitives, there are hundreds of possible combinations, resulting in hundreds of possible effects. Thus, many of the effects you've grown accustomed to in raster-based programs are possible to achieve in SVG.

10

Q&A

Q Creating filter effects seems difficult and tricky. Is there a method similar to PhotoShop's filter application where I can press a button and a drop shadow appears on my artwork?

A Filters can seem a little intimidating upon introduction, but their results far outweigh the steeper learning curve. Nonetheless, some SVG WYSIWYG editors, such as JASC WebDraw and Adobe Illustrator 10, offer the ability to select from pre-defined filter effects to apply to your artwork. You should still familiarize yourself with how each primitive works, as you may need to fine-tune the results of these programs' code.

Q SVG filter effects look awesome, but I don't have a clue how to achieve the results of filters such as an emboss or a multiply. Is there a resource to show different filter combinations and possibilities?

A While no definitive resource exists for such matters, you can visit this book's companion Web site, www.svgnow.com, for a series of examples showing different filter combinations. Your best bet may be to look at examples at a site such as this to get an idea of ways to recreate effects you've seen in PhotoShop and elsewhere.

Workshop

The Workshop is designed to help you anticipate possible questions, review what you've learned, and begin learning how to put your knowledge into practice.

Quiz

1. The outcome of any filter primitive can be named by defining the value of which attribute?

2. What filter primitive is used to combine turbulence effects with artwork?

3. True or False: Filter effects modify both the applied object and the background imagery by default.

4. To reference the alpha channel of an object, what value is used for a filter primitive's `in` attribute?

5. True or False: The `filterUnits` attribute should have a value of `userSpaceOnUse` to have your viewport match the shape of your content *after* an effect has been applied.

Answers

1. The `result` attribute is used to name the output of a filter primitive, allowing other primitives to perform their functions based on this output (as opposed to existing unmodified artwork).

2. The `feComposite` filter primitive allows you to combine another filter primitive's results with existing artwork in a number of ways. By using `feComposite`, the `feTurbulence` primitive can be visually melded with the artwork to which it is being applied.

3. False. By default, filter effects modify only the artwork to which they are applied, not the "background" artwork (any artwork lying below the applied artwork). To allow the effects of the filter to spill over onto the background artwork, you must use the `enable-background` attribute.

4. To reference the alpha channel of an object, a filter primitive's `in` attribute must use the `SourceAlpha` value.

5. True. By using `userSpaceOnUse`, the entire coordinate system is open to work with, whereas using `objectBoundingBox` prevents any effects from running outside of the object's original bounding coordinates.

Exercises

1. Change the operator function in the `feComposite` example to see the different results possible.

2. Adjust the `stdDeviation` settings of the blur primitive. Make an extreme motion blur by changing the values to "`0 100`".

3. Play with the settings for the turbulence effects. By changing the disparity in values between `numOctaves` and `baseFrequency`, you can get an incredible range of possible effects.

Hour 11

Images

As you've read, SVG efficiently handles vector artwork display and transmission. Luckily, many graphics you create can be displayed in a vector format. Any flat, graphic imagery, in fact, is best suited for SVG's vector format.

There will, however, be many situations wherein you will need to include photographic imagery within your artwork. Consider, for instance, a news network site, such as CNN.com. Although a large portion of their imagery is bold, colorful vector artwork, they also house several photographic images. Not being able to include photos on such a site would be somewhat preposterous.

Thankfully, SVG has a method of referencing and loading other image formats to accommodate designers' needs to include raster imagery. The `image` element, rather appropriately named, allows developers to reference external image files.

In this hour, you will learn the following:

- The difference between raster and vector imagery
- How to reference external images using the image element
- Supported image formats

Once you've learned to incorporate external images into your SVG document, you will have finished learning the basics of creating static SVG content. The next group of chapters will introduce animation and interaction, but before you move on to such exciting matters, you should learn about the interesting possibilities external image inclusion offers.

Using the `image` Element

Using images in SVG is similar to using images in HTML. By using an element to reference an image, you can load an external file into your document for display. A familiarity with HTML will actually be helpful, as you will recognize some of the attributes and logic needed to reference and place an external image.

The syntax of the `image` element is similar to that of the `use` element. The `image` element uses the `xlink:href` attribute to reference an outside image file, the x and y attributes to determine the top left placement of the image, and the `width` and `height` attributes to determine the dimensions of the image. Thus, your image tag at its most basic level will appear as

```
<image xlink:href="imageURL' x="x1' y="y1" width="widthUnits"
height="heightUnits"/>.
```

The `width` and `height` attributes are important, as they have an impact on the quality of the image display. By and large, the graphics you will be referencing with the `image` element will be raster-based images. As explained before, raster images are fixed images; their appearance is constrained to a particular size and resolution, and each pixel has its own color definition.

Because of the fixed nature of raster images, any distortions to their size or shape can produce unpleasant results. As the image was not created for alternate sizes or shapes, the image distorts according to its new attributes. The most common, and annoying, distortion most Web users will encounter is images stretched larger than they were intended, resulting in blurry or pixilated views of the original image. This result reflects poorly on the discerning eye of the designer/developer. (Images scaled smaller than their original size sometimes appear OK, though, especially when scaled proportionally, meaning that the height scales in proportion to the width of the image.)

Thus, setting the `height` and `width` values of the `image` element to match the values of the original image becomes important for the SVG developer. Unless you are intentionally trying to distort the image's appearance, you will need to gather the appropriate values for the image's dimensions.

The easiest method of finding these values (in pixels) for bitmap images is to open the desired image in your Internet browser. In most cases, the dimensions of the image will appear in the browser's title bar (or in the Properties panel, available upon right/control-clicking the image). You can also open the image(s) in a graphic editing program, such as Adobe PhotoShop or GraphicConverter. (For a list of freeware tools available for both Mac and PC users, visit this book's companion website, www.svgnow.com, and check out the "Tools" section.)

Once you have gathered the dimensional values of the image, you can insert these values into the height and width attributes of the image element. Unlike HTML, however, you do not have the choice of ignoring the width and height values; if you do not provide values for these attributes, the referenced image will not display.

This book's news center graphic includes a reference to an external graphic—an advertisement for this book linking to Amazon.com. To learn how to use this element, you can create a small example referencing this file.

FIGURE 11.1

The image to be placed in this book's final news center graphic is an advertisement for this book.

First, copy the code from Listing 10.7 and paste it into a new document (Listing 11.1). Delete all style sheet and content information from the body of this new document. Next, you will need to create an image element (line 6). As the image to be displayed is on a remote server, your xlink:href value will need to reference an outside URL— http://www.svgnow.com/images/svgnow/tysvg24hrs-ad.gif.

The image size is a common Internet advertisement format—88 pixels wide by 60 pixels tall. For the sake of this example, you can place the image in the center of the document. To calculate the appropriate x and y values, simply subtract 44 pixels from 250 (half of the document's 500-unit width minus half of the image's width) and 30 pixels from 150 (half of the document's 300-unit height minus half of the image's width). The resulting coordinates (206,120), plus the image's dimensions, can be plugged into the appropriate x, y, width, and height values.

LISTING 11.1 Images Can Be Placed in Your SVG Document by Using the `image` Element

```
01: <?xml version="1.0" standalone="no"?>
02: <!DOCTYPE svg PUBLIC "-//W3C//DTD SVG 1.0//EN"
            "http://www.w3.org/TR/2001/REC-SVG-20010904/DTD/svg10.dtd">
03:
04: <svg  width="500" height="300">
05:
06:         <image id="AdImage" x="206" y="120" width="88" height="60"
                    xlink:href="http://www.svgnow.com/images/svgnow/tysvg24hrs-
                    ad.gif"/>
07:
08: </svg>
```

Line 6 declares the `image` element with the proper x and y coordinates, as well as the `xlink:href` to the image. The result of this code is shown in Figure 11.2.

FIGURE 11.2

Images can be placed in your SVG document by using the image *element.*

Adding images is truly as simple as referencing them via the `image` element. However, not every image can be added to an SVG document.

Allowed Filetypes

According to the W3C recommendation, SVG-compliant viewers need provide support only for the display of PNG, JPEG, and SVG image formats. PNG and JPEG formats are common file formats for raster imagery, but several other image formats exist (some more prevalent than others).

For example, the GIF (Graphic Interchange Format) format is certainly the most prevalent image type on the Internet. Originally developed by CompuServe to significantly reduce graphic file sizes, the GIF format has come under scrutiny in the last several years. Its creator has considered suing corporations and developers that do not pay a royalty for the use of the technology. Since such royalties were never collected before, the Web development community reacted in outrage, and the outcome of this matter has yet to be decided.

As such, the W3C has mandated only that JPEG and PNG (the remaining major image format players) be supported. The creator of an SVG viewer may support formats such as GIF and TIFF, however. Adobe has provided support for GIF in its Adobe SVG Viewer plug-in. As such, Listing 11.1's example can be shown. Please keep in mind, though, that other viewer vendors may choose to support GIF and similar technologies at their discretion.

SVG in SVG

SVG's image element can also reference external SVG files. This support is added to allow SVG files to incorporate other SVG files just as they would another graphic. In the same manner that an SVG document can render with a JPEG file inside, so too can it render an SVG document inside an SVG document.

There is no change in syntax for the `image` element to support SVG inclusion. Rather, the `xlink:href` value should point to an SVG document instead of a JPEG or PNG file. The `x`, `y`, `width`, and `height` attributes still accept the same values and operate in the same manner.

So what is the value of placing an SVG file within an SVG file? This question has many possible answers. By allowing developers to link and render outside SVG files, multiple developers can be working simultaneously. Later, their individual works can be collectively displayed through one larger master SVG document.

Common graphical images may be kept in external SVG files and referenced by the image element. This is somewhat similar in concept to using symbols, except that instead of keeping your reused content within a `defs` element in your SVG document, you would keep this group of artwork in an external file.

Also, you may not have permission to copy and edit someone else's SVG document. In such cases, you may be able to secure rights to display their document untouched within your SVG document.

Whatever the motivation, the SVG recommendation accommodates the need of developers to include other SVG documents. Keep in mind, however, not every SVG viewer supports this ability yet. Though the recommendation mandates conformance to this matter, most SVG viewers are still under some form of development. The Adobe SVG Viewer, for instance, is still unable to render external animated SVG files using the `image` element as of the 3.0 release. It can, however, place an external static SVG document.

11

Will this change in the future? Absolutely. In the short term, however, you will need to code your documents according to this limitation.

Summary

Support for the display of raster imagery is still required, as nearly all photographic images are encoded in such a manner. SVG supports the inclusion of raster images, as well as its own vector imagery, through the use of the image element. Using familiar syntax, the image element allows SVG viewers to render imagery within SVG documents.

Image formats such as JPEG and PNG are supported, whereas other formats, such as GIF, may be supported on a case-by-case basis, depending on each SVG viewer vendor's decision. External SVG files can also be placed using the image element, allowing different SVG files to be collected together within one document.

With the completion of this hour, you've finished Part II, and you're now ready to move into Part III: Bringing SVG to Life. Hour 12, "Time," will introduce you to the concepts behind the handling of time in SVG. Subsequent chapters will then familiarize you with animation, interaction, and more.

Q&A

Q Why not simply paste the code of the linked SVG file within the master SVG document?

A You may encounter situations where the linked SVG documents are using a different DTD, competing class names, and so forth. In such cases, linking to the outside documents allows them to display according to their directions inside the new environment. Linking thus can save a significant amount of work on the part of the developer.

Q I've placed an unsupported image type in my SVG document and it still renders correctly. How is this possible?

A SVG viewers can support additional image formats. To remain SVG compliant, they must provide a basic level of JPEG, PNG, and SVG support. However, they are free to add support for other images.

Workshop

The Workshop is designed to help you anticipate possible questions, review what you've learned, and begin learning how to put your knowledge into practice.

Quiz

1. What attribute does the image element require to determine the location of an external image file?

2. True or false: Every conformant SVG viewer must be able to display JPEG images.

3. Which common image format found on the Web does not have mandated support?

Answers

1. The image element uses the xlink:href attribute to designate an external file for placement.

2. True. Every conformant viewer must be able to render external JPEG, PNG, and SVG documents.

3. The W3C recommendation does not require the GIF format to be supported. However, many viewers will provide support for this format of their own accord.

Exercise

The image element accepts certain style properties, such as display and opacity. Try applying the opacity property value of 0.5 to the image element in Listing 11.1. Create a set element that returns the opacity of the image to 100% (via a value of 1) when a user's cursor passes over the image (using the mouseover event suffix).

11

PART III

Bringing SVG to Life

Hour

HOUR 12

Time

For this hour, you will step back from the practical application of code to review a concept that will be fundamental in making your SVG content interactive.

With any technology that defines motion and interaction, you will need to have a system of measuring and addressing time to handle animation. In terms of SVG, animation is considered an action that occurs beyond an object's initial static display (such as an adjustment in size, visibility, color, position, and so forth). For an animation to occur (that is, for a ball to bounce or a drop-down menu to unfold), a viewer must know when to initiate the action. In some instances, you will want an animation to occur at a fixed time. For example, 5 seconds after your SVG loads, a ball should begin bouncing. In another instance, you may want that same ball to bounce once a button is pressed.

In this hour, you will learn a number of concepts critical to the animation and interaction functions discussed in the next several hours. These concepts include the following:

- How SVG interprets time
- How to notate time

- How to define multiple points in time
- How to use events instead of specific time values

To illustrate these concepts, some examples in this hour may include animation and interaction elements you have not yet learned. These instances are for illustration purposes only, and you will learn all about interaction, animation, and more in the next several hours.

Understanding How Time Unfolds in SVG

SVG handles timing and events largely using SMIL 2.0's timing and synchronization syntax. For those unfamiliar, SMIL (Synchronized Multimedia Integration Language) is another W3C effort to define interactive and animated content in XML. SMIL allows developers the ability to integrate audio, video, animation, and more using an XML grammar.

The most common use of SMIL that you've likely encountered is in the RealPlayer application. Generally, any interactive content you experience in the RealPlayer (outside of plain video feeds) is authored using SMIL. In this instance, SMIL is used to synchronize audio and video with time or other events, such as a user pressing a button.

Thankfully, the W3C puts a lot of effort into the portability of their languages; understanding the syntax of one W3C language invariably assists in understanding the syntax of another. SMIL 2.0 was created with the express intent of allowing other XML technologies to use its syntax to define such multimedia presentations.

Rather than using a more abstract, frame-based system (such as broadcast or Flash), SVG operates using true time measurements. Hours, minutes, seconds, and milliseconds are all acceptable forms of time measurement. To designate a numeric value with one of these time measurements, you will need to add the correct SVG notation to the value. Table 12.1 shows how SVG notates time values.

TABLE 12.1 Time Values

Time Value	SVG Notation
Hours	h
Minutes	min
Seconds	s
Milliseconds	ms

So, for instance, if you were to create a bouncing ball animation and have it animate for 5 minutes, your time value would be 5min.

If you leave your time value as strictly a number, such as 5, your value will be interpreted as seconds because seconds is the default unit of time measurement.

In some cases you will need to define time that extends beyond a single notation's measurement, such as 5 hours, 5 minutes, 5 seconds, and 5 milliseconds. If you wanted your ball to bounce for such a precise measurement, you could break down the value into a smaller unit of measurement to encompass the larger units. Thus, you could use one of the following notations: 18305.005s, 18305.005, or 18305005ms. You likely will not wish to spend your time doing the math to determine such large values, though.

Thankfully, time can also be notated in "full clock value" notation. By using colons to separate three two-digit values, you can designate more precise time measurements. Using full clock value, you can notate this time as 05:05:05.005. Note that milliseconds do not get their own colon-separated value, but rather rely on a decimal-point addition to the "seconds" value.

Time is used to define multiple points in an animation: the start, stop (or duration), and any points in between. Time is applied to animation elements (which you will learn about in the next several hours) via specific attributes. The first three time-based attributes are listed in Table 12.2; multiple points in time are defined using the keyTimes attribute (defined in the next section).

TABLE 12.2   Time-Based Attributes

Attribute Name	Attribute Description
begin	At what point the event begins
end	At what point the event ends
dur	The duration of the event

Important note: If you do not designate a begin value, the animation will occur upon the loading of the document.

The end and dur attributes are alternate attributes that determine when an animation ceases its action. Whereas the end attribute specifies an exact time (generally in relation to the loading of the document), the dur attribute defines a time in relation to the begin attribute value. Obviously, these two attributes don't work well together, as they could each give an event a different point in time to cease action.

In each animation you create, you will need to determine whether you will use the `end` or `dur` attribute, depending on your preference or need in the situation. In cases where the length of your animation is critical, using the `dur` attribute will allow you to quickly adjust the animation's start point (`begin`) while not affecting the length of the playback. In other cases, you may have a definitive point upon which the animation should end; in such instances, fixing the `end` value will allow you to adjust the length of the animation without letting the animation's playback extend past a specific time.

The syntax for your time events will then take the form of `timeAttribute="x"`, where `timeAttribute` is `begin`, `end`, or `dur`, and `x` is a time value, such as `5s`. It is important to note that your time attributes do not need to use the same time notation for their values. For instance, one animation event could properly render `begin="1s"` and `dur="00:03:00"`.

An example of applying such attributes, using the `dur` attribute to define the length, is as follows:

```
<animate begin="3s" dur="5.5s"/>
```

To create the same animation using the `end` attribute, your code would appear like the following:

```
<animate begin="3s" end="8.5s"/>
```

In each case the animation starts 3 seconds after the SVG document has loaded and completes 8.5 seconds after the same load. (The `animate` element will be discussed again later in Hour 15, "Animation.")

Using `keyTimes`

To understand the need for the `keyTimes` attribute, picture a circle fading slowly from black to 50% transparent. If the circle fades at a consistent pace, you will need only one animation, defining the beginning and ending points of both time and the object's transparency.

Now, if you wanted the circle to fade from black to 50% transparent in 2 seconds but then slowly fade to 100% transparent over 6 more seconds, you may consider creating two separate animations: one handling the fade of the circle from black to 50% transparent, the second from 50% black to 100% transparent.

Using `keyTimes`, however, the same task can be accomplished in one fell swoop. The `keyTimes` attribute accepts multiple values, separated by semicolons, allowing different animation values to synchronize with specific time points over the animation's duration.

The number of values in the keyTimes attribute list should mirror the number of values in the same element's values attribute list (to be discussed in Hour 15), as a value's position in the keyTimes list relates to the same position in the values list. The numbers, however, must range from 0 to 1, where 0 corresponds to the initial time value of the animation (the start) and 1 corresponds to the final value (the end). Because keyTimes does not accept specific time values, it still relies on begin and end attributes to define the span of time to which its values relate.

Thus, the resulting code would appear similar to the following code. Remember, both the animate element and the attributeName attribute, alongside the keyTimes and values attributes, will be defined later in Hour 15, "Animation."

```
<animate attributeName="opacity" begin="3s" dur="5.5s" keyTimes="0; 0.25; 1"
         values="1; 0.5; 1"/>
```

The values in the keyTimes list parallel the values in the values list; thus, at the keyTimes' value of 0 (or the beginning of the stretch of time), the opacity of the circle is defined as 1 (the first value in the values list). As you remember from Hour 7, opacity, like keyTimes, is defined on a scale of 0 to 1, 1 equaling 100% opaque. The second value in the keyTimes list is 0.25, which translates to 1.375 seconds (25% of 5.5 seconds). This value parallels the values value of 0.5; thus, the circle is 50% opaque 1.375 seconds into the animation.

To better illustrate the use for keyTimes, examine the rolling ball animation in Figure 12.1. At the beginning of the animation (at 0 seconds), the ball is in a stationary position. As time moves forward, the ball begins to slowly move up the hill. To make the animation more realistic, the animator assumes that gravity would prevent the ball from rolling up the hill at the same speed it would roll down. Hence, the ball takes 8.5 seconds to move to the top of the hill, and only 2.5 seconds to roll down.

FIGURE 12.1

An animation of a ball rolling, dependent on keyTimes to control the speed of its rolling.

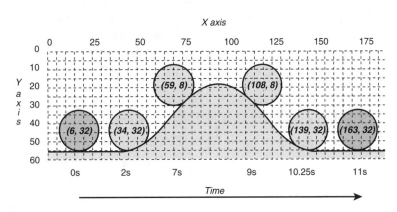

Rather than creating five separate animations to accommodate the different speeds between each position in the rotating ball's path, you can use keyTimes with an animation element (Hour 14) to match your balls' coordinates with their appropriate time value. For instance, by listing the ball's coordinates in a values list, such as values="17,43; 45,43; 70,20; 120,20; 145,43; 175,43" (positions taken from Figure 12.1), and then listing the times corresponding to each point in a keyTimes list, your animation element can synchronize the coordinates with the time value. Doing the math to convert the time values (also listed in Figure 12.1) to proportional values between 0 and 1, your result would look like this: keyTimes="0; 0.18; 0.63; 0.81; 0.93; 1".

The resulting code would look similar to Listing 12.1.

LISTING 12.1 Using keyTimes to Control Multiple Animations

```
01: <?xml version="1.0" standalone="no"?>
02: <!DOCTYPE svg PUBLIC "-//W3C//DTD SVG 1.0//EN"
03:    "http://www.w3.org/TR/2001/REC-SVG-20010904/DTD/svg10.dtd">
04:
05: <svg width="500" height="300">
06:
07: <circle id="ball" cx="17" cy="43" r="25"/>
08: <animateTransform xlink:href="#ball" attributeName="transform" type="translate"
09:        begin="0s"
10:        dur="11s"
11:        keyTimes="0; 0.18; 0.63; 0.81; 0.93; 1"
12:        values="17,43; 45,43; 70,20; 120,20; 145,43; 175,43"/>
13:
14: </svg>
```

Without knowledge of the animation elements and their according attributes, this may be a bit difficult to comprehend at first. The important items to focus on here are how the begin and end/dur attributes work, as well as how the keyTimes and values attributes relate to each other. Don't worry; further animation examples and lessons using keyTimes will be covered in Hour 15. There are still event dependencies to review before diving into actual examples.

Using Time Dependencies

You've just seen how the begin and end attributes were based on time, but in many instances, you will want these attributes triggered by another event. An event can be a number of things, including a user's mouse movements, an animation ending, or a user pressing a key.

For instance, rather than having your ball animation (from Figure 12.1) roll down the hill after 8.5 seconds, you may want it to wait until another animation has finished playing. Using event suffixes (declarations added to an `id` value after a period), you can trigger animations to occur based on other events. By replacing the time-based values of the `begin`, `end`, or `dur` attributes, another event can trigger an animation to occur.

Thus, rather than using a time value to determine when the event begins, you can now use other events to trigger your animations or other interactions. Table 12.3 details only a portion of the available event suffixes. (If you're familiar with JavaScript, you'll notice many of these are common to JavaScript's event suffixes.)

TABLE 12.3 Event Suffixes

Event Suffix	Suffix Description Action Will Be Triggered by...
begin	...the start of the designated event.
end	...the end of the designated event.
click	...the user making a mouse click on the designated object.
mouseover	...the user placing the mouse pointer over the designated object.
mouseout	...the user moving the mouse pointer away from the designated object.
mouseup	...the user releasing the mouse button while over the designated object.
mousedown	...the user pressing the mouse button while over the designated object.

Events can be referenced using their `id` attribute values. For instance, if you wanted your bouncing ball animation to begin after pressing a "Start" button (an object labeled with `id` attribute "StartButton"), you would set the `begin` attribute value of the animation to `StartButton.click`. By referencing events via their `id` attribute, you have access to a number of possible triggering combinations.

The following code illustrates this concept (please keep in mind that you would need to populate the elements with their defining attributes in place of the ellipsis):

```
<circle id="Ball" ... />
<rect id="StartButton" ... />
<animate id="BounceBall" begin="StartButton.click" ... />
```

By setting the `begin` value of the `animate` element to an event (by adding the event suffix to an object's `id` value), the animation will not occur until the user interacts with the SVG document. The same thing could be done to the end value; instead of providing a fixed end for the animation, the animation could continue along until another event triggered its cessation.

12

Allowing developers to use events to determine an animation's beginning and end points keeps SVG in parity with other interactive formats (such as Flash and Shockwave). Using events instead of time can have many useful purposes, as well. In some cases, you may want to encourage a user to participate with your content, and thus an event-based animation rewards the user for engaging your content. On the other hand, if you have a wild and busy animation playing, you may want to provide a user with the ability to disable the animation playback to allow for easier reading of the content.

Summary

To extend SVG beyond the static display of still graphics, a unified system of measuring time and action becomes necessary. Time in SVG, just as in day-to-day life, unfolds in a linear fashion, and is measured in a similar manner (seconds, minutes, hours, and so forth). Events may occur at either a designated time or in relation to another event. By setting an event to occur in relation to another, user-based interaction becomes possible (that is, rollovers and linking), making SVG operate comparably to Flash and other interactive technologies. Using time-based events, on the other hand, makes SVG content similar in nature to animated GIFs or video.

Now that you understand the general concept of how time and events unfold, it's on to actual application of this concept. The next hour will introduce you to simple interaction, such as the final "Start" button example in this chapter.

Q&A

Q Why doesn't SVG use a frame-based animation system?

A SVG's animation system is largely based on SMIL (Synchronized Multimedia Integration Language), another W3C recommendation used to define animation in XML syntax. By using SMIL as a foundation, SVG can handle a variety of possible animation techniques, including (but not limited to) frame-based animation.

Q Instead of `begin` and `end` attributes, why not use a `keyTimes` attribute for every animation and interaction element?

A `keyTimes` provides a great means for defining multiple actions within one element. However, the `set` animation element cannot use this attribute. Also, the syntax for the `keyTimes` and `values` attributes results in code that requires some deciphering on the part of a developer. By splitting the attribute value (a point in time) from the attribute name (`begin` or `dur`), the developer has to think harder to understand the code. If the code can just as easily be written with `begin` and `end` attributes, you should seriously consider helping both yourself (and future developers who may have to read your code) by opting for the easier route.

Workshop

The Workshop is designed to help you anticipate possible questions, review what you've learned, and begin learning how to put your knowledge into practice.

Quiz

1. How is time measured in SVG?

2. When not specified with notation, what is the default unit of time measurement?

3. What unit is used to separate an event suffix from an event name?

4. What attribute's values must parallel the number of values in the `keyTimes` attribute?

Answers

1. Time is measured in real time units in SVG, whether in milliseconds, seconds, minutes, or hours.

2. The default unit of time measurement is seconds. A time value with no notation is then considered to refer to seconds. Thus, a value of `5` is identical to `5s`.

3. A period separates an event name from an event suffix (for example, `Button.click`).

4. The `keyTimes` attribute requires the `values` attribute to have the same number of attribute values to match a modification to a specific time value.

Exercises

1. Dissect some of your favorite online animations and applications. Begin thinking in terms of how different actions are dependent on very specific events occurring beforehand.

2. Make a quick "cheat-sheet" diagramming all the possible event suffixes. A full list is available in Chapter 16.2 of the W3C SVG recommendation (available at `http://www.w3.org/TR/SVG/`).

12

Hour 13

Interaction

It almost goes without saying: interactive elements often make for more engaging content than static, unmoving elements. SVG not only provides the language to define vector content display, but also the language to define how that content interacts with itself and other outside elements.

In SVG, animation and interaction controls are created using an appropriate element (such as set, animate, animateTransform, animateMotion, and animateColor). Though in some cases you can define an object's interactivity by locating an interactive element within an object's element, SVG does not require the object and the interactive control to be located next to each other in the code. This affords two very helpful benefits:

- Reduced chance for errors—By separating the object and the interaction, you run into less likelihood of mistakenly editing the wrong property. For instance, if your interaction element had a similar attribute name as one of your object element's attributes, you may mistakenly edit the interaction element's attribute when meaning to edit the object element's attribute.

- Easier identification of code—With interaction elements separated from their applied objects by space within the SVG code, you can group all interaction elements together. This makes it easier to find and edit interaction elements (without mistakenly editing the original objects), as you won't need to pick through large, unrelated sections of code.

In this hour, you'll learn

- how to make pop-up devices and links to other sites
- how to change an item's display (disappearance) and its color
- ways to apply your timing and event trigger knowledge
- fundamental concepts of animation

Hyperlinks

Hyperlinks in SVG are quite similar to HTML's hyperlinking system. Hyperlinks let users click on an item and move to another page or location in a manner that generally relates to the name (or image) of the clicked item.

Just as in HTML, hyperlinks are created using the a element. Also, the a element surrounds the content that will serve as the clickable object(s). However, instead of using the HTML href attribute, SVG uses the xlink:href attribute. (You briefly encountered this attribute in Hour 11, "Images," where it was used to reference an image location.) This attribute is actually a carryover from the Xlink technology. XLink can be thought of as the XML hyperlink destination technology. (For more information on XLink, you can visit www.w3.org/tr/xlink.) Using XLink's xlink:href attribute, the syntax for a hyperlink in SVG is

```
<a xlink:href="destinationLink">…</a>
```

By closing the a element, only the content contained within this element becomes "hot," or linkable.

To try SVG's linking system, you can begin by creating hyperlinks to actual sites or stories on the Internet for this book's news center graphic (Listing 13.1). In Listing 13.1's code, there are a series of references (lines 29, 32, 35, and 38) to the newspaper icon symbol (lines 18 through 25) To illustrate the use of hotlinking, these icons are linked to an external site. (As the purpose of this example is to show the function of the link, the destination URL can be changed at your desire.) Containing each icon within an a element will hotlink them and create a graphic that moves into the world of interaction (lines 28, 31, 34, and 37). The results of this listing are shown in Figure 13.1.

LISTING 13.1 Using the a Element to Hyperlink Newspaper Icons

```
01: <?xml version="1.0" standalone="no"?>
02: <!DOCTYPE svg PUBLIC "-//W3C//DTD SVG 1.0//EN"
03:    "http://www.w3.org/TR/2001/REC-SVG-20010904/DTD/svg10.dtd">
04:
05: <svg  width="500" height="300">
06:
07:        <style type="text/css">
08:                <![CDATA[
09:                        .FillFFFFFF{fill:#FFFFFF;}
10:                        .Fill000000{fill:#000000;}
11:                        .Stroke000000{stroke:#000000;}
12:                        .StrokeWidth1{stroke-width:1;}
13:                        .StrokeWidth1Point5{stroke-width:1.5;}
14:                ]]>
15:        </style>
16:
17:        <defs>
18:                <g id="IconPaper" class="FillFFFFFF Stroke000000 StrokeWidth1">
19:                        <rect id="PaperOutline" x="0" y="0" width="13"
                                        height="10"/>
20:                        <rect id="PaperPhoto" x="7.5" y="5" width="3" height="5"/>
21:                        <line id="PaperHeadline" x1="2" y1="2.5" x2="11" y2="2.5"
22:                                class="StrokeWidth1Point5"/>
23:                        <line id="PaperLine1" x1="2" y1="5" x2="5.5" y2="5"/>
24:                        <line id="PaperLine2" x1="2" y1="7" x2="5.5" y2="7"/>
25:                </g>
26:        </defs>
27:
28:        <a xlink:href="http://www.nytimes.com/">
29:                <use id="StoryLink1Icon" xlink:href="#IconPaper" x="225" y="168"/>
30:        </a>
31:        <a xlink:href="http://www.adbusters.com/">
32:                <use id="StoryLink2Icon" xlink:href="#IconPaper" x="225" y="198"/>
33:        </a>
34:        <a xlink:href="http://www.justgive.org/">
35:                <use id="StoryLink3Icon" xlink:href="#IconPaper" x="225" y="228"/>
36:        </a>
37:        <a xlink:href="http://www.apple.com/hotnews/">
38:                <use id="StoryLink4Icon" xlink:href="#IconPaper" x="225" y="257"/>
39:        </a>
40:
41: </svg>
```

13

FIGURE 13.1

*Though not visually
impressive, the
four icons compose
the book's first
interactive example.*

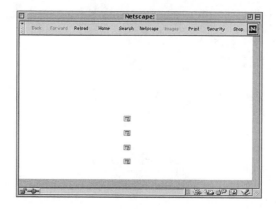

When you click on one of the newspapers, your browser will hop to the appropriate link. As the a element encloses the icons, you'll notice that your mouse pointer changes to the system-default hand. This convention lets users know that the item their mouse pointer is over is actually clickable.

Using the set Element

Now comes the fun part. One of the most basic animation and interaction elements is the set element. The set element doesn't so much animate items as it explicitly changes their attributes. As such, it provides a perfect example of basic interaction.

Taking advantage of what you learned with timing and event triggers in the last hour, you can use the set element to modify elements or groups in a number of ways. For example, you can make an item disappear, flip over, change color, change position, and more.

The set element uses several common attributes to operate. These are detailed in Table 13.1.

TABLE 13.1   set Element Attributes

set *Attribute*	*Attribute Function*
xlink:href	Similar to the use element, set usually relies on the xlink:href attribute to determine which object will be modified.
attributeName	The attributeName value defines which attribute of the designated object to modify.
to	The to value describes the desired state of the modified attribute.

continues

TABLE 13.1 Continued

set *Attribute*	*Attribute Function*
begin	The begin value determines when the set element's action takes place.
end	The end value hinges the duration of the set element on another event or action. (Optional; used in place of dur.)
dur	The dur value determines the duration of time of the set element. (Optional; used in place of end.)

Changing Colors

Changing an object's color is a simple example of the set element.

To illustrate the change, you can modify the color of the sun in the news center graphic. To do so, you will need to match the attributes of the set element reviewed above to the appropriate values described in Table 13.2.

TABLE 13.2 Modification Values for the News Center Graphic

set *Attribute*	*Attribute Value*
xlink:href	#RingOuter
attributeName	fill
to	red
begin	00:00:02
dur	3s

This produces the following code:

```
<set id="SunColorChange" xlink:href="#Sun" attributeName="fill"
     to="red" begin="00:00:02" dur="3s"/>
```

Note the use of the "pound" symbol (#) in the xlink:href value. As you saw in the use element, the "pound" symbol tells the SVG viewer to look *within* the SVG file for the labeled item. If you did not include the "pound" symbol, the set element can reside anywhere within the SVG content area. In the case of Listing 13.2, it has been placed at the end of the file (line 30). As mentioned in previous hours, it is wise to develop conventions for your coding. In the case of this book's examples, all interactive elements are placed at the end of the file for convenience's sake.

13

LISTING 13.2   Using the set Element to Change the Color of the Sun

```
01: <?xml version="1.0" standalone="no"?>
02: <!DOCTYPE svg PUBLIC "-//W3C//DTD SVG 1.0//EN"
03:   "http://www.w3.org/TR/2001/REC-SVG-20010904/DTD/svg10.dtd">
04:
05: <svg  width="500" height="300">
06:
07:       <style type="text/css">
08:             <![CDATA[
09:                    .FillFFFFFF{fill:#FFFFFF;}
10:                    .Fill99CCFF{fill:#99CCFF;}
11:                    .FillFFFF00{fill:#FFFF00;}
12:             ]]>
13:       </style>
14:
15:       <defs>
16:             <g id="Cloud">
17:                    <circle cx="24" cy="36" r="15"/>
18:                    <circle cx="41" cy="26" r="17"/>
19:                    <circle cx="90" cy="40" r="13"/>
20:                    <circle cx="105" cy="31" r="13"/>
21:                    <ellipse cx="75" cy="20" rx="27" ry="20"/>
22:                    <ellipse cx="56" cy="50" rx="25" ry="18"/>
23:             </g>
24:       </defs>
25:
26:       <rect id="Sky" x="10" y="45" width="200" height="245"
                 class="Fill99CCFF"/>
27:       <circle id="Sun" cx="105" cy="160" r="56" class="FillFFFF00"/>
28:       <use id="Cloud1" xlink:href="#Cloud" x="-20" y="80"
                 class="FillFFFFFF"/>
29:       <use id="Cloud2" xlink:href="#Cloud" x="150" y="150"
                 class="FillFFFFFF"/>
30:
31:       <set id="SunColorChange" xlink:href="#Sun"
32:             attributeName="fill"
33:             to="red"
34:             begin="00:00:02"
35:             dur="3s"/>
36:
37: </svg>
```

To illustrate the use of the set element, first copy the code from Listing 8.1 (the example with the sun and clouds over the blue sky) and paste it into a new document. Next, place the set element (line 30) after the graphical content on lines 26 through 29, and provide it with a name (SunColorChange) using the id attribute.

The set element's xlink:href attribute tells it to modify the object named Sun (the circle on line 27). As the attributeName value is fill, this set element will be adjusting the color of the fill of that object from its original value (a yellow defined via the FillFFFF00 class) to red (defined on line 33 via the to attribute).

The timing of this change is described using the begin and dur attributes (lines 34 and 35, respectively). According to these two attributes, the Sun object's fill will change from its original yellow to red two seconds after the document loads (line 34) and remain red for 3 seconds (line 35) before reverting back to its original yellow color. The result of this code is shown in Figure 13.2.

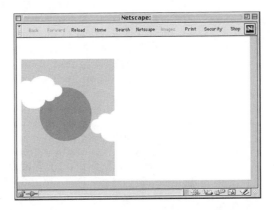

FIGURE 13.2

By using the set *element, the color of the sun is changed to red for three seconds.*

As discussed in the last hour, animation and interaction elements can be set to begin on an event, rather than a time value. To illustrate how the set element can play off other events, you can have the cloud on the left of your previous example change colors once the sun has finished changing red.

To do so, you'll first have to follow a series of steps:

- Duplicate the original set element
- Rename the duplicate element's id value to better reflect its function (such as Cloud1ColorChange)
- Change the duplicate element's begin value from a time value to an event value

As you learned in the previous hour, an event can be defined using an element's id value, coupled with an event suffix. In the case of this example, you will want this second set element to begin once the original element (SunColorChange) completes its action (described using the end event suffix). Thus, the begin value should be defined as SunColorChange.end. With these changes made, the cloud's color change will wait until the sun's color change is complete (see Listing 13.3).

13

LISTING 13.3   Using the set Element to Change the Color of the Cloud After the Sun Changes Color

```
01: <?xml version="1.0" standalone="no"?>
02: <!DOCTYPE svg PUBLIC "-//W3C//DTD SVG 1.0//EN"
03:   "http://www.w3.org/TR/2001/REC-SVG-20010904/DTD/svg10.dtd">
04:
05: <svg  width="500" height="300">
06:
07:        <style type="text/css">
08:                <![CDATA[
09:                        .FillFFFFFF{fill:#FFFFFF;}
10:                        .Fill99CCFF{fill:#99CCFF;}
11:                        .FillFFFF00{fill:#FFFF00;}
12:                ]]>
13:        </style>
14:
15:        <defs>
16:                <g id="Cloud">
17:                        <circle cx="24" cy="36" r="15"/>
18:                        <circle cx="41" cy="26" r="17"/>
19:                        <circle cx="90" cy="40" r="13"/>
20:                        <circle cx="105" cy="31" r="13"/>
21:                        <ellipse cx="75" cy="20" rx="27" ry="20"/>
22:                        <ellipse cx="56" cy="50" rx="25" ry="18"/>
23:                </g>
24:        </defs>
25:
26:        <rect id="Sky" x="10" y="45" width="200" height="245" class="Fill99CCFF"/>
27:        <circle id="Sun" cx="105" cy="160" r="56" class="FillFFFF00"/>
28:        <use id="Cloud1" xlink:href="#Cloud" x="-20" y="80" class="FillFFFFFF"/>
29:        <use id="Cloud2" xlink:href="#Cloud" x="150" y="150" class="FillFFFFFF"/>
30:
31:        <set id="SunColorChange" xlink:href="#Sun"
32:                attributeName="fill"
33:                to="red"
34:                begin="00:00:02"
35:                dur="3s"/>
36:
37:        <set id="Cloud1ColorChange" xlink:href="#Cloud1"
38:                attributeName="fill"
39:                to="#339933"
40:                begin="SunColorChange.end"
41:                dur="1.5s"/>
42:
43: <vg>
```

In Listing 13.3, you can see the effects of such a modification. Begin by copying the code from Listing 13.2 and pasting it into a new document. Next, copy the original `set` element (line 31) and paste it after the original (line 37). As described before, change the name (`id`) of this element to better reflect its purpose (`Cloud1ColorChange`) and point the element towards the `Cloud1` object (using the `xlink:href` attribute) instead of the `Sun` object.

Second, change the `to` value from `red` to `#339933` (line 39). This will determine the cloud's fill to be a green and illustrate the ability to use different color definitions within the `set` element. Finally, change the `begin` value to `SunColorChange.end` (to have this `set` element begin once the other element completes) and the `dur` value to any length of time (such as `1.5s`). The resulting image will appear similar to Figure 13.2; however, once the sun switches back to yellow, the cloud on the left will appear green for 1.5 seconds.

Not only can you have the `set` element begin or end according to an event or a specific time, you can merge both event- and time-based values to further specify the `begin` or `end` values. To combine these values, you must add a plus symbol, "+," between the two values. Thus, for a `begin` attribute value, your syntax would be *objectId.begin+Xs*.

To illustrate this blending of event-based and time-based actions, you can have the cloud on the right from the previous examples change colors one second after the sun *begins* changing colors. You'll use a statement similar to the event-based action to signify the start of the object: `SunColorChange.begin`.

However, to add the additional time value to the event, as suggested earlier, you'll add `+1s` to the end of the attribute value, thus resulting in `SunColorChange.begin+1s`. By duplicating the second `set` element (`Cloud1ColorChange`) in Listing 13.3 and modifying it to begin according to this new `begin` value, your code will appear similar to Listing 13.4.

LISTING 13.4   Using Both Time- and Event-Based Actions to Trigger the `set` Element

```
01: <?xml version="1.0" standalone="no"?>
02: <!DOCTYPE svg PUBLIC "-//W3C//DTD SVG 1.0//EN"
03:    "http://www.w3.org/TR/2001/REC-SVG-20010904/DTD/svg10.dtd">
04:
05: <svg  width="500" height="300">
06:
07:        <style type="text/css">
08:                <![CDATA[
09:                        .FillFFFFFF{fill:#FFFFFF;}
10:                        .Fill99CCFF{fill:#99CCFF;}
11:                        .FillFFFF00{fill:#FFFF00;}
12:                ]]>
```

13

continues

LISTING 13.4   Continued

```
13:        </style>
14:
15:        <defs>
16:              <g id="Cloud">
17:                    <circle cx="24" cy="36" r="15"/>
18:                    <circle cx="41" cy="26" r="17"/>
19:                    <circle cx="90" cy="40" r="13"/>
20:                    <circle cx="105" cy="31" r="13"/>
21:                    <ellipse cx="75" cy="20" rx="27" ry="20"/>
22:                    <ellipse cx="56" cy="50" rx="25" ry="18"/>
23:              </g>
24:        </defs>
25:
26:        <rect id="Sky" x="10" y="45" width="200" height="245" class="Fill99CCFF"/>
27:        <circle id="Sun" cx="105" cy="160" r="56" class="FillFFFF00"/>
28:        <use id="Cloud1" xlink:href="#Cloud" x="-20" y="80" class="FillFFFFFF"/>
29:        <use id="Cloud2" xlink:href="#Cloud" x="150" y="150" class="FillFFFFFF"/>
30:
31:        <set id="SunColorChange" xlink:href="#Sun"
32:              attributeName="fill"
33:              to="red"
34:              begin="00:00:02"
35:              dur="3s"/>
36:
37:        <set id="Cloud1ColorChange" xlink:href="#Cloud1"
38:              attributeName="fill"
39:              to="#339933"
40:              begin="SunColorChange.end"
41:              dur="1.5s"/>
42:
43:        <set id="Cloud2ColorChange" xlink:href="#Cloud2"
44:              attributeName="fill"
45:              to="#993399"
46:              begin="SunColorChange.begin+1s" />
47:
48: </svg>
```

To create this code, first copy the code from Listing 13.3 and paste it into a new document. Duplicate the set element on lines 37 through 41 and rename the id value to Cloud2ColorChange (line 43 in Listing 13.4). Next, change the xlink:href attribute value from Cloud1 to Cloud2 so that this element modifies the cloud on the right of the sun (line 43).

After making this change, modify the `begin` value to match the value described earlier: `SunColorChange.begin+1s` (line 46). Next, change the value of the `to` attribute to specify a different color, such as a purple (#993399 in line 45). Finally, to make this element's color change permanent, simply remove the `dur` attribute and its value. Without a specified ending, a `set` element's modification will remain after its occurrence as long as the document remains open.

By using a combination of time- and event-based actions, you can gain greater control over your document's interaction and animations.

Rollovers

As you can see, using the `set` element isn't too complicated. Building on this element, you can create a rollover for the news center graphic. Whenever a user moves her cursor over your semi-transparent advertising area, the area will turn to full opacity.

Since a user can move over an object at any time, you will need to trigger the `set` element to mouse actions rather than a time value. As you saw in the last hour, there are several opportunities for mouse interaction. In this case, `mouseover` and `mouseout` are appropriate, as you're concerned with mouse position, not mouse action (like button-clicking).

To experiment with creating a rollover, you can create an example that alters the opacity of an object depending on the location of the mouse cursor. To begin, copy the code from Listing 5.1 (the first rectangle you drew) and paste it into a new document (Listing 13.5). Alter the dimensions and coordinates of the rectangle by changing the `x`, `y`, `width`, and `height` attribute values, and then give the object a name using the `id` attribute (line 7). Next, make the rectangle semi-transparent by applying an `opacity:0.5` style to the object (line 8).

With the simple rectangle now complete, you can begin to create the `set` element that will serve as the rollover command. First, associate the element with the rectangle using the `xlink:href` attribute (line 10). Next, supply the `attributeName` attribute with a value of `opacity` to have the element adjust the transparency of the selected object (line 11).

To turn the semi-transparent object to an opaque object, supply the `to` attribute with a value of 1 (line 12). Finally, give the `begin` and `end` attributes the respective values of `Button.mouseover` and `Button.mouseout` (lines 13 and 14). These values will coordinate the `set` element's action according to the position of the mouse pointer in relation to the `Button` object (the rectangle). Figure 13.3 shows a rectangle whose opacity has been changed by a mouse event.

13

LISTING 13.5   Creating a Rollover Using the set Element

```
01: <?xml version="1.0" standalone="no"?>
02: <!DOCTYPE svg PUBLIC "-//W3C//DTD SVG 1.0//EN"
03:    "http://www.w3.org/TR/2001/REC-SVG-20010904/DTD/svg10.dtd">
04:
05: <svg  width="500" height="300">
06:
07:        <rect id="Button" x="200" y="110" width="100" height="80"
08:               style="opacity:0.5"/>
09:
10:        <set xlink:href="#Button"
11:              attributeName="opacity"
12:              to="1"
13:              begin="Button.mouseover"
14:              end="Button.mouseout"/>
15:
16: </svg>
```

FIGURE 13.3

The set *element can change the opacity of an object based on mouse events. This illustration shows a rectangle with 100% opacity once the mouse cursor is over the top of the object.*

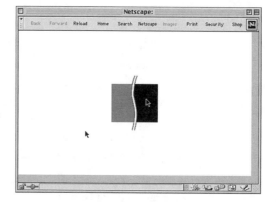

By tying the set element to mouse events, you are able to accomplish common interactive design conventions such as rollovers. Changing opacity isn't the only modification the set element can perform upon a rollover, either. Any modification that the set element can perform can be tied to mouse events. For instance, rather than changing the opacity of an object, the set element could enable the display of an object with a drop shadow behind a navigation item, shift the location of an object, or modify the radius of a circle or ellipse.

Pop-up Devices

Another popular interaction design device that can be replicated using the set element is the pop-up box (see Listing 13.6). To demonstrate this by creating a pop-up credit box, you will need to duplicate and modify the set command used to change opacity. Rather than changing opacity, though, the command will need to change display (as the pop-up isn't visible until initiated). Rather than occurring on mouseovers (the .mouseover event suffix), the new action will occur on mouseclicks (the .click event suffix).

Whenever a user clicks on a button (line 31), a little screen should appear in the center of the screen. This can occur by using the set element to change the display attribute, the command setting the visibility of an object, from none to inline (line 37). As this box should appear only on mouse click, you'll need to hide the box from view as the default using the display:none style command on the original object (line 32).

To allow for the pop-up box to be closed, you will need to create a box within the newly displayed pop-up box as the "close" button: once a user presses it, the pop-up box will vanish (line 34). By setting the end value of the set element to the clicking of this box (line 37), the pop-up box will disappear again. Also, to visually reinforce that the pop-up box resides on a layer above the artwork, you can apply the drop shadow filter you created in Hour 10 (line 19). Your code, once rendered, will appear similar to Figure 13.4.

LISTING 13.6   Creating a Pop-up Device Using the set Element

```
01: <?xml version="1.0" standalone="no"?>
02: <!DOCTYPE svg PUBLIC "-//W3C//DTD SVG 20010904//EN"
            "http://www.w3.org/TR/2001/REC-SVG-20010904/DTD/svg10.dtd">
03:
04: <svg  width="500" height="300">
05:
06:        <style type="text/css">
07:                <![CDATA[
08:                        .FillFFFFFF{fill:#FFFFFF;}
09:                        .Fill666666{fill:#666666;}
10:                        .Fill99CCFF{fill:#99CCFF;}
11:                        .Stroke000000{stroke:#000000;}
12:                        .StrokeWidth1{stroke-width:1;}
13:                        .FilterDropShadow{filter:url(#DropShadow);}
14:                        .DisplayNone{display:none;}
15:                ]]>
16:        </style>
17:
18:        <defs>
19:                <filter id="DropShadow" filterUnits="userSpaceOnUse">
20:                        <feGaussianBlur in="SourceAlpha" stdDeviation="10"
21:                                result="shadow"/>
22:                        <feOffset dx="10" dy="10" in="shadow" result="shadow"/>
23:                        <feMerge>
24:                                <feMergeNode in="shadow"/>
25:                                <feMergeNode in="SourceGraphic"/>
```

continues

13

LISTING 13.6   Continued

```
26:                        </feMerge>
27:                    </filter>
28:        </defs>
29:
30:        <rect id="Bkgd" x="0" y="0" width="500" height="300"
                    class="Fill99CCFF"/>
31:        <rect id="Button" x="380" y="220" width="100" height="60"
                    class="FillFFFFFF"/>
32:        <g id="PopupCredits" class="DisplayNone">
33:                <rect id="PopupBackground" x="125" y="75" width="250"
                    height="150"
                    class="FillFFFFFF StrokeWidth1 Stroke000000
                    FilterDropShadow"/>
34:                <rect id="PopupCloseBox" x="225" y="195" width="50"
                    height="15"
                    class="Fill666666"/>
35:        </g>
36:
37:                <set id="PopupCloseBoxOpen" xlink:href="#PopupCredits"
                        attributeName="display"
                        from="none" to="inline"
                        begin="Button.click"
                        end="PopupCloseBox.click"/>
38:
39: </svg>
```

FIGURE 13.4

The set *element can be used to create a pop-up box.*

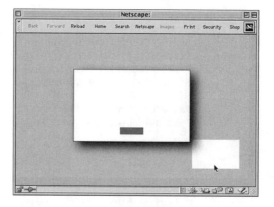

The set element can be used to create a variety of common interaction devices, such as the pop-up "window", as well as many other conventions. When wondering how to create a certain interactive device in SVG, try to dissect a device down to its basic functions. For example, in the case of a rollover, you can determine that you will need a command to adjust the display of an object while the mouse pointer is above an object. Depending on the complexity of the rollover, you may need more than one set element to accomplish your desired interactive device. After reviewing these functions, you may see that the set element can re-create these common devices. (For an example, see Exercise 2 at the end of this hour.)

Keep in mind, however, that the set element cannot accomplish every interactive device. In some cases, you may need to use an animation element to address gradual changes between two or more states (to be covered in Hour 15), as the set element only operates between two distinct states; in others, there may be not be an easy solution to the problem. Don't worry, though. There is almost always a way to accomplish an action you've seen elsewhere. Just keep in mind that the complexity of an interactive device often affects the complexity of the solution.

Summary

SVG's basic interaction controls allow developers to accomplish many of the same results that existing technologies have produced. Although hyperlinking remains largely similar to HTML's original model of using the a element, more complex forms of interaction are possible using the set element.

SVG's hyperlinking abilities allow it to take advantage of one of the most basic of interaction functions (and certainly *the* function that drove the usefulness of the Internet). By using hyperlinks, SVG documents can point to other existing content in order to supplement the original content.

There's no reason to think of an SVG document as a "walled garden." This metaphor was often used to describe the original online communities, where users could view only their communities' content. Rather, SVG can point users to outside content (whether another SVG document or otherwise) just as easily as HTML or Flash.

The set element, on the other hand, makes the experience within the SVG document more engaging. By allowing developers the ability to modify SVG content after its initial load, this element can generally handle most of the distinct visual changes between two states (such as painting, position, and visibility) common to interactive design. In fact, coupled with transformations (covered in the next hour), the set element can perform seemingly endless changes on your content.

13

Q&A

Q Can SVG pop up a new window to contain a hyperlink?

A Certainly. Just like XHTML, the a element accepts the `target` attribute. Simply add `target="new"` to your a element, and your link will open in a new window.

Q Can a `set` element accept more than one `begin` value?

A Yes; simply separate your `begin` values with a semicolon, and you can have a `set` element start on various events or times.

Workshop

The Workshop is designed to help you anticipate possible questions, review what you've learned, and begin learning how to put your knowledge into practice.

Quiz

1. Which element handles hyperlinking in SVG?

2. The `set` element initiates on the time or event listed in which attribute?

3. True or false: The `xlink:href` attribute for the `set` element determines which object will be modified.

4. True or false: The `set` element must appear at the end of the document.

5. True or false: You can use only one `set` element per document.

Answers

1. The a element establishes a hyperlink.

2. The `begin` attribute's value determines when the `set` element initiates.

3. True. The `xlink:href` attribute's value (another element's `id` value) tells the `set` element which element to modify.

4. False. The `set` element can be placed anywhere within the document. It is recommended that you pick a consistent position in your documents to house your interactive elements to make editing easier.

5. False. You can add as many `set` elements as you desire.

Exercises

1. Make a simple frame-by-frame animation using the set element to control the cx value of the sun in Listing 13.2.

2. Using examples from this chapter as a guide, repurpose Listing 13.6 to become a drop-down menu (similar to your operating system's menu bar). First, strip the "Close" button and drop shadow filter information from the document. Then, modify the coordinates and dimensions of the rectangle that serves as the pop-up activation button to span the top of your SVG document (similar in appearance to a menu bar). Subsequently, change the coordinates and dimensions of the rectangle that served as the pop-up device; now it should reflect the appearance of a drop-down menu hanging from the bottom of the menu bar. Finally, insert the newspaper icons with their hotlinks from Listing 13.1 inside the drop-down menu's group. With these changes made, you will have replicated the basic functionality of a drop-down menu (a device with links inside that appears only upon command).

13

HOUR 14

Transforms

After symbols, transformations are the feature that most maximizes the possibilities of a single graphics object. Whereas symbols allow you to reuse an object multiple times within a document, transformations allow you to modify the existing coordinate system of an object. By moving, scaling, skewing, or rotating an object, or all (or some) of the above, a transformation can dramatically change an object's original appearance.

In this hour, you will learn how to

- Move artwork
- Scale artwork
- Skew artwork
- Rotate artwork
- Combine transformations

Once you learn how to transform your artwork, you will be able to apply some powerful distortions to your content. What's more, combined with symbols and animations (which you will learn about in the next hour), transformations can extend the use of your original artwork to accomplish more impressive visual results.

Introduction to Transformations

Transformations are distortions to your artwork that are calculated before a viewer renders your SVG document. Thus, a square that is rotated 45° will appear to someone viewing your document as a diamond; unless they examine your code, they will be unaware of the fact that a transformation was applied.

Transformations are applied as attributes to other elements, such as shapes, groups, or instances. Most often you will see a transformation applied to groups surrounding objects or symbol instances to maximize the usefulness of a transform. By modifying a symbol instance instead of the original, your original artwork will retain its intended properties; instances of that artwork can be modified by a transformation to adjust its appearance according to the instance's needs.

To apply a transformation, the `transform` attribute is applied to the element of the artwork you wish to modify. The attribute's value consists of a combination of a transformation property (which determines the function of the alteration) and a numerical value(s). The transformation properties that compose the possible functions are listed in Table 14.1.

TABLE 14.1   Transform Attribute Properties

Transform Properties	Property Function
translate	Moves an object
scale	Enlarges or reduces the size of an object
rotate	Rotates an object clockwise or counterclockwise
skewX	Skews an object along the x axis
skewY	Skews an object along the y axis
matrix	Performs a series of transformations simultaneously

Transforms are applied to objects using the syntax

```
transform="TransformProperty(A)",
```

where "*TransformProperty*" is one of the six values listed in Table 14.1, and "*A*" is the modifying value(s) for the particular transformation property. Thus, if you were to apply a move function on a circle, your code would appear similar to

```
<rect cx="50" cy="50" width="15" transform="translate(10,10)"/>,
```

effectively moving the object 10 units down and to the right.

Transforming with the `translate` Property

The most common transformation is `translate`—the function that moves an object a set distance from its original coordinates. To move an object, you will need to apply `transform="translate(x,y)"` to your desired element. In this case, "*x,y*" refers to the horizontal and vertical distance from the *object's* original x,y coordinates, not from the SVG document's (0,0) coordinates.

To demonstrate, you can move the sun in the news center graphic 50 units up and 50 units to the left. First, copy the code from Listing 13.2 and paste it into a new document. Next, add `transform="translate(-50,-50)"` to the `circle` element (line 28) that defines the sun's shape. This is shown in Listing 14.1.

LISTING 14.1 Using the `translate` Transformation to Alter the Position of the Sun

```
01: <?xml version="1.0" standalone="no"?>
02: <!DOCTYPE svg PUBLIC "-//W3C//DTD SVG 1.0//EN"
03:    "http://www.w3.org/TR/2001/REC-SVG-20010904/DTD/svg10.dtd">
04:
05: <svg  width="500" height="300">
06:
07:        <style type="text/css">
08:                <![CDATA[
09:                        .FillFFFFFF{fill:#FFFFFF;}
10:                        .Fill99CCFF{fill:#99CCFF;}
11:                        .FillFFFF00{fill:#FFFF00;}
12:                ]]>
13:        </style>
14:
15:        <defs>
16:                <g id="Cloud">
17:                        <circle cx="24" cy="36" r="15"/>
18:                        <circle cx="41" cy="26" r="17"/>
19:                        <circle cx="90" cy="40" r="13"/>
20:                        <circle cx="105" cy="31" r="13"/>
21:                        <ellipse cx="75" cy="20" rx="27" ry="20"/>
22:                        <ellipse cx="56" cy="50" rx="25" ry="18"/>
23:                </g>
24:        </defs>
25:
26:        <rect id="Sky" x="10" y="45" width="200" height="245" class="Fill99CCFF"/>
27:        <circle id="Sun" cx="105" cy="160" r="56" class="FillFFFF00"
28:                transform="translate(-50,-50)"/>
29:        <use id="Cloud1" xlink:href="#Cloud" x="-20" y="80" class="FillFFFFFF"/>
30:        <use id="Cloud2" xlink:href="#Cloud" x="150" y="150" class="FillFFFFFF"/>
31:
32: </svg>
```

14

Figure 14.1 shows the results of this code: the sun is now closer to the top left corner and obscured by the left cloud.

FIGURE **14.1**

Using the translate *transformation to alter the position of the sun.*

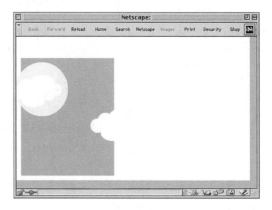

The translate property is likely the easiest-to-use of the many transform attributes, as all it requires is a simple knowledge of x and y positioning. As you begin to use the other properties, you will need to dust off those old math skills.

Transforming with the scale Property

Scaling objects is handled by applying

```
transform="scale(x,y)"
```

to your desired object. In this case, "x,y" refers to the horizontal scale and vertical scale of the applied object (not x and y positioning as with the translate property). To scale an object uniformly, you need include only the x value, as the y value will be assumed to be the same.

In each case, the value of 1 is equivalent to "100%." So, to apply a scale transformation that is twice as large as the original object, you would apply transform="scale(2)". Reductions are thus handled using decimal values; to apply a scale transformation making an object half as big as the original object, you would apply transform="scale(0.5)".

To illustrate this property, you can scale the sun's height and width. Using Listing 14.1 as a starting point, simply change the transformation property (line 28) from translate to scale. Next, change the property values to accommodate a horizontal scale of 120% (1.2) and a vertical scale of 50% (0.5). Your code should then appear similar to Listing 14.2.

LISTING 14.2   Using the `scale` Transformation to Alter the Width and Height of the Sun

```
01: <?xml version="1.0" standalone="no"?>
02: <!DOCTYPE svg PUBLIC "-//W3C//DTD SVG 1.0//EN"
03:    "http://www.w3.org/TR/2001/REC-SVG-20010904/DTD/svg10.dtd">
04:
05: <svg  width="500" height="300">
06:
07:        <style type="text/css">
08:                <![CDATA[
09:                        .FillFFFFFF{fill:#FFFFFF;}
10:                        .Fill99CCFF{fill:#99CCFF;}
11:                        .FillFFFF00{fill:#FFFF00;}
12:                ]]>
13:        </style>
14:
15:        <defs>
16:                <g id="Cloud">
17:                        <circle cx="24" cy="36" r="15"/>
18:                        <circle cx="41" cy="26" r="17"/>
19:                        <circle cx="90" cy="40" r="13"/>
20:                        <circle cx="105" cy="31" r="13"/>
21:                        <ellipse cx="75" cy="20" rx="27" ry="20"/>
22:                        <ellipse cx="56" cy="50" rx="25" ry="18"/>
23:                </g>
24:        </defs>
25:
26:        <rect id="Sky" x="10" y="45" width="200" height="245" class="Fill99CCFF"/>
27:        <circle id="Sun" cx="105" cy="160" r="56" class="FillFFFF00"
28:                transform="scale(1.2,0.5)"/>
29:        <use id="Cloud1" xlink:href="#Cloud" x="-20" y="80" class="FillFFFFFF"/>
30:        <use id="Cloud2" xlink:href="#Cloud" x="150" y="150" class="FillFFFFFF"/>
31:
32: </svg>
```

Figure 14.2 shows the results of this code: a flattened and widened sun in the top right corner of the sky.

You'll note that the sun seemed to shift its original coordinates. This is because all transformations are applied *before* the applied object is rendered. In other words, all of the object's properties are filtered through the transformation before being displayed. Hence, the x and y positions of your original element will shift according to the transformation. In the case of Listing 14.2, the `cx` position of 105 was scaled 120% to 126, and the `cy` position of 160 was scaled 50% to 80.

14

FIGURE **14.2**

Using the scale
*transformation to
alter the width and
height of the sun.*

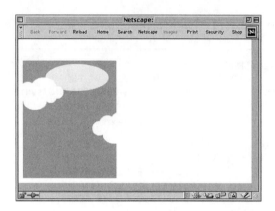

Later in this hour, you will learn how to use a second transformation on the same object, allowing you to keep your object in its same location while applying a distortion.

Transforming Using the skewX and skewY Properties

For those unfamiliar with the concept of skewing, here's a brief introduction. Skewing is, for all intents and purposes, simultaneously stretching and tilting an object only along an axis; oftentimes, if an object has been skewed, it appears to have been tilted at an angle.

Skewing comes in most handy when trying to create an isometric perspective. (Isometric perspective, often recognized in ancient Chinese paintings, bends one axis to create the appearance of depth.) To illustrate this concept, Figure 14.3 shows the lightning bolt you created in Hour 5 skewed 45° along the X axis.

FIGURE **14.3**

*Skewing an object tilts
the artwork at a
specified angle along
an axis. In this exam-
ple, the artwork has
been skewed 45° along
the x-axis.*

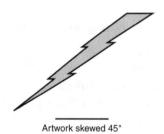

Original artwork   Artwork skewed 45°

There are two skew properties available: skewX and skewY, each representing a skew along a given axis. Skewing objects horizontally is handled by applying transform="skewX(z)" to your desired element, while transform="skewY(z)" skews objects vertically. In both cases, "z" refers to the angle of the skew.

To show skewing in action, you can skew the sun from the previous example horizontally 15°. First, copy the code of Listing 14.2 and paste it into a new document. Next, modify the transform attribute on the sun object to reflect the skew command: skewX(15) (shown on line 28 in Listing 14.3 below). The result of your code will appear similar to Figure 14.4.

LISTING 14.3 Using the skew Transformation to Alter the Tilt of the Sun

```
01: <?xml version="1.0" standalone="no"?>
02: <!DOCTYPE svg PUBLIC "-//W3C//DTD SVG 1.0//EN"
03:    "http://www.w3.org/TR/2001/REC-SVG-20010904/DTD/svg10.dtd">
04:
05: <svg  width="500" height="300">
06:
07:         <style type="text/css">
08:                 <![CDATA[
09:                         .FillFFFFFF{fill:#FFFFFF;}
10:                         .Fill99CCFF{fill:#99CCFF;}
11:                         .FillFFFF00{fill:#FFFF00;}
12:                 ]]>
13:         </style>
14:
15:         <defs>
16:                 <g id="Cloud">
17:                         <circle cx="24" cy="36" r="15"/>
18:                         <circle cx="41" cy="26" r="17"/>
19:                         <circle cx="90" cy="40" r="13"/>
20:                         <circle cx="105" cy="31" r="13"/>
21:                         <ellipse cx="75" cy="20" rx="27" ry="20"/>
22:                         <ellipse cx="56" cy="50" rx="25" ry="18"/>
23:                 </g>
24:         </defs>
25:
26:         <rect id="Sky" x="10" y="45" width="200" height="245" class="Fill99CCFF"/>
27:         <circle id="Sun" cx="105" cy="160" r="56" class="FillFFFF00"
28:                 transform="skewX(15)"/>
29:         <use id="Cloud1" xlink:href="#Cloud" x="-20" y="80" class="FillFFFFFF"/>
30:         <use id="Cloud2" xlink:href="#Cloud" x="150" y="150" class="FillFFFFFF"/>
31:
32: </svg>
```

14

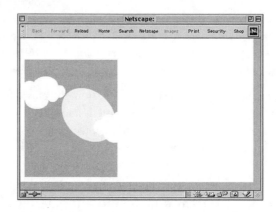

FIGURE **14.4**

Using the skewX *transformation to alter the skew of the sun.*

The skewY property produces a similar result, except that it operates along the vertical axis. To see its results, copy the code from Listing 14.3 and paste it into a new document. Next, alter line 28's transform attribute. Instead of the previous skewX value, change the value to skewY(-60). The –60° angle will skew the artwork up the axis (in accordance with SVG's inverted Y axis). Your code should now look like Listing 14.4. The result will mirror Figure 14.5.

LISTING 14.4   Using the skewY Transformation to Alter the Tilt of the Sun

```
01: <?xml version="1.0" standalone="no"?>
02: <!DOCTYPE svg PUBLIC "-//W3C//DTD SVG 1.0//EN"
03:    "http://www.w3.org/TR/2001/REC-SVG-20010904/DTD/svg10.dtd">
04:
05: <svg  width="500" height="300">
06:
07:        <style type="text/css">
08:               <![CDATA[
09:                        .FillFFFFFF{fill:#FFFFFF;}
10:                        .Fill99CCFF{fill:#99CCFF;}
11:                        .FillFFFF00{fill:#FFFF00;}
12:               ]]>
13:        </style>
14:
15:        <defs>
16:               <g id="Cloud">
17:                        <circle cx="24" cy="36" r="15"/>
18:                        <circle cx="41" cy="26" r="17"/>
19:                        <circle cx="90" cy="40" r="13"/>
20:                        <circle cx="105" cy="31" r="13"/>
21:                        <ellipse cx="75" cy="20" rx="27" ry="20"/>
22:                        <ellipse cx="56" cy="50" rx="25" ry="18"/>
```

continues

LISTING 14.4   Continued

```
23:                          </g>
24:              </defs>
25:
26:              <rect id="Sky" x="10" y="45" width="200" height="245" class="Fill99CCFF"/>
27:              <circle id="Sun" cx="105" cy="160" r="56" class="FillFFFF00"
28:                          transform="skewX(15)"/>
29:              <use id="Cloud1" xlink:href="#Cloud" x="-20" y="80" class="FillFFFFFF"/>
30:              <use id="Cloud2" xlink:href="#Cloud" x="150" y="150" class="FillFFFFFF"/>
31:
32: </svg>
```

FIGURE 14.5

Using the skewY
transformation to
alter the vertical skew
of the sun.

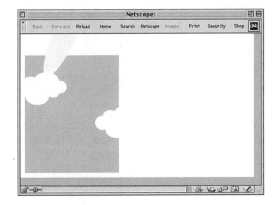

The skew properties work in terms of 90° increments. In fact, using a 90° value often makes the applied object seem to disappear. This is because if the artwork were tilted to a complete 90° angle, it would appear similar to a piece of paper on its side: imperceptible and seemingly gone. Values greater than 90° are possible, however. The result varies, as each increment of 90° results in the same "disappearing" effect, and the tilt is applied in an opposite direction from the previous 90° increment's result. The skew property also accepts negative values for its angle, which have a similar result as values between 91° and 180°, as well as 271° and 380°.

Transforming Using the rotate Property

Rotation is possible by applying transform="rotate(A)" to your desired element. In this case, "A" refers to the angle of the rotation. A positive angle value will rotate an object in a clockwise direction, whereas a negative value defines a counterclockwise direction. The rotation will occur around the object's top-left corner (the (0,0) coordinates).

14

As you can imagine, the sun from previous examples might not be a good test case for rotation. Instead, you can rotate a simple object like a rectangle in the center of your document. As Listing 13.5 used such a shape, open that document, copy its code, and paste it into a new document. Next, add a transform attribute to the rect element (line 6 in Listing 14.5) and supply it with a rotate(15) value. This modification will produce a result similar to Figure 14.6, where the rectangle has been rotated 15° from and according to its top left corner.

LISTING 14.5   Using the rotate Transformation to Spin a Rectangle

```
01: <?xml version="1.0" standalone="no"?>
02: <!DOCTYPE svg PUBLIC "-//W3C//DTD SVG 20010904//EN"
             "http://www.w3.org/TR/2001/REC-SVG-20010904/DTD/svg10.dtd">
03:
04: <svg  width="500" height="300">
05:
06:         <rect x="200" y="110" width="100" height="80" transform="rotate(15)"/>
07:
08: </svg>
```

FIGURE 14.6

Using the rotate *transformation to spin a square.*

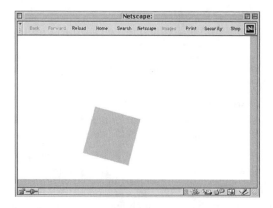

Just as you saw with the scale, skewX, and skewY transformations, the applied object's coordinate space is affected by the application of the transform attribute. The transform is calculated according to the top left corner of the object, the same as all objects in SVG. In the case of the rotated square, the x and y coordinates of the top left starting point of the square were calculated by rotating the object's x and y attribute values 45° before the square was rendered.

Applying Multiple Transform Operations

As explained in the scaling section (and as you saw just now in the rotation section), applying transformations can result in odd coordinate shifts. In such cases, you will often want to apply more than one transformation effect to an object.

There are two methods for applying multiple transformations to an object: additive `transform` properties and the `matrix` property. The `matrix` property, which was mentioned briefly in Table 14.1, is an elaborate mathematical formula for applying a number of transformations.

> If you are feeling brave of heart, you can learn more about matrix transformations in Chapter 7.4 of the W3C's SVG recommendation at
> `http://www.w3.org/tr/svg/`.

As this book is focused on fundamentals, you will focus here on additive `transform` properties (as they are much easier to decipher). Additive transformations are a listing of multiple transformation properties within one `transform` attribute. To incorporate multiple transformation properties, simply separate them with a space within the `transform` attribute value list. For instance, the syntax for three transformation properties within one attribute would be

```
transform="TransformProperty1(A) TransformProperty2(B) TransformProperty3(C)"
```

Thus, if you wanted to apply a `translate`, `rotate`, and `scale` property to the rectangle in Listing 14.5, you would list the properties and their values within the `transform` attribute's value as follows:

```
<rect x="200" y="110" width="100" height="80"
      transform="translate(10 10) rotate(15) scale(0.5)"/>
```

To demonstrate this ability in practice, consider the illustration of the sun in this book's final news center graphic (shown in Figure 1.1). Rather than being a simple circle, it has a number of points around the edge, as is common for many renderings of sunshine. Rather than drawing each of these points individually, you could use a series of symbols with different `transform` combinations to create the sun's many points, as shown in Figure 14.7.

As this example is a bit more complex than some of the others, it has been divided into smaller chunks. You will be able to explore this example similar to the order of the steps leading to the example shown in Figure 14.7.

14

FIGURE **14.7**

*Using symbols in
conjunction with
transformations, the
sunshine illustration
can be created without
attempting to plot
the coordinates for
each point.*

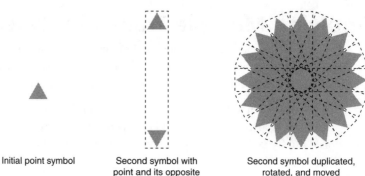

Initial point symbol   Second symbol with   Second symbol duplicated,
                              point and its opposite   rotated, and moved

(Dotted lines represent symbol grouping)

First, copy the code from Listing 14.5 and paste it into a new document. Next, strip out the cloud symbol, instances, and related style. Then, using the sun circle and sky rectangle as a relational guide, draw a simple triangle using the polygon element to represent the sun's top-most point (see line 15 in Listing 14.6 following), filling it with the same yellow used for the sun's circle. As the point will eventually be used only as a repeatable symbol, simply plot its coordinates from the top-left corner of the document (thus making math calculations easier later). Figure 14.8 shows the creation of the triangle in the upper left corner of the browser window.

LISTING 14.6   Creating the First Point for the Sunshine Illustration

```
01: <?xml version="1.0" standalone="no"?>
02: <!DOCTYPE svg PUBLIC "-//W3C//DTD SVG 20010904//EN"
            "http://www.w3.org/TR/2001/REC-SVG-20010904/DTD/svg10.dtd">
03:
04: <svg  width="500" height="300">
05:
06:        <style type="text/css">
07:                <![CDATA[
08:                        .Fill99CCFF{fill:#99CCFF;}
09:                        .FillFFFF00{fill:#FFFF00;}
10:                ]]>
11:        </style>
12:
13:        <rect id="Sky" x="10" y="45" width="200" height="245"
                class="Fill99CCFF"/>
14:        <circle id="Sun" cx="105" cy="160" r="56" class="FillFFFF00"/>
15:        <polygon id="SunRay" points="7.5,0 0,15 15,15" class="FillFFFF00"/>
16:
17: </svg>
```

FIGURE **14.8**

Creating the first triangle "ray" for the sunshine illustration.

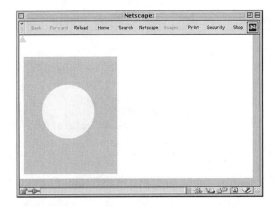

Having created the simple sun "ray", it's now time to make it a symbol. Moving the triangle, which was dubbed SunRay in the example, into the defs section makes it a symbol ready for referencing. The next step is to create another symbol that uses two instances of SunRay: one in its normal position, the second rotated 180° and moved down the length of the sun. As the base of the point isn't curved to match the arc of the sun's center, the example uses a value (–138 in line 17 below) that accommodates for the base of each point to remain within the circle (thus making the points and circle appear as one mass).

In the following example (Listing 14.7), SunRay has become a symbol (line 14), and the second symbol, SunRay1 (line 15), has been created using the two instances of SunRay: one unchanged and the other rotated and placed in vertical alignment down from the original. To accomplish the rotation and placement necessary for this second triangle, you will need to combine a translate and rotate property (line 17). You can see how this will look in Figure 14.9 (note the second triangle below the first).

LISTING 14.7   Using Transformations, the Triangle Symbol Is Placed Twice in Relation to the Sunshine Illustration

```
01: <?xml version="1.0" standalone="no"?>
02: <!DOCTYPE svg PUBLIC "-//W3C//DTD SVG 20010904//EN"
            "http://www.w3.org/TR/2001/REC-SVG-20010904/DTD/svg10.dtd">
03:
04: <svg  width="500" height="300">
05:
06:        <style type="text/css">
07:                <![CDATA[
08:                        .Fill99CCFF{fill:#99CCFF;}
09:                        .FillFFFF00{fill:#FFFF00;}
10:                ]]>
11:        </style>
```

continues

14

LISTING 14.7 Continued

```
12:
13:         <defs>
14:                 <polygon id="SunRay" points="7.5,0 0,15 15,15" class="FillFFFF00"/>
15:                 <g id="SunRay1" class="FillFFFF00">
16:                         <use xlink:href="#SunRay"/>
17:                         <use xlink:href="#SunRay" x="-15" y="-138"
                                    transform="rotate(180)"/>
18:                 </g>
19:         </defs>
20:
21:         <rect id="Sky" x="10" y="45" width="200" height="245"
                    class="Fill99CCFF"/>
22:         <circle id="Sun" cx="105" cy="160" r="56" class="FillFFFF00"/>
23:         <use xlink:href="#SunRay1"/>
24:
25: </svg>
```

FIGURE 14.9

Using transformations, the triangle symbol is placed twice in relation to the sunshine illustration.

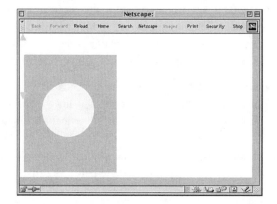

Refer back to Figure 14.7, which shows how the SunRay1 dual triangle symbol will need to be duplicated and rotated around the center of the sun. Though you could certainly duplicate the SunRay1 symbol several times and plot the placement for each modified symbol (after the rotate transformation is applied), it would amount to a lot of math work. As SVG coordinate systems are always plotted from the top-left corner, each instance of the SunRay1 symbol would have its own starting coordinate. Considering that the center point of the SunRay1 symbol is (7.5,69), you would need to determine 12 unique coordinates for the sunshine's 24 points (comprised of 12 dual point symbols).

Obviously, this is more work than a simple sunshine illustration is worth. Instead, you can apply a translate function to the SunRay1 symbol so as to move its artwork half its width (7.5 pixels) and height (69 pixels) left and upwards. This effectively moves the center point of the artwork from (7.5,69) to (0,0), as shown in Figure 14.10.

By moving the center point of the symbol through translating its position, you need worry only about the rotation angle to be applied to each symbol. The coordinate location of each instance will be the same—the center point of the sun's circle (whose coordinates you already have).

Knowing both the sun's center point coordinates and the distance to offset the symbol, you can modify Listing 14.7 appropriately. First, add the translate function to the SunRay1 symbol (line 15 in Listing 14.8). Then alter the coordinates of the use element that places the symbol to reflect the center point of the sun (line 23), as shown in Figure 14.11.

FIGURE 14.10

Using a translate *transformation, the* SunRay1 *symbol's center point is moved to (0,0).*

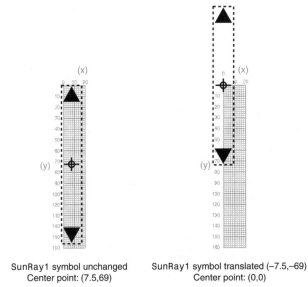

SunRay1 symbol unchanged
Center point: (7.5,69)

SunRay1 symbol translated (–7.5,–69)
Center point: (0,0)

(Dotted lines represent symbol grouping)

LISTING 14.8   Having Translated the Symbol's Artwork, the Point Symbol Is Centered to the Sun's Center Point

```
01: <?xml version="1.0" standalone="no"?>
02: <!DOCTYPE svg PUBLIC "-//W3C//DTD SVG 20010904//EN"
            "http://www.w3.org/TR/2001/REC-SVG-20010904/DTD/svg10.dtd">
03:
04: <svg  width="500" height="300">
05:
06:         <style type="text/css">
```

14

continues

LISTING 14.8 Continued

```
07:                    <![CDATA[
08:                        .Fill99CCFF{fill:#99CCFF;}
09:                        .FillFFFF00{fill:#FFFF00;}
10:                    ]]>
11:            </style>
12:
13:            <defs>
14:                    <polygon id="SunRay" points="7.5,0 0,15 15,15" class="FillFFFF00"/>
15:                    <g id="SunRay1" transform="translate(-7.5,-69)" class="FillFFFF00">
16:                            <use xlink:href="#SunRay"/>
17:                            <use xlink:href="#SunRay" x="-15" y="-138"
                                    transform="rotate(180)"/>
18:                    </g>
19:            </defs>
20:
21:            <rect id="Sky" x="10" y="45" width="200" height="245"
                    class="Fill99CCFF"/>
22:            <circle id="Sun" cx="105" cy="160" r="56" class="FillFFFF00"/>
23:            <use xlink:href="#SunRay1" transform="translate(105,160)"/>
24:
25: </svg>
```

FIGURE 14.11

Having translated the symbol's artwork, the point symbol is centered to the sun's center point.

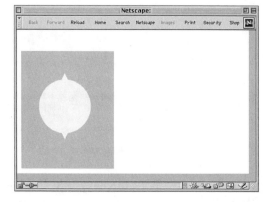

Now comes the fun part. You will create the remainder of the sun points by duplicating the use element 11 times to reflect the total of 24 points (see lines 24 through 34 in Listing 14.9). In each case, you will need to add a second transform attribute to the attribute list—rotate. To create the desired result (shown in Figure 14.12), each duplicate element will need to use an increment of 15° for its rotation value.

LISTING 14.9 Multiple Transformations on Each Instance of the Sunray Symbols Allow for Quick Placement

```
01: <?xml version="1.0" standalone="no"?>
02: <!DOCTYPE svg PUBLIC "-//W3C//DTD SVG 20010904//EN"
              "http://www.w3.org/TR/2001/REC-SVG-20010904/DTD/svg10.dtd">
03:
04: <svg  width="500" height="300">
05:
06:        <style type="text/css">
07:                <![CDATA[
08:                        .Fill99CCFF{fill:#99CCFF;}
09:                        .FillFFFF00{fill:#FFFF00;}
10:                ]]>
11:        </style>
12:
13:        <defs>
14:                <polygon id="SunRay" points="7.5,0 0,15 15,15" class="FillFFFF00"/>
15:                <g id="SunRay1" transform="translate(-7.5,-69)" class="FillFFFF00">
16:                        <use xlink:href="#SunRay"/>
17:                        <use xlink:href="#SunRay" x="-15" y="-138"
                                transform="rotate(180)"/>
18:                </g>
19:        </defs>
20:
21:        <rect id="Sky" x="10" y="45" width="200" height="245" class="Fill99CCFF"/>
22:        <circle id="Sun" cx="105" cy="160" r="56" class="FillFFFF00"/>
23:        <use xlink:href="#SunRay1" transform="translate(105,160)"/>
24:        <use xlink:href="#SunRay1" transform="translate(105,160) rotate(15)"/>
25:        <use xlink:href="#SunRay1" transform="translate(105,160) rotate(30)"/>
26:        <use xlink:href="#SunRay1" transform="translate(105,160) rotate(45)"/>
27:        <use xlink:href="#SunRay1" transform="translate(105,160) rotate(60)"/>
28:        <use xlink:href="#SunRay1" transform="translate(105,160) rotate(75)"/>
29:        <use xlink:href="#SunRay1" transform="translate(105,160) rotate(90)"/>
30:        <use xlink:href="#SunRay1" transform="translate(105,160) rotate(-75)"/>
31:        <use xlink:href="#SunRay1" transform="translate(105,160) rotate(-60)"/>
32:        <use xlink:href="#SunRay1" transform="translate(105,160) rotate(-45)"/>
33:        <use xlink:href="#SunRay1" transform="translate(105,160) rotate(-30)"/>
34:        <use xlink:href="#SunRay1" transform="translate(105,160) rotate(-15)"/>
35:
36: </svg>
```

By accommodating multiple functions within one attribute, transform is able to apply complex visual changes with clarity and minimal code.

14

FIGURE 14.12

Multiple transformations on each instance of the sunray symbols allow for quick placement.

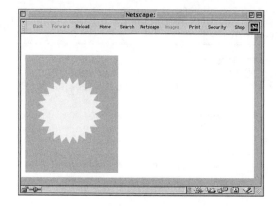

Summary

Transformations offer a great deal of control over several visual arrangement matters. Allowing developers to move, rotate, scale, and skew objects provides a greater flexibility in manipulating imagery comparable to other graphics technologies. By combining several transform functions, you can minimize code and accomplish complex distortions.

Q&A

Q The matrix attribute wasn't covered in this book. What is this attribute used for?

A The matrix attribute applies multiple transformations to an object using what is termed a "current transformation matrix," a series of table values multiplied together to produce a complex result.

Q Can transformations be animated?

A Yes, they can. Hour 15 will explain how to use the animateTransform element, which can transition between different transform attribute values.

Workshop

The Workshop is designed to help you anticipate possible questions, review what you've learned, and begin learning how to put your knowledge into practice.

Quiz

1. Which attribute is used to apply transformations to objects?

2. True or false: Transformations affect an object's initial coordinate system.

3. How many transform functions exist?

4. True or false: multiple `transform` properties require multiple `transform` attributes to be applied to one object.

5. What sort of changes do the skew functions apply to artwork?

Answers

1. The `transform` attribute is used to apply transformations to an element.

2. True. Any transformation factors into an object's coordinate system. For instance, a rotation applies not only to the position of an object, but also to its initial coordinates.

3. There are six `transform` functions: `translate`, `rotate`, `scale`, `skewX`, `skewY`, and `matrix`.

4. False. One `transform` attribute can contain multiple `transform` attribute values, accommodating several functions within one element.

5. Skew functions distort artwork by shifting its coordinates only along one axis, generally resulting in a slanted perspective.

Exercises

1. Rebuild the sun graphic from previous examples using the `translate` function instead of x and y coordinates to determine placement.

2. Try using both the `skewX` and `skewY` functions on an object, such as a cloud, from previous examples. Use the `translate` function to offset the center point of the artwork so that the skewing does not offset it.

14

HOUR 15

Animation

Animation has long been considered a crowning achievement in Web graphics. Bringing static imagery to life with motion, an intelligent application of animation can evoke a feeling, a message, or a meaning. Not wanting to limit SVG, the W3C incorporated a series of animation abilities into their creation based on SMIL's functionality.

To introduce you to SVG's animation capabilities, you will learn the following in this hour:

- How motion unfolds
- Animating basic attribute value transitions
- Animating along a motion path
- Animating a transformation
- Animating color transitions

Having familiarized yourself with transformations and the set element (which is actually an animation element) in the previous two hours, you are already aware of much of the syntax behind animation elements. With both of these hours fresh in your mind, you'll be able to whip through this hour and begin bringing your content to life.

Understanding Motion

SVG offers five animation elements, each with its own focus, as detailed in Table 15.1.

TABLE 15.1   Animation Elements

Element	Function
animate	Alters the values of attributes
animateMotion	Moves objects along a path
animateTransform	Animates a transformation property
animateColor	Shifts colors
set	Switches the value(s) of an attribute

The fifth animation element, set, should look familiar, as you learned about it in Hour 13, "Interaction." The set element is used for handling most of the distinct visual changes between two attribute states. The remaining four elements generally do the same; however, these elements transition between the two (or more) visual states, whereas the set element creates an abrupt change.

Although you won't be using each animation element in this book's final example, a brief review of these four remaining elements will strengthen your understanding of your options in the future. Before diving in, though, keep in mind that these four animation elements are beholden to the same time and interaction syntax discussed in Hour 12, "Time." Time measurements and event-based triggers are still allowed and can be designated for animation elements just as they were allowed for the set element.

Animating Basic Attribute Transitions

Altering attributes is what the animate element focuses on. Virtually any attribute with a numerical value can be animated, from width to letter-spacing, x to r; the animate element can cause certain non-numerical attributes to be animated, too. The animate element needs several attributes to operate correctly. These attributes are detailed in Table 15.2.

TABLE 15.2 `animate` Element Attributes

Attribute	Function
xlink:href	Similar to the `set` command, the `xlink:href` attribute value determines which object will be modified.
attributeName	The `attributeName` value tells the animation element which attribute of the designated object to modify.
from	The `from` value describes the initial state of the animated attribute at the start of the animation.
to	The `to` value describes the final state of the animated attribute at the end of the animation.
begin	The `begin` value determines when the `animate` command takes place. (Optional.)
end	The `end` value extends the length of the `animate` command to match another event or action. (Optional; Used in place of `dur`.)
dur	The `dur` value determines the duration of time of the `animate` command. (Optional; Used in place of `end`.)

Using these attributes, the `animate` element has the following syntax:

```
<animate xlink:href="#A" attributeName="B" from="C" to="D" begin="E" end="F"/>
```

In this case, *A* represents the name of the item the animation is applied to, *B* represents the attribute whose values will be animated, *C* represents the initial attribute value, *D* represents the final attribute value, *E* represents the time measurement defining the start of the animation, and *F* represents the final time measurement determining when the animation ends.

Thus, an example of this syntax, where an object's x attribute value was animated from 10 units to 247 units (effectively moving the object across the screen), beginning 2 seconds after the SVG document loads and finishing 3 seconds later, would translate into

```
<animate xlink:href="#Sky" attributeName="x" from="10" to="247" begin="2s"
        ends="5s"/>
```

The `animate` element's attributes look like and perform very similarly to the `set` element's attributes. The important distinction, however, is between what the `set` element performs and what the `animate` element performs. The `set` element abruptly changes an attribute from one setting to another, whereas `animate` transitions (or "tweens," as the concept is known to Flash users) between one setting and another.

For example, the final example of Hour 13 (Listing 13.6) showed a pop-up immediately becoming visible once a button was pressed; there were no intermediate values between being hidden and being fully visible. The animate element, on the other hand, could fade in the pop-up box (using the opacity attribute instead of the display attribute).

To get a sense of how the animate element works, you can begin with a simple example. By animating the radius of the sun in the previous examples, you can begin to see how simple (yet powerful) the animate element is.

First, copy the code from Listing 13.2 and paste it into a new document (see Listing 15.1). Next, change the set element to an animate element (line 31) to perform the correct operation. Then change the attributeName value to r so your animation adjusts the radius of the circle (see line 32).

Next, add the from attribute to define the value from which the animation begins its transition (line 33). Match this attribute value with the circle's radius value so that the animation begins from the circle's original size. On line 34, change the to attribute's value to 86 (or any number larger than the original circle element's radius value). The begin, dur, and xlink:href attribute values can remain the same. Figure 15.1 shows how this will look.

LISTING 15.1   Using the animate Element to Gradually Grow the Sun

```
01: <?xml version="1.0" standalone="no"?>
02: <!DOCTYPE svg PUBLIC "-//W3C//DTD SVG 20010904//EN"
03:    "http://www.w3.org/TR/2001/REC-SVG-20010904/DTD/svg10.dtd">
04:
05: <svg  width="500" height="300">
06:
07:        <style type="text/css">
08:                <![CDATA[
09:                        .FillFFFFFF{fill:#FFFFFF;}
10:                        .Fill99CCFF{fill:#99CCFF;}
11:                        .FillFFFF00{fill:#FFFF00;}
12:                ]]>
13:        </style>
14:
15:        <defs>
16:                <g id="Cloud">
17:                        <circle cx="24" cy="36" r="15"/>
18:                        <circle cx="41" cy="26" r="17"/>
19:                        <circle cx="90" cy="40" r="13"/>
20:                        <circle cx="105" cy="31" r="13"/>
21:                        <ellipse cx="75" cy="20" rx="27" ry="20"/>
22:                        <ellipse cx="56" cy="50" rx="25" ry="18"/>
```

continues

15

LISTING 15.1   Continued

```
23:                    </g>
24:            </defs>
25:
26:            <rect id="Sky" x="10" y="45" width="200" height="245" class="Fill99CCFF"/>
27:            <circle id="Sun" cx="105" cy="160" r="56" class="FillFFFF00"/>
28:            <use id="Cloud1" xlink:href="#Cloud" x="-20" y="80" class="FillFFFFFF"/>
29:            <use id="Cloud2" xlink:href="#Cloud" x="150" y="150" class="FillFFFFFF"/>
30:
31:            <animate id="SunRadiusChange" xlink:href="#Sun"
32:                    attributeName="r"
33:                    from="56"
34:                    to="86"
35:                    begin="00:00:02"
36:                    dur="3s"/>
37:
38: </svg>
```

FIGURE 15.1

Using the animate *element, the radius of the sun gradually grows larger over a three-second timeframe.*

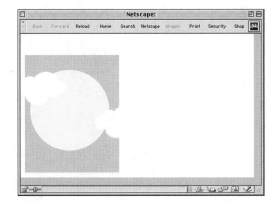

Notice how the sun's circle jumped back to its original size at the end of the duration of the animation. You can control the final visual state of an animation by using the fill attribute. The fill attribute has two possible attribute values: freeze and remove.

The default value is remove, and it results in what you just experienced with your example: The animated object will return to its predefined state once its animation has been completed. The freeze value, on the other hand, captures the last value (to) of the animation and holds it on screen, even after the animation has reached its end.

If you do not supply a `fill` attribute and value pair to your animation elements, the SVG viewer will automatically assume a `fill` attribute with a value of `remove`.

Thus, in the case of the previous example, you can insert `fill="freeze"` in your animate element (line 37 in Listing 15.2) to prevent the sun's radius from returning to its original size of 56; instead, it will hold at `to`'s value of 86.

LISTING 15.2 Adding the `freeze` Value to the `fill` Attribute

```
01: <?xml version="1.0" standalone="no"?>
02: <!DOCTYPE svg PUBLIC "-//W3C//DTD SVG 20010904//EN"
03:    "http://www.w3.org/TR/2001/REC-SVG-20010904/DTD/svg10.dtd">
04:
05: <svg  width="500" height="300">
06:
07:      <style type="text/css">
08:           <![CDATA[
09:                     .FillFFFFFF{fill:#FFFFFF;}
10:                     .Fill99CCFF{fill:#99CCFF;}
11:                     .FillFFFF00{fill:#FFFF00;}
12:           ]]>
13:      </style>
14:
15:      <defs>
16:           <g id="Cloud">
17:                     <circle cx="24" cy="36" r="15"/>
18:                     <circle cx="41" cy="26" r="17"/>
19:                     <circle cx="90" cy="40" r="13"/>
20:                     <circle cx="105" cy="31" r="13"/>
21:                     <ellipse cx="75" cy="20" rx="27" ry="20"/>
22:                     <ellipse cx="56" cy="50" rx="25" ry="18"/>
23:           </g>
24:      </defs>
25:
26:      <rect id="Sky" x="10" y="45" width="200" height="245" class="Fill99CCFF"/>
27:      <circle id="Sun" cx="105" cy="160" r="56" class="FillFFFF00"/>
28:      <use id="Cloud1" xlink:href="#Cloud" x="-20" y="80" class="FillFFFFFF"/>
29:      <use id="Cloud2" xlink:href="#Cloud" x="150" y="150" class="FillFFFFFF"/>
30:
31:      <animate id="SunRadiusChange" xlink:href="#Sun"
32:           attributeName="r"
33:           from="56"
```

continues

15

LISTING 15.2   Continued

```
34:                       to="86"
35:                       begin="00:00:02"
36:                       dur="3s"
37:                       fill="freeze"/>
38:
39: </svg>
```

In this case, once the sun has expanded, the screen holds the larger version of the sun. The fill attribute, though its name is somewhat confusing, becomes necessary in those instances where you wish to maintain the animation's final appearance.

Unless you designate fill="freeze", the animation elements assume the remove value.

Animating an Object's Location

The animate element allows for the transition of an object between one state and another. One application of this element would be moving an object from one point to another. The animate element would smoothly move the object from the first point to the second point in a straight line.

To demonstrate this, copy the code of the previous example (Listing 15.2) and paste it into a new document. Alter the animate element to modify the x attribute (line 32 in Listing 15.3) of Cloud1, the leftmost cloud (line 31). Have the cloud move from its original x location (–20) to a place off to the right of the sky rectangle (something like 200). This can be done by altering the from and to values according to these two new positions (lines 33 and 34 respectively). You can see how this will look in Figure 15.2.

LISTING 15.3   Using the animate Element to Move an Object Along a Straight Line

```
01: <?xml version="1.0" standalone="no"?>
02: <!DOCTYPE svg PUBLIC "-//W3C//DTD SVG 20010904//EN"
03:    "http://www.w3.org/TR/2001/REC-SVG-20010904/DTD/svg10.dtd">
04:
05: <svg  width="500" height="300">
06:
07:        <style type="text/css">
08:               <![CDATA[
09:                       .FillFFFFFF{fill:#FFFFFF;}
10:                       .Fill99CCFF{fill:#99CCFF;}
```

continues

LISTING 15.3   Continued

```
11:                                    .FillFFFF00{fill:#FFFF00;}
12:                    ]]>
13:            </style>
14:
15:            <defs>
16:                    <g id="Cloud">
17:                            <circle cx="24" cy="36" r="15"/>
18:                            <circle cx="41" cy="26" r="17"/>
19:                            <circle cx="90" cy="40" r="13"/>
20:                            <circle cx="105" cy="31" r="13"/>
21:                            <ellipse cx="75" cy="20" rx="27" ry="20"/>
22:                            <ellipse cx="56" cy="50" rx="25" ry="18"/>
23:                    </g>
24:            </defs>
25:
26:            <rect id="Sky" x="10" y="45" width="200" height="245" class="Fill99CCFF"/>
27:            <circle id="Sun" cx="105" cy="160" r="56" class="FillFFFF00"/>
28:            <use id="Cloud1" xlink:href="#Cloud" x="-20" y="80" class="FillFFFFFF"/>
29:            <use id="Cloud2" xlink:href="#Cloud" x="150" y="150" class="FillFFFFFF"/>
30:
31:            <animate id="Cloud1Move" xlink:href="#Cloud1"
32:                    attributeName="x"
33:                    from="-20"
34:                    to="200"
35:                    begin="0s"
36:                    dur="5s"/>
37:
38: </svg>
```

FIGURE 15.2

Use the animate *element to move the left cloud across the sky along a straight line.*

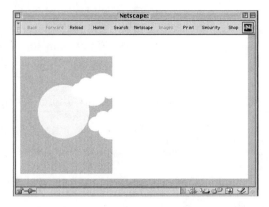

Using the animate element in this fashion provides a quick and easy way of moving an object along a straight path. There are many times, though, where you will need to move an object along a free-form path. The animateMotion element does just that, moving an object along a "motion path" that is defined using the commands for the path element. In this case, however, the motion path's data is described within a required path attribute, as opposed to the d property needed for the path element.

The animateMotion element uses many of the same attributes as the animate element while introducing another: the path attribute. Its structure looks like this:

```
<animateMotion xlink:href="#A" path="B"/>,
```

where *A* represents the object to be animated and *B* represents the motion path data (using the syntax and commands from the path element).

To illustrate the animateMotion element, try having the cloud move down and across the front of the sun. You will need to use the animateMotion element in place of the previous animate element, supplying it with a path that forms a semicircular line from the cloud's original location.

First, copy Listing 15.3 and paste it into a new document. Change the animate element into an animateMotion element (line 31 in Listing 15.4) and then delete the from and to attributes (and their corresponding values). Add a path attribute (line 32) and supply it with the path data for a curved arc (in this example, the path information has been supplied for you). Continue to have the animation start immediately upon load (line 33's begin="0s"), but change the duration (line 34) to last 11 seconds (dur="11s"); remember, many of the time controls from the animate element work with the animateMotion element. Figure 15.3 shows the cloud moving along its path over the sun.

LISTING 15.4   Using the animateMotion Element to Move an Object Along a Motion Path

```
01: <?xml version="1.0" standalone="no"?>
02: <!DOCTYPE svg PUBLIC "-//W3C//DTD SVG 20010904//EN"
03:   "http://www.w3.org/TR/2001/REC-SVG-20010904/DTD/svg10.dtd">
04:
05: <svg  width="500" height="300">
06:
07:       <style type="text/css">
08:               <![CDATA[
09:                       .FillFFFFFF{fill:#FFFFFF;}
10:                       .Fill99CCFF{fill:#99CCFF;}
11:                       .FillFFFF00{fill:#FFFF00;}
12:               ]]>
13:       </style>
14:
15:       <defs>
16:               <g id="Cloud">
17:                       <circle cx="24" cy="36" r="15"/>
```

continues

LISTING 15.4   Continued

```
18:                                    <circle cx="41" cy="26" r="17"/>
19:                                    <circle cx="90" cy="40" r="13"/>
20:                                    <circle cx="105" cy="31" r="13"/>
21:                                    <ellipse cx="75" cy="20" rx="27" ry="20"/>
22:                                    <ellipse cx="56" cy="50" rx="25" ry="18"/>
23:                    </g>
24:            </defs>
25:
26:            <rect id="Sky" x="10" y="45" width="200" height="245" class="Fill99CCFF"/>
27:            <circle id="Sun" cx="105" cy="160" r="56" class="FillFFFF00"/>
28:            <use id="Cloud1" xlink:href="#Cloud" x="-20" y="80" class="FillFFFFFF"/>
29:            <use id="Cloud2" xlink:href="#Cloud" x="150" y="150" class="FillFFFFFF"/>
30:
31:            <animateMotion id="Cloud1Move" xlink:href="#Cloud1"
32:                    path="M0,0 C25,80 180,30 300,20"
33:                    begin="0s"
34:                    dur="11s"
35:
36: </svg>
```

FIGURE 15.3

The left cloud moves across the sky and sun along an arced path using the animateMotion *element's motion path.*

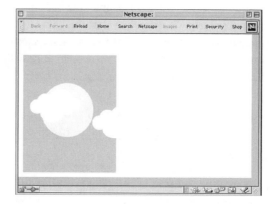

You can also apply a rotate attribute to the animateMotion element, which can rotate your object to follow the shape of the path. The rotate attribute uses one of three values that represent an angle: auto, auto-reverse, and a value. auto takes its value from the direction of the motion path; auto-reverse uses the opposite angle. A user-specified value will also rotate the object along the path according to the angle of the supplied value.

To illustrate this attribute, take the same cloud and rotate it along the curved motion path. First, copy the code from Listing 15.4 and paste it into a new document (see Listing 15.5). Next, add the rotate attribute (line 35) and supply it with a rotate value of auto. Figure 15.4 shows the rotated cloud.

LISTING 15.5   Adjusting an Object's Angle to Match the Motion Path

```
01: <?xml version="1.0" standalone="no"?>
02: <!DOCTYPE svg PUBLIC "-//W3C//DTD SVG 20010904//EN"
03:    "http://www.w3.org/TR/2001/REC-SVG-20010904/DTD/svg10.dtd">
04:
05: <svg  width="500" height="300">
06:
07:         <style type="text/css">
08:                 <![CDATA[
09:                         .FillFFFFFF{fill:#FFFFFF;}
10:                         .Fill99CCFF{fill:#99CCFF;}
11:                         .FillFFFF00{fill:#FFFF00;}
12:                 ]]>
13:         </style>
14:
15:         <defs>
16:                 <g id="Cloud">
17:                         <circle cx="24" cy="36" r="15"/>
18:                         <circle cx="41" cy="26" r="17"/>
19:                         <circle cx="90" cy="40" r="13"/>
20:                         <circle cx="105" cy="31" r="13"/>
21:                         <ellipse cx="75" cy="20" rx="27" ry="20"/>
22:                         <ellipse cx="56" cy="50" rx="25" ry="18"/>
23:                 </g>
24:         </defs>
25:
26:         <rect id="Sky" x="10" y="45" width="200" height="245" class="Fill99CCFF"/>
27:         <circle id="Sun" cx="105" cy="160" r="56" class="FillFFFF00"/>
28:         <use id="Cloud1" xlink:href="#Cloud" x="-20" y="80" class="FillFFFFFF"/>
29:         <use id="Cloud2" xlink:href="#Cloud" x="150" y="150" class="FillFFFFFF"/>
30:
31:         <animateMotion id="Cloud1Move" xlink:href="#Cloud1"
32:                 path="M0,0 C25,80 180,30 300,20"
33:                 begin="0s"
34:                 dur="11s"
35:                 rotate="auto"/>
36:
37: </svg>
```

By the very fact that the animateMotion element requires the usage of path data, it becomes a bit more difficult to visualize its effect when reviewing the code. Nonetheless, this element provides a powerful means of moving an object around in a free-form manner.

FIGURE 15.4

The animateMotion *element's* rotate *attribute enables the cloud to turn according to the direction of the motion path.*

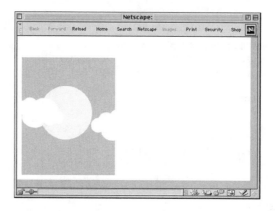

Animating a Transformation

Hour 14 introduced you to transformations and the amazing changes they spawn. Building on this knowledge, you can extend transformations by animating them. The animateTransform element does just that by applying animated transform actions to an object.

Any of the six transform functions can be animated using animateTransform. The element uses a syntax very similar to those of the previous two animation elements, as the following shows:

```
<animateTransform xlink:href="#A" attributeName="transform" type="B"
        from="C" to="D" begin="E" dur="F" />.
```

In this syntax, all the attributes similar to animate and animateMotion are consistent with their counterparts; with animateTransform, however, your attributeName value will remain transform.

There is an important new attribute added to the list: type. type tells the element which transformation property will be animated. There are only six possible values for type, and these are the same six transform functions: translate, rotate, scale, skewX, skewY, and matrix. The values listed in the from and to attributes are relative to this operator, as they define the result of the type value's function.

To see the animateTransform element in action, you can build an animation that skews the sun to its right for 5 seconds. Taking Listing 15.5 as the departure point, you can replace its animateMotion element with animateTransform (line 30 in Listing 15.6). Set the type value to skewX, and provide a to value of 45 (with an initial from value of 0 so the animation starts smoothly). Finish it off with a begin and dur value (or an end value in place of dur), and you're ready to watch the sun slide around. Figure 15.5 shows the sun skewed by the animateTransform element.

LISTING 15.6   Transitioning Between One Transformation Value and Another
with `animateTransform`

```
01: <?xml version="1.0" standalone="no"?>
02: <!DOCTYPE svg PUBLIC "-//W3C//DTD SVG 20010904//EN"
          "http://www.w3.org/TR/2001/REC-SVG-20010904/DTD/svg10.dtd">
03:
04: <svg  width="500" height="300">
05:
06:      <style type="text/css">
07:              <![CDATA[
08:                      .FillFFFFFF{fill:#FFFFFF;}
09:                      .Fill99CCFF{fill:#99CCFF;}
10:                      .FillFFFF00{fill:#FFFF00;}
11:              ]]>
12:      </style>
13:
14:      <defs>
15:              <g id="Cloud">
16:                      <circle cx="24" cy="36" r="15"/>
17:                      <circle cx="41" cy="26" r="17"/>
18:                      <circle cx="90" cy="40" r="13"/>
19:                      <circle cx="105" cy="31" r="13"/>
20:                      <ellipse cx="75" cy="20" rx="27" ry="20"/>
21:                      <ellipse cx="56" cy="50" rx="25" ry="18"/>
22:              </g>
23:      </defs>
24:
25:      <rect id="Sky" x="10" y="45" width="200" height="245" class="Fill99CCFF"/>
26:      <circle id="Sun" cx="105" cy="160" r="56" class="FillFFFF00"/>
27:      <use id="Cloud1" xlink:href="#Cloud" x="-20" y="80" class="FillFFFFFF"/>
28:      <use id="Cloud2" xlink:href="#Cloud" x="150" y="150" class="FillFFFFFF"/>
29:
30:      <animateTransform id="SunSkew" xlink:href="#Sun"
                  attributeName="transform"
                  type="skewX"
                  from="0"
                  to="45"
                  begin="0s"
                  dur="5s"/>
31:
32: </svg>
```

As you just saw, animating transformations isn't difficult. You may find that you wish to supply your transformation animation with more than one set of transitions, though. For instance, in this past example, you made the sun slide from its existing position to a skewed position to the right, at which point the animation ended. Instead, you may want to transition the sun back to its original state after it reaches its far-right position.

FIGURE 15.5

The animateTransform *element is used to animate the horizontal skew of the sun.*

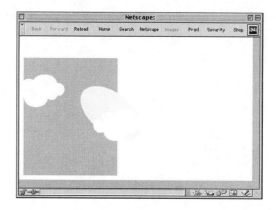

This could surely be done by adding a second animateTransform element to your document. The animateTransform element could be set to begin upon the completion of the first animation element and transition the sun from 45° back to 0°. The result of such a solution would appear similar to:

```
<animateTransform id="SunSkewOut" xlink:href="#Sun" attributeName="transform"
        type="skewX" from="0" to="45" begin="0s" dur="5s"/>
<animateTransform id="SunSkewIn" xlink:href="#Sun" attributeName="transform"
        type="skewX" from="45" to="0" begin="5s" dur="5s"/>
```

By using such a solution, however, the golden rule of coding—make your code as lean and efficient as possible—would be broken.

In this case, there is a way to make such an animation leaner and more efficient. All the animation elements can use the values attribute in place of from and to. Whereas from and to define two distinct points in an animation (the start and stop properties of the object being animated), values accepts multiple points in the progression of an animation. The syntax for this attribute is simply a series of values separated by semicolons. The result of this more optimized method will appear similar to

```
<animateTransform id="SunSkew" xlink:href="#Sun" attributeName="transform"
        type="skewX" values="0; 45; 0" begin="0s" dur="10s"/>
```

To try this out, alter Listing 15.6 by removing the from and to attributes and replacing them with a values attribute (line 34 in Listing 15.7). Provide this attribute with a value of 0; 45; 0 to allow the skewX transformation to transition from the sun's original state to a skewed state and then back to the original state. Lastly, keep the dur value at 5s to speed along the animation (line 36).

LISTING 15.7   Transitioning the `animateTransform` Between Several Transformation Values

```
01: <?xml version="1.0" standalone="no"?>
02: <!DOCTYPE svg PUBLIC "-//W3C//DTD SVG 20010904//EN"
03:    "http://www.w3.org/TR/2001/REC-SVG-20010904/DTD/svg10.dtd">
04:
05: <svg  width="500" height="300">
06:
07:         <style type="text/css">
08:                 <![CDATA[
09:                         .FillFFFFFF{fill:#FFFFFF;}
10:                         .Fill99CCFF{fill:#99CCFF;}
11:                         .FillFFFF00{fill:#FFFF00;}
12:                 ]]>
13:         </style>
14:
15:         <defs>
16:                 <g id="Cloud">
17:                         <circle cx="24" cy="36" r="15"/>
18:                         <circle cx="41" cy="26" r="17"/>
19:                         <circle cx="90" cy="40" r="13"/>
20:                         <circle cx="105" cy="31" r="13"/>
21:                         <ellipse cx="75" cy="20" rx="27" ry="20"/>
22:                         <ellipse cx="56" cy="50" rx="25" ry="18"/>
23:                 </g>
24:         </defs>
25:
26:         <rect id="Sky" x="10" y="45" width="200" height="245" class="Fill99CCFF"/>
27:         <circle id="Sun" cx="105" cy="160" r="56" class="FillFFFF00"/>
28:         <use id="Cloud1" xlink:href="#Cloud" x="-20" y="80" class="FillFFFFFF"/>
29:         <use id="Cloud2" xlink:href="#Cloud" x="150" y="150" class="FillFFFFFF"/>
30:
31:         <animateTransform id="SunSkew" xlink:href="#Sun"
32:                 attributeName="transform"
33:                 type="skewX"
34:                 values="0; 45; 0"
35:                 begin="0s"
36:                 dur="5s"/>
37:
38: </svg>
```

By replacing these attributes with the `values` attribute (line 34), new possibilities emerge. Whereas before you could animate only between two values, you now can add a series of values to be animated using a specific transformation function.

You'll notice, however, when the document is being viewed that the time spans between the initial value and the second and between the second and final values are the same. As the example ran for 5 seconds, the time between successive values is 2.5 seconds. In some cases, you may want nonuniform time lapses between values.

For instance, in this same example, you may decide that between the first and second values 4.25 seconds should elapse, leaving only 0.75 seconds left for the sun to transition back to its original state. Coding this sort of time control to correlate with a specific value in a values list requires the keyTimes attribute, which was initially mentioned in Hour 12.

As mentioned in that chapter, the keyTimes attribute relates a specific time value to a specific animation attribute's value. This is done by having the same number of values in your keyTimes attribute as in the values attribute. For every value in the values list, the SVG viewer will look to match the corresponding time value in the keyTimes list.

Using the previous example, Listing 15.7, you can add a keyTimes attribute to the document (see line 35 in Listing 15.8). The previous example had three values in its values list, 0; 45; 0 (line 34), and your new list of keyTimes values will need to match this.

If you want the first leg of the animation (the transition between angles 0 and 45) to last 4.25 seconds, you need to convert this time value to a number between 0 and 1. To do so, divide 4.25 by 5 (the duration of the animation). This value, 0.85, will become the second value in your keyTimes list, resulting in the final code: keyTimes="0; 0.85; 1" (line 35). Your animation should now play back with a slow skewing of the sun and a quick snap back to its original position after 4.25 seconds.

LISTING 15.8 Transitioning the animateTransform at Different Rates Using the keyTimes Attribute

```
01: <?xml version="1.0" standalone="no"?>
02: <!DOCTYPE svg PUBLIC "-//W3C//DTD SVG 20010904//EN"
03:     "http://www.w3.org/TR/2001/REC-SVG-20010904/DTD/svg10.dtd">
04:
05: <svg  width="500" height="300">
06:
07:         <style type="text/css">
08:                 <![CDATA[
09:                         .FillFFFFFF{fill:#FFFFFF;}
10:                         .Fill99CCFF{fill:#99CCFF;}
11:                         .FillFFFF00{fill:#FFFF00;}
12:                 ]]>
13:         </style>
14:
15:         <defs>
16:                 <g id="Cloud">
17:                         <circle cx="24" cy="36" r="15"/>
18:                         <circle cx="41" cy="26" r="17"/>
19:                         <circle cx="90" cy="40" r="13"/>
```

continues

LISTING 15.8 Continued

```
20:                              <circle cx="105" cy="31" r="13"/>
21:                              <ellipse cx="75" cy="20" rx="27" ry="20"/>
22:                              <ellipse cx="56" cy="50" rx="25" ry="18"/>
23:                     </g>
24:              </defs>
25:
26:              <rect id="Sky" x="10" y="45" width="200" height="245" class="Fill99CCFF"/>
27:              <circle id="Sun" cx="105" cy="160" r="56" class="FillFFFF00"/>
28:              <use id="Cloud1" xlink:href="#Cloud" x="-20" y="80" class="FillFFFFFF"/>
29:              <use id="Cloud2" xlink:href="#Cloud" x="150" y="150" class="FillFFFFFF"/>
30:
31:              <animateTransform id="SunSkew" xlink:href="#Sun"
32:                     attributeName="transform"
33:                     type="skewX"
34:                     values="0; 45; 0"
35:                     keyTimes="0; 0.85; 1"
36:                     begin="0s"
37:                     dur="5s"/>
38:
39: </svg>
```

Seeing keyTimes in action, you can begin to get an idea of the number of subtle animations possible. Rarely do events in reality unfold in a rhythmic, equally spaced manner, nor should your animations be bound by such constraints. Just be sure to remember to match the number of values in your keyTimes and values lists, as well as to figure your math correctly for the keyTimes values.

Animating Color Transitions

The last animation element, animateColor, seems a bit redundant, as its function is easily duplicable using the animate element. Nonetheless, animateColor exists, and it allows you to transition an object's color between a variety of hues.

Using the same syntax as the animate element, animateColor's code looks like this:

```
<animateColor xlink:href="#A" attributeName="fill" from="B" to="C" begin="D"
       end="E"/>.
```

Just as before, A represents the id of the object to be modified, D the time at which the animation should begin, and E the time at which the animation should cease. B represents the initial color value and C represents the final color value. Using these attributes, you could define a change in the sky's color with the following code:

```
<animateColor xlink:href="#Sky" attributeName="fill" from="#99CCFF" to="#318131"
       begin="0s" end="5s"/>.
```

The `attributeName` attribute can accept values that determine color application, such as `fill` and `stroke`. Also, just as you saw with the `animateTransform` element, you can replace `from` and `to` with the `values` attribute, allowing multiple color transitions to occur.

To quickly view this element in action, you can take the previous example and modify it. As you modified the color of the sun in Hour 13, apply a 10-point stroke to the sun with a lighter value than the sun's yellow. To do so, you'll need to add two new classes to your file (lines 11 and 12 in Listing 15.9) and then apply them to your `circle` element (line 28). Then replace the `animateTransform` element with the `animateColor` element, swapping the values list's values with a number of colors near the yellow hue (line 32).

In this example, you can leave off the `keyTimes` attribute. Designate the `attributeName` value to modify `stroke`, and you're done. Figure 15.6 shows one frame of the result: the sun's outline with an often-changing stroke color.

LISTING 15.9   Transitioning the `animateColor` Element Between a Series of Colors

```
01: <?xml version="1.0" standalone="no"?>
02: <!DOCTYPE svg PUBLIC "-//W3C//DTD SVG 20010904//EN"
          "http://www.w3.org/TR/2001/REC-SVG-20010904/DTD/svg10.dtd">
03:
04: <svg  width="500" height="300">
05:
06:      <style type="text/css">
07:              <![CDATA[
08:                      .FillFFFFFF{fill:#FFFFFF;}
09:                      .Fill99CCFF{fill:#99CCFF;}
10:                      .FillFFFF00{fill:#FFFF00;}
11:                      .StrokeFFFF99{stroke:#FFFF99;}
12:                      .StrokeWidth10{stroke-width:10;}
13:              ]]>
14:      </style>
15:
16:      <defs>
17:              <g id="Cloud">
18:                      <circle cx="24" cy="36" r="15"/>
19:                      <circle cx="41" cy="26" r="17"/>
20:                      <circle cx="90" cy="40" r="13"/>
21:                      <circle cx="105" cy="31" r="13"/>
22:                      <ellipse cx="75" cy="20" rx="27" ry="20"/>
23:                      <ellipse cx="56" cy="50" rx="25" ry="18"/>
24:              </g>
25:      </defs>
26:
27:      <rect id="Sky" x="10" y="45" width="200" height="245" class="Fill99CCFF"/>
```

continues

15

LISTING 15.9   Continued

```
28:          <circle id="Sun" cx="105" cy="160" r="56"
                     class="FillFFFF00 StrokeFFFF99 StrokeWidth10"/>
29:          <use id="Cloud1" xlink:href="#Cloud" x="-20" y="80" class="FillFFFFFF"/>
30:          <use id="Cloud2" xlink:href="#Cloud" x="150" y="150" class="FillFFFFFF"/>
31:
32:          <animateColor id="SunColorChange" xlink:href="#Sun"
                     attributeName="stroke" values="#FFFF99; #FFFFFF; #FFCC00;
                     #FFFF33; #FFFF99" begin="0s" dur="5s"/>
33:
34:  </svg>
```

FIGURE 15.6

*The sun's color shifts
between a series of
hues thanks to the
animateColor ele-
ment's instructions.*

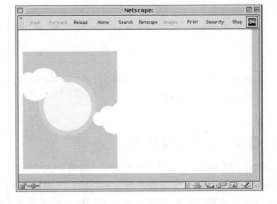

As you can see, animateColor's effects could be easily duplicated by using the
animate element with the very same attributes and attribute values. Regardless,
the animateColor element *quickly* signals to other developers (or yourself) the function of the animation.

Repeating Animations

You will often find yourself developing animations that need to loop repeatedly. SVG
offers two attributes for the elements that control animation repetition: repeatDur and
repeatCount. Each accepts one numerical value to designate the number of repetitions.

The repeatDur attribute tells the animation element to continue looping the animation
for a set period of time. For instance, if your skew example is set to animate for 5 seconds and is given a repeatDur value of 11 seconds, the 5-second skewing will be
repeated twice and reset to its original position 1 second into the third repeat.

repeatDur is used to allow repetition to occur only within a given time frame.

The repeatCount attribute, on the other hand, designates how many times a complete animation should repeat. In the same example, should your sun be set to skew for five seconds and your repeatCount value set to 11, the five-second bounce will be repeated 11 times (resulting in a 55-second animation). The loop will be played through completely for each repetition, regardless of time.

repeatCount is used to define a precise number of repetitions.

In either instance, using a value of indefinite for these attributes will loop the animation for as long as the document is open.

Frame-Based Animation

As mentioned earlier, SVG is quite different from Flash in terms of how it handles time and animation. Whereas Flash uses frames to establish its animation, SVG makes no assumptions as to how animation and time will unfold (other than the most basic assumption of a linear progression of time); the developer is left to make such determinations.

When the time-precise animation controls do not handle your requirements, you can still count on the tried-and-true nature of frame-based animation. Keep in mind, however, that the term *frame* is used loosely in SVG; no such "frame" exists. Frames will *appear* to be used by displaying groups at set intervals; whenever one group is displayed, the others are not.

To accomplish this, you can use the set element you learned about in Hour 13; set is actually considered an animation element in the W3C's SVG recommendation. Using this element, you can have groups appear and disappear based on precise numerical values (or in relation to other events), one after the other. In many ways, this is comparable to a "flip-book," a series of static images that, when viewed quickly in succession, appear to be moving.

This book has a very simple example of how to create such an effect; in the final news center graphic (Figure 1.1), there is a thunderstorm illustration with flashing lightning. This lightning bolt needs to flash intermittently, just as lightning would in the real world.

To build this example, you can create a document based on Listing 15.9's sky and cloud. You'll want to change the color of the sky and cloud to better match the environment of a thunderstorm, so you'll need to add two new values to your style sheet (lines 8 and 9 in Listing 15.10):

```
.Fill664785{fill:#664785;}
.FillFFFF00{fill:#FFFF00;}.
```

To make the scene more ominous, delete one of the cloud's uses, and center and scale the remaining cloud toward the top of the sky (line 27).

```
<use id="RainCloudForeGround" xlink:href="#Cloud" x="10" y="40"
        class="FillCCCCCC" transform="scale(1.5)"/>
```

Add to this document's `defs` section Figure 5.8's lightning bolt `polygon` illustration (line 23), and then instantiate the bolt with a `use` element, placing the bolt in the center of the sky (line 28).

```
<use id="Lightning1" xlink:href="#LightningBolt1" x="100" y="170"/>
```

With the scene now built, you can begin plotting the course of your animation. For the sake of this example, you can figure that the lightning should appear after 0.5 seconds, flashing quickly first (another 0.5 seconds), disappearing again for 0.25 seconds, and then flashing on screen again for 4 seconds before looping through the same cycle again.

Reiterating these events in terms of frames, the first frame would be empty (starting at 0 seconds and ending at 0.5 seconds), the second frame would show the lightning bolt (starting at 0.5 seconds and ending at 1 second), the third frame would also be empty (starting at 1 second and ending at 1.25 seconds), and the fourth and final frame would contain the lightning bolt (starting at 1.25 seconds and ending at 5.25 seconds). Knowing the time values desired, you can begin creating `set` elements to flash the lightning off and on.

First, you'll need to create `Frame1` (the id value signifying the first frame), the `set` element that hides the lightning bolt for the initial 0.5 seconds (line 32). To hide the bolt, you will need to adjust the `display` attribute, changing the value from `inline` to `none` (as you learned in previous chapters). The command should last for 0.5 seconds, and it will need to begin at 0 seconds to start upon the loading of the SVG document. Also, as the animation is to play through again once the fourth frame is finished, you can add a second value to the begin attribute: `Frame4.end`. This value tells `Frame1` to execute again once the `Frame4` `set` element has finished executing. (`.end` is one of the event handler suffixes that you learned about in Hours 12 and 13.) To accommodate two values in the

begin attribute, you need to separate them with a semicolon. The result of your first
frame should appear as

```
<set id="Frame1" xlink:href="#Lightning1" attributeName="display"
        from="inline" to="none" begin="0s;Frame4.end" dur="0.5s" />
```

With the first frame out of the way, you can duplicate Frame1 and rename the duplicate
Frame2 (line 31). Frame2 will also modify the display attribute, but will switch the values, going from none to inline. Again, the duration should be set to 0.5 seconds, and the
element should begin upon the end of Frame1's execution (Frame1.end). Frame 2 should
appear as

```
<set id="Frame2" xlink:href="#Lightning1" attributeName="display"
        from="none" to="inline" begin="Frame1.end" dur="0.5s" />
```

The remaining two frames can be created by duplicating Frame1 and Frame2, renaming
the Frame1 duplicate Frame3 (line 32) and renaming the Frame2 duplicate Frame4 (line 33).
Each should be set to begin upon the completion of the previous element, and both
should have their durations changed to the times listed previously. With that complete,
you are ready to watch your frame-by-frame animation unfold. Figure 15.7 shows what a
frame of this animation will look like.

LISTING 15.10   Creating a Frame-by-Frame Animation Using the set Element

```
01: <?xml version="1.0" standalone="no"?>
02: <!DOCTYPE svg PUBLIC "-//W3C//DTD SVG 20010904//EN"
             "http://www.w3.org/TR/2001/REC-SVG-20010904/DTD/svg10.dtd">
03:
04: <svg  width="500" height="300">
05:
06:        <style type="text/css">
07:                <![CDATA[
08:                        .Fill664785{fill:#664785;}
09:                        .FillFFFF00{fill:#FFFF00;}
10:                        .FillCCCCCC{fill:#CCCCCC;}
11:                ]]>
12:        </style>
13:
14:        <defs>
15:                <g id="Cloud">
16:                        <circle cx="24" cy="36" r="15"/>
17:                        <circle cx="41" cy="26" r="17"/>
18:                        <circle cx="90" cy="40" r="13"/>
19:                        <circle cx="105" cy="31" r="13"/>
20:                        <ellipse cx="75" cy="20" rx="27" ry="20"/>
```

continues

LISTING 15.10 Continued

```
21:                             <ellipse cx="56" cy="50" rx="25" ry="18"/>
22:                 </g>
23:                 <polygon id="LightningBolt1" class="FillFFFF00"
                         points="13,0 4,25 8,25 2,48 6,48 0,72 18,44 14,44 25,21
                         20,21 32,0"/>
24:         </defs>
25:
26:         <rect id="Sky" x="10" y="45" width="200" height="245" class="Fill664785"/>
27:         <use id="RainCloudForeGround" xlink:href="#Cloud" x="10" y="40"
                     class="FillCCCCCC" transform="scale(1.5)"/>
28:         <use id="Lightning1" xlink:href="#LightningBolt1" x="100" y="170"/>
29:
30:         <set id="Frame1" xlink:href="#Lightning1"
                     attributeName="display"
                     from="inline" to="none"
                     begin="0s;Frame4.end"
                     dur="0.5s" />
31:         <set id="Frame2" xlink:href="#Lightning1"
                     attributeName="display"
                     from="none" to="inline"
                     begin="Frame1.end"
                     dur="0.5s" />
32:         <set id="Frame3" xlink:href="#Lightning1"
                     attributeName="display"
                     from="inline" to="none"
                     begin="Frame2.end"
                     dur="0.25s" />
33:         <set id="Frame4" xlink:href="#Lightning1"
                     attributeName="display"
                     from="none" to="inline"
                     begin="Frame3.end"
                     dur="4s" />
34:
35: </svg>
```

FIGURE 15.7

Frame-by-frame animations are used to create effects such as the flashing of this lightning bolt.

Using the set element in such a manner allows for an effect similar to broadcast television or traditional animation. When "frames" are turned off and on so quickly that viewers cannot distinguish a lapse, they interpret the images as one cohesive progression.

Summary

Animation can certainly inject your SVG documents with life. With all the possible elements and various attributes that allow fine-tuning, virtually any animation conceivable can be replicated in SVG. Figuring out which animation element to use, however, is the challenge.

Remember that each animation has its own focus. animate focuses on transitioning between values of a specific attribute. animateMotion deals only with moving an object along a motion path, allowing more freeform movement than animate can allow. animateTransform transitions an object between various transformation states. Finally, animateColor simply shifts an object's color from one state to another.

Old-fashioned frame-by-frame animation is possible as well. By intelligently using the set element, you can turn on a series of objects in succession, creating the impression of animation or movement. Whether through tricks such as this or just the animation elements themselves, you will be hard-pressed to find an animation that SVG cannot handle.

Q&A

Q Are there elements, attributes, or properties that cannot be animated?

A Certainly. Time, for instance, cannot be changed; for example, you cannot animate the duration of another animation. Chapter 19.2.15 of the SVG Recommendation (http://www.w3.org/TR/2001/REC-SVG-20010904/) gives a list of items that can be animated. Also, for each item listed, the recommendation states clearly whether it can be animated or not. If you become frustrated with an animation, be sure to check the recommendation to see whether your animation is indeed possible. Also, check the release notes of the SVG viewer you are using to make sure it can handle such animation at its present version.

Q My animation is playing back choppily. What's wrong with my code?

A The SVG viewers currently available to the public are not fully optimized for performance comparable to Flash animation. Although this can be frustrating initially, keep in mind that this performance bottleneck will be overcome soon. Adobe's

SVG Viewer, for instance, has seen tremendous improvements in speed with each release. Also, Hour 24 covers some common problems and provides suggestions for making your code perform well in today's situations.

Workshop

The Workshop is designed to help you anticipate possible questions, review what you've learned, and begin learning how to put your knowledge into practice.

Quiz

1. What additional attribute does the `animateTransform` element need that the other animation elements do not?

2. The `keyTimes` attribute depends on which attribute for relating its time values with specific events?

3. The `dur` attribute can be used in place of which other attribute?

4. What attribute is common to all animation elements and is used to determine which object will be modified?

5. What does the animation elements' `fill` attribute determine?

Answers

1. The `animateTransform` element needs the `type` attribute to determine which transformation function will be performed.

2. The `values` attribute coordinates its values (specific attribute values) with a matching `keyTimes` value.

3. Both the `dur` and `end` attributes determine the length of an animation and can be used interchangeably, but not simultaneously.

4. The `xlink:href` attribute tells an animation element which object to modify.

5. The animation elements' `fill` attribute determines how an object is displayed upon the ending of an animation.

Exercises

1. Use `keyTimes` and `values` with the `animate` element. Alter some of the initial examples in this chapter by adding additional values and time points using these two attributes.

2. Rebuild the frame-by-frame example of the lightning bolt flashing using only one `set` element with `keyTimes` and `values`. As you will only have one `set` element, you can add a `repeatCount` attribute to it, allowing it to cycle endlessly.

Part IV
Text and Typography

Hour

Hour 16

Formatting

SVG's handling of type stands in stark contrast to HTML's handling. Designers who have always complained (somewhat rightfully) about the lack of typographic control in HTML will benefit the most from SVG's detailed level of control.

In this hour, you will learn how to

- Include text within an SVG document
- Change the size, spacing, and justification of your text
- Create groups of text and give them margins
- Bind text to a path

Understanding Text with SVG

SVG provides for all of HTML's font controls, such as

- Font designation (as well as alternative font designation)
- Type size
- Alignment
- Color

However, it adds to this list by supporting

- True font designation (through referencing font outline packages)
- Letter and word spacing
- Rendering control (whether aliased or anti-aliased)
- Binding type to a path

What's more, SVG's typographic functionality can be extended with other font technologies. For instance, SVG uses its own SVG fonts to define a typeface's character outlines, but you are not confined to this technology to embed typefaces. You can choose to use CSS2's WebFonts or Adobe's CEF technology if you are so inclined.

With CEF, you can export your entire typeface as binary data, which can be parsed by the Adobe SVG Viewer. The CEF format generally offers smaller file sizes than SVG Fonts, as it does not have to use the same plain-text syntax to define its shapes and allows developers to use one external typeface across several SVG documents. The downside to the technology is that only the Adobe viewer can display the CEF typefaces. As of press time for this book, many developers are using Adobe's CEF technology, as it is the easiest and quickest method of getting typefaces exported into an SVG-ready format. (For more information on CEF technology, please visit www.adobe.com/svg/.)

Hour 17, "Typefaces," will cover typeface designation, exporting typefaces to SVG-viewable fonts, and altering the display quality of type.

Before you dive into using type in your graphics, you should review the list of terms to be used in this group of chapters. For those unfamiliar with typographic vocabulary, Figure 16.1 illustrates various terms to be used, and Table 16.1 defines them.

FIGURE 16.1
Typography uses a variety of specific terms to specify its control.

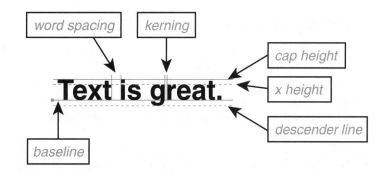

16

TABLE 16.1 Text Terms

Term	Description
Baseline	The invisible rule on which all typographic forms align the base of their letterforms.
Descender	The portions of letters such as *g* and *y* that extend below the baseline.
x height	The invisible rule on which the tops of most lowercase letterforms align.
Cap height	The invisible rule on which all capital letters align the tops of their letterforms.
Leading	The amount of space, measured in points, between baselines, determining the space between rows of type (handled by the `dy` attribute).
Kerning	The amount of space determined by typographic designers to be optimal between letter pairs (for example, the distance between the letters *T* and *e* in "Text"). Most fonts have "kerning pairs," which establish the amount of space for every possible character combination. Traditionally, kerning is applied specifically to a combination of two letters.
Letter spacing	Often confused with kerning, the amount of space between characters in addition to the amount determined by kerning. Letter spacing is applied across a body of text, providing an equal amount of space between adjacent letters.
Word spacing	Determines the space between words.

Including Text in Your Document

Text in SVG is handled considerably differently than in HTML. The name HTML (Hypertext Markup Language) alone suggests considerable concern as to the handling of text; the name SVG (Scalable Vector Graphics) suggests an emphasis elsewhere. Whereas HTML is focused on formatting text, with the addition of graphics as a postscript to the language, SVG focuses largely on the precise visual presentation of content, whether it is graphics or text.

SVG's attention to detail in how it displays its text comes at a price. Whereas the vagaries of HTML allow massive amounts of text to be freely formed and resized according to the user's environment, SVG requires precise coordinates for each line of text. This level of control allows SVG code to define complex typographical functions unavailable in other Web technologies. However, SVG is not well suited for handling large bodies of text; instead, SVG is accommodating of other XML technologies (such as XHTML) that can handle the management of such text.

SVG's handling of text may seem awkward at first. Whereas HTML assumes that text should wrap according to the dimensions of the user's browser window, SVG makes no such assumptions. In fact, SVG doesn't even support text wrapping or multiline text formatting (what most designers view as a text box, where text conforms to a set width and flows vertically as long as needed). Rather, SVG's support for text is really more focused on how text is included in *graphics*—short, little bursts of information (generally on one or two lines).

So what does this mean for you as an SVG developer or designer? Ironically, the very emphasis on the graphic nature of SVG is what makes the format best suited for designers concerned about the appearance of their text. By allowing designers precise control over the presentation of their type, SVG is forced to sacrifice some of the flexibility and assumptions inherent in HTML.

To provide an example of the difference between SVG's and HTML's handling of text, consider the example in Figure 16.2.

In HTML, the text would be encoded in one large block, with the user's browser interpreting the display and occasionally wrapping lines according to the code's specifications as to font, size, and justification.

In SVG, however, the code is very different. Each line is hard-coded beforehand, similar to the way a book's lines never change. Line breaks, if there are any (in this case, there are not), are where they are; no bending or flexing of the viewer's window bumps words to a new line.

An SVG viewer makes no assumptions about wrapping text. With the lack of information defining where and how each line should be broken and placed, the text appears as one

FIGURE 16.2

Text is displayed in a different manner between HTML and SVG.

> Scalable Vector Graphics (SVG) is an amazing new format engineered to provide both designers and developers a flexible manner to encode graphic information in an easy-to-read, standards-based XML grammar.

> Scalable Vector Graphics (SVG) is an amazing

HTML presentation of the following code:

```
<html>

    <body>
    Scalable Vector
    Graphics (SVG) is an
    amazing new format
    engineered to provide
    both designers and
    developers a flexible
    manner to encode
    graphic information in
    an easy-to-read,
    standards-based XML
    grammar.
    </body>

</html>
```

SVG presentation of the following code:

```
<svg>

    <text x="15" y="20">
    Scalable Vector
    Graphics (SVG) is an
    amazing new format
    engineered to provide
    both designers and
    developers a flexible
    manner to encode
    graphic information in
    an easy-to-read,
    standards-based XML
    grammar.
    </text>

</svg>
```

16

long line. Although SVG is similar to HTML in that it does rely on the code to establish its font, size, and justification, it also relies on the code to determine its exact placement within the document. There is no guessing as to margins or location with SVG; each must be defined beforehand in code.

Text is inserted in a document, rather straightforwardly, by using the `text` element. The text to be displayed is contained within the element's open and close tags. The element often uses two attributes to define its content's placement: the x and y attributes.

The function of these two attributes is somewhat similar to that of the x and y attributes of the `rect` element, with one major difference. Whereas the `rect` element's x and y attributes define the location of the top left corner of the rectangle, the `text` element's x and y attributes define the location of the text insertion point.

The y attribute effectively establishes the baseline's coordinate on the Y-axis, whereas the x attribute determines the position on the X-axis where text begins. (Remember, the baseline is the invisible line upon which most text characters sit upon; see Figure 16.1.) Unless specified otherwise, text will flow in a positive direction to the right of the x attribute value's coordinate. (You will learn how to specify text alignment later in this hour.)

Thus, the syntax for this element is

```
<text x="A" y="B">…</text>
```

In this case, *A* and *B* represent the coordinates of the text insertion point (that is, in this case, the leftmost edge of the text's baseline).

To test this, try creating a simple document with the `text` element. As this is just a quick test, just place the element at the coordinates (100,100) (done by populating the element's x and y attributes; see line 6 in Listing 16.1), and provide a couple lines of sample text (lines 7 and 8) before closing off the element (line 9).

LISTING 16.1   Inserting Type onto a Single Line Using the `text` Element

```
01: <?xml version="1.0" standalone="no"?>
02: <!DOCTYPE svg PUBLIC "-//W3C//DTD SVG 20010904//EN"
            "http://www.w3.org/TR/2001/REC-SVG-20010904/DTD/svg10.dtd">
03:
04: <svg  width="500" height="300">
05:
06:        <text x="100" y="100">
07:                This is an example of SVG text.
08:                It is bold, fresh, and odor-free!
09:        </text>
10:
11: </svg>
```

The result of this code is shown in Figure 16.3.

FIGURE 16.3

Text is inserted in an SVG document using the text *element.*

The size, weight, and typeface that your viewer uses to present this example's result may vary considerably from Figure 16.3. Such specifications are determined by your viewer (or viewer's container, such as a browser) and can generally be set in such an environment's settings or preferences. Specifying the display, however, is possible and will be covered later in this chapter and in the next.

As mentioned before, an SVG viewer does not know to wrap text, even if the lines are broken within the code as you see in Listing 16.1. So how can you create multiple lines of text? The simplest way involves making as many text elements as you have lines of text.

For instance, in Listing 16.1, if you wanted to break lines 7 and 8 so that the final display's result was on one line, you could create two separate text elements. The first element will contain line 7 (lines 6 through 8 in Listing 16.2), and the second element will contain line 8 (lines 9 through 11 in Listing 16.2). Obviously, the y value for the second text element will need to change to position the baseline of the second line under the first.

16

LISTING 16.2   Creating Multiple Lines of Text Using Multiple text Elements

```
01: <?xml version="1.0" standalone="no"?>
02: <!DOCTYPE svg PUBLIC "-//W3C//DTD SVG 20010904//EN"
            "http://www.w3.org/TR/2001/REC-SVG-20010904/DTD/svg10.dtd">
03:
04: <svg  width="500" height="300">
05:
06:        <text x="100" y="100">
07:                This is an example of SVG text.
08:        </text>
09:        <text x="100" y="115">
10:                It is bold, fresh, and odor-free!
11:        </text>
12:
13: </svg>
```

The result of this code is shown in Figure 16.4.

FIGURE 16.4

Multiple text *elements can be used to create multiple lines of text.*

Text Boxes

Having successfully created multiline text, try selecting the text within your viewer's window. Just as in HTML, when your cursor nears text, it changes to an I-beam cursor, allowing you to select the type. You will notice in this case, though, that you are capable of selecting only one line of text, not both. This is because SVG viewers consider each text element to be a unique and independent chunk of text.

Naturally, you will have instances where you will want to create a continuous chunk of text (such as a paragraph to allow users to select and copy the whole text). To accommodate this, SVG offers a text subelement: tspan. The tspan element serves as a child of a master text element. This means that you can insert multiple tspan elements within one text element, and an SVG viewer will render them as one continuous block of text.

The syntax for tspan is identical to that for text:

```
<tspan x="A" y="B">…</tspan>.
```

As before, A and B represent the coordinates of the leftmost point of the text's baseline. As tspan contains its own set of baseline coordinates, any coordinates given to the master text element via the x and y attributes will be ignored; thus, when using tspan elements within a text element, you can leave the x and y attributes off the text element.

Try creating a document with tspan elements by modifying Listing 16.2. Move each line of text within its own tspan element, and transfer the x and y attributes and values over to the tspan elements. After you do so, your code should appear similar to Listing 16.3.

LISTING 16.3 Creating Multiple Lines of Text That Are Selectable Together

```
01: <?xml version="1.0" standalone="no"?>
02: <!DOCTYPE svg PUBLIC "-//W3C//DTD SVG 20010904//EN"
            "http://www.w3.org/TR/2001/REC-SVG-20010904/DTD/svg10.dtd">
03:
04: <svg  width="500" height="300">
05:
06:      <text>
07:              <tspan x="100" y="100">
08:                     This is an example of SVG text.
09:              </tspan>
10:              <tspan x="100" y="115">
11:                     It is bold, fresh, and odor-free!
12:              </tspan>
13:      </text>
14:
15: </svg>
```

At first glance, you will not be able to discern any changes to your new document; Listings 16.2 and 16.3 should render exactly the same. However, the latter document will allow multiple line selection. In fact, you should be able to select and copy the text, allowing for pasting within another application.

Adjusting Margins and Leading with the dx and dy Attributes

Now that you're able to add text, and consistent blocks of text, you can investigate adding margins to your text. In certain cases, you may find that offsetting your text from an edge or indenting certain lines of text becomes necessary. To accomplish this, there are two optional attributes that can be added to the tspan element: dx and dy. Both of these attributes determine the offset of the leftmost edge of the baseline; dx moves the edge horizontally, and dy moves the baseline vertically. Each accepts only numerical values to determine the amount of offset.

One example of the use of these attributes is indenting the first line of a text block, similar to a newspaper or book's handling of text. To try such an alteration, take Listing 16.3 as a starting point. Because an indentation in the left edge of the text would entail only a horizontal move of the first line, you only need to add a dx element to your first tspan element (see line 7 in Listing 16.4).

LISTING 16.4   Adding an Indent to tspan Elements by Using the dx Attribute

```
01: <?xml version="1.0" standalone="no"?>
02: <!DOCTYPE svg PUBLIC "-//W3C//DTD SVG 20010904//EN"
           "http://www.w3.org/TR/2001/REC-SVG-20010904/DTD/svg10.dtd">
03:
04: <svg  width="500" height="300">
05:
06:     <text>
07:             <tspan x="100" y="100" dx="15">
08:                     This is an example of SVG text.
09:             </tspan>
10:             <tspan x="100" y="115">
11:                     It is bold, fresh, and odor-free!
12:             </tspan>
13:     </text>
14:
15: </svg>
```

As you can tell from Figure 16.5, the first line of text is now indented.

Just as the dx attribute is used to define the adjustment of the character insertion point's
position on the X-axis, the dy attribute defines the same along the Y-axis. Thus, by determining the vertical distance between one line of text and another, the dy attribute can be
used to define line position in terms of leading (rather than coordinates).

Consider your previous example (Listing 16.4). To define the starting point of each line,
you added x and y attributes to each tspan element (lines 7 and 10); these attributes'
values designated the coordinates of the character insertion point of each line of text.
Although this method allows precise placement of your text, should you decide to move
your text block up 10 units, you would need to modify both y attribute values.

The value of the dy attribute comes to light in such situations. Instead of defining each
tspan element with a y attribute, you can apply the y attribute to the text group's master
text element; relative positioning between each line of text can be addressed then using
the dy attribute.

The value of the dy attribute will determine the vertical distance between the element it
belongs to and the previous element. By defining the text line's vertical position in terms
of distance from the previous line instead of precise coordinate locations, you are effectively determining the leading of your text.

To see the dy attribute in application, copy the code from Listing 16.4 and paste it into a
new document (Listing 16.5). Delete the dx attribute and its value, and move the y
attribute and its value from the first tspan element (line 8) and place it inside the text
element (line 7). This will determine the baseline's position on the Y-axis.

Next, delete the y attribute and its value from the second tspan element (line 11). Add a
dy attribute to this element (also line 11), and supply it with a value that provides an
optimal vertical distance between its line of text and the previous line, such as 15 units,

to mirror the distance defined in the previous example. Finally, to further show the value of the dy attribute, duplicate the second tspan element (line 14). The result of this code should appear similar to Figure 16.6.

LISTING 16.5   Determining the Vertical Spacing Between Lines of Text Using the dy Attribute

```
01: <?xml version="1.0" standalone="no"?>
02: <!DOCTYPE svg PUBLIC "-//W3C//DTD SVG 20010904//EN"
03:    "http://www.w3.org/TR/2001/REC-SVG-20010904/DTD/svg10.dtd">
04:
05: <svg  width="500" height="300">
06:
07:        <text y="100">
08:              <tspan x="100">
09:                      This is an example of SVG text.
10:              </tspan>
11:              <tspan x="100" dy="15">
12:                      It is bold, fresh, and odor-free!
13:              </tspan>
14:              <tspan x="100" dy="15">
15:                      Just add letters and mix.
16:              </tspan>
17:        </text>
18:
19: </svg>
```

FIGURE 16.6

Lines of text can have their leading adjusted using the dy attribute.

Now, with this code created, if you alter the y attribute value of the text element, the baselines of the subsequent tspan elements are calculated against the new value. Though the value of such an optimization may seem small when viewed in terms of three lines of text, larger bodies will invariably benefit from the use of the dy attribute to define leading instead of coordinate position.

Size

One of the most common changes you will make to your text is determining its point size. Point size is applied via a style property. By applying the `font-size` property to a `text` or `tspan` element, you can specify the size of the enclosed text. The property's syntax

`font-size:x`

allows for a variety of inputs for the numerical value and its input identifier (*x*). The most common are points (`pt`) and pixels (`px`), as these are the measurement values used in most design programs. (The identifiers are the same as those listed in the "units of measurement" chart in Hour 4.) Thus, if you want text that is 12 points in size, you would apply the following style command: `font-size:12pt`.

To change the point size of the example you've already done, take Listing 16.3 and add a style class for 18-point text: `font-size:18pt` (see line 8 in Listing 16.6). Then apply this class to your `text` element (line 12), which will pass this style information to its contained `tspan` elements, rendering both lines as 18-point type.

LISTING 16.6   Type Size Can Be Changed Using the `font-size` Style Property

```
01: <?xml version="1.0" standalone="no"?>
02: <!DOCTYPE svg PUBLIC "-//W3C//DTD SVG 20010904//EN"
            "http://www.w3.org/TR/2001/REC-SVG-20010904/DTD/svg10.dtd">
03:
04: <svg  width="500" height="300">
05:
06:         <style type="text/css">
07:                 <![CDATA[
08:                         .FontSize18{font-size:18pt;}
09:                 ]]>
10:         </style>
11:
12:         <text class="FontSize18">
13:                 <tspan x="100" y="100">
14:                         This is an example of SVG text.
15:                 </tspan>
16:                 <tspan x="100" y="115">
17:                         It is bold, fresh, and odor-free!
18:                 </tspan>
19:         </text>
20:
21: </svg>
```

Figure 16.7 illustrates this code, showing the text's size increased to 18 points.

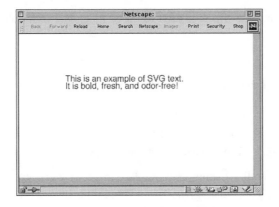

FIGURE 16.7

Type size can be changed using the font-size *style property.*

Subsequently, you could create another style command with a different point size and apply it to one of the tspan elements. As you learned in Hour 6's review of style application, SVG renders the style command closest to the element. Thus, if you have a point size declaration on the master text element and a point size declaration on a child tspan element, the tspan's declaration will be the one rendered.

Spacing

In the review of the terminology of typography at the beginning of this chapter, the differences between kerning and letter spacing were discussed. SVG offers control over both; however, specific control over kerning is more complex than the subject matter of this book permits. Hence, the more common and easy-to-apply alteration, spacing, will be covered in this book.

If you're truly a typographic fanatic, review the second exercise at the end of this chapter for a quick and dirty method of kerning between letter pairs. Or, if you'd like to learn more about SVG's defined method of kerning, read Chapter 20.7 of the W3C SVG Recommendation, "The hkern and vkern elements."

As mentioned earlier, there are two types of spacing in SVG: letter spacing and word spacing. Letter spacing determines a uniform distance to be inserted between letters, thus "spacing" the letters from each other. Word spacing is quite similar, except that it modifies only the space between words.

To apply either of these effects to text, you need to apply a style command. Letter spacing uses the syntax

`letter-spacing:x`

Word spacing uses the syntax

`word-spacing:x`

In each case, *x* represents a numerical value that can include a measurement unit suffix (same as `font-size`). If no measurement unit is specified, pixels (px) are assumed.

To try these out, modify Listing 16.6. Replace the `font-size` style class with two new classes (lines 8 and 9 in Listing 16.7)—one providing 10-pixel letter spacing (`letter-spacing:10`) and the other 10-pixel word spacing (`word-spacing:10`). Then apply the `letter-spacing` class to your first `tspan` element (line 14) and the `word-spacing` class to your second `tspan` element (line 17). When you load the result in your viewer (Figure 16.8), you will see that the first row of text is uniformly spaced between letters and words (as the space between words is technically a blank letter), whereas the second row has large spaces between the words.

LISTING 16.7   The Spacing Between Letters and Words Can Be Changed with Style Applications

```
01: <?xml version="1.0" standalone="no"?>
02: <!DOCTYPE svg PUBLIC "-//W3C//DTD SVG 20010904//EN"
            "http://www.w3.org/TR/2001/REC-SVG-20010904/DTD/svg10.dtd">
03:
04: <svg  width="500" height="300">
05:
06:      <style type="text/css">
07:            <![CDATA[
08:                  .FontLetterSpacing10{letter-spacing:10;}
09:                  .FontWordSpacing10{word-spacing:10;}
10:            ]]>
11:      </style>
12:
13:      <text>
14:            <tspan x="100" y="100" class=" FontLetterSpacing10">
15:                  This is an example of SVG text.
16:            </tspan>
17:            <tspan x="100" y="115" class=" FontWordSpacing10">
18:                  It is bold, fresh, and odor-free!
19:            </tspan>
20:      </text>
21:
22: </svg>
```

FIGURE 16.8

The spacing between letters and words can be changed with style applications.

By increasing the space between words and letters, you can add some "air" to your text. This can come in useful for both headlines and instances where your type is very small. When type is small, anti-aliasing (smoothing of the edges) can blend letters together, making them difficult to read (see Hour 17 for a more in-depth discussion of anti-aliasing). Thus, having `letter-spacing` styles to apply can significantly increase the legibility in such instances.

Be careful, though, with your application of spacing. If you apply too much space between letters and words, people may not make the connections and read the words as random individual letters. Or, as in the case of the previous example, if more space is added, people may begin to group text vertically instead of horizontally if the baselines remain close together.

Justification

Another common typographic adjustment is text alignment. In certain instances, you may wish to have multiple lines of text align along their centers or their right edges. To accommodate this urge, you can use the `text-anchor` style. This property is defined with the syntax

```
text-anchor:x
```

where x is one of three values: `start`, `middle`, or `end`. The first value, `start`, rarely needs to be applied, as it is the assumed value. (Every example you've seen thus far automatically started the text from the leftmost edge.) The `middle` value centers the text, and the `end` value aligns the right (or "end") edges. All of these values refer to alignment of the text according to the x and y attribute values of the text's `text` or `tspan` elements.

To try this adjustment yourself, take Listing 16.6 and swap the spacing classes with a
text-anchor class. Set the value of the text-anchor property to middle to align
the text lines along their centerpoints (line 8 in Listing 16.8), and then apply the class
to the text element (line 12). Now both lines will appear to be centered according to
their tspan's x attribute value (see Figure 16.9). (Because the two lines of text were so
similar in length in Listing 16.7, the second line was reduced in this example for a more
dramatic effect.)

LISTING 16.8   Aligning Text Using the text-anchor Style Property

```
01: <?xml version="1.0" standalone="no"?>
02: <!DOCTYPE svg PUBLIC "-//W3C//DTD SVG 20010904//EN"
            "http://www.w3.org/TR/2001/REC-SVG-20010904/DTD/svg10.dtd">
03:
04: <svg  width="500" height="300">
05:
06:        <style type="text/css">
07:                <![CDATA[
08:                        .FontTextAnchorMiddle{text-anchor:middle;}
09:                ]]>
10:        </style>
11:
12:        <text class="FontTextAnchorMiddle">
13:                <tspan x="100" y="100">
14:                        This is an example of SVG text.
15:                </tspan>
16:                <tspan x="100" y="115">
17:                        It is bold.
18:                </tspan>
19:        </text>
20:
21: </svg>
```

FIGURE 16.9

*Text can be aligned
using the* text-anchor
style property.

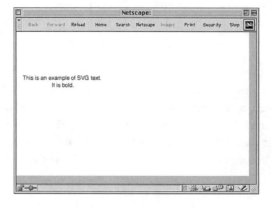

It is important to remember the difference in syntax and vocabulary between SVG and
HTML when handling justification (and virtually all other font and text manipulations).
Whereas HTML uses "center" and "right" to describe its alignment, SVG uses "middle"
and "end"; subtle changes like this may take a while to become accustomed to.

Text Along a Path

16

When desktop publishing tools first hit the mainstream market in the 1980s, applying
gradients and wrapping text along a path were two of the hottest functions every designer
wanted to play with. Twenty years have passed, and thankfully the desire to use these
effects incessantly has waned. However, no self-respecting graphics tool or technology
would be complete without the obligatory text-on-a-path function.

SVG doesn't let the graphics community down; text-on-a-path is handled by the
textPath element. The textPath element is contained within the text element and references an outside path to render the text along. The syntax for the element

```
<textPath xlink:href="#pathID">…</textPath>
```

requires that a path with an id value of *pathID* (or whatever name you give the path)
exist in the document.

To experiment with this element, you can wrap a short chunk of text around the raindrop
path you created in Listing 5.11. If you remember correctly, this example first illustrated
the use of relative path commands.

First, copy the code from Listing 5.11 and paste it into a new document. When you view
this file in your browser, you will see that the drop is located in the far top left corner and
is rather small. First, you can scale the path by a factor of 2 using the transform attribute
(line 8 in Listing 16.9); then, as this path was drawn using relative coordinates (by using
lowercase path commands), you can give the drop new starting coordinates (line 9) to
center it on the page, and the remaining coordinates will render according to this new
location.

With the path established, you can move this data (lines 8 through 13) into the definitions
area (defs) and begin work on the text. The next step will be to create a text element
(line 16) and a textPath element inside that (line 17). Link your textPath element to the
id value Raindrop (the id value of the path element on line 8), and insert a line of text
within this element (line 18). With this step, your textPath document is complete, and the
results can be seen in Listing 16.9.

LISTING 16.9   Wrapping Text Around a Path to Create Interesting Results

```
01: <?xml version="1.0" standalone="no"?>
02: <!DOCTYPE svg PUBLIC "-//W3C//DTD SVG 20010904//EN"
03:    "http://www.w3.org/TR/2001/REC-SVG-20010904/DTD/svg10.dtd">
04:
05: <svg  width="500" height="300">
06:
07:      <defs>
08:              <path id="RainDrop" transform="scale(2)"
09:                     d="M100,50
10:                     c 0,0 -16,24 -16,33
11:                     c 0,9 7,15 16,15
12:                     c 9,0 16,-7 16,-15
13:                     c 0,-9 -16,-33 -16,-33"/>
14:      </defs>
15:
16:      <text>
17:              <textPath xlink:href="#RainDrop">
18:                     Raindrops keep falling on my head.
19:              </textPath>
20:      </text>
21:
22: </svg>
```

Figure 16.10 shows the text wrapping around the raindrop path.

FIGURE 16.10

Text can be wrapped around a path to create interesting results.

The `textPath` element allows you to wrap your text along a path for the length of the path. If your text runs longer than the length of your path, it will be displayed only up to the point of the end of the path. You can also add any sort of typographic control, such as size, justification, or typeface, to further manipulate the display of the text on the path.

Summary

Text in SVG is somewhat different from the HTML medium that so many developers are accustomed to. However, if you are familiar with CSS and design programs, the level of typographic control will seem both familiar and welcome. The ability to set the size, spacing, justification, and indentation, as well as bind text to a path, not only keeps SVG on par with other technologies (such as HTML and CSS), but elevates it above the capabilities of other technologies.

In the next Hour, you'll learn to use specific typefaces with your SVG documents to communicate additional information beyond the message of the text alone.

16

Q&A

Q I really need my text to wrap automatically. Is there truly no way for SVG to handle this?

A The technology itself is not really capable of managing this function. However, SVG developer Kevin Lindsey has posted a method that accomplishes this on some level. You can access his examples and documentation at `http://www.kevlindev.com`. Even if you are uninterested in text wrapping, Lindsey provides some amazing examples of the possibilities of SVG.

Q How do I change the color of my text?

A The `text` element and its child elements (`tspan` and `textPath`) accept the same `fill` and `stroke` style properties as any other SVG object. Apply `fill` and `stroke` classes to text elements the same as you would to any other object.

Workshop

The Workshop is designed to help you anticipate possible questions, review what you've learned, and begin learning how to put your knowledge into practice.

Quiz

1. True or false: SVG's text handling is similar to HTML's.
2. What element must the `tspan` element reside within?
3. Type size in SVG is assigned using what style property?
4. What value does the `text-anchor` style property require to center text?
5. True or false: The default unit of measurement for the `letter-spacing` style property is the centimeter.

Answers

1. False. SVG handles text in a completely different manner than HTML and does not include the ability to wrap text based on window dimensions.

2. The `tspan` element is a child of the `text` element. Multiple `tspan` elements can reside within the `text` element to create a text block of multiple lines.

3. Type size is applied using the `font-size` style property.

4. The `middle` value is assigned to the `text-anchor` style property to align lines of text along their centerpoints.

5. False. The default unit of measurement for the `letter-spacing` style property is the pixel.

Exercises

1. Try simulating kerning the letter pairs in the word "Josephine" by using `tspan` elements and their associated `dx` attributes. Surround each letter in the word with a `tspan` element. Move the letters closer or farther from each other by modifying their dx positions, starting with the second letter ("o") and moving right towards the final letter ("e"). First, contract the letters very close together, and then experiment with adding more air between the letters. Examine how the legibility of the word (as a word, not a series of letters) increases or decreases depending on the changes you make.

2. Replace the `path` data in Listing 16.8 with some of the other path data you've created (such as the lightning bolt). Examine the differences in how the text's letterforms move around soft arcs and sharp edges.

HOUR 17

Typefaces

Having text rendered in a specific typeface can communicate a visual message in addition to the text's message. Designers have long enjoyed the flexibility of computer-aided design, with extensive letterform control just a few mouse clicks away. When HTML and subsequent online technologies emerged, all that had been viewed as beautiful and promising with digital technology was thrown out the window; suddenly, precise layouts and typographic control were a thing of the past. Generalities ruled the online world.

Choosing between Verdana and Times New Roman often felt like choosing the lesser of two evils in communicating typographically on the Web. Whereas most online standards have fallen short of providing true typographic solutions, SVG stands as a real contender in this arena. By being able to use a specific typeface and have it render for *every* viewer (not just Netscape 4.73 PC users), SVG is beginning to bring online viewing up to the standards that the offline world has enjoyed for centuries. Thus, in the minds of designers, SVG's typographic control puts it in an entirely different class of interactive technologies.

In this hour, you will learn a considerable amount about typefaces and their inclusion in SVG. Specifically, you will learn

- The fundamental concepts of typefaces
- How to apply generic font classifications to your text
- How to apply system fonts to your text
- Creating and using SVG Fonts
- How to alter the quality of your typeface display

Having just learned in the last hour how to incorporate text into your documents, you are now ready to explore how to finesse that text's appearance.

Understanding Typefaces

How does SVG allow for true typeface display across all viewers? What separates this technology from previous standards? To start with, SVG was designed with the express goal of supporting actual typefaces beyond what a user has installed on his or her machine. To accommodate this, SVG was created to accept its own SVG Fonts format, as well as existing typeface standards such as CSS2's WebFonts. Both formats allow designers to encode the typefaces used in their work into a format that an SVG viewer can understand.

Neither format is similar to system fonts, which actually reside on an end user's computer. System fonts generally contain information, such as bitmaps, that optimize typeface display at specific sizes and contain complex kerning-pair information. SVG Fonts, on the other hand, contain only the letterform outlines of specific characters in a typeface. In some cases, an SVG Font may contain only one character; in others, it may contain several or all characters in a typeface. By being composed of only outlines, SVG Fonts can scale cleanly to any size, but they cannot contain "hinting" information that optimizes display at different point sizes.

Because of this, SVG allows for the use of alternative technologies to handle typeface encoding and inclusion. Developers can use the CSS2 WebFonts technology, the Adobe CEF (Compact Embedded Font) technology, or other technologies capable of interfacing with the SVG specification. These alternative technologies also contain outline information, but may have more optimized methods of storing characters and may carry hinting information.

For more information on WebFonts, visit www.w3.org/tr/rec-css2/fonts.html.

The ability to encode specific typefaces for display on all potential SVG viewers is obviously quite beneficial to designers. Suddenly, the specificity of print is available to Web graphics, and the former confinements of typeface selection make previous technologies seem somewhat antiquated. This is, however, not to say that SVG cannot take advantage of the generalities that HTML and other technologies enjoy in typeface specification. For instance, SVG can reference a user's system fonts or a typeface classification to display text.

Font Classifications

To begin learning how to specify typefaces, you can explore the use of system fonts and classifications. This will seem, in many ways, like familiar terrain, as HTML uses a similar method. Fonts, whether system or encoded, are applied to text elements using the font-family style property. This property, like most others, uses a very simple syntax:

font-family:*name*

where *name* is the name of a system font, a font classification, or an encoded font's name.

Font classifications are general categories used to describe a type. There are six common font classification families: proportional, serif, sans-serif, monospace, cursive, and fantasy. Fonts such as Times New Roman, Bodoni, and Palatino are serif fonts. As a designer/developer, you know that an end user's computer has *a* serif font; you just don't know which font that may be. By using a classification term, you can ensure that text is at least rendered in the general appearance of a classification family (such as serif).

Often, a user can specify the typeface to be used for each classification by changing the browser's settings. Most users, however, leave the application's settings alone. In such cases, using the font classifications instead of specific names will often result in the following interpretations:

Font Classification	Mac	PC
Proportional	Times New Roman	Courier New
Sans-Serif	Helvetica	Arial
Serif	Times New Roman	Times New Roman
Monospace	Courier New	Courier New
Cursive	Geneva	Comic Sans
Fantasy	Comic Sans	Broadway BT

17

For anyone who has coded HTML before, such font classifications will seem familiar. HTML provides no ability to ensure that every viewer sees the same typeface, so many developers have resorted to using these classifications (sometimes as a fallback in case specific designated typefaces are not on a user's machine).

Because of this familiarity, using font classifications serves as a good beginning point in the application of typefaces to SVG text. To begin learning, you can modify the code in Listing 16.7, where you learned about letter- and word-spacing. First create two font-family classes: one for serif fonts (serif) and one for sans-serif fonts (sans-serif) (see lines 8 and 9 in Listing 17.1). Next apply the serif class to the first line of text (line 14) and the sans-serif class to the second line of text (line 17).

With those classes applied, the first line of text will likely render in Times New Roman, and the second line will likely render in Arial or Helvetica (depending on your computer platform). The result should appear similar to Figure 17.1.

LISTING 17.1   Displaying Text According to a Typographic Classification

```
01: <?xml version="1.0" standalone="no"?>
02: <!DOCTYPE svg PUBLIC "-//W3C//DTD SVG 20010904//EN"
            "http://www.w3.org/TR/2001/REC-SVG-20010904/DTD/svg10.dtd">
03:
04: <svg  width="500" height="300">
05:
06:       <style type="text/css">
07:               <![CDATA[
08:                       .FontSerif{font-family:serif;}
09:                       .FontSansSerif{font-family:sans-serif;}
10:               ]]>
11:       </style>
12:
13:       <text>
14:               <tspan x="100" y="100" class="FontSerif">
15:                       This is an example of SVG text.
16:               </tspan>
17:               <tspan x="100" y="115" class="FontSansSerif">
18:                       It is bold, fresh, and odor-free!
19:               </tspan>
20:       </text>
21:
22: </svg>
```

FIGURE 17.1

The two different type-
faces are applied using
generic font classifica-
tion names.

With the `font-family` property applied to your text, it can appear within a specific range
of typefaces. This ensures that the general appearance of the type is maintained regardless of what fonts an end user may have.

System Fonts

The `font-family` property allows for more than just font classifications. You can also
apply system fonts (fonts already on an end user's computer) to your SVG text. Using
the same property as before, you can apply specific font names by using `font-`
`family:'fontName'`, where *fontName* is the specific name of a typeface. Note, however,
that the font name is surrounded by single or double quote marks; this allows you to
include spaces within a typeface name.

For instance, the typeface Times New Roman should be applied as `'Times New Roman'`,
because `'TimesNewRoman'` is not recognized by the operating system as the name of that
typeface. Often you can find the name of a font in your word processing or design program by perusing the names in the pull-down list of available fonts. Again, be sure to
note any spaces or suffixes, such as "MS" in "Comic Sans MS." Referring to `'Comic`
`Sans'` will not apply Comic Sans MS.

Obviously, there can be a number of different names for one typeface (as in the Comic
Sans example). Thus, there is a method with which you can designate more than one font
name to a `font-family` property. Similar to the manner in which HTML handles the
determination of typefaces, you can list multiple font names, separated by commas,
within the `font-family` property. The syntax remains the same:

```
font-family:'fontName1','fontName2','fontName3'
```

Fonts should be listed in descending order, as the first font in the list that *can* be applied *will* be applied. Thus, it often makes good design sense to add one of the font classification names at the end of a `font-family` property. For instance, should you want to apply the font Arial to your text, consider applying `font-family:'Arial',sans-serif`. (Remember, the font classification names do not need quote marks surrounding them.)

To explore this property, you can apply different fonts to each line of text in the previous example. You can add specific typefaces to your code, ensuring that a viewer will render them if available.

Modifying Listing 17.1, add `'Times New Roman'` to your first `font-family` class (line 8 in Listing 17.2) and `'Charcoal'` and `'Helvetica'` to your second `font-family` class (line 9). Finish your example by changing your class names (and the subsequent references to them in lines 14 and 17). Figure 17.2 shows the result.

LISTING 17.2 Displaying Text According to a Typographic Classification

```
01: <?xml version="1.0" standalone="no"?>
02: <!DOCTYPE svg PUBLIC "-//W3C//DTD SVG 20010904//EN"
            "http://www.w3.org/TR/2001/REC-SVG-20010904/DTD/svg10.dtd">
03:
04: <svg  width="500" height="300">
05:
06:        <style type="text/css">
07:                <![CDATA[
08:                    .FontTimes{font-family:'Times New Roman',serif;}
09:                    .FontCharcoal{font-
                            family:'Charcoal','Helvetica',sans-serif;}
10:                ]]>
11:        </style>
12:
13:        <text>
14:                <tspan x="100" y="100" class="FontTimes">
15:                        This is an example of SVG text.
16:                </tspan>
17:                <tspan x="100" y="115" class="FontCharcoal">
18:                        It is bold, fresh, and odor-free!
19:                </tspan>
20:        </text>
21:
22: </svg>
```

FIGURE 17.2

To accommodate for a range of viewer environments wherein certain fonts may not be installed, these two text lines both have specific typefaces and a generic font classification.

17

By using multiple font names within one `font-family` property, you increase the chances that an end user sees your SVG text in the typeface you planned. Most Mac users have Charcoal installed, whereas PC users do not. Therefore, any machine that does not have Charcoal installed will check to see if it has Helvetica installed. However, as most PCs do not have Helvetica installed either, the viewer will opt for the system's default sans-serif font.

SVG Fonts

With system fonts and font classifications under your belt, it's time to dive into one of the real joys of SVG: true typeface encapsulation for display across *all* viewers. The SVG recommendation requires that all viewers be able to use and display the SVG Fonts standard. This standard, similar to Web Fonts and other font definition technologies, allows you to contain vector outline information for letterforms within an SVG framework.

The SVG Fonts standard may seem a bit odd at first to anyone unfamiliar with font creation. All font systems (such as TrueType, OpenType, and even SVG Fonts) use a square grid from which they calculate the coordinates of any typeface's characters. In the case of SVG Fonts, a 1,000-by-1,000-unit grid is used to determine character placement.

In abstract terms, you can think of each character in a font as having an invisible square behind it. The placement of a character within its square determines how it aligns with other characters. Characters are plotted within this square on coordinates based on the 1,000-by-1,000-unit box. Thus, a letterform that maximizes the space of its square (such as the capital letter *W*, which is very wide as well as tall) may well be 1,000 units tall and 1000 units wide; a slender letterform (such as the lowercase letter *i*) may only be 650 units tall and 150 units wide. Such discrepancies in maximizing the width of the character grid are important to note inasmuch as they affect the consistency of your letters' kerning.

There is a key difference between the coordinate spaces of SVG and SVG Fonts, however. In SVG Fonts the y-axis increases in positive value going up (not down as in SVG).
This will certainly throw you for a loop when you try to plot your artwork after having
become familiar with SVG's system.

To make sense of this concept, examine Figure 17.3. The Helvetica letter *A* is plotted
according to the SVG Fonts system of a 1,000-unit grid, with the y value increasing as
the letterform rises.

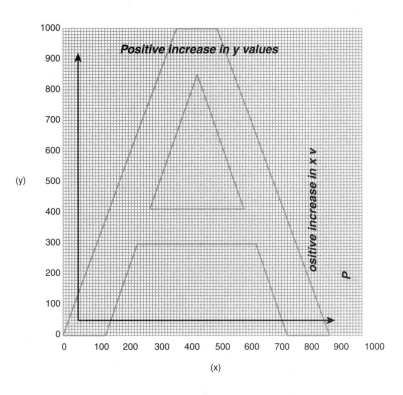

FIGURE 17.3

*SVG Fonts characters
are plotted on a
1,000-by-1,000-unit
character grid whose
y values increase in
the upward direction.*

As the character grid square is always defined as 1,000 units by 1,000 units (no matter
what type size has been designated), the coordinates of a letterform adjust in relation to
the interpolation of the type size divided by 1,000. For example, if you have designated
your typeface to display at 24 points, each unit on the square grid (invisible behind the
square) is 0.024 points.

The coordinates for a character within the character grid never change despite the changing
of the text's type size. Rather, these coordinates are converted to a point value that *does*
change based upon the type size applied. Consider Figure 17.4. The Helvetica *A* has a

coordinate value of (450,850) for the inner point of the *A*'s counterform (the shape defining the inner area of a letter). This value does not change; however, when the letter is displayed at 24-point type size, the coordinates are converted to the SVG coordinates (10.8,20.4). These numbers can be found, again, by dividing the type size value by 1,000 and then multiplying that number by the character's coordinate values. (Thus $450 \times 0.024 = 10.8$, and $850 \times 0.024 = 20.4$.)

FIGURE 17.4

The coordinates for the letter A within the character grid never change despite the changing of the text's type size.

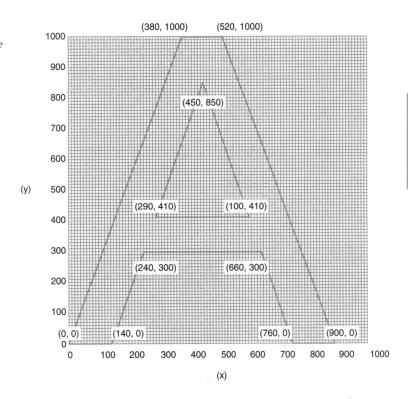

Using SVG Fonts

Now that you know how characters are plotted in SVG Fonts, you'll need to know how to apply this information. SVG Fonts are stored within SVG using the `font` element and its series of child elements. Every SVG Font is contained between the `font` element's tags:

```
<font>…(Your font data here)…</font>
```

The `font` element can actually contain a number of child elements that can be used to more precisely determine the display of your font. For the sake of your finishing this book in 24 hours, this chapter will focus on the two necessary child elements: `font-face` and `glyph`.

If you would like to learn about the other child elements, review Chapter 20 of the W3C SVG recommendation.

The `font-face` element is used to name your font. As you learned earlier in this chapter, fonts are applied by referencing their proper name, such as Comic Sans MS. To allow you to name your font, the `font-face` element uses the `font-family` attribute. The value you use for this attribute determines how you should reference your font in your `font-family` style property later. (Keep in mind that if you give your font the same name as a system font, such as Times New Roman, your viewer will not be able to use the system font.) Because the sole requirement of this element is to name your font, you can use one closed element tag: `<font-face font-family="Your font name"/>`.

Next up is the `glyph` element. This element is used to define the character outlines for each letter in your typeface. The `glyph` element uses the `unicode` attribute to designate which character is being defined. (Unicode is a standard, similar to ASCII, used to designate a character in platform-agnostic code.) Thus,

```
<glyph unicode="a">…</glyph>
```

is used to define the lowercase letter *a*.

If you are more familiar with XML hexadecimal names for every character, such as ÷ for the ÷ character, you can also use this convention. Thus, your code would look like

```
<glyph unicode="&#247;">…</glyph>
```

Within the `glyph` element there are two methods of defining the actual character shape. You can use the `d` attribute within an empty `glyph` element (that is, `<glyph/>`), or you can enclose your artwork within the `glyph` element's two tags. The `d` attribute accepts path data, using the same syntax and commands as the `path` element's `d` attribute, and allows you to define your characters via compound path data (often the type exported by programs such as Adobe Illustrator and CorelDraw).

The syntax for this method,

```
<glyph unicode="a" d="pathData"/>
```

is the most common, although you can also draw your characters using any shape element (`rect`, `circle`, `ellipse`, `line`, `polyline`, `polygon`, and `path`) contained between the `glyph` element's tags. Your syntax with this method is as follows:

```
<glyph unicode="a">…Your shape elements here…</glyph>
```

You can also mix and match the different methods of storing glyph data. For instance, you can store the data for the letter *a* as d attribute values while building the letter *b* from shape elements.

As you will generally use more than one letter per font, you can add as many glyph elements as you have letters. Thus, your font's code will often appear as follows:

```
<font>
    <font-face font-family="Font Name"/>
    <glyph unicode="a" d="pathData"/>
    <glyph unicode="b">
            <!--shape elements -->
    </glyph>
    <glyph unicode="c" d="pathData"/>
</font>
```

To apply this knowledge, you can create a very simple SVG Font. First, you will need to plot the coordinates of your letterforms just as you would any path or polygon element. For the sake of this example, you will create just two letters: the uppercase *T* and the lowercase *a*. To illustrate both types of glyph data, the *T* will be created using a continuous path, and the *a* will be shaped from two rectangles.

Figure 17.5 shows these two letterforms plotted out. With the coordinates in hand, you can begin creating your font element.

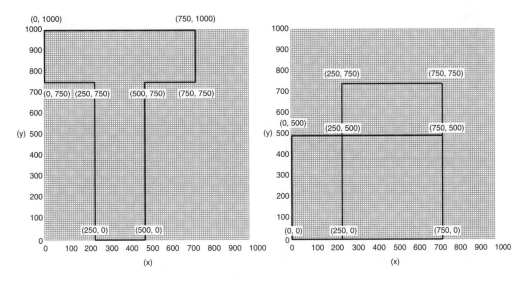

FIGURE 17.5

Plotting your typeface characters as you would your path *data allows you to quickly transfer coordinates into your* glyph *element.*

In Listing 17.3, you begin to create your font by storing the font element within the defs element (line 13). After naming the font with the font-family attribute (line 14), you can begin to bring the coordinates from Figure 17.5 into their appropriate glyph element. The letter *T* is defined via absolute path data on line 15, whereas *a* uses the two rectangles on lines 17 and 18 to define its very basic shape.

After defining the SVG Font, you need only apply the typeface with the font-family style property to the text (line 8). As you have created just two letterforms, only the letters described in the font will appear, regardless of what text exists in the text element (line 23).

LISTING 17.3 Defining the Shapes of Each Letterform

```
01: <?xml version="1.0" standalone="no"?>
02: <!DOCTYPE svg PUBLIC "-//W3C//DTD SVG 20010904//EN"
            "http://www.w3.org/TR/2001/REC-SVG-20010904/DTD/svg10.dtd">
03:
04: <svg  width="500" height="300">
05:
06:      <style type="text/css">
07:            <![CDATA[
08:                 .FontFirstSVGFont{font-family:'My First SVG Font';}
09:            ]]>
10:      </style>
11:
12:      <defs>
13:            <font>
14:                  <font-face font-family="My First SVG Font"/>
15:                  <glyph unicode="T"
                         d="M0,1000 L750,1000 L750,750 L500,750
                         L500,0 L250,0 L250,750 L0,750"/>
16:                  <glyph unicode="a">
17:                       <rect x="0" y="0" width="750" height="500"/>
18:                       <rect x="250" y="0" width="500"
                              height="750"/>
19:                  </glyph>
20:            </font>
21:      </defs>
22:
23:      <text x="100" y="100" class="FontFirstSVGFont">Tasty</text>
24:
25: </svg>
```

Figure 17.6 illustrates the results of this code.

FIGURE 17.6

Creating an SVG Font is merely a matter of defining the shapes of each letterform.

Sadly, two letterforms fall far short of an impressive typeface, and a method where you must define each letter isn't too realistic for every project you develop. Thankfully, there are tools out there to convert existing typefaces to SVG Fonts. As of press time, the only product with a cross-platform solution for exporting typefaces as SVG Fonts is CorelDraw 10. Batik offers a converter for TrueType fonts that runs on Windows and Java environments. Other vendors are at work on such tools, and perhaps by the time you pick up this book there will be several options available to you.

There are other solutions available as well. Adobe has created the CEF format (short for Compact Embedded Font). As you learned last hour, CEF Fonts offer small file sizes but are currently usable only via the Adobe SVG Viewer. Adobe does plan, however, to open the specification for the format at some point to allow developers to support the format in other viewers.

As a final note on fonts, to help you get started designing SVG with typefaces other than system fonts, Jay Vidheecharoen of Red Eye Type (`www.redeyetype.com`) has agreed to provide several of his popular typefaces as both SVG and CEF Fonts free of charge for your noncommercial use. To download these typefaces, visit `www.svgnow.com`. There you will find links to these typefaces, as well as other examples using the Adobe CEF technology.

Kerning

Although SVG Fonts provide the amazing ability of packaging typefaces for display across all viewers, there are some limitations to this technology. The very fact that SVG Fonts contain information only about a character's shape in its relation to the 1,000-by-1,000-unit character grid leaves some features common to system fonts lacking.

Obviously, a slender letterform has considerable extra space remaining in its square. This is where kerning comes in handy. Consider the word *Hello*. The letters *H*, *e*, and *o* are all similar in width, whereas the two *l*'s have only a fraction of that width. Using the abstract concept of the literal square behind each letter, odd gaps would occur between the letters placed next to each other to assemble the word.

Depending on where the *l* was placed in its square, a full letter's space may occur between the two *l*'s and between one of the *l*'s and its neighboring letter. However, the *H* and *e* would have a comfortably tight spacing. Because of this inconsistency in spacing (based on the characters' varying widths), kerning was developed to adjust these spaces. In a sense, kerning allows the characters' squares to overlap when necessary to create a uniform distance.

This type of kerning, however, comes at the expense of calculating every possible character combination. This can be an unbelievably enormous task. The work involved in kerning every letter combination for optimal display is tremendous. Consider a font that has only 26 lowercase letters. These letters have 26 possible pair combinations. Thus, a font with only 26 letters needs 676 kerning pairs (26 letters multiplied by 26 possibilities).

SVG Fonts offers the ability for you to encode kerning information, but the reality of the matter is you will likely never have the time to investigate a typeface's every kerning combination. As such, this aspect falls outside of this book's scope. However, if you are interested, you can read more about kerning and other options available for SVG Fonts in Chapter 20 of the W3C SVG Recommendation.

Type Quality

As you've surely noticed upon viewing any of your documents, SVG renders all objects with anti-aliasing as a default. If you are not familiar with the concept of aliasing and anti-aliasing, a brief overview is in order.

Aliasing refers to the display quality of objects where no edges are smoothed or softened. This often leads to a look that appears bit-mapped or hard-edged. Although this was the default display of computer monitors for years, the past decade has seen a push for the softening of onscreen edges to more accurately mimic the appearance of offscreen edges. As arcs and curves must be rendered onscreen as a series of pixels, a method called anti-aliasing was created to soften the harsh ragged edges of curve rendering.

Anti-aliasing is a method of interpolating the colors on either side of an edge and creating a fine blend between the colors along this edge. This blend reduces the sharp contrast of the edge and results in an aesthetic most viewers find preferable.

There are cases, however, when anti-aliasing can be unwelcome. In displaying small point sizes, such as 7- or 8-point text, anti-aliasing blurs edges that are already close together so that they become unreadable. There may also be cases where you wish to create a hard-edged, low-quality look to your type.

In either case, there is a solution. The text-rendering style property can be applied to a text element or its children to determine the degree of anti-aliasing performed on type. The property's syntax is

```
text-rendering:propertyValue
```

where propertyValue is one of four values that determines the priority of four rendering functions (anti-aliasing, legibility, speed, and character shapes):

Text-Rendering Value	Display Priority
auto	Anti-aliasing
optimizeSpeed	Quick rendering without anti-aliasing
optimizeLegibility	A mixture of character shapes and anti-aliasing
geometricPrecision	Letterform shapes

To try this property out, you can modify Listing 17.1. Simply swap the two style classes with a single text-rendering:optimizeSpeed class (line 8), apply the style to the first tspan element (line 13) so that you can see a difference between the results, and you're done. Listing 17.4 shows the modifications, and Figure 17.7 shows the results.

LISTING 17.4 Changing Type Display Quality

```
01: <?xml version="1.0" standalone="no"?>
02: <!DOCTYPE svg PUBLIC "-//W3C//DTD SVG 20010904//EN"
             "http://www.w3.org/TR/2001/REC-SVG-20010904/DTD/svg10.dtd">
03:
04: <svg  width="500" height="300">
05:
06:      <style type="text/css">
07:              <![CDATA[
08:                     .FontAlias{text-rendering:optimizeSpeed;}
09:              ]]>
10:      </style>
11:
12:      <text">
13:              <tspan x="100" y="100" class="FontAlias>
14:                     This is an example of SVG text.
15:              </tspan>
16:              <tspan x="100" y="115">
```

continues

LISTING 17.4 Continued

```
17:                              It is bold, fresh, and odor-free!
18:                </tspan>
19:        </text>
20:
21: </svg>
```

FIGURE 17.7

The first line of text appears crisp, unlike the softer-edged (anti-aliased) text below it.

By adding the text-rendering property to your text, your type can be forced to display without anti-aliasing. Although the number of times you will need to use this effect will likely be small, you will at least have the ability to override the default anti-aliased display, which can sometimes destroy the intent of your visual message.

Summary

Using specific typefaces with your SVG documents gives you the ability to communicate additional information beyond the message of the text alone. SVG is one of the few technologies available to designers that allows them not only to specifically reference fonts by name (similar to XHTML), but to actually encode the entire typeface so that all viewers see the exact same typographic display (similar to Flash).

What's more, SVG offers a standardized method for encoding typefaces using its SVG Fonts scheme. By saving letterforms as unique vector-based glyphs, able to be referenced just like a system font, SVG Fonts allow typefaces to be displayed in any point size across all viewers.

Having now completed Part IV of this book, "Text and Typography," you have finished learning the basics of SVG authoring. The remainder of this book will focus on refining the material you've learned and teaching you ways to extend SVG beyond its basic capabilities. In the next section, Part V, "Using JavaScript to Unleash SVG," you will learn how to use JavaScript to both enhance SVG's animation capabilities and create a dynamic graphic. With this knowledge, you will hopefully begin to envision creative ways that SVG can interact with other technologies.

Q&A

Q Does SVG come bundled with any fonts I can use?

A SVG is not a technology that comes "bundled"; it is a recommendation, allowing anyone to develop code using it, and does not exist as a software package able to be purchased. Thus, no fonts are bundled and ready to use with SVG. However, you can visit `http://www.svgnow.com/` to download freely available CEF and SVG Fonts, able to be used with the Adobe SVG Viewer.

Q How do I create CEF fonts?

A Currently, only Adobe products, such as Illustrator, have the ability to create CEF fonts. You will need to use one of their programs to create the CEF. Both Illustrator 9 and 10 come with excellent tutorials explaining the various settings available for exporting CEF fonts. Remember, however, that CEF fonts can be viewed only with the Adobe SVG Viewer.

Q Flash can embed fonts in its documents as well. What's so special about SVG's ability to retain typographic information?

A One of the reasons Flash is so popular with designers is its ability to embed typefaces within its exported SWF files. The main difference, then, between the two is that SVG's font information is available to edit and share.

For instance, SVG stores its characters within the `glyph` element in syntax that is easily discernible (if you already know SVG). A designer can then quickly modify a single character if the supplied typeface does not provide the desired results—a feat not easily replicated in Flash (without a font creation program, such as Macromedia's long-defunct Fontographer).

Also, according to the SVG Recommendation, an SVG Font stored in one file can be accessed by other SVG documents. Although this feature is not yet supported by the Adobe viewer (referencing CEF files is currently possible), the ability to reduce file sizes and downloads by eliminating duplicate content is a welcome feature. Currently, Flash embeds its typographic information in each file it exports; it has no way to share that font across several files.

17

Workshop

The Workshop is designed to help you anticipate possible questions, review what you've learned, and begin learning how to put your knowledge into practice.

Quiz

1. What do the letters CEF stand for?

2. True or false: SVG viewers will attempt to render text aliased unless otherwise directed.

3. What child element does the font element use to define individual characters in an SVG Font typeface?

4. True or false: The glyph element can only accept path data to define its character's shape.

Answers

1. CEF is an acronym for Adobe's Compact Embedded Font.

2. False. By default, viewers will render all objects, text included, with anti-aliased edges.

3. The glyph element is used to define each individual character.

4. False. The glyph element can accept both path data and any drawing elements.

Exercises

1. Modify Listing 17.3, where you created an SVG Font, to use the typographic properties you learned about in the last chapter. By adding letter spacing, type size, and alignment properties to your text, you can see how SVG Fonts work similarly to your system fonts.

2. SVG Fonts allow for a missing-glyph element to define the display of any character not covered by a glyph in the typeface. This element uses the same syntax as the glyph element, minus the faculty for a unicode attribute. Try creating a unique character to represent the lack of a character, and add this null character either via the d attribute or through enclosure of drawing elements. It's important to remember that the missing-glyph element is a child of the font element; make sure it stays within the font tags!

3. Download one of the free SVG Fonts available on www.svgnow.com. Copy the font element into one of your document's defs sections, and begin applying this typeface to one of your text experiments.

PART V

Using JavaScript to Unleash SVG

Hour

HOUR **18**

JavaScript

Congratulations. As of the completion of Hour 17, you've covered the basics of coding SVG. The remainder of this book will deal with some more advanced topics as well as some tips on how to make your development process a bit easier.

Anyone who has done some serious code work on the Web has, at some point, run into JavaScript. Whether for image rollovers, animation, or interfacing with another technology, JavaScript has proven to be a relatively easy method to extend possibilities on the Web.

SVG also has the ability to work with JavaScript, or, more accurately, ECMAScript. ECMAScript is an open standard scripting language, whereas JavaScript is a scripting language created by Netscape that is based upon ECMAScript and that adds a few additional features. As JavaScript is the most commonly used scripting language amongst Web developers, this hour and the next will focus on it.

There are endless possibilities for using JavaScript to enhance SVG, which are limited really only by your imagination. JavaScript can pass values between documents, check user-inputted data for errors, initiate commands on an end-user's machine, and more. This hour will focus on using JavaScript to enhance usability and animation, while the next hour will use it to create a dynamic SVG graphic.

Neither of the hours in this part will go into exceptional detail on the workings of JavaScript. Rather, they will focus on setting up your SVG to work with the technology. Though all attempts will be made to explain the function and use of the scripts you will see, these two hours are dependent on some knowledge of JavaScript.

There are books devoted solely to teaching JavaScript, including *Sams Teach Yourself JavaScript in 24 Hours* and *Sams Teach Yourself JavaScript in 21 Days*.

All that said, it is still recommended that you read these hours, as they will provide you with ideas for other possibilities using SVG. At the very least, you will learn how to set up your SVG code for JavaScript interaction. Following are the main topics you will cover in this hour:

- How to use JavaScript scripts in SVG
- Detecting the presence of an SVG viewer
- Creating JavaScript-powered SVG animations

Using Scripts in SVG

Just in case you're completely in the dark on Web scripting, a script is a program written in a scripting language (JavaScript, for example) that carries out some kind of task within a Web page or other document, such as an SVG document. Although we're focusing on JavaScript, there are other types of scripting languages in use these days, including Microsoft's VBScript (Visual Basic Script). Scripts of any sort are added to an SVG file using the `script` element. To identify the scripting language, such as "JavaScript," you can add a `type` attribute with the appropriate value (the MIME type of the scripting language).

For instance, if you were inserting a JavaScript script, you would add the following code to your SVG document:

```
<script type="text/javascript">...</script>
```

Your script would be contained between the `script` tags where the three dots appear in the example.

If you prefer to store your scripts in separate files, you can opt to link an SVG document to an external script file by adding an `xlink:href` attribute. This attribute allows the `script` element to take advantage of an external script file. Your syntax would reflect this change, as the following code demonstrates:

```
<script type="text/javascript" xlink:href="scriptFile.js"/>
```

In this example, `scriptFile.js` represents the URI of the external script file; notice that it is assigned to the `xlink:href` attribute. Also, since an external script file doesn't involve you placing any script code in your document, you can simply use an empty `script` element, as the example demonstrates.

> The syntax for referencing external script files in HTML documents is a little different than the approach used in SVG documents, as you learn a little later in the hour.

18

Although external scripts can be handy in some situations, the scripts you create in this hour and the next will be embedded directly within the `script` tags; external scripts are primarily useful when you acquire them from somewhere else. When contained between the `script` tags, your script will also need to be enclosed within CDATA tags to accommodate the strict rules of XML. SVG viewers are required to be able to process JavaScript functions, but JavaScript's syntax does not follow XML's syntax conventions. As such, if your script is not wrapped inside CDATA, your viewer will encounter an error trying to parse the script's data as SVG code.

Thus, if you are embedding your script into your SVG document, your syntax should be as follows:

```
<script type="text/javascript">
   <![CDATA[
   your JavaScript code goes here
   ]]>
</script>
```

By wrapping your scripts like this, you can be assured that your JavaScript will be read as JavaScript and not as invalid SVG code.

You can place the `script` element just about anywhere within an SVG document, similar to the `defs` and `style` elements, as long as it remains between your `svg` element's tags.

Scripts can also be added to HTML documents, allowing external information to be passed to your SVG document. Examples of this approach to Web scripting will be shown in the "Viewer Detection" section of this hour as well as in the "Dynamic Content" section of the next hour.

Viewer Detection

With the proliferation of Flash sites came the proliferation of "plug-in detection scripts." These detection scripts consisted of code that could be used to detect the computer platform, browser vendor and version, and plug-in vendor and version. By checking these attributes, a Web page could redirect users that didn't have the technology necessary to correctly view the advanced content. For example, you could have different versions of a Web site that were targeted to browsers based upon their capabilities.

Such detection scripts have become commonplace with the widespread use of Flash, which hasn't always been such a standard part of Web browsers. No one wants a user to arrive at a Web page only to see a broken graphic due to a missing plug-in. Although Flash has become a standard across most Web browsers, SVG still has not quite achieved such a status. For this reason, developers have begun to create detection scripts for SVG viewers. Knowing the reluctance of Web users to install plug-ins and browser add-ins on their own, such a feature can help boost the odds of users seeing your SVG content. For example, if your detection script determines that an SVG viewer is not installed, you can direct the user to a download source for an SVG viewer plug-in and/or explain that your content is SVG-enhanced. Explaining the benefits of your content might encourage users to allow the plug-in to be installed.

The Adobe SVG Viewer is the most-installed viewer on the market at the moment and is the viewer used throughout this book to test examples. For this reason, you should consider downloading Adobe's viewer detection scripts, which are available at http://www.adobe.com/svg/workflow/autoinstall.zip. It's probably a good idea to download the files and store them locally on your machine and/or Web server. This takes the load off of Adobe's servers when a user views your SVG content and also helps speed up your Web pages because the files are available directly from your site.

Downloading the Adobe package results in two files available for your use: svgcheck.js and svgcheck.vbs. These two files are external script files that provide viewer detection scripts in JavaScript and VBScript, respectively. Since the focus of this hour is using JavaScript with SVG, we'll be working only with svgcheck.js. This script is responsible for analyzing your system and allowing a Web page to load uninhibited if everything is OK, or, if not, for taking a user to the Adobe SVG Viewer download page if it can't automatically download and install the plug-in itself.

To use the svgcheck.js script, after "unzipping" the downloaded script file with a decompression program (such as WinZIP), you will need to place the script in a directory accessible to your HTML and SVG content. For the sake of this example, you can safely store the script file in the same directory as your HTML and SVG documents.

After placing the script file alongside your other documents, you will need to add a script reference to the external script file within your HTML document's <head> element tags:

```
<script language="JavaScript" src="svgcheck.js"/>
```

Note how this element uses a different syntax than SVG's script element, which looks like this:

```
<script type="text/javascript" xlink:href="scriptFile.js"/>
```

The difference between these two approaches of referencing external scripts has to do with differences between HTML and SVG. HTML scripts are referenced using the language and src attributes of the script element, whereas SVG scripts are referenced using the type and xlink:href attributes of SVG's script element.

Simply referencing an external script file is important, but it doesn't completely take care of business. This is because you must somehow invoke the code in a script in order for the script to do anything. This usually involves calling a function within a script that carries out a certain task, such as looking to see if an SVG viewer is available. The svgcheck.js script includes a function named checkAndGetSVGViewer() that is responsible for looking to see if an SVG viewer is available and for automatically downloading the viewer if it is not. You must call the function from an internal script that is placed directly in the HTML document, like the following code snippet:

```
<script language="JavaScript">
   <!--
   checkAndGetSVGViewer();
   // -->
</script>
```

At this point, you've referenced an external script containing the important function checkAndGetSVGViewer(), and you've called the function so that the viewer check actually takes place. With this script in place, your HTML document is capable of detecting whether an end-user has the latest version of the Adobe SVG Viewer installed and of helping initiate the download and installation process if it is not.

Listing 18.1 shows the internal script code combined with the external svgcheck.js script reference in an HTML document. Using the embed element you learned about at the end of Hour 3, "Viewing SVG," you can reference an SVG file (line 11). For this example, the HTML document references the SVG file listing1802.svg, which you will learn about in a moment.

18

LISTING 18.1   Referencing an Adobe JavaScript Script to Test Whether an End-User Has His SVG Viewer Installed

```
01: <html>
02:         <head>
03:                 <script language="JavaScript" src="svgcheck.js"></script>
04:                 <script language="JavaScript">
05:                         <!--
06:                                 checkAndGetSVGViewer();
07:                         // -->
08:                 </script>
09:         </head>
10:         <body>
11:                 <embed src="listing1802.svg" width="500" height="300"
                        type="image/svg+xml"
                        pluginspage="http://www.adobe.com/svg/viewer/install/">
12:         </body>
13: </html>
```

If you have the Adobe SVG Viewer plug-in installed when you open this HTML document, you should see a graphic image appear, courtesy of the listing1802.svg document. However, if you're testing this file on a machine without the Viewer installed, you'll see the script go into action and attempt to resolve the missing viewer problem.

If you would like further information on Adobe's detection script and auto-install functionality, check out http://www.adobe.com/svg/workflow/autoinstall.html. This Web site will obviously contain the latest information and news about their scripts.

Enhancing Animation Performance

One of the most useful tasks you can rely on JavaScript to perform is that of animation. JavaScript is very adept at injecting animation into otherwise static graphics. Even though SVG supports animation, it can be advantageous in terms of performance to use JavaScript as a means of adding animation to SVG documents. This has to do with the fact that most Web browsers are optimized to execute JavaScript code very efficiently.

When you use JavaScript to animate an SVG document, the browser's JavaScript engine handles the chore of carrying out the SVG animation, generally resulting in speed and performance improvements. To test this possibility, you can apply some object-oriented JavaScript to the news center graphic to animate the clouds over the sun and sky. (Again, keep in mind that this hour will not cover an entire JavaScript step-by-step tutorial.)

There are a number of possible methods to use JavaScript to animate an SVG document. This book will use an object-oriented method developed by Jim Moore. Mr. Moore worked with the author of this book on the BattleBots SVG projects and has repeatedly found clever ways of enhancing the function of SVG content through JavaScript. As such, his script (Listing 18.3), which you will learn about in a moment, reflects an efficient method of handling the animation.

Before diving into his example, you should understand the logic behind the animation. Using Listing 15.3 as a base (where you began to explore SVG animation by animating a cloud across the sky), Mr. Moore decided to use a different approach of moving an image between two points. This time around there are two clouds so there are two variables (cloud1 and cloud2) that define the leftmost and rightmost boundaries of the clouds. To move the clouds, you then increase or decrease their x value (based upon the direction of the cloud) between these two points. Mr. Moore then built on this approach by adding logic into the script to sense when a cloud reached a boundary so that it could start again. This gives the effect of the clouds constantly drifting along. Figure 18.1 shows a graphical interpretation of such a concept.

FIGURE 18.1

By defining boundaries for the clouds, you can carefully control the extents of their animation.

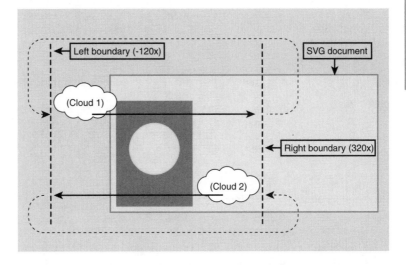

To create this example yourself, open and resave Listing 15.3, and remove the animate element so that your document is no more than a static image of the clouds over the sun and sky. As you have been naming all your artwork's elements with id values in your examples, you are in good shape to add JavaScript code for the animation; this is because JavaScript will rely on the names of these id values to determine the targets of its commands. Listing 18.2 shows the code for this static image, including the id values on the cloud objects (lines 27 and 28).

LISTING 18.2   In Order to Apply Script Code to Objects in an SVG Document, the
Objects Must Have Unique ID Values

```
01: <?xml version="1.0" standalone="no"?>
02: <!DOCTYPE svg PUBLIC "-//W3C//DTD SVG 1.0//EN"
            "http://www.w3.org/TR/2001/REC-SVG-20010904/DTD/svg10.dtd">
03:
04: <svg  width="500" height="300">
05:
06:        <style type="text/css">
07:                <![CDATA[
08:                        .FillFFFFFF{fill:#FFFFFF;}
09:                        .Fill99CCFF{fill:#99CCFF;}
10:                        .FillFFFF00{fill:#FFFF00;}
11:                ]]>
12:        </style>
13:
14:        <defs>
15:                <g id="Cloud">
16:                        <circle cx="24" cy="36" r="15"/>
17:                        <circle cx="41" cy="26" r="17"/>
18:                        <circle cx="90" cy="40" r="13"/>
19:                        <circle cx="105" cy="31" r="13"/>
20:                        <ellipse cx="75" cy="20" rx="27" ry="20"/>
21:                        <ellipse cx="56" cy="50" rx="25" ry="18"/>
22:                </g>
23:        </defs>
24:
25:        <rect id="Sky" x="10" y="45" width="200" height="245"
                    class="Fill99CCFF"/>
26:        <circle id="Sun" cx="105" cy="160" r="56" class="FillFFFF00"/>
27:        <use id="Cloud1" xlink:href="#Cloud" x="-20" y="80"
                    class="FillFFFFFF"/>
28:        <use id="Cloud2" xlink:href="#Cloud" x="150" y="150"
                    class="FillFFFFFF"/>
29:
30: </svg>
```

At this point, you have a basic SVG document that describes a static image of a sky with
a sun and a couple of clouds. The task now is to animate the clouds by adding JavaScript
code. First, you will need to add a `script` element that declares the script as type
JavaScript, and subsequently you will need to include CDATA tags within this element so
that you don't violate the rules of XML. Just to recap, following is an example of what
this script template code should look like:

```
<script type="text/javascript">
    <![CDATA[
    ]]>
</script>
```

You saw this code earlier in the hour, so it should be somewhat familiar. You're now ready to begin placing script code within the CDATA section of the script element. The first code to be added is responsible for creating variables that control the animation; these variables are different from SVG element attributes, such as the id values of objects. As you will be moving both clouds, you will need one variable to represent each; in this case, these variables are named cloud1 and cloud2 to be similar in name to the SVG id values but not conflict with their spelling (Remember: SVG's id values are case sensitive.). You will also need a variable to tell the script where to target its actions (svgdoc)—this is the SVG document itself. These three variables are coded like the following:

```
var svgdoc;
var cloud1;
var cloud2;
```

Before going any further, it is important to note, for those unfamiliar with JavaScript, that these variable names are determined solely by you. In other words, you can change these names to virtually anything you'd like, as long as you use the names consistently throughout the entire script.

After declaring the variables, you can create the first function, which is just a grouping of code that carries out a given task. In this case, the function is called Cloud(), and its task consists of initializing the data fields for a cloud object. More specifically, the Cloud() function accepts a few pieces of information that it then uses to construct an object that represents each cloud in the script. Following is the code for the Cloud() function:

```
function Cloud(name, direction, bounds_left, bounds_right) {
    this.direction = direction;
    this.element = svgdoc.getElementById(name);
    this.x = parseInt(this.element.getAttribute('x'));
    this.bounds_left = bounds_left;
    this.bounds_right = bounds_right;
}
```

This function accepts four pieces of information when it is called:

1. The name of the object (name)
2. The direction the object is traveling (direction)
3. The left boundary for the object (bounds_left)
4. The right boundary for the object (bounds_right)

These four pieces of information are then used to create a cloud object that can be easily accessed and manipulated throughout the remainder of the script. The word this that appears throughout the code is object-oriented programming terminology that refers to the object being created. Although it's not important for you to understand object-oriented

18

programming, you should hopefully be able to grasp the concept of the Cloud() function creating a cloud object that we can now manipulate by changing information, such as its horizontal position.

Having established the Cloud() function, you now need to create another function titled initVars(). This function initializes the script and gets the animation started. More specifically, it calls the Cloud() function to create a couple of clouds, and then it sets the animation interval for the clouds to determine how fast they move. Following is the code for the initVars() function:

```
function initVars(evt){
    svgdoc = evt.getTarget().getOwnerDocument();
    cloud1 = new Cloud('Cloud1', true, -120, 320);
    cloud2 = new Cloud('Cloud2', false, -120, 320);
    top.setInterval(moveCloud1, 50);
    top.setInterval(moveCloud2, 70);
}
```

The second line of this code obtains the SVG document, which is stored in the svgdoc variable; if you recall, this variable is used in the Cloud() function to create the cloud objects. Speaking of the Cloud() function, it is called twice in a row to create two cloud objects (cloud1 and cloud2). Notice that four values are passed into the Cloud() function; they are separated by commas. These four values correspond to the object name, direction, left boundary, and right boundary that you learned about earlier. The differing values for the direction (true and false) indicate that one cloud is moving left while the other is moving right.

Near the end of the initVars() function, you'll notice that a function named setInterval() is called a couple of times. This function accepts two values: the name of a function to be called at regular intervals and the amount of time (in milliseconds) between each interval. So, the function moveCloud1() is set to be called once every 50 milliseconds, whereas moveCloud2() gets called every 70 milliseconds. These two functions are responsible for slightly changing the positions of the clouds and are ultimately responsible for the animation.

Following is the code for the moveCloud1() and moveCloud2() functions:

```
function moveCloud1() {
    moveCloud(cloud1);
}

function moveCloud2() {
    moveCloud(cloud2);
}
```

As you can see, these functions are surprisingly simple. In fact, all they do is call another function, moveCloud(), and pass it one of the cloud objects. Of course, this means that the moveCloud() function must be doing the real animation work. Following is the code for the moveCloud() function:

```
function moveCloud(cloud) {
  if (cloud.direction) {
        cloud.x = (cloud.x+1);
  } else {
        cloud.x = (cloud.x-1);
  }

  if (cloud.direction) {
        if (cloud.x >= cloud.bounds_right) cloud.x = cloud.bounds_left;
  } else {
        if (cloud.x <= cloud.bounds_left) cloud.x = cloud.bounds_right;
  }

  cloud.element.setAttribute('x', cloud.x);
}
```

The moveCloud() function is divided into three main sections of code that perform the following tasks:

1. Move the cloud by altering its X position
2. Check to see if the cloud is outside of the boundaries, correcting if necessary
3. Set the cloud's position changes

The first section of code checks to see which direction the cloud is moving and then increases or decreases its X position accordingly. The second section of code checks to see if the cloud has reached a boundary, in which case its position is reset. And finally, the next to last line of code sets the changes to the cloud's position by calling the setAttribute() function, which is a built-in JavaScript function.

You just about have all of the pieces of the JavaScript puzzle to put this animation together. The only missing ingredient is a small piece of script code that gets the whole animation started. Surprisingly enough, this code must be placed directly in the <svg> tag for the document, like this:

```
<svg width="500" height="300" onload="initVars(evt);">
```

Notice in this code that there is an attribute named onload that is set to the value initVars(evt). The onload attribute determines what, if any, JavaScript code is to be executed when the document is first loaded. In this case, the initVars() function is called, which is enough to set in motion the entire animation.

18

You now have everything you need to combine the script code with the static SVG image from Listing 18.2 to create a complete SVG animation. Listing 18.3 shows the code for the newly improved SVG document with JavaScript animation.

LISTING 18.3   Using JavaScript to Handle Animation

```
01: <?xml version="1.0" standalone="no"?>
02: <!DOCTYPE svg PUBLIC "-//W3C//DTD SVG 1.0//EN"
             "http://www.w3.org/TR/2001/REC-SVG-20010904/DTD/svg10.dtd">
03:
04: <svg  width="500" height="300" onload="initVars(evt);">
05:
06:        <style type="text/css">
07:                <![CDATA[
08:                        .FillFFFFFF{fill:#FFFFFF;}
09:                        .Fill99CCFF{fill:#99CCFF;}
10:                        .FillFFFF00{fill:#FFFF00;}
11:                ]]>
12:        </style>
13:
14:        <script type="text/javascript">
15:                <![CDATA[
16:                        // variables
17:                                var svgdoc;
18:                                var cloud1;
19:                                var cloud2;
20:
21:                        // Object definitions
22:
23:                                function Cloud(name, direction, bounds_left,
                                        bounds_right) {
24:                                this.direction = direction;
25:                                this.element =
                                        svgdoc.getElementById(name);
26:                                this.x =
                                        parseInt(this.element.get
                                        Attribute('x'));
27:                                this.bounds_left = bounds_left;
28:                                this.bounds_right = bounds_right;
29:                                }
30:
31:                        // Javascript functions
32:                                function initVars(evt){
33:                                        svgdoc =
                                                evt.getTarget().get
                                                OwnerDocument();
34:                                        cloud1 = new Cloud('Cloud1', true,
                                                -120, 320);
```

continues

LISTING 18.3 Continued

```
35:                                    cloud2 = new Cloud('Cloud2', false,
                                           -w120, 320);
36:                                    top.setInterval(moveCloud1, 50);
37:                                    top.setInterval(moveCloud2, 70);
38:                            }
39:
40:                            function moveCloud1() {
41:                                    moveCloud(cloud1);
42:                            }
43:
44:                            function moveCloud2() {
45:                                    moveCloud(cloud2);
46:                            }
47:
48:                            function moveCloud(cloud) {
49:                                    if (cloud.direction) {
50:                                            cloud.x = (cloud.x+1);
51:                                    } else {
52:                                            cloud.x = (cloud.x-1);
53:                                    }
54:
55:                                    if (cloud.direction) {
56:                                            if (cloud.x >=
                                                    cloud.bounds_right)
                                                    cloud.x = cloud.
                                                    bounds_left;
57:                                    } else {
58:                                            if (cloud.x <=
                                                    cloud.bounds_left)
                                                    cloud.x =
                                                    cloud.bounds_right;
59:                                    }
60:
61:                                    cloud.element.setAttribute('x',
                                            cloud.x);
62:                            }
63:
64:                    ]]>
65:            </script>
66:
67:            <defs>
68:                    <g id="Cloud">
69:                            <circle cx="24" cy="36" r="15"/>
70:                            <circle cx="41" cy="26" r="17"/>
71:                            <circle cx="90" cy="40" r="13"/>
72:                            <circle cx="105" cy="31" r="13"/>
73:                            <ellipse cx="75" cy="20" rx="27" ry="20"/>
74:                            <ellipse cx="56" cy="50" rx="25" ry="18"/>
75:                    </g>
```

18

continues

LISTING 18.3 Continued

```
76:        </defs>
77:
78:        <rect id="Sky" x="10" y="45" width="200" height="245"
               class="Fill99CCFF"/>
79:        <circle id="Sun" cx="105" cy="160" r="56" class="FillFFFF00"/>
80:        <use id="Cloud1" xlink:href="#Cloud" x="-20" y="80"
               class="FillFFFFFF"/>
81:        <use id="Cloud2" xlink:href="#Cloud" x="150" y="150"
               class="FillFFFFFF"/>
82:
83: </svg>
```

Though this code admittedly looks a little overwhelming at first, keep in mind that some of what you're seeing is the original SVG document. The script code appears between lines 14 and 65 and consists entirely of the code you've already covered in this section. The only new code that you haven't really seen are the comments that help to organize the script (lines 16, 21, and 31). JavaScript comments are used to add documentation to script code and don't actually perform any other useful function. These comments appear as double slash marks (//) followed by text and are somewhat akin to XML's <!-- --> tags. Anything following the // on the same line serves as a comment in JavaScript; there is no closing to the convention other than a line break.

With the animation document complete, you can open two separate browser windows and view Listing 18.3 next to Listing 14.3. Your JavaScript-enhanced animation should look similar to the all-SVG animation and hopefully should run a little smoother.

As you can see from this example, using JavaScript to animate your SVG content certainly isn't easier than using SVG's own animation controls. That is, unless you're a JavaScript wiz who's just now learning SVG. However, JavaScript's performance exceeds SVG's to enough of an extent that you may want to consider using it in the near future if you require animation-intensive SVG. The hope is that eventually SVG viewers will render pure SVG animations as efficiently as they do JavaScript-powered animations.

Summary

One of the tremendous values of using an open-standards technology, such as SVG, is its interoperability with other technologies. Often times, if SVG cannot accomplish something, or cannot accomplish it in a manner you find acceptable, you can use another technology to work with SVG to meet your needs. In this case, you have seen how JavaScript can be used to detect whether an SVG viewer is available to display embedded content and improve the performance of its animation. These are but a few examples of the possibility of JavaScript interaction with SVG.

Hour 19 will show one final example for this book: using JavaScript to simulate how SVG graphics can be made dynamic. Other uses can be found and are listed online at this book's companion site: `http://www.svgnow.com`.

Q&A

Q JavaScript looks pretty exciting. Where can I learn more about it?

A As mentioned before, SAMS Publishing has a line of titles available on this subject. If you can't wait to get to the bookstore, check out the W3Schools' online JavaScript tutorial at `http://www.w3schools.com/js/`. They have a series of easy-to-understand, self-taught classes that are available free-of-charge.

Q Is it possible to create animations, such as the one in this hour using scripting languages, other than JavaScript?

A Yes. There are a variety of different scripting languages supported on the Web that you could use to create SVG animations. For example, Microsoft's VBScript is a strong competitor of JavaScript that can do pretty much anything JavaScript can do. If you happen to have a background in BASIC, you might consider taking a look at VBScript. To learn more, visit the W3Schools' online VBScript tutorial at `http://www.w3schools.com/vbscript/`. There are also several good SAMS Publishing titles on VBScript.

18

Workshop

The Workshop is designed to help you anticipate possible questions, review what you've learned, and begin learning how to put your knowledge into practice.

Quiz

1. True or False: All scripts to be used with SVG must be placed inside the SVG document.
2. How are scripts called upon to execute once an SVG document loads?
3. True or False: JavaScript and ECMAScript are the same thing.

Answers

1. False. SVG can access both internal and external scripts. External scripts can be accessed through the `xlink:href` attribute.

2. Using the `onload` attribute with your `svg` element, you can designate a JavaScript function to initiate once the document has finished loading.

3. False. JavaScript and ECMAScript are so *similar* that just about everyone thinks they are the same. JavaScript is a scripting language developed by Netscape, whereas ECMAScript is the conversion of JavaScript into a standard by the ECMA.

Exercises

Modify the JavaScript in Listing 18.3 to do the following:

1. Increase the speed (hint: reduce the millisecond values in lines 36 and 37). And,

2. Change the top cloud's boundaries so that it begins looping before it reaches the edge of the sky (hint: change the final pixel value in line 34). And,

3. Alter the direction of the clouds so that they move vertically instead of horizontally (hint: change all references to x position).

HOUR 19

Using JavaScript to Create Dynamic Content

Truly one of the most exciting aspects of SVG is its ability to easily create dynamic graphics, which are graphics whose content is somehow driven by external data. In fact, SVG stands apart from Flash in terms of its ability to accept a range of data sources. Data sources for SVG can be built using free, standards-based tools, such as JavaScript, or expensive commercial environments, such as Oracle application servers.

This hour will focus on how to create dynamic SVG content that can be driven by data sources. In the process, you will be able to see an example of how to use JavaScript to pass user-input values to an SVG file. By the end of the hour, you will have seen the use of dynamic graphics and will hopefully have a strong sense of what is possible with this technology.

Specifically, in this hour you will see

- An introduction to dynamic graphics
- How to prepare SVG graphics for dynamic content
- An example of using JavaScript to pass data to an SVG graphic
- Workflow suggestions for creating dynamic graphics

Understanding Dynamic Graphics

It's important to evaluate the specific needs of a project to determine if it stands to gain functionality or efficiency from using dynamic graphics.

Dynamic graphics are graphics that are generated on the fly (meaning they are generated upon their rendering, not beforehand), typically by combining quantitative data with graphical imagery. A good example of a dynamic graphic is a bar graph that is rendered when it is loaded based upon ever-changing numeric data. Dynamic graphics are different from standard graphics in that they aren't stored in static files, such as .gif or .jpg files. Rather, they exist as a pairing of graphic content and data that merge together to form a final image. This image can be changed by modifying the data and refreshing/ republishing the image.

These graphics are generally created as templates, with specific areas defined for population from an outside data source. Looking at a graphic template, you might have some difficulty visualizing what your final image may look like simply because the image isn't complete. This is because the image will generally have "holes" in places where content should reside in its final form. Your data that feeds the dynamic image may look rather bland, as it will not yet have been stylized. If the data for the dynamic image resides in a database, it may not be readily visible at all.

To determine the need for dynamic graphics, you will need to consider how often you republish similar static graphics. Most charts and financial graphics are graphics that, though looking very similar, are republished weekly (if not daily) to continue plotting the progress or decline of certain information. As such, someone must recreate the same graphic every day by modifying certain points or figures to reflect any changes.

Such repeated work, which is often performed by a graphic designer, becomes tedious and an inefficient means of publishing information. Instead, by creating a master template and a series of rules, these images can be recreated with a simple data update (whether text, image, or otherwise). More specifically, a rule might designate that a numeric value for a company's stock price appear at a certain position and in a certain font, along with an arrow indicating whether the stock has risen or fallen. The numeric stock price and arrow image are considered part of the data update that takes place to "refresh" the dynamic image.

For a solid example of the value of dynamic graphics, consider the 2000 elections. Every news station and newspaper in the USA published a map of Florida voting district results time and time again after each district released its recounts. Each time numbers were released to these organizations:

1. A reporter would need to gather the new figures and provide them to a graphic artist. Then,

2. A graphic artist would open the most recent version of the map, update the figures to reflect the changes, and save a new version. Then,

3. A copy editor would then need to check the new image for accuracy against the new numbers. If there were any errors, the process would return to step 2. If not, then,

4. The graphic would be published.

Although a relatively straightforward process, consider that none of these steps are particularly efficient; it takes an appreciable amount of time and human effort to carry out each step.

By removing the artist from the data-entry process, valuable human resources are conserved and the artist is made available for more pressing projects. The timeframe needed to publish this content is also greatly reduced. Anyone familiar with this process can vouch for the tedium and annoyance inherent in repetitive text corrections to graphics; the likelihood for misspellings and errors increases significantly when the graphic visually changes in imperceptible increments.

Other possible uses for dynamic graphics include

- Visualizing an employee's weekly time distribution across several projects based on timesheet figures

- A stylized presentation of stock market performance, updated every fifteen minutes with each information release

- A mosaic that is made of an association of several random images drawn from an ever-increasing pool of user-uploaded artwork

Though dynamic graphics can be a time saver in the examples listed above, there are many cases of when dynamic graphics are inappropriate. Virtually all the examples in this book have static (that is, unchanging) content and were never intended to change. As such, taking the time to separate your content from your graphic template and then reintegrating the two becomes a time-*waster*.

Unless your graphic will be frequently updated or requires a technical solution to determine its presentation, you are best suited to develop static graphics. Keep in mind, though, that static graphics can still have animation and interactive functions; they simply do not require external content to display correctly.

19

Designing SVG for Dynamic Content

Designing your graphics to accommodate dynamic content is not all that different from designing them for static content. The difference lies more in your planning than in your execution. Your graphics must be able to accommodate variable chunks of content, which usually means allowing space for dynamic data to be integrated alongside predefined graphics.

By the very nature of a dynamic graphic, the artist has relinquished control of reviewing every possible iteration of her graphic. For example, if the designer provides a 50-pixel wide by 50-pixel tall hole for an advertisement within an Arts Nouveau–style design that accommodates user-submitted artwork, the designer must be comfortable with the prospect of a crude crayon-style illustration being placed within those borders. In other words, the artist is allowing part of the graphic to be defined dynamically by another person or possibly by an automated application.

Because dynamic graphics can produce odd results, most dynamic graphics should be designed so that only select individuals have access that allows them to change data and subsequently publish the image. Even with these precautions, the designer must create a graphic that accommodates various content possibilities.

For instance, if your corporate intranet has a funny photo and caption that change daily based upon the intern's latest Web-surfing expedition, you will need to design your graphic to have room for several scenarios. On some days, this intern may write two words for the caption; on others, they may write two paragraphs. You should always design your graphics for the worst-case scenario, allowing for the maximum characters or screen real estate the content can occupy.

Once designed, you should experiment by populating your graphic with

1. Too much content
2. Too little content
3. The perfect amount of content

You can then use these examples for two purposes:

- To fine tune your design to better handle the extremes
- To help educate the content production team as to the consequences of their work

With a clear idea of how their work impacts the visual presentation, most content production teams will work harder to massage their material into attractive solutions. Without this sort of idea, they may just think you're a bad designer!

Preparing Your Graphic for Dynamic Content

After you have stylized your content and arranged your artwork, you will need to uniquely identify all your objects that will be accepting external content. For instance, if you have a `text` element that will contain a dynamic headline, you should provide that element with an `id` value, such as `NewsStory1Headline`. By providing these objects with a definitive, unique label, you can target your content to its appropriate destination.

After identifying all objects in a graphical image that are to be dynamically driven, you can prepare your graphic for its yet-to-come content. Most designers choose to design their dynamic graphics as static graphics originally, using fake text and imagery to visualize the final result; then, after the design is approved, they delete the placeholder imagery and content before exporting.

In some cases, however, you may need to delete the placeholder imagery at a later time. For instance, if you use a program like Adobe Illustrator or Corel Draw to design your graphic, you will likely export the SVG code from the program (rather than attempting to hand-code the design while looking at a printout). For most of your elements, you will need these programs to export the style properties of the placeholder content so that the dynamic content will assume these properties upon its inclusion. After its style properties have been transferred to an empty object, you can delete the placeholder content.

For instance, in the case of the dynamic headline, you might export the graphic from Illustrator with a bogus headline like "SVG Scores Again!" and the unique identifier NewsStory1Headline. Once exported, you can delete the mock headline within this object, knowing that the style information is still retained, ready to be applied to the dynamic headline upon processing. Figure 19.1 shows the result of such an effort in both code and imagery.

```
<rect x="0" y="0" width="150" height="30" class="FillBeige"/>
<use xlink:href="StarIcon" x="5" y="5" style="FillRed"/>
<text style="FontSize18 FontUniversExtraCond">
        <tspan id="HeadlineText" x="35" y="25">SVG Scores Again!</tspan>
</text>
```

**Orginal artwork with dynamic content's substitute text
(noted via the "HeadlineText" id value) and resulting code**

```
<rect x="0" y="0" width="150" height="30" class="FillBeige"/>
<use xlink:href="StarIcon" x="5" y="5" style="FillRed"/>
<text style="FontSize18 FontUniversExtraCond">
        <tspan id="HeadlineText" x="35" y="25"> </tspan>
</text>
```

**Final SVG template with dynamic content's tspan element
left without content for dynamic inclusion and resulting code**

19

FIGURE 19.1

A graphic's dynamic elements can be visually mimicked initially to determine placement and appearance before removing such substitutions for the final graphic template.

Localizing SVG Graphics

Taking the concept of dynamic graphics one step further, you can "localize" your graphics based upon a user's preferred language. By designing your textual content to draw upon an external data source, your graphic can appear in one of the many languages to which your content has been translated.

For instance, if both English- and Spanish-speaking users frequent your SVG-designed site, you could run a detection script that determines the operating system language of the user. If the user is Spanish-speaking, the graphical navigation bars and page titles could change to accommodate his familiar language.

Such a possibility is quite a selling point for designing your graphical content in SVG. Database-driven content solutions have long been touted for reducing the cost and maintenance of multiple-language environments. With SVG, graphics now have the same flexibility and translation opportunities that textual content has enjoyed. A designer needs to create only one graphic template, and the back-end system could populate it with the appropriate text. The time savings in terms of just image production and copy-editing become significant when viewed in this perspective.

As a final note on localization, keep in mind that text isn't the only form of communication. As the old saying goes, a picture is worth a thousand words. Make sure that you test your designs on your various audiences before going live with several language translations.

Keep in mind that the pairing of translated words with your English-original artwork may make for awkard, unintentional messages. Make certain that your artwork is appropriate for the audiences targeted, and, if not, provide alternative artwork for some locations. If you're able to swap textual content according to user-preference, you're also technically able to switch visual content.

Creating Dynamic Content

Now that I've hopefully sold you on the benefits of dynamic graphics, you're probably curious as to how they are created. There are a number of possible tools you can use to generate dynamic SVG graphics. Solutions range in price from free technologies like XSLT, PHP, and XHTML to low-cost means like ASP and all the way up to high-priced solutions like an Oracle back-end system.

Each solution has its own requirements and various means of integrating the SVG template and the external content. As such, this book can deal only with the generalities of how to create dynamic content. A number of groups are working together to find new ways of creating dynamic SVG graphics, and you can find further information online in SVG developer groups.

To provide you with a concrete example of dynamic graphics, this hour contains a modification of this book's news center weather graphic (Figure 1.1). Weather information changes daily, and thus this graphic provides a great example for creating a dynamic image out of weather data.

Ben Strawbridge, another developer who worked closely with this book's author, created this example. Mr. Strawbridge has created a number of dynamic SVG solutions for commercial and research purposes and provided a logical fit for this book's example. More examples of his work are available online at www.svgnow.com, as well as at his site, www.benstrawbridge.com.

To quickly illustrate dynamic SVG creation, this example relies on JavaScript to pass variables between an HTML form and an SVG document. The stripped-down news center SVG document relies on the HTML form to determine which weather forecast image is displayed as well as the high and low temperatures. To simplify matters, the HTML document that passes the variables to the SVG document also embeds the dynamic SVG graphic; because of this, you can see your changes instantly.

Creating this example requires two separate documents: an SVG template (Listing 19.1) and a JavaScript-enhanced HTML document (Listing 19.2). As with the previous hour, a basic knowledge of JavaScript will help you to understand the logic behind the scripting portion of this example. However, it isn't a necessity. The JavaScript code in this example is relatively straightforward and isn't too difficult to follow. In fact, you may find yourself reusing the code in your own projects to suit your own needs.

19

To create the first document, the SVG file, you can blend two previous examples together. The sunny sky illustration can be garnered from Listing 15.3, whereas the code for the thunderstorm can be found in Listing 15.10. Before getting into the code to create the SVG document combining these two weather-related scenes, you must include a style sheet that provides important styles that are used by the two scenes in the SVG document. Following is the code for this style sheet:

```
<style type="text/css">
   <![CDATA[
      .FillFFFFFF{fill:#FFFFFF;}
      .Fill99CCFF{fill:#99CCFF;}
      .FillFFFF00{fill:#FFFF00;}
      .Fill333333{fill:#333333;}
      .Fill664785{fill:#664785;}
      .FillFFFF00{fill:#FFFF00;}
      .FillCCCCCC{fill:#CCCCCC;}
```

```
        .FillOpacityPoint25{fill-opacity:0.25;}
        .FillOpacityPoint75{fill-opacity:0.75;}
        .FontFamilyArialNarrow{font-family:'ArialNarrow',san-serif;}
        .FontFamilyArialBlack{font-family:'Arial-Black',san-serif;}
        .FontSize14{font-size:14;}
        .FontSize36{font-size:36;}
        .TextAlignRight{text-anchor:end;}
        .DisplayNone{display:none;}
    ]]>
</style>
```

This style sheet isn't really doing anything too fancy; it mainly establishes some fill colors, transparency settings, and font characteristics that are used throughout the remainder of the SVG document. Of much more interest are the two graphical objects that indicate the visual weather forecast. These are the "Sunny" and "Rainy" weather forecast graphics (taken from Listings 15.3 and 15.10, respectively, and modified so that the background rectangles do not share the same id value), whose code follows:

```
<g id="Sunny" class="DisplayNone">
    <rect id="BlueSky" x="10" y="45" width="200" height="245"
          class="Fill99CCFF"/>
    <circle id="Sun" cx="105" cy="160" r="56" class="FillFFFF00"/>
    <use id="Cloud1" xlink:href="#Cloud" x="-20" y="80" class="FillFFFFFF"/>
    <use id="Cloud2" xlink:href="#Cloud" x="150" y="150" class="FillFFFFFF"/>
</g>

<g id="Rainy" class="DisplayNone">
    <rect id="DarkSky" x="10" y="45" width="200" height="245"
          class="Fill664785"/>
    <use id="RainCloudForeGround" xlink:href="#Cloud" x="10" y="40"
          class="FillCCCCCC" transform="scale(1.5)"/>
    <use id="Lightning1" xlink:href="#LightningBolt1" x="100" y="170"/>
</g>
```

These two graphics are used to provide a visual representation of a weather forecast: sunny or rainy. Unlike the previous version of these graphics, the class attribute is now set to DisplayNone, which results in the graphics not being displayed initially. The idea is to prevent either image from displaying until the user has selected a preference for one using the HTML form. You might have noticed that these graphical objects are dependent on a few predefined SVG graphical components, which you originally saw in Hour 14. Following is the code for these components just in case your memory is a little fuzzy:

```
<defs>
    <g id="Cloud">
        <circle cx="24" cy="36" r="15"/>
        <circle cx="41" cy="26" r="17"/>
        <circle cx="90" cy="40" r="13"/>
        <circle cx="105" cy="31" r="13"/>
        <ellipse cx="75" cy="20" rx="27" ry="20"/>
        <ellipse cx="56" cy="50" rx="25" ry="18"/>
```

```
    </g>
    <polygon id="LightningBolt1" class="FillFFFF00"
        points="13,0 4,25 8,25 2,48 6,48 0,72 18,44 14,44 25,21 20,21 32,0"/>
</defs>
```

The next component of the weather graphic is a box containing textual elements for the high and low temperature values, as well as their labels. Following is the code for the box, text objects, and labels:

```
<g id="TempBar">
    <rect id="BarStatistics" x="10" y="245" width="200" height="45"
            class="Fill333333 FillOpacityPoint25"/>
    <g id="WeatherStats" class="FillOpacityPoint75">
        <text class="FontFamilyArialNarrow FontSize14">
            <tspan x="16" y="280">HIGH:</tspan>
            <tspan x="110" y="280">LOW:</tspan>
        </text>
        <text class="FontFamilyArialBlack FontSize36">
            <tspan x="50" y="280" id="high_text"> </tspan>
            <tspan x="142" y="280" id="low_text"> </tspan>
        </text>
    </g>
</g>
```

There are a few interesting things about this code worth pointing out. First of all, notice that the entire temperature graphic is grouped together under a <g> tag with an id of TempBar. The box itself is a rect with an id of BarStatistics. The text objects consist of two labels ("HIGH:" and "LOW:") and their respective placeholders for the dynamically provided high and low temperature values (high_text and low_text). After applying separate typographic information (font family and font size) to each text object, the SVG document is complete. Listing 19.1 shows the complete code for this SVG document, which is now ready to receive dynamic data.

LISTING 19.1 An SVG Document That Is Properly Designed to Accept Dynamic Data

```
01: <?xml version="1.0" standalone="no"?>
02: <!DOCTYPE svg PUBLIC "-//W3C//DTD SVG 1.0//EN"
            "http://www.w3.org/TR/2001/REC-SVG-20010904/DTD/svg10.dtd">
03:
04: <svg  width="500" height="300">
05:     <style type="text/css">
06:         <![CDATA[
07:             .FillFFFFFF{fill:#FFFFFF;}
08:             .Fill99CCFF{fill:#99CCFF;}
09:             .FillFFFF00{fill:#FFFF00;}
10:             .Fill333333{fill:#333333;}
11:             .Fill664785{fill:#664785;}
```

continues

LISTING 19.1   Continued

```
12:                .FillFFFF00{fill:#FFFF00;}
13:                .FillCCCCCC{fill:#CCCCCC;}
14:                .FillOpacityPoint25{fill-opacity:0.25;}
15:                .FillOpacityPoint75{fill-opacity:0.75;}
16:                .FontFamilyArialNarrow{font-family:'ArialNarrow',
                        san-serif;}
17:                .FontFamilyArialBlack{font-family:'Arial-Black',
                        san-serif;}
18:                .FontSize14{font-size:14;}
19:                .FontSize36{font-size:36;}
20:                .TextAlignRight{text-anchor:end;}
21:                .DisplayNone{display:none;}
22:            ]]>
23:        </style>
24:
25:        <defs>
26:            <g id="Cloud">
27:                <circle cx="24" cy="36" r="15"/>
28:                <circle cx="41" cy="26" r="17"/>
29:                <circle cx="90" cy="40" r="13"/>
30:                <circle cx="105" cy="31" r="13"/>
31:                <ellipse cx="75" cy="20" rx="27" ry="20"/>
32:                <ellipse cx="56" cy="50" rx="25" ry="18"/>
33:            </g>
34:            <polygon id="LightningBolt1" class="FillFFFF00"points="13,0 4,25 8,25,
                    2,48 6,48 0,72 18,44 14,44 25,21 20,21 32,0"/>
35:        </defs>
36:
37:        <g id="Sunny" class="DisplayNone">
38:            <rect id="BlueSky" x="10" y="45" width="200" height="245"
                    class="Fill99CCFF"/>
39:            <circle id="Sun" cx="105" cy="160" r="56" class="FillFFFF00"/>
40:            <use id="Cloud1" xlink:href="#Cloud" x="-20" y="80"
                    class="FillFFFFFF"/>
41:            <use id="Cloud2" xlink:href="#Cloud" x="150" y="150"
                    class="FillFFFFFF"/>
42:        </g>
43:
44:        <g id="Rainy" class="DisplayNone">
45:            <rect id="DarkSky" x="10" y="45" width="200" height="245"
                    class="Fill664785"/>
46:            <use id="RainCloudForeGround" xlink:href="#Cloud" x="10" y="40"
                    class="FillCCCCCC" transform="scale(1.5)"/>
47:            <use id="Lightning1" xlink:href="#LightningBolt1" x="100" y="170"/>
48:        </g>
49:
50:        <g id="TempBar">
51:            <rect id="BarStatistics" x="10" y="245" width="200" height="45"
                    class="Fill333333 FillOpacityPoint25"/>
```

continues

LISTING 19.1   Continued

```
52:          <g id="WeatherStats" class="FillOpacityPoint75">
53:            <text class="FontFamilyArialNarrow FontSize14">
54:              <tspan x="16" y="280">HIGH:</tspan>
55:              <tspan x="110" y="280">LOW:</tspan>
56:            </text>
57:            <text class="FontFamilyArialBlack FontSize36">
58:              <tspan x="50" y="280" id="high_text"> </tspan>
59:              <tspan x="142" y="280" id="low_text"> </tspan>
60:            </text>
61:          </g>
62:      </g>
63:
64: </svg>
```

A quick look at this listing shows that the code snippets you've seen thus far for the SVG document are now combined into a cohesive document. Lines 5 through 23 contain the CSS style sheet for the document, while lines 25 through 35 contain the predefined graphics objects used by the sunny (lines 37–42) and rainy (lines 44–48) forecast graphics. Finally, the temperature bar graphic is described in lines 50 through 62.

With your SVG file complete and admittedly a little sparse-looking, you can begin to create the surrounding HTML and JavaScript code that finishes up the dynamic image. Using HTML code that you saw back in Hour 3, you can embed your SVG file within the HTML document by referencing the name of the SVG document (`listing1901.svg` in this case). Rather than flip back to Hour 3, take a look at the following code, which embeds the `listing1901.svg` document in an HTML document:

```
<embed src="listing1901.svg" id="weather" name="weather" height="300"
    width="500" type="image/svg+xml"
    pluginspage="http://www.adobe.com/svg/viewer/install/">
```

The most important parts of this embed element are the id and name attributes; the lack of standards-adherence in browsers has resulted in you having to use multiple approaches of identifying objects in a Web page. In this case, it means using both the id and name attributes to carry out the same task—uniquely identifying the weather SVG document.

The Web page for this example consists of a table that is used to organize the user interface used to enter dynamic data and the actual SVG graphic. More specifically, the user interface, which consists of form controls, appears on one row of a table, whereas the SVG graphic appears on another row. The table's first row includes a form named

19

dynamichandler, which accepts a user's submissions for both high and low temperatures, as well as their selection of either a rainy or sunny illustration. Following is the
HTML code for this table row:

```
<tr height="99">
    <form name="dynamichandler">
        <td>
            Today's High<br/>
            <input type="text" name="high_temp" size="5"><br/>
        </td>
        <td>
            Today's Low<br/>
            <input type="text" name="low_temp" size="5"><br/>
        </td>
        <td>
            <input type="radio" id="forecast" name="forecast"
                    value="Sunny">Sunny<br/>
            <input type="radio" id="forecast" name="forecast"
                    value="Rainy">Rain<br/>
        </td>
        <td>
            <a href="#" onclick="setSVG();setForecast();"><strong>set
                    svg</strong></a>
        </td>
    </form>
</tr>
```

A quick study of this code reveals that it establishes a user interface consisting of text
input fields for the high and low temperatures, as well as radio buttons for selecting the
forecast. The trigger for submitting the form is created with an <a> tag that is tied to
the text "set svg." So, clicking the text "set svg" results in the data entered into the
form being used to update the dynamic graphic. Notice that the onclick attribute of the
<a> tag makes function calls to the setSVG() and setForecast() functions, which are
script functions that you create in a moment.

If you recall from the previous hour, you must enclose script code within a script element when you create JavaScript functions. Only one variable, svgdoc, is used by the
script code in the following example:

```
var svgdoc;
```

This variable is used to keep track of the SVG document so that the script can access and
feed data to the dynamic graphic. The first script function you must create is called
initSVGvars() and is responsible for taking care of a couple of initialization tasks:

```
function initSVGvars(){
    svgdoc = document.embeds["weather"].getSVGDocument();
    forecastLen = document.dynamichandler.forecast.length;
}
```

The first task of the initSVGvars() function is to access the SVG document and store it away in svgdoc for later access. The second task involves determining the number of form elements with the name forecast. If you recall, forecast elements are radio buttons that represent optional forecasts (sunny, rainy, and so on). By determining the number of forecast elements, the script allows you to add more forecast graphics (snowy, cloudy, and so on) without having to alter the code.

The next function to be created, setSVG(), passes along the high and low temperature values to the SVG graphic, as follows:

```
function setSVG(){
    newHigh = document.dynamichandler.high_temp.value;
    newLow = document.dynamichandler.low_temp.value;
    if(svgdoc.getElementById('high_text').getFirstChild().getNodeValue()
            !=newHigh)svgdoc.getElementById('high_text').getFirstChild()
            .setData(newHigh);
    if(svgdoc.getElementById('low_text').getFirstChild().getNodeValue()
            !=newLow)svgdoc.getElementById('low_text').getFirstChild()
            .setData(newLow);
}
```

The beginning of this function takes the values submitted in the dynamichandler form's high_temp and low_temp fields and gives them the variable names newHigh and newLow respectively. The remainder of the function checks to see if the values in the newHigh and newLow variables are different than the high_text and low_text SVG elements' contents. If so, it replaces the old values with the new values in the SVG document.

The final function, setForecast(), sets the forecast image to be displayed:

```
function setForecast() {
    for(i=0; i<forecastLen; i++)
        if (document.dynamichandler.forecast[i].checked==true) {
            svgdoc.getElementById(document.dynamichandler.forecast[i].value).
            setAttribute("style", "display:inline;");
        }
        else {
            svgdoc.getElementById(document.dynamichandler.forecast[i].value).
            setAttribute("style", "display:none;");
        }
}
```

This function first takes the number of forecast selection inputs (radio buttons) and runs them through an if/then statement that verifies whether any of the inputs have been checked. If an input has indeed been checked, the SVG object with the same value name (in this case, either Rainy or Sunny) as the checked input is made visible. Any SVG objects with the value names of unchecked inputs are hidden, which makes sense because only one forecast graphic can be visible (selected) at any given time.

19

As you learned in the previous hour, most JavaScript scripts require some kind of initiation in order to start running and executing code. In the case of the weather example HTML document, this is accomplished by calling the initSVGvars() function in the onload attribute of the HTML's body element. The code for this task looks like the following:

```
<body onload="initSVGvars();" bgcolor="#FFFFFF">
```

If you recall from earlier in this discussion, the initSVGvars() function performs some necessary overhead required of the other functions that control the dynamic SVG document. With this function call in place, your document is complete, and you're just about ready to view the successful results by loading the HTML document in a Web browser. Before doing that, however, take a look at the complete code listing for the weather forecast HTML document (Listing 19.2).

LISTING 19.2 An HTML Document That Dynamically Updates the Weather Forecast SVG Document Using JavaScript

```
01: <html>
02:    <head>
03:        <script language="JavaScript" type="text/javascript">
04:            <!--
05:                var svgdoc, forecastLen;
06:                function initSVGvars(){
07:                    svgdoc =document.embeds["weather"].getSVGDocument();
08:                    forecastLen = document.dynamichandler.forecast.length;
09:                }
10:                function setSVG(){
11:                    newHigh = document.dynamichandler.high_temp.value;
12:                    newLow = document.dynamichandler.low_temp.value;
13:                    if(svgdoc.getElementById('high_text')
                            .getFirstChild().getNodeValue()!=newHigh)
                            svgdoc.getElementById('high_text')
                            .getFirstChild().setData(newHigh);
14:                    if(svgdoc.getElementById('low_text')
                            .getFirstChild().getNodeValue()!=newLow)svgdoc.
                            getElementById('low_text').getFirstChild()
                            .setData(newLow);
15:                }
16:                function setForecast(){
17:                    for(i=0; i<forecastLen; i++)
18:                        if (document.dynamichandler.forecast
                                [i].checked==true){
19:                            svgdoc.getElementById(document.dynamichandler.
                                    forecast[i].value).setAttribute("style",
                                    "display:inline;");
20:                        }else{
```

continues

LISTING 19.2   Continued

```
21:                              svgdoc.getElementById(document.dynamichandler.
                                     forecast[i].value).setAttribute("style",
                                     "display:none;");
22:                        }
23:                     }
24:              //-->
25:           </script>
26:        </head>
27:        <body onload="initSVGvars();" bgcolor="#FFFFFF">
28:           <table bgcolor="#CCCCCC" cellpadding="12" cellspacing="0" border="0">
29:              <tr height="99">
30:                 <form name="dynamichandler">
31:                    <td>
32:                       Today's High<br/>
33:                       <input type="text" name="high_temp" size="5"><br/>
34:                    </td>
35:                    <td>
36:                       Today's Low<br/>
37:                       <input type="text" name="low_temp" size="5"><br/>
38:                    </td>
39:                    <td>
40:                       <input type="radio" id="forecast"
                                    name="forecast"value="Sunny">Sunny<br/>
41:                       <input type="radio" id="forecast"
                                    name="forecast"value="Rainy">Rain<br/>
42:                    </td>
43:                    <td>
44:                       <a href="#" onclick="setSVG();setForecast();">
                                    <strong>set svg</strong></a>
45:                    </td>
46:                 </form>
47:              </tr>
48:              <tr>
49:                 <td colspan="4">
50:                    <embed src="listing1901.svg" id="weather" name="weather"
                                 height="300" width="500" type="image/svg+xml"
                                 pluginspage="http://www.adobe.com/
                                 svg/viewer/install/">
51:                 </td>
52:              </tr>
53:           </table>
54:        </body>
55: </html>
```

19

The complete code listing for the weather forecast HTML document reveals how the JavaScript code fits into the HTML code as well as the SVG document reference. Lines 3 through 25 contain all of the script code that drives the dynamic graphic, while lines 28 through 53 describe the table that houses the user interface and SVG graphic for the complete example. With the complete code in hand, you're ready to see the results of your hard work by viewing the HTML document in a Web browser.

Upon viewing the HTML document, you will see a somewhat empty page with several HTML form elements at the top of a gray table (Figure 19.2). After entering numerical values for the high and low temperatures, as well as selecting your choice for the weather forecast, you need only click the "set svg" link. Pressing this link fires off the appropriate JavaScript functions (setSVG() and setForecast()) and instantly updates the embedded SVG document, resulting in a complete weather illustration (Figure 19.3). You can then repeatedly update this SVG document by altering the values of the temperature and forecast and clicking the "set svg" link.

FIGURE 19.2

Upon initial load, the dynamic SVG image is set to hide its content, leaving a sparse page.

If you're the curious sort, you'll likely try inputting non-numeric values into the high and low temperature fields. The resulting display can be quite bizarre and obviously inappropriate. If your dynamic content should consist only of specific values (that is, only numbers, no more than three characters in length, and so on), you could add an additional JavaScript that checks your HTML forms for valid values.

FIGURE 19.3

After submitting values to the HTML form, the SVG document instantly updates, revealing the appropriate content.

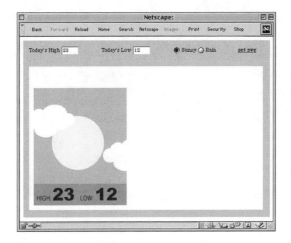

Summary

Dynamic graphics offer designers and developers a way of presenting ever-changing data in an attractive and efficient manner. Instead of relying on manpower to generate each version of the graphic anew, dynamic graphics use a content source to populate a visual template. This separation can help reduce errors and production time, allowing for attractive content to reach its audience more quickly.

Several means exist for passing dynamic content to an SVG document and subsequently rendering it. Technologies ranging from the simple to the complex and the free to the expensive allow developers a slew of options when determining the best means of publishing dynamic graphics. By providing this multitude of options, SVG stands apart from Flash and other technologies, empowering developers to make decisions appropriate for their needs. As you learned in this hour, JavaScript offers a reasonable and relatively simple solution for creating dynamic SVG content.

19

Q&A

Q I would like to create dynamic graphics using XSLT and other open-standards technologies. Are there resources that can explain this specific method?

A There are a number of XSLT-generated SVG examples available online. Visit this book's companion Web site at www.svgnow.com to find links to these and other resources.

Q **If JavaScript can create dynamic graphics for free, why would I use any other technology?**

A JavaScript was able to handle one type of dynamic content creation. Other types of graphics may rely on content stored in a database instead of user-submitted values. In such cases, JavaScript may not be the most efficient or versatile technology to pass content into an SVG document.

Workshop

The Workshop is designed to help you anticipate possible questions, review what you've learned, and begin learning how to put your knowledge into practice.

Quiz

1. When creating dynamic graphics, what factors should you keep in mind while designing?
2. True or False: You should develop every graphic to accept dynamic content.
3. What is localization?
4. Dynamic content requires SVG elements to be named with what attribute?

Answers

1. Designers should design their dynamic graphics with the extreme content usage in mind. Thinking through how users can inadvertently destroy the integrity of the graphic with sub-par content can help you plan alternatives to avoid unacceptable results.
2. False. Not every graphic is suitable for dynamic content, and time could be wasted preparing each graphic for external content inclusion.
3. Localization refers to altering your content to match different regions' needs. Most often, this refers to changing the language used in the graphics to make the content understandable to the appropriate audience.
4. Dynamic graphics rely on the `id` value to match content with its appropriate location.

Exercise

Create a third possibility for the dynamic example in this hour. As the `setForecast()` function processes an indefinite number of options, you can add another selection input to your HTML form and another hidden illustration group in your SVG document. Be sure that the value of the new selection input matches the `id` value of the new illustration.

PART VI

SVG Mastery

Hour

HOUR **20**

Organizing and Optimizing Your Code

As you've surely seen by now, whether reviewing HTML code or SVG code, there are a number of different ways to handle the development process and the arrangement of code. The direction in this book has been arrived at through the author's development of several existing commercial applications of SVG. It is important to keep in mind that there are numerous other ways to arrange your code beyond the direction of this book.

For instance, in Hours 13 and 15, you were taught to keep all your animation and interaction elements separate from your content and at the end of the document. This is but one method of handling code arrangement; there are other, and possibly somewhat better, methods available to you.

This hour will focus on some tips concerning the actual development process, somewhat removed from the specifics of the SVG recommendation. Thus, this hour will help design and development teams find an efficient manner in which to begin an SVG project.

You will also learn how to organize and optimize your code, making editing and reviewing your documents considerably easier. These tips are based on experience, but they aren't must-follow rules.

Specifically, you will learn the following lessons this hour:

- Separation of design and engineering
- SVG development processes
- Coding with basic elements to clarify the function of your code
- Detailing code
- Commenting code
- Annotating documents
- Using consistent terminology
- Locating document elements
- Attribute organization
- Style sheet organization
- Compressing your SVG documents

Every developer has his or her own preference on code organization and structure. The only definitive rule regarding these issues is to make sure you establish a consistent set of organization and structure rules to your documents.

Separation of Design and Engineering

One of the greatest hurdles that many Web development shops face is the coordination of their design, architecture, and engineering teams. Each team believes it should have the most control over the project, and each team often spends valuable time waiting for another to finish so that they can begin their work.

If you are already familiar with many Web development processes, Figure 20.1 will appear quite recognizable. After initial creative exploration and direction has been completed, a development team is assembled and prepared for the scope of the project. In many cases, an architecture group then begins structuring content and user pathways. Once complete, the design team comes back in, developing the appearance and strengthening the structure established. After completing the designs and producing the artwork, the engineering team is then able to begin building the HTML and back-end systems to facilitate the structure and design.

FIGURE 20.1

Current Web development processes leave teams waiting for each other to complete tasks, extending development time.

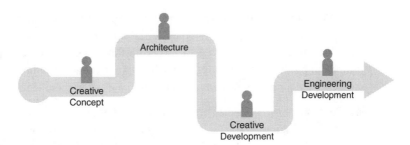

At this point, the creative and architecture teams generally sit idle, or begin development on another project. This results in an information loss, as the knowledge of these teams becomes somewhat inaccessible. As the engineering team is put under the gun to meet their project deadlines, communication with the other teams begins to dwindle out of necessity for completion.

This sort of arrangement leads to an awful lot of inefficiency. As anyone familiar with the process knows, this also creates a significant amount of tension between the teams. Each team is anxious to begin work *and* be consulted throughout the process.

These tensions and inefficiencies have an opportunity to be remedied when developing SVG content. SVG can certainly be developed in a similar fashion to HTML and other Web technologies, but it offers a chance at a different path. Rather than staggering development stages, it actually allows concurrent development (similar to the process outlined in Figure 20.2).

FIGURE 20.2

SVG's unique structure allows for all teams to work simultaneously, potentially reducing development time.

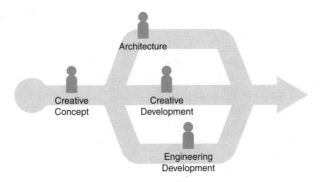

20

SVG's development cycle is somewhat similar to that of Flash, except that designers are often the ones left to code Flash content. In this case, after initial creative exploration and direction has been completed, the development team is assembled and prepared for the scope of the project (just as before). Not long after an architecture group begins structuring content and user pathways, the design and engineering teams can begin.

As SVG is little more than styled content, engineers can begin building the substructure of the SVG code, using simple blocks or groups to represent content and graphical chunks. The design team can get to work on fleshing out their concepts as the architecture team produces finished segments. The engineering team then continues to build, referencing the emerging designs for animation and interaction elements.

Rather than using completed artwork or content, they can develop their code more efficiently by thinking more abstractly about their work. For instance, if a designer begins scoping an animation of a spaceship careening across the screen, the engineer can produce a simple rectangle and begin animating it along a simple path. Once the design is complete, the designer can provide the engineer with the path and style information for both the spaceship and its motion path. The engineer then simply swaps the rectangle with the ship data and the simple motion path with the more complex version. Figure 20.3 provides a graphic look at this example.

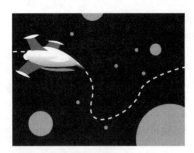

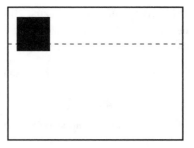

Final spaceship scene with motion path (above) and SVG code (below)

```
<svg width="500"height="300"

  <g id="Background">
    <!--several different elements building sky and planets-->
  </g>

  <g id="Spaceship">
    <!--several different elements building spaceship-->
  </g>

  <animateMotion xlink:href="#Spaceship"
    path="complex path data"/>

</svg>
```

Initial development with basic motion path (above) and SVG code (below)

```
<svg width="500"height="300"

  <g id="Background">
    <rect x="0" y="0" width="500" height="300"
      style="fill:white"/>
  </g>

  <g id="Spaceship">
    <rect x="20" y="20" width="100" height="100"/>
  </g>

  <animateMotion xlink:href="#Spaceship"
    path="M0,100 L500, 100"/>

</svg>
```

FIGURE 20.3

The design and engineering teams can simultaneously develop the final graphic (at left). The engineering team can begin working on a simple prototype (at right) that can later house the actual content.

By allowing all development teams to work simultaneously, information can be passed efficiently between teams, and overall development time can be reduced. This leaves some extra breathing room to fix mistakes or refine material further, an option for which every development team has always wished.

With a high-level view of how to work side-by-side, you can begin looking a bit deeper at how this process really works.

Development Process

Though you have learned how to draw basic shapes, paths, and polygons, and apply filters to your objects, the reality is that you will likely continue to use your drawing tools to create your design work. Applications such as Adobe Illustrator 10, CorelDraw 10, and JASC WebDraw 1.0 allow you to create your imagery in a WYSIWYG (What You See Is What You Get) environment, removing you from the underlying code. Just as most designers couldn't program their designs in the PostScript language, the reality is that most won't be programming their artwork in SVG code either.

Frankly, this is a good thing. Designers don't think in terms of variables and coding requirements any more than engineers think in terms of amorphous shapes moving around. Using tools such as those listed previously, designers are able to develop their material in the manner that makes the most sense to them. In return, these tools produce code that can be manipulated and understood by engineers.

As such, using the abstract method briefly outlined above provides an excellent way for designers and engineers to work alongside each other. Rather than waiting for the finished artwork to be produced, engineers can begin producing simple prototypes of the SVG document by using basic shapes and symbols.

Coding with Basic Elements

Although WYSIWYG tools ease the development of complex artwork, they generally produce code that, though sound and correct, isn't necessarily what an engineer would like it to be. For instance, in Adobe Illustrator, every shape (such as a square, oval, or freeform path) is exported as a path. Though logical for freeform paths, basic shapes become rather confusing to interpret when seen in the form of several abstract points in path data.

Whenever possible, and whether handled by a designer or engineer, it will behoove you to replace basic shapes produced as path elements with their appropriate SVG elements. Though this may seem a bit fussy, consider the amount of time you may spend reviewing your code. If you encounter line after line after line of path data, your eye begins to stop discerning the differences between them. However, one line may be the simple rectangle you are looking for, whereas the surrounding lines are complex freeform shapes. Having the rectangle stand out as a rect element allows for quicker mental processing of what the code intends to display.

To compare the difference between the two styles of coding artwork, compare Listings 20.1 and 20.2. Listing 20.1 is the illustration of a house (Figure 20.4) as Adobe Illustrator would export basic shapes. Listing 20.2 is the same illustration, with the same shapes drawn using basic elements.

LISTING 20.1   The Code Generated by Adobe Illustrator for the Illustration in Figure 20.4 Using path Elements

```
01: <?xml version="1.0" standalone="no"?>
02: <!DOCTYPE svg PUBLIC "-//W3C//DTD SVG 1.0//EN"
            "http://www.w3.org/TR/2001/REC-SVG-20010904/DTD/svg10.dtd">
03:
04: <svg  width="500" height="300">
05:
06:        <style type="text/css">
07:                <![CDATA[
08:                       .FillFFFFFF{fill:#FFFFFF;}
09:                ]]>
10:        </style>
11:
12:        <g id="structure">
13:                <path id="roof" d="M144,66L72,0L0,66H144z"/>
14:                <path id="block" d="M22,60v80h100V60H22z"/>
15:        </g>
16:        <g id="windows" class="FillFFFFFF">
17:                <path id="pane1" d="M55,42h9v9h-9V42z"/>
18:                <path id="pane2" d="M80,42h9v9h-9V42z"/>
19:                <path id="pane3" d="M55,65h9v9h-9V65z"/>
20:                <path id="pane4" d="M80,65h9v9h-9V65z"/>
21:        </g>
22:        <g id="door">
23:                <path id="frame" class="FillFFFFFF"
                        d="M88,91v41H55V91H88z"/>
24:                <path id="handle"
                        d="M59,112.999c0-2.208,1.791-3.999,4-3.999
                        s4,1.791,4,3.999S65.209,117,63,117
                        S59,115.208,59,112.999z"/>
25:        </g>
26:
27: </svg>
```

LISTING 20.2   The Illustrator Code Edited to Use Basic Shape Elements

```
01: <?xml version="1.0" standalone="no"?>
02: <!DOCTYPE svg PUBLIC "-//W3C//DTD SVG 1.0//EN"
            "http://www.w3.org/TR/2001/REC-SVG-20010904/DTD/svg10.dtd">
03:
04: <svg  width="500" height="300">
05:
06:        <style type="text/css">
07:                <![CDATA[
08:                     .FillFFFFFF{fill:#FFFFFF;}
09:                ]]>
10:        </style>
11:
12:        <g id="structure">
13:                <polygon id="roof" points="144,66 72,0 0,66"/>
14:                <rect id="block" x="22" y="60" width="100" height="80"/>
15:        </g>
16:        <g id="windows" class="FillFFFFFF">
17:                <rect id="pane1" x="55" y="42" width="9" height="9"/>
18:                <rect id="pane2" x="80" y="42" width="9" height="9"/>
19:                <rect id="pane3" x="55" y="65" width="9" height="9"/>
20:                <rect id="pane4" x="80" y="65" width="9" height="9"/>
21:        </g>
22:        <g id="door">
23:                <rect id="frame" class="FillFFFFFF"
                        x="55" y="91" width="33" height="41"/>
24:                <circle id="handle" cx="63" cy="113" r="4"/>
25:        </g>
26:
27: </svg>
```

FIGURE 20.4

This illustration of a house can be rendered by path data or basic shape elements. Basic shapes are easier to understand when quickly perusing code.

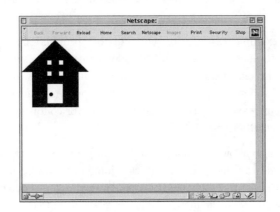

20

Some will argue that this adds an excessive amount of time to the development process. Keep in mind, however, that should your design team need to nudge specific objects around even slightly, recalculating each coordinate within path data can be exceedingly time consuming. For instance, consider the door handle (id value: doorhandle) in Listing 20.1. Should your designer need to move the handle up two pixels, you have two options if you are resigned to only using the exported code: 1) recalculate every coordinate, or 2) apply a transformation to the element.

By using basic shape elements, such a change will require minimal effort. Rather than changing roughly ten coordinates, you can change one cy value of the doorhandle circle. For one such change, the modifications seem somewhat pointless. However, when you're dealing with dozens of changes (especially late in a project cycle), such modifications will seem like lifesavers. In all cases, if you have the time and ability to swap abstract path data with basic SVG elements, you will be doing yourself (and any subsequent viewer of your code) a great service.

Detailing Code

Though using basic shape elements can help you and other developers more easily discern the rendering function of an element, such elements can't always provide you with the information you need to understand the visual function of the element.

Using id attributes can certainly assist in this problem. The id attribute not only serves the function as a code identifier, but it also sometimes acts as a nametag for developers. Though naming every element may seem like a tedious task, the alternative (selectively changing each object's style or removing it to see which object was changed) is far more painful.

In the previous example, Listing 20.2, you will note the addition of id attributes on every graphical element. Such nametags allow development teams to speak the same language. For instance, in the same example, each square making up the window is labeled with the word "pane," followed by a number. If the development team agrees to a nomenclature for their naming system early on, the possibility for confusion over which object is pane3 becomes greatly reduced.

The id attribute also allows for quick searching of your document. By knowing the names used for the id values, you can quickly jump to a specific area to make modifications. Such a means of accessing specific content within large code documents can result in significant timesavings. Picture trying to make a change to the third window pane in the house illustration if your document contained no id attributes, no basic shape elements, and a multitude of other graphical elements (as most of your documents will); the challenge would be dreadful.

The drawback of the id attribute is that it often resides at a distance from the element name. As such, you may spend more time trying to find the id value (when quickly scanning the code) than you would spend reviewing element names. Also, the id attribute's values must conform to the XML id attribute rules (that is, no spaces, special characters, and so forth).

Terminology

There was a reason the discovery of the Rosetta stone was so widely heralded in its time. Being able to communicate in the same language is important if you wish to share ideas with others. Though SVG obviously provides an unchanging language to describe its elements, attributes, properties, and functions, it provides no such rules for its user-inputted values. As in any environment without rules, chaos reigns supreme.

Developers have taken advantage of this freedom to name id values in whatever manner they choose. Because of this, any developer unfamiliar with a document's code must attempt to decipher the original developer's naming system when, in fact, there may be none.

Rather than adding to this sort of confusion, you should strongly consider developing a consistent naming convention. For instance, the author has found that using a system where an object is described with several terms, starting with the general and then moving towards the specific, can clearly identify it.

As an example, consider the illustration of the house. When a document is as small as Listing 20.2, there doesn't seem to be a need to describe each object in detail in its id value. However, if this document had several buildings with different shapes, naming the first house's doorframe "frame" wouldn't make much sense. All the buildings have a doorframe; why does the first one own such a general term?

Instead, finding a system that describes this particular doorframe in the most general terms down to the specifics may provide a more understandable system. Consider a name that describes the frame in its relationship to the house and in the house's relationship to the document. A name such as Bldg1DoorFrame meets these requirements; first, it describes which building it belongs to (Bldg1), then which component of that building it belongs to (Door), and then finally describes the specific object itself (Frame).

20

Using such a system for the entire document would result in an outcome similar to Listing 20.3.

LISTING 20.3   By Modifying the `id` Values of Listing 20.2, the Content Is More Easily Recognizable in Relation to Other Content

```
01: <?xml version="1.0" standalone="no"?>
02: <!DOCTYPE svg PUBLIC "-//W3C//DTD SVG 1.0//EN"
             "http://www.w3.org/TR/2001/REC-SVG-20010904/DTD/svg10.dtd">
03:
04: <svg width="500" height="300">
05:
06:       <style type="text/css">
07:               <![CDATA[
08:                       .FillFFFFFF{fill:#FFFFFF;}
09:               ]]>
10:       </style>
11:
12:       <g id="Bldg1Structure">
13:               <polygon id="Bldg1StructureRoof" points="144,66 72,0 0,66"/>
14:               <rect id="Bldg1StructureBlock" x="22" y="60" width="100"
                       height="80"/>
15:       </g>
16:       <g id="Bldg1Windows" class="FillFFFFFF">
17:               <rect id="Bldg1WindowPane1" x="55" y="42" width="9"
                       height="9"/>
18:               <rect id="Bldg1WindowPane2" x="80" y="42" width="9"
                       height="9"/>
19:               <rect id="Bldg1WindowPane3" x="55" y="65" width="9"
                       height="9"/>
20:               <rect id="Bldg1WindowPane4" x="80" y="65" width="9"
                       height="9"/>
21:       </g>
22:       <g id="Bldg1Door">
23:               <rect id="Bldg1DoorFrame" class="FillFFFFFF"
                       x="55" y="91" width="33" height="41"/>
24:               <circle id="Bldg1DoorHandle" cx="63" cy="113" r="4"/>
25:       </g>
26:
27: </svg>
```

By changing each `id` value to follow this system, your `id` attribute value can reveal details about its associated element otherwise obscured by the textual landscape of code. In fact, if such a system is followed when creating the other buildings, the system will take on further meaning and usefulness. If you were assigned the task of modifying the width of the third building's second windowpane, you could quickly do a "Find" on the name `Bldg3WindowPane3`. By knowing a document's naming scheme, you can expedite a number of search and retrieval functions.

Again, such naming systems may seem unnecessary on such a small scale as this document. However, when used in a document where more than one object can be mistaken due to having similar names, the system's value will shine through. For a better example, demonstrating the scope and use of this system, refer to Hour 23's listing of this book's final example—the news center graphic.

Commenting Code

Commenting can also provide an excellent means of communicating the intent of your code. Using comments, you can actually write your thoughts in plain English. If a set of animation elements performs related actions, it may help to place a comment line above and below the code, explaining these elements' function.

Listing 20.4 shows how comments can be used in two different manners. In the first example (lines 12 and 29), the comment is used to wrap content, signifying the start and stop of a visual object. The second manner is actual plain-text description of the nearby content (lines 13 and 18). In such a case, the comment can clarify things that may not be self-evident (such as why your elements are named in a certain fashion). Both methods allow other developers to have a clear idea of the intent of your code.

LISTING 20.4 Comments Can Shine Light on Your Thoughts and Naming Systems

```
01: <?xml version="1.0" standalone="no"?>
02: <!DOCTYPE svg PUBLIC "-//W3C//DTD SVG 1.0//EN"
         "http://www.w3.org/TR/2001/REC-SVG-20010904/DTD/svg10.dtd">
03:
04: <svg  width="500" height="300">
05:
06:      <style type="text/css">
07:           <![CDATA[
08:                .FillFFFFFF{fill:#FFFFFF;}
09:           ]]>
10:      </style>
11:
12:      <!-- START HOUSE ILLUSTRATION -->
13:      <!-- The house illustration needs only one class (white
              for the door and windows), as the bulk of its shapes
              will automatically be filled black as a default. -->
14:      <g id="structure">
15:           <polygon id="roof" points="144,66 72,0 0,66"/>
16:           <rect id="block" x="22" y="60" width="100" height="80"/>
17:      </g>
18:      <!-- The following window panes are numbered in order
              of left to right, top to bottom. -->
19:      <g id="windows" class="FillFFFFFF">
20:           <rect id="pane1" x="55" y="42" width="9" height="9"/>
21:           <rect id="pane2" x="80" y="42" width="9" height="9"/>
22:           <rect id="pane3" x="55" y="65" width="9" height="9"/>
23:           <rect id="pane4" x="80" y="65" width="9" height="9"/>
24:      </g>
```

continues

20

LISTING 20.4 Continued

```
25:        <g id="door">
26:            <rect id="frame" class="FillFFFFFF"
                    x="55" y="91" width="33" height="41"/>
27:            <circle id="handle" cx="63" cy="113" r="4"/>
28:        </g>
29:        <!-- END HOUSE ILLUSTRATION -->
30:
31: </svg>
```

Lastly, note how lines 12 and 29 describe, in a consistent language, the beginning and ending of the house illustration. Using a similar semantic style in your comments can reduce the amount of time you or other developers may face deciphering the document's naming system. By using comments, basic shapes, and `id` attributes, you can assure other developers (and quite possibly yourself) an easier time sorting through your code.

Annotating Documents

Another method of commenting your code involves the `title` and `desc` elements. The `title` and `desc` elements allow developers to provide descriptive text on both a document and object level. Similar to the comment, the `title` and `desc` elements can accept plain text content between their tags. These two elements, though not required, are encouraged for several reasons.

- Other developers, upon examining your code, will be able to discern a greater amount of context for your document.

- Some SVG viewers will use title element content as "tool-tip" text, meaning that when a user's cursor is over an object with a `title` element, the `title` element's contents display in a box above the content.

- By providing your document and elements with the `title` and `desc` elements, your SVG content is more accessible to those with limited viewing capabilities, such as the visually impaired.

The `title` element is used to verbally name both an SVG document and its objects. The syntax for the element is `<title>Titling goes here.</title>`. Although it can be located almost anywhere within the `svg` element's tags, the `title` element used to describe the document generally follows the `svg` element. Additional `title` elements can be inserted within other elements, thus creating a child element that quickly describes an object (or group of objects).

To illustrate the use of the `title` element, copy the code from Listing 20.2 and paste it into a new document. To name the entire SVG document, insert a `title` element below the `svg` element (line 7 in Listing 20.5). Provide an illustrative name that gives a reader enough detail about the document (line 8), and close the `title` element (line 9).

As the `title` element also works on content, you can name objects within your document as well. Try this by inserting a `title` element within the `windows` group (line 22). As this `title` falls within a group, it should be used to name the group's content (not the document's). Provide an appropriate name (line 23), and close the element (line 24).

LISTING 20.5 Using the `title` Element, Documents and Objects Can Be Labeled in a Manner That Assists Other Developers and the Handicapped

```
01: <?xml version="1.0" standalone="no"?>
02: <!DOCTYPE svg PUBLIC "-//W3C//DTD SVG 1.0//EN"
03:     "http://www.w3.org/TR/2001/REC-SVG-20010904/DTD/svg10.dtd">
04:
05: <svg  width="500" height="300">
06:
07:         <title>
08:                 A graphic illustration of a simple home.
09:         </title>
10:
11:         <style type="text/css">
12:                 <![CDATA[
13:                         .FillFFFFFF{fill:#FFFFFF;}
14:                 ]]>
15:         </style>
16:
17:         <g id="structure">
18:                 <polygon id="roof" points="144,66 72,0 0,66"/>
19:                 <rect id="block" x="22" y="60" width="100" height="80"/>
20:         </g>
21:         <g id="windows" class="FillFFFFFF">
22:                 <title>
23:                         Windowpanes above the door.
24:                 </title>
25:                 <rect id="pane1" x="55" y="42" width="9" height="9"/>
26:                 <rect id="pane2" x="80" y="42" width="9" height="9"/>
27:                 <rect id="pane3" x="55" y="65" width="9" height="9"/>
28:                 <rect id="pane4" x="80" y="65" width="9" height="9"/>
29:         </g>
30:         <g id="door">
31:                 <rect id="frame" class="FillFFFFFF"
32:                         x="55" y="91" width="33" height="41"/>
33:                 <circle id="handle" cx="63" cy="113" r="4"/>
34:         </g>
35:
36: </svg>
```

20

The result of these two `title` additions will make no effect on the display of your SVG document, as neither the `title` nor `desc` elements' contents are rendered as graphical content. The three possibilities where users might encounter your `title` content are as follows:

1) If a user views your document's source code, the title content is visible in the text.

2) Some SVG viewers will display the content as tool-tip text.

3) If a user views your SVG file as a stand-alone document within a viewer, a viewer's window title bar may display the content.

The `desc` element is used to verbally describe an SVG document and/or its objects. The syntax for the element is `<desc>`*Descriptive text goes here.*`</desc>`. Although it can be located almost anywhere within the `svg` element's tags, the `desc` element used to describe the document generally follows the `title` element (which often follows the `svg` element). Additional `desc` elements can be inserted within other elements, thus creating a child element that expounds on the purpose of an object (or group of objects).

To illustrate the `desc` element, copy your code from Listing 20.5 and paste it into a new document. As the content of the `title` element you previously created only speaks to what is rendered, you can add text that explains the purpose of the file: this document was originally created to show how basic shape elements were more descriptive than `path` elements in certain instances. Thus, to further describe the document, create a `desc` element directly following your `title` element (line 10 in Listing 20.6). Insert your descriptive text (line 11), and close the element (line 12).

Just as with the `title` element, the `desc` element can be used to describe specific content. Take advantage of this ability by further describing an object within your file. Insert a `desc` element within the `door` group (line 34), provide text that describes the function of the group's content (line 35), and close the element (line 36).

LISTING 20.6 Using the `desc` Element, Documents and Objects Can Be Further Described in Plain Text

```
01: <?xml version="1.0" standalone="no"?>
02: <!DOCTYPE svg PUBLIC "-//W3C//DTD SVG 1.0//EN"
03:    "http://www.w3.org/TR/2001/REC-SVG-20010904/DTD/svg10.dtd">
04:
05: <svg  width="500" height="300">
06:
07:        <title>
08:                A graphic illustration of a simple home.
09:        </title>
```

continues

LISTING 20.6   Continued

```
10:            <desc>
11:                    An illustration of a simple house is created using basic SVG
                          elements.
12:            </desc>
13:
14:            <style type="text/css">
15:                    <![CDATA[
16:                            .FillFFFFFF{fill:#FFFFFF;}
17:                    ]]>
18:            </style>
19:
20:            <g id="structure">
21:                    <polygon id="roof" points="144,66 72,0 0,66"/>
22:                    <rect id="block" x="22" y="60" width="100" height="80"/>
23:            </g>
24:            <g id="windows" class="FillFFFFFF">
25:                    <title>
26:                            Windowpanes above the door.
27:                    </title>
28:                    <rect id="pane1" x="55" y="42" width="9" height="9"/>
29:                    <rect id="pane2" x="80" y="42" width="9" height="9"/>
30:                    <rect id="pane3" x="55" y="65" width="9" height="9"/>
31:                    <rect id="pane4" x="80" y="65" width="9" height="9"/>
32:            </g>
33:            <g id="door">
34:                    <desc>
35:                            The house's door is created using only two elements:
                                a rectangle for the door and a circle for the door
        handle.
36:                    </desc>
37:                    <rect id="frame" class="FillFFFFFF"
38:                            x="55" y="91" width="33" height="41"/>
39:                    <circle id="handle" cx="63" cy="113" r="4"/>
40:            </g>
41:
42: </svg>
```

20

Just as with Listing 20.5, your desc content will not render, resulting in the same visual output as Figure 20.4. Despite the lack of impact on the visual result of your code, the title and desc elements are very useful to developers (yourself included if you forget the purpose of your code) and some handicapped users. By adding these elements to your documents, you can help ensure that your documents are viewable and understandable to a larger audience.

The extent to which you use these elements is truly at your discretion. Providing a title and description for every element you create may be more time consuming than the effort is worth. As a general rule of thumb, consider prioritizing the addition of the following elements:

- Document level (foremost importance)
- Major groups of content
- Individual elements (least importance)

Locating Document Elements

Finding a consistent location for items that do not display, such as style sheets, symbol libraries, fonts (or other encoded CDATA), and animation elements, can tremendously ease time spent editing a document. By ensuring future editors of your code (this includes you) a dependable location to find certain elements, valuable time can be spent modifying code, not searching for it.

This book's examples utilize a consistent method of organizing document elements. This method organizes content in the following order:

1. Document data (`<?xml>`, `<!DOCTYPE>`, and so forth)
2. Annotation (`<desc>`)
3. Stylesheet (`<style>`)
4. Symbol libraries (`<defs>`, `<symbol>`, and so forth)
5. Document content (`<rect>`, `<path>`, and so forth)
6. Animation and interaction (`<animate>`, `<set>`, and so forth)

Not to belabor this point, but this method is only one possible system. Knowing the system of a document's author, though, can provide a developer expedient access to specific content.

Attribute Organization

Similar in importance to the arrangement of your document's different elements is the arrangement of your elements' attributes. In Listing 20.2, you hopefully saw the value of using basic shape elements to ease the understanding of an element's function. Providing an ordering for your attributes produces similar results.

Consider the following two examples:

LISTING 20.7 Elements with Various Locations for Their Attributes Result in a Confusing Read

```
<rect id="Box1" x="10" y="10"
    width="125" height="125"/>
<rect x="53" height="25" y="98"
    width="11" id="Box2"/>
```

LISTING 20.8 By Using Consistent Locations for Attributes, Understanding an Element's Location Is Possible Much More Quickly

```
<rect id="Box1" x="10" y="10"
    width="125" height="125"/>
<rect id="Box2" x="53" y="98"
    width="11" height="25"/>
```

The ease of interpreting the elements in Listing 20.8 almost needs no explanation. Each element lists its attributes in the same manner as the other, making comparisons and quick scanning easily possible.

Listing 20.7, on the other hand, is several times more confusing. The id value loses its ability to quickly convey the sense of the element because it is hard to find. The remaining attributes are jumbled, and comparisons between the two elements become more difficult to make.

Even on a scale of merely two elements, such consistent arrangement of attributes makes sense. Considering nearly all of your SVG documents will contain dozens, if not hundreds, of elements, a structured order to your attributes becomes necessary.

Style Sheet Organization

In Hour 6, you learned how to organize your style sheets by grouping together similar styles, thus making it easier to find, add, or edit related classes. It also created a system that was easy to duplicate between documents, allowing anyone editing or reviewing your document to determine a class's name without having to root through the actual style sheet.

Your SVG files will likely contain numerous selectors. If your styles are not organized, it becomes difficult to quickly scan over a list of selector names and discern the style appropriate for a specific use.

20

To alleviate such issues, you can group style rules according to their function. In Hour 6, the instance was given where you had a style sheet with ten classes that represented different fill colors, four classes that represented four stroke colors, and two classes that determined an object's visibility. In such a case, you should group these classes according to their function rather than arranging them in a haphazard fashion (such as a stroke rule in between two fill rules).

Compression

Although SVG benefits developers by exposing its code for both perusal and editing (similar to HTML), its raw code base can result in files that are larger than contemporary formats (such as Flash and GIF). Knowing that file size will still be an issue for some time to come due to bandwidth considerations, the W3C opted to allow a compressed form of SVG.

SVGZ is the acronym used for compressed SVG documents. The "Z" in SVGZ references the "Z" in GZIP, the type of compression used for SVG (as GZIP files generally end with a ".gz" suffix). GZIP is a compression technology originally developed for Unix. It is now an open standard itself: a likely reason why the technology was chosen over other compression technologies.

An SVGZ file is no more than a regular SVG document compressed using the GZIP format. Though its code is no longer editable in this format (as it is compressed), every SVG viewer is capable of displaying its contents in the exact same manner as the uncompressed file. Thus, using SVGZ for your SVG documents once the documents are complete makes considerable sense. Your documents, once compressed, display and perform exactly as before, only now they are a fraction of the file size.

GZIP compression is not a one-way street. An SVG document encoded with the GZIP technology can be easily decompressed, resulting in the same file as the original. In other words, you run no risk of losing your content by compressing your SVG documents.

So what tools can you use to GZIP your SVG documents? The following options exist for the Macintosh and PC:

- As always, the PC platform has a number of possible solutions available. The creator of GZIP, Jean-loup Gailly, has created an appropriately named application, gzip, to handle GZIP compression on the PC. Similar to the Mac version, drag and drop your SVG documents onto the application and the files will be compressed (You can download GZIP free from www.gzip.org).

- On the Macintosh, Jean-loup Gailly's MacGZIP is a freeware utility that can both compress and decompress files in the GZIP format. By simply dragging your SVG documents onto the MacGZIP application, you can quickly create GZIP files (You can download MacGZIP free from persephone.cps.unizar.es/general/gente/spd/gzip/.) Also, StuffIt Deluxe (the primary commercial compression/decompression suite on the Macintosh platform) offers a GZIP encoding option (StuffIt Deluxe is avilable for download and purchase from www.aladdinsys.com.)

It is important to note that in both cases you will need to rename your files. SVGZ files should end with the ".svgz" extension to be interpreted correctly. In the case of these applications, your files will generally end in ".svg.gz," as ".gz" is the suffix attached to GZIP files.

Once you have changed the file name to reflect the ".svgz" suffix, your new compressed documents are ready for viewing. You should experiment with GZIP compression on the examples you have already made (as well as the book's final example in Hour 23). After compressing your files, compare the file sizes to get an idea of the savings GZIP compression offers.

Many 10-kilobyte files can be reduced to two kilobytes, equaling file size savings of close to 80%. Keep in mind, however, that the smaller the file size of the original uncompressed file, the less significant the results of compression.

Summary

Anyone can code an SVG document. Coding an SVG document that makes sense to other developers, however, separates a marketable developer from the masses. Especially when considering team environments, producing code that is legible, well structured, and well documented makes you a valuable asset. Though your teammates may not think to thank you for your efforts, you can be certain they will remember to scorn you for your lack of foresight if you neglect such coding efficiency.

Considering that you will likely want to review your work at a later point, such organization can be justified for selfish reasons, too. Whatever your motivation, the time spent organizing your document is similar to the time spent maintaining your car. You can avoid changing the oil for a period of time, but when things actually break down, their severity is magnified by the amount of neglect.

You can choose to ignore such tips on organization and optimization, and you will likely continue to produce code that works and displays fine. But come one critical deadline where you can't find the cause of an error or determine the function of an object, and you may sorely regret your short-sightedness.

The suggestions in this hour have provided you with concrete steps you can take to minimize your development team's headaches when working on SVG projects. All of these suggestions come from practical experience working in a team environment and trying to determine the most efficient method to develop SVG. As such, these suggestions are a culmination of the findings from this experience. If you have other experiences, or experiences that further prove the usefulness of these suggestions, be sure to drop the author a line at author@svgnow.com.

20

Q&A

Q How detailed should an engineer's prototype be?

A The prototypes discussed in this hour should truly be as simple and basic as possible. Use rectangles to serve as virtually all content to be used on the page. If animation or interaction will occur, use the appropriate element, but don't worry about populating every attribute. For instance, the prototype should not concern itself with the motion path to be used; rather, it should contain *a* motion path to prove the design's ability to be executed.

Q Our design and engineering teams do not get along well nor do they see the value in working concurrently. Can we develop SVG in the same fashion as we've used before?

A Certainly. However, before you throw out the idea completely, consider running two teams on a project. Have one team work concurrently, while the other works in a traditional fashion. Measure the success of both approaches, and see which truly works better for your teams. As with all the points in this hour, these are suggestions, not hard-and-fast rules. Find the method that works best for your team, but always keep your eyes open for potentially stronger models.

Q My office uses a different code organizational structure than the one recommended in this book. Which should I use?

A This hour's suggestions on code organization are just that—suggestions. If your colleagues already have a system that works, you will generally want to stick to theirs. Unless an existing system is extremely flawed, you generally cause more damage by introducing competing systems (thereby producing *no* system).

Q At what point does a document need such an organizational system?

A Rather than determining a point at which you decide to begin implementing a cohesive system, always start with a system that is as expandable as possible. You will never be able to foresee every organizational problem that may arise, but avoiding even the small ones saves you time in the long run.

Workshop

The Workshop is designed to help you anticipate possible questions, review what you've learned, and begin learning how to put your knowledge into practice.

Quiz

1. What is the value of having development teams working concurrently?

2. True or False: Engineers can begin developing prototype SVG documents after seeing rudimentary design approaches.

3. What is the value of naming every element with the `id` attribute?

4. True or False: You must comment all of your code for it to work correctly.

5. True or False: SVG does not require a consistent naming convention.

Answers

1. When development teams (such as creative, architecture, and engineering) work in parallel, you can generally shave time off the production cycle. Also, as all teams are working simultaneously, their ability to share critical knowledge with the other groups is increased (as there is no delay in transmission).

2. True. By working abstractly with simple shapes initially, engineers can focus on creating optimized code. Once the artwork is finished, they can replace their placeholder imagery with the actual designed content.

3. The `id` attribute not only allows SVG content to be referenced internally by animation and interaction elements, but it also lets development teams use a common language to describe content. The designer and engineer will be able to use the same names to describe an object, thus reducing the possibility of mistakes and frustration.

4. False. Commenting code is optional, but can greatly increase the chances you or another developer can understand the intent of your code.

5. True. Providing a consistent naming convention is not a mandate of the W3C recommendation. Rather, it becomes a mandate amongst developers once excessive time is spent trying to determine the intent of a developer who did not use a convention.

Exercises

1. If you work as part of a development team, try working in tandem with your counterpart (if you are a designer, work with an engineer; if an engineer, then a designer; and so forth) on a basic SVG project. For instance, as you saw in Hours 18 and 19, JavaScript integration can take some serious thought. Have the designer sketch an idea for an SVG animation. Then, while the designer is producing the artwork, the engineer should begin developing the JavaScript and basic SVG code. Combine the respective accomplishments, and measure the effectiveness of this teamwork.

2. If you own a WYSIWYG SVG drawing application (such as Illustrator or CorelDraw), export some of your existing designs (don't go for the super-complicated ones first) as SVG. Open a copy of the code in your editor and begin replacing the path elements with basic shape elements. When finished, compare the two sets of code to see the value of such an exercise. Better yet, pass the two

20

documents to two engineers, and give them three specific tasks to change objects in the artwork. Do not refer to the objects by id value, but rather by their appearance in a print-out. Measure which code base allows for faster editing.

3. Try and develop a new naming convention for the example in Listing 20.3. Make sure your system can accommodate similar objects (such as other buildings or additional components to each building). For instance, what happens to this example when a second window is added to the house?

HOUR **21**

Using Adobe Illustrator to Create Artwork

As with HTML and other technologies, the layperson couldn't care less about the SVG code needed to generate graphics. In fact, the more removed they can be from the actual code, the better. Unfortunately, the bulk of WYSIWYG HTML editors have ruined a good thing; the code these editors generate often requires more work to fix than it would have taken to hand-code in the first place.

In the last hour, you learned how the visual aspects of SVG creation could be separated from the more technical aspects by allowing designers to develop the artwork while the engineering team developed the interactive prototype. The integration of these two separate tracks requires some effort, though, and this hour will begin to outline some steps designers can take while working within Adobe Illustrator (the most used WYSIWYG SVG editor). By adhering to these steps, you are more likely to produce SVG code that will ease the blending of these two development paths.

Although many developers may bemoan tools that separate code from its appearance, software vendors, such as Adobe, Corel, and Jasc, have worked hard to create a new breed of WYSIWYG SVG tools that do not suffer from the same pitfalls to which their HTML predecessors succumbed. No graphical editor will ever create code the exact way you want it, however, so having a few tricks up your sleeve before using the programs will eliminate some of the headaches you may otherwise experience.

As Adobe Illustrator is the tool nearly all design professionals already use, this hour will focus on tips for SVG creation in this program. The decision to focus on this one tool among many was not chosen lightly. Corel, Jasc, and others are putting out high-quality tools to author SVG, some matching and some surpassing Illustrator's capabilities. As such, the decision was based on the tool most likely to be in the possession of this book's audience.

Several of the tips in this hour and the next were published in an alternative format by the author during 2000 and 2001 while he led a research & development team at New York–based Iguana Studios. The tips were culled from experience creating SVG content for the *BattleBots* Web site. (*BattleBots* is Comedy Central's robotic combat show, comparable in nature to the WWF but with robots instead of wrestlers. It can be found online at `www.battlebots.com`.)

All caveats aside, this hour will focus on helping you expedite SVG creation using either Adobe Illustrator 9 or 10 (for both Macintosh and Windows platforms). This hour will not serve as a step-by-step guide to every feature of Illustrator nor to Illustrator's every SVG option. Rather, it will focus on examples, drawn from commercial experience using the tool, that can significantly reduce time spent modifying the exported code.

Specifically, you will learn the following in this hour:

- Matching your Illustrator layer names to your SVG document's `id` values
- Maintaining accurate artwork position between your Illustrator and SVG documents
- Converting Illustrator-export style selectors into more easily decipherable selector names
- Precisely positioning artwork to reduce coordinate clutter and file size
- Reducing unnecessary artwork from your Illustrator document before exporting an SVG document
- Optimizing masked content for export
- Cleaning up Illustrator's code export

Layers

Likely the most common annoyance when exporting Illustrator artwork into SVG is the misshapen `id` values generated by the names in the Layers palette. As most designers think in plain English and not in possible XML-compatible `id` attribute values, the names used for each layer in the palette (which convert into an object or group's `id` value) often result in bizarre output.

When using Illustrator 9, any layer name with spaces will export with the text "_x_200_" replacing the space. As such, "Bldg 1 Window" will export as "Bldg_x_200_1_x_200_Window." Such an oddity results in not only an addition of 7 bytes for each space in all of your layer names, but also nearly illegible `id` values. Figure 21.1 shows the bizarre results of leaving spaces in your Illustrator layer names.

FIGURE 21.1

Leaving spaces in your layer names results in bizarre name conversions when your SVG code is exported.

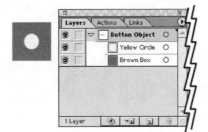

The remedy for this issue is simple: make sure to never use spaces in your layer names. This rule isn't too hard to remember when you create *new* artwork in Illustrator; the problem really manifests itself when you open *legacy* artwork (which may contain hundreds of layer names). Of course, if changing every layer name in Illustrator is problematic, you can find every instance of "_x_200_" within your code and replace it with an underscore or nothing at all. Figure 21.2 shows the result of the "no space" policy: `id` values that are legible and parallel to their Illustrator layer name counterpart.

FIGURE 21.2

By deleting all spaces in your layer names, your layer names and SVG `id` values remain consistent when your SVG code is exported.

21

Illustrator 10 also offers a further resolution to this matter. As a default, it converts spaces to underlines. Thus, "Bldg 1 Window" will be output as "Bldg_1_Window" in version 10. Also, you can change your Units preferences (Edit > Preferences > Units & Undo. . .) from the default "Object ID" to "XML ID," thus forcing your layer names to adhere to XML's naming conventions. With this option set, you can be assured that the id values your design team is referring to have the same names as the values your engineering team uses. Figure 21.3 shows this option within the "Units & Undo. . ." preference pane.

FIGURE 21.3

Changing your Units preferences in Illustrator 10 to "XML ID" forces your layer names to adhere to XML's naming conventions.

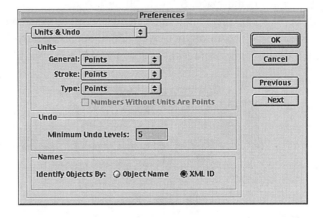

Whether using Illustrator 10's remedy or not, it makes good sense to begin naming all your Illustrator layer names using either no spaces or using underscores in place of spaces. By getting in this habit now, you can ensure you won't have to deal with the time-consuming task of name conversion on that awesome file you'll be exporting next year.

Another issue relating to layers is Illustrator's inclusion of all layer data upon export. Although this may seem like common sense, most designers haven't needed to clean up their artwork before exporting for raster formats. Anything that wasn't visible in your Illustrator file wouldn't suddenly appear when exported as a GIF.

Visually, this still holds true when Illustrator exports SVG. However, every layer, whether hidden or revealed, exports into your SVG document. Layers that were hidden in Illustrator will have a `display` property value of `none` upon export, thus hiding them from display but retaining their data within the code. Figure 21.4 shows how hidden layers within an Illustrator document still produce code in the exported SVG document.

If you have only one small layer hidden, this may be no large matter. If you have dozens of complex layers, though, your SVG document's file size will be much larger than necessary. As shaving bytes off file size can mean the difference in a user waiting around for your content to load or leaving for another site, it is in your best interest to strip as much unnecessary information as possible from your documents. You can do this easily via a graphical user interface in Illustrator, or you can manually delete the data by hand.

Not only is the "by hand" method more time consuming, but mistakes can also be made more easily. Remember, every object that is hidden will retain style information that describes its appearance should it be revealed. Thus, you may end up exporting a number of style classes that needn't be in your master style sheet.

FIGURE 21.4

Leaving hidden layers in your Illustrator file upon export will result in unnecessary exported code, cluttering your document.

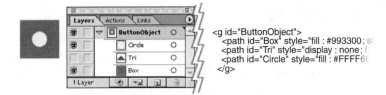

Finally, before exporting, be certain to ungroup your content as much as possible. Excessive grouping in Illustrator results in excessive grouping in your SVG file. Though some grouping will benefit your understanding of how some elements relate to each other, hundreds of nested groups (groups within groups) may become more complex than you can manage. Try and balance your need for grouping items upon export with the need to reduce your code size as much as possible.

Style

Illustrator has a unique method of applying style to objects. When exporting SVG, Illustrator creates a series of styles beginning with st and ending in a sequentially building number. Though creating small style names shaves a number of bits off the file size, it also creates a problem for developers who are trying to understand what style names reference what style properties. Consider performing a global find & replace on your SVG document. Replace each st# instance with a more illustrative name.

For instance, if st7 fills an object with #336699, replace all instances of st7 with "Fill336699." Be certain to start the find-and-replace task with the last style, as replacing st1 will catch both st1 and the first three characters of st10. Also, be sure not to use underscores in your style names, as CSS has strict rules for class names. Your viewer will display a "Bad CSS descriptor" error if you create a class name that isn't compatible.

Before instantly finding & replacing all these style names, be cautious. These tips require added work to the initial development of your SVG files but reduce many stumbling blocks later. It is very important to note, however, that these tips should be applied only

21

to your final exported documents. As you are unable to label your styles within Illustrator as of version 10, future exports will ignore any changes you have made to style names and replace them with the default Illustrator naming convention, making many of your previous efforts worthless. Thus, it is advisable to make these adjustments as late in the process as possible. (After overwriting your hard work once, you'll be certain to perform this task only when the artwork is final and complete.)

Positioning

Illustrator, just like SVG, is a pixel-precise application. Although the bulk of the world may not care if a rectangle's top left corner is at (5.76389,45.8012), you can bet your inheritance that the designer does care if that is the original intent. As such, SVG allows designers to fuss with their code to their hearts' content.

However, there are some unexpected side effects of both Illustrator's and SVG's precision. What may *look* like perfect alignment between two abutting objects in Illustrator may actually be off by 0.00001 of a pixel. Although Illustrator's display engine may make your artwork appear correctly, you have no such guarantees with every SVG viewer. The 0.00001–pixel difference may be enough to cause a different application of anti-aliasing on each object.

Such a display difference may be enough to make the objects look askew, thus ruining your effect. To resolve such a matter, be sure to align both X- and Y-axes' edges when possible before exporting your artwork.

You can also ensure proper alignment and placement of your artwork by using the Transform palette in Illustrator. By using whole numbers for the top left coordinates, width, and height when possible, your code will be dramatically easier to understand (and significantly smaller in size). You can also be assured that your objects are in correct placement by comparing their X and Y values after clicking on the top left corner of the nine-box matrix in the left quadrant of the palette. (This box determines where the X and Y values are calculated.) Figure 21.5 shows the Transform palette and its matrix selector with comparable artwork but different values.

FIGURE 21.5

Illustrator's Transform palette allows you to precisely place your artwork (as in the rectangle at right) before exporting, resulting in simpler values.

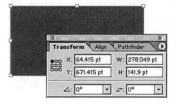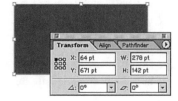

Most designers and illustrators haven't needed to worry about the page location of their artwork. A group of artwork can reside in the center of the page or in the top-right corner; the artwork is generally positioned in a page layout program, such as Quark XPress.

SVG does worry about the location of your artwork, and thus Illustrator exports your artwork in relation to its relation to the top-left corner of the artwork's bounding box. Figure 21.6 shows how the bounding box relates to Illustrator artwork.

FIGURE 21.6

Illustrator sets the (0,0) coordinates of its exported artwork based upon the top-left edge of the artwork's bounding box.

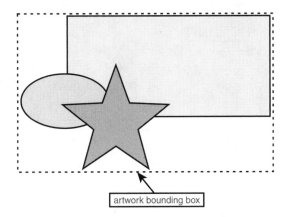

artwork bounding box

As such, your artwork may not appear in the location you had originally intended (unless, of course, your artwork was aligned with the upper-leftmost corner of your artboard). There is a method, though, to ensure that your artwork exports from Illustrator according to its page position.

Ensuring correct page position is a three-step process. First, set your Illustrator document layout definitions to the exact size of the SVG you will be exporting. This can be done using the Document Setup dialog box, available under the file menu, or at document startup, using the New Document dialog box. Figure 21.7 shows these two dialog boxes.

FIGURE 21.7

Set your document's artboard size to the same dimensions as your final SVG by using either the Document Setup or the New Document dialog boxes.

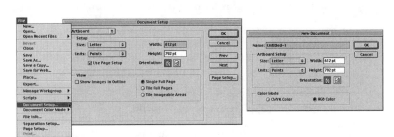

21

Next, set your Illustrator document's (0,0) point (via the ruler's corner tool) to the top left corner of your artboard's page. The (0,0) coordinate is set to the lower-left corner of the page by default. You need only to click and drag the dotted crosshairs in the upper left corner of the rulers to make such an adjustment. Figure 21.8 shows this coordinate change process in action.

FIGURE 21.8

Set your document's top-left coordinates to (0,0) using the ruler's corner tool.

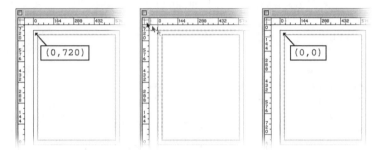

Finally, create a box with no fill or stroke that conforms to the size of your artboard (which should always be set to the final size of your SVG). Label this layer **BoundingBox**, or something along those lines. Any time you export components of your artwork from your file, be sure to keep your BoundingBox layer, and these components will retain their x and y values in relation to the original SVG document.

Once exported, you can delete the BoundingBox object, as it will not be needed in your SVG document. It will have ensured, however, that your artwork is placed in its appropriate position within the document's framework.

This trick will almost always guarantee pixel-precise placement. The exception to this rule is when your document contains masked content that bleeds over the artboard's left and top edges *before* being masked. If such content exists, the exported SVG uses the top left coordinates of the mask's original content, not the mask's coordinates. As such, you will notice white margins to the left and top of your exported file.

There are several resolutions to this issue.

First, you can delete the masked content, not the mask itself, from your file before your first export. After this, export only the mask's content. You can then move the mask's content into position using a translate command, and then paste your content inside the mask using the clipPath or mask elements.

Your second option is to trim your masked content before exporting, effectively eliminating the need for a mask. By using the Pathfinder's tools, such as Subtract, you can "punch" your artwork so that it does not extend past its mask's edges (remembering that there will be no mask when this task is completed). Figure 21.9 shows these tools within the Pathfinder palette.

FIGURE 21.9

By using the Pathfinder's tools, you can punch your artwork out of its mask.

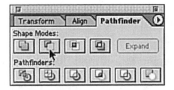

Also, remove all points outside of the artboard. In cases where your paths extend past the artboard, simply drag their points (or cut the path) to the artboard's edge. As mentioned before, the SVG file will contain all of the Illustrator document's elements. If information that won't be visible in the final image is taken out or trimmed down, your file will be much smaller and easier to understand.

Cleaning Up Your Code

Be sure to avoid exporting complex blends from Illustrator. SVG currently has no way to define complex, multi-directional blends comparable to Illustrator's Gradient Mesh or object blend. If you export a complex blend from Illustrator, your blend will comprise (potentially) hundreds of unique paths, representing each step of the gradation.

Such a result will be both code-heavy and nearly incomprehensible. Although visually you may achieve your result, the resulting code may warrant an alternative solution.

In Hour 20, you learned to code your artwork with basic shape elements when possible. A similar rule holds true in Illustrator: Try to create your artwork as simply as possible.

For instance, if you are creating a table, draw one large rectangle, and then draw simple lines that can easily be duplicated, instead of many boxes that must line up exactly. Not only does the former method create smaller files, but it also eliminates possible room for errors when you export code.

As you read earlier, a 0.00001 pixel shift may result in odd anti-aliasing, destroying your intended visual result. By thinking through your artwork, you may reduce the amount of code necessary to render your masterpiece and help prevent possible errors.

Also, there is a trick to facilitate converting your exported elements to basic shape elements. Currently, Illustrator does not export its circles and rectangles into these elements, but there is a workaround. Simply label your path with a convention similar to `ObjectIDName_Rect23x56y10h10z`. By adding the x, y, width, and height values, as well as the basic shape name, designers can help their engineering team quickly convert path data into basic shape elements.

21

Lastly, upon final export of your code, set the decimal value in export options to "1" when no curves are being used. Decimal points determine the precision of your point placement. If you are using straight lines that don't have slight gradations in angle or curves, you should use exact positioning and set your decimal range export value to "1."

If you've set all your objects to use precise whole-numbered coordinates, this option will not matter much. However, if you have objects with coordinates like (41.89234,71.459235), a simple method such as this can automatically reduce your code export by producing (41.9,71.5).

The decimal setting can be changed in Illustrator 10 by clicking on the "Advanced" button in the SVG Options dialog box upon saving your document as an SVG file. Illustrator 9 generates SVG by using the Export option (under the File menu), where a dialog box with a pull-down menu for decimal places automatically appears upon pressing Export. Figure 21.10 shows both of these options.

FIGURE 21.10

Both versions of Illustrator offer means of reducing the amount of data exported by reducing the number of possible decimal places.

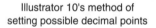
Illustrator 10's method of   Illustrator 9's method of
setting possible decimal points   setting possible decimal points

Summary

Using Adobe Illustrator to create your SVG content allows beautiful design work to enter the SVG sphere. Although any code created by Illustrator can certainly be created by hand, the amount of time required to plot all the coordinates and shapes of most design work would be monumental.

As such, knowing how to effectively create and export your Illustrator artwork can further increase the usefulness of this tool. By having designers name and manage layers, use precise coordinates and document sizes, trim masked content, and clean up style sheet exports, engineers can focus on what they do best, rather than having to deal with excessive cleanup.

Q&A

Q **Why bother deleting hidden layers from an Illustrator file before exporting it as an SVG document?**

A Although it is true that an end-user viewing your SVG in a viewer will not see any artwork that was hidden in Illustrator, there are several reasons to delete this data beforehand. First, excess data that will not be displayed results in extra download and loading time, which users will likely not appreciate, for negligible content. Second, that hidden content can be made visible if a user modifies your code. If the layer was hidden for privacy reasons, you will be sorely surprised when users extract information that wasn't intended for them.

Workshop

The Workshop is designed to help you anticipate possible questions, review what you've learned, and begin learning how to put your knowledge into practice.

Quiz

1. What corner of Illustrator's artboard reflects the (0,0) coordinate by default?

2. True or False: Reducing decimal places in your exported code does not affect file size.

3. How can a designer set the precise placement of an object in Illustrator?

Answers

1. The bottom left corner is Illustrator's default (0,0) location. Using the ruler's corner point tool can change this.

2. False. By reducing the number of possible values in each coordinate, you can significantly reduce your file size.

3. By using Illustrator's Transform palette, a designer can plot precise coordinates for an object's placement and dimensions.

21

Exercises

1. Try creating the house illustration used in Figure 20.4 within Illustrator. Name your layers according to the convention shown in this hour's "Cleaning Up Your Code" section. After listing your coordinates within the layer name and exporting the file, open the SVG code in a text editor and change the `path` data into basic shape elements by referring to the `id` value's information.

2. After exporting an Illustrator document as SVG, try to perform the style sheet cleanup detailed in this hour. Convert the class names to a convention similar to the one outlined in Hour 6. Remember to find & replace the largest numbered names first!

Hour 22

Overcoming Common Problems

Hour 21 detailed how to handle fine-tuning your Illustrator documents for exporting your code. This chapter, however, will detail some common problems you may encounter while creating SVG documents; whether in Illustrator or by hand. To help you overcome some of the possible roadblocks, you will cover topics such as

- Animation
- Typography
- Display
- Style sheets
- AOL image display

Animation

One of the most common complaints users have of SVG is its performance when handling animation. The Adobe SVG Viewer, for one, calculates the plug-in screen's redraw area based on the bounding box of the edges of all moving or changing objects. Thus, if you create an SVG that has movement in all four corners of the screen, the entire plug-in screen is forced to redraw for every frame of the animations. As the plug-in has not yet been optimized for display, animation performance drops dramatically when large areas are forced to redraw.

It is important to remember that SVG has not yet reached the maturity of fifth-generation Flash. Rather, vendors like Adobe and IBM have worked to create viewers that can match the specification's requirements first and foremost. After functionality is in place, performance optimization will likely take next priority.

Nonetheless, you've got SVG animations you want to create! There are a couple of tricks to pulling off high-performance animation. If you need to have multiple animations display simultaneously, try breaking your image into multiple SVGs, and then reassemble the pieces together in HTML.

An example of this would be a diagram of a football game, where players are running, cheerleaders are jumping, and fans are waving, all at the same time. Rather than creating one large sluggish file, try to create three separate files—one for each group of animation.

Alternatively, if you can design your screen so that all animation occurs in one area, the plug-in will need only redraw a small area. The football game analogy isn't a likely candidate for this method, but could be if you staggered your animation so that the screen redraw would only be occurring at one place at a time.

Probably the biggest drain on animation performance involves filter effects. If at all possible, avoid animating filters or objects with applied filters for the time being. The amount of calculations that need to be applied for filters significantly exceeds that of standard vector artwork. Animating these effects, or having objects move over an area with applied effects, compounds these calculations exponentially.

The number of calculations necessary to render an object's display is important as it is impacted by a user's computer. Older, slower machines, though capable of rendering SVG graphics, may not be able to process enough information to calculate both the artwork and its filter effects at the speed desired.

Because of this, moving an object with a drop shadow will most likely result in the user seeing only the start and stop frame of the animation on a slower machine. Small, selective animations of filters have produced some beautiful results, but when applied to larger, more complex examples, some disappointing results have emerged. Try to design your animations, especially those involving filter effects, with older machines in mind. The bulk of the computing audience is not using state-of-the-art, high-clock-speed graphics machines. Unless your target audience is design professionals, you should create your animations accordingly.

Another trick in optimizing animation playback is to turn non-moving imagery into a JPEG or PNG. The Adobe SVG Viewer displays animations much better if it doesn't need to continuously recalculate static information (now a JPEG or PNG) behind a moving object. This tip is obviously a last resort, as converting your artwork into a raster format removes all the benefits SVG offers, and SVG viewer animation performance should certainly be resolved in the near future (as both vendors optimize their viewers and users purchase faster CPUs).

Lastly, you may want to avoid stroke information when animating an object, whether as the moving object or as the object underneath. As strange as it may sound, redrawing objects with fills but without strokes results in a much faster display. Similar to an issue in Flash, if you can convert your strokes to paths before exporting from Illustrator, you'll generally see better results.

Again, this trick offers performance benefits in the short-term, but destroys your ability to manipulate one object with several style commands. Using this method, every object with a stroke becomes two objects—one object representing the stroke (which is actually now a filled object) and another representing the fill.

Each successive version of SVG viewers moves closer to optimal playback. As such, do not become disheartened by some of today's limitations. In the course of this book's writing, several performance boosts have already been accomplished, and several more are likely within the next year.

Until viewer performance is optimized, though, be cautious of complicated animations that affect the entire document. Such results are not bound to impress audiences or developers, so instead, try and focus on animations that are possible with today's technology. By creating graphics that intelligently use the technology for what it can do today, you can help ensure that viewers will be improved in the future *and* that more people are likely to adopt the technology.

Typography

SVG's ability to apply actual typefaces to your text is an obvious step up in the design capabilities of on-screen technology. However, some bizarre occurrences can emerge in the way SVG applies typeface information to text.

When displaying typography, the Adobe SVG Viewer will first load the text and afterwards apply the CEF font definitions to the `text` element. This often results in a "flickering" effect, as the text initially displays in the default system font and then "jumps" to the appearance of the applied CEF typeface.

To help reduce this flickering, consider embedding the font data within your SVG. Rather than linking to an external CEF or SVG Font, you can contain this information within your SVG document. Encoding this information within the document and *before* your document's visual content will ensure that the typeface's outline information is loaded before the text to which it is applied. This effectively eliminates any text flickering.

By getting rid of the need for accessing an outside file to apply font information, your typeface will appear instantly. Keep in mind, however, that including your font information in your files will add significantly to your file size and scroll time within your code. You will also need to include the same large chunk of typographic information in every SVG document that needs that font.

Display

SVG content is known for its high-quality, resolution-independent display, but it nonetheless has some issues that can easily be resolved with some foresight on the developer's part. Issues such as poor object `opacity` performance, anti-aliasing, and inconsistent document edges can be rectified with the following tips.

The `opacity` style property is incredibly useful to fade items in and out in SVG. However, viewer display performance may suffer, rendering clumsily if you are fading a large quantity of objects.

To improve this handling, try using both the `fill-opacity` and `stroke-opacity` descriptors for each object rather than a global `opacity` property. For some reason, the Adobe SVG Viewer is able to render such transparency calculations faster than with the global `opacity` property.

In some cases, SVG's default smoothing of edges (anti-aliasing) can distort your artwork in negative ways. For example, you may have line-work that needs to appear crisp, such as a table. If your table was created with several abutting rectangles, the default anti-aliasing will make overlapping edges appear thicker and/or darker than non-overlapping edges.

This is due to the visual multiplication of anti-aliased edges. The anti-aliased material is semi-transparent, so when two anti-aliased edges align, their two semi-transparent materials become less transparent, resulting in a thicker and/or darker line.

In such cases, disabling the anti-aliasing effect on these objects can result in a sharper display. To apply an aliased, or crisp-edged, display to an element, use the shape rendering:optimizeSpeed style class. This property and value combination will affect only the objects to which it is applied; the rest of your document will display with the smooth, anti-aliased edges to which you are accustomed.

The final display issue that this hour will cover is the odd edges that sometimes can occur around your SVG document. Many developers have found that a rectangle the size of the SVG dimensions can be used to create a background color for their document. Though a clever trick, as SVG has no method of defining a document background otherwise, unexpected results may occur.

As you know, SVG anti-aliases every object unless specified otherwise. A rectangle set to the dimensions of the document will also see its edges anti-aliased, sometimes resulting in edges that are lighter than the rectangle's solid fill. This is generally noticeable only when your SVG is placed within an XHTML document, as the edge will contrast against the page background.

The solution to this problem is quite easy. All you need do is extend your background beyond the document's inherent viewBox dimensions. Simply extend your background rectangle several units (whether user units, pixels, points, and so on) in every direction beyond the viewBox's area. The viewBox will mask the excess information, and the light edges will disappear.

Listing 22.1 uses the problematic rectangle, whereas Listing 22.2 shows the small but important differences in dimensions and position that eliminate this issue from occurring. (Remember that the visual differences will be discerned only when the SVG files are viewed within an HTML/XML document. You will likely be unable to see a difference if you simply load the SVG files directly into your browser.)

LISTING 22.1 Using a Rectangle, You Can Create a Solid Background Color

```
01: <?xml version="1.0" standalone="no"?>
02: <!DOCTYPE svg PUBLIC "-//W3C//DTD SVG 20001102//EN"
            "http://www.w3.org/TR/2000/CR-SVG-20001102/DTD/svg-20001102.dtd">
03:
04: <svg  width="500" height="300">
05:
06:        <rect id="Background" x="0" y="0" width="500" height="300"
                   style="fill:#336699"/>
07:
08: </svg>
```

Listing 22.2   Altering the Rectangle's Dimensions and Position, You Can Ensure a Consistently Solid Background Color

```
01: <?xml version="1.0" standalone="no"?>
02: <!DOCTYPE svg PUBLIC "-//W3C//DTD SVG 1.0//EN"
            "http://www.w3.org/TR/2001/REC-SVG-20010904/DTD/svg10.dtd">
03:
04: <svg  width="500" height="300">
05:
06:         <rect id="Background" x="-10" y="-10" width="520" height="320"
                    style="fill:#336699"/>
07:
08: </svg>
```

Using this method to expand the shape of the background rectangle, you can be assured of consistent tone across your SVG's background.

Style Sheet Organization

Although Hours 6 and 20 stressed naming and organizing your style sheets, there are two additional and important factors to keep in mind. By consolidating both style classes and style applications, you can reduce the size of your code.

The first of these matters, consolidating style classes, involves reducing the size of your style sheet and class attribute values. For example, if you are using only one font style for your entire document (that is, every instance of text should be 16-point Helvetica, aligned center, with 20-point letter spacing), you should consolidate all font classes into one style, eliminating duplicate information.

Listings 22.3 and 22.4 show the difference between a consolidated class definition (22.4) and an unconsolidated one (22.3).

Listing 22.3   When All Text Elements in a Document Use the Same Font Styles, Class Application Gets Overly Replicated

```
01: <?xml version="1.0" standalone="no"?>
02: <!DOCTYPE svg PUBLIC "-//W3C//DTD SVG 1.0//EN"
            "http://www.w3.org/TR/2001/REC-SVG-20010904/DTD/svg10.dtd">
03:
04: <svg  width="500" height="300">
05:
06:         <style type="text/css">
07:                 <![CDATA[
08:                         .FontFamilyHelvetica{font-family:'Helvetica',sans-serif}
```

continues

LISTING 22.3   Continued

```
09:                              .FontSize16{font-size:16}
10:                              .FontLetterSpacing2{letter-spacing:2}
11:                              .FontAlignCenter{text-anchor:middle}
12:                              ]]>
13:         </style>
14:
15:         <text x="250" y="100" class="FontFamilyHelvetica
                  FontSize16 FontLetterSpacing2 FontAlignCenter">
16:              This is an example of SVG text.
17:         </text>
18:         <text x="250" y="115" class="FontFamilyHelvetica
                  FontSize16 FontLetterSpacing2 FontAlignCenter">
19:              It is bold and fresh!
20:         </text>
21:
22: </svg>
```

LISTING 22.4   By Consolidating Several Style Properties into One Class, Class Application Can Be Simplified

```
01: <?xml version="1.0" standalone="no"?>
02: <!DOCTYPE svg PUBLIC "-//W3C//DTD SVG 1.0//EN"
           "http://www.w3.org/TR/2001/REC-SVG-20010904/DTD/svg10.dtd">
03:
04: <svg  width="500" height="300">
05:
06:         <style type="text/css">
07:                 <![CDATA[
08:                     .MasterFontStyle{font-family:'Helvetica',sans-serif;
                        font-size:16;
                        letter-spacing:2;
                        text-anchor:middle}
09:                 ]]>
10:         </style>
11:
12:         <text x="250" y="100" class="MasterFontStyle">
13:              This is an example of SVG text.
14:         </text>
15:         <text x="250" y="115" class="MasterFontStyle">
16:              It is bold and fresh!
17:         </text>
18:
19: </svg>
```

Removing excess class applications decreases file size, speeds up screen display, and makes your files easier to understand.

The second matter to consider when optimizing your document's style is to consolidate style *application* when possible. For instance, in Listing 22.4, lines 12 and 15 have class applications that are the same. You can consolidate their styles by enclosing both objects within a `MasterFontStyle`-applied group.

Thus, by consolidating these two applications of the same style, you can reduce size and clutter in your document. Listing 22.5 shows such a grouping.

LISTING 22.5 Using a Group with a Class Applied Eliminates the Need to Apply the Same Class to Each of Its Enclosed Elements

```
01: <?xml version="1.0" standalone="no"?>
02: <!DOCTYPE svg PUBLIC "-//W3C//DTD SVG 1.0//EN"
            "http://www.w3.org/TR/2001/REC-SVG-20010904/DTD/svg10.dtd">
03:
04: <svg  width="500" height="300">
05:
06:        <style type="text/css">
07:                <![CDATA[
08:                        .MasterFontStyle{font-family:'Helvetica',sans-serif;
                           font-size:16;
                           letter-spacing:2;
                           text-anchor:middle}
09:                ]]>
10:        </style>
11:
12:        <g class="MasterFontStyle">
13:                <text x="250" y="100">
14:                        This is an example of SVG text.
15:                </text>
16:                <text x="250" y="115">
17:                        It is bold and fresh!
18:                </text>
19:        </g>
20:
21: </svg>
```

Rather than having every object within a group refer to the same class, apply the class to the enclosing group and remove the class from the individual objects.

AOL Image Display

22

Last and most annoyingly in any how-to book comes the section on how to make your content work with America Online (AOL). AOL is notorious for providing a software package and platform that destroys almost every designer's dreams for consistent display.

Image quality has always been a problem for AOL browsers due to a somewhat hidden feature in their software. AOL's servers compress every graphic that a user requests to view (such as images in a Web page) before serving the images back to the user's browser in AOL's proprietary image format. This is always the case, except in the very rare instance that an AOL user has altered the application's preference to turn off this extra compression. As such, any static GIF or JPEG actually becomes an AOL graphic before being viewed. Designers who have checked AOL to see how their sites display are likely familiar with the bizarre changes such compression can cause within HTML.

The result, however, for those viewing SVG files with linked GIF or JPEG images using an SVG viewer while in an AOL browser is the lack of display of these images. The SVG document will continue to load without problems, except that no graphic (nor any trace of a graphic, such as an empty white box) will appear.

There are two ways to work around this issue. First, if you are using a GIF (and thus depending on the Adobe SVG Viewer or any other GIF-capable viewer), consider converting it into an animated GIF. AOL cannot recompress animated GIFs, and thus lets them pass through their servers unmodified. You can simply add a duplicate frame to your GIF, adding a negligible amount of file size, and it will appear no different than it had before (as it is animating between identical frames).

The alternate solution is to embed the image within the SVG file. Programs like Adobe Illustrator allow you to convert raster image data into binary code, which can then be parsed by a viewer as regular image data within the `image` element.

To do this, simply place the formerly external files in an Illustrator document. In Illustrator 9, upon exporting the Illustrator file as an SVG, be sure to select "Embed Raster Images" in the "Raster Image Location" dropdown menu. In Illustrator 10, simply select "Embed" under the "Images" option in the SVG Options dialog box that appears upon saving. Either way, the resulting file will contain the binary data in place of a URI to an image location.

Certain elements, such as PNG alpha channel transparency, will not convert correctly upon export, as the Illustrator binary export does not retain the original graphic format. Rather, the image (whether originally GIF, JPEG, PNG, TIFF, or otherwise) is exported as a JPEG.

Although pestering vendors to fix their wares to become standards-compliant is always a worthwhile cause, AOL has long proven its comfort with ignoring developers's requests. A larger issue than standards conformance and software glitches exists, however. According to their own numbers, AOL has over 6 million subscribers, and their demographic is an audience of technically unsavvy users.

So, even if AOL began shipping new versions of their software with this extra compression removed, several years will pass before even 75% of their users upgrade their software. As such, developers are stuck with this problem and must develop ways to circumvent this issue (and others that will invariably arise).

Troubleshooting Issues

Whether new to SVG or an experienced developer, you will likely encounter some interesting quirks while developing SVG content. These quirks may be the result of various issues that may not be visible upon first glance. Before throwing your hands in the air in defeat, try and determine the possible cause of the issue by asking the following questions:

- Is the problem simply a limitation of the SVG specification? SVG was created to handle specific problems, not every problem. You should double check the specification to see if what you're attempting is even possible.

- Is the problem related to the viewer you are using? Most viewers do not currently have support for the entire W3C recommendation. First, check to see if you're using the latest release of the vendor's viewer. Second, check your vendor's release notes for your particular viewer. Either the viewer may not officially support the feature you are looking for, or you may have found a bug.

- Is the problem related to third-party software? Though the SVG recommendation and certain viewers may technically support your desired effects, third-party software may get in the way. For instance, not every browser has feature parity, and viewers may be limited not by their own technology but rather another's. Again, check your viewer vendor's release notes or FAQs to see if the issue is documented.

Whatever the issue may be, always be sure to check developer groups, such as the svg-developers list on Yahoo! Groups (http://groups.yahoo.com/group/svg-developers/) to see if others have encountered your issue and how they may have handled it. If your problem isn't noted anywhere, then by all means it needs to be. Depending on the issue, post your comments to the appropriate vendor, whether the W3C, a software vendor, a third-party vendor, or a user group.

Summary

The tips to fine-tune your SVG content, thus resolving some common problems, come about from the experience of trying to solve these issues while within a client's deadline. As such, some of the tips may seem more like quick fixes than hard-and-fast rules.

Though these tips solve several issues you are likely to encounter, any developer that seriously attempts to code SVG (or any comparable technology) is certain to encounter a perplexing problem. Just remember to run through the battery of troubleshooting questions before throwing in the towel. Keep in mind that most problems arise from being too close to a situation; by reviewing these simple questions, you may gain the perspective necessary to resolve your issue.

With all of these tips, though, plus the previous hours' instruction, you do have all the knowledge you need to get started creating SVG. The next hour will cover the book's final example, where each lesson learned in this book culminates into one piece.

Q&A

Q Does a computer's processor have any bearing on my animation performance?

A Absolutely. Computer processing speed will impact your animation's performance for some time, until SVG viewers have been fully optimized. Even then, a base level of processor performance will likely be necessary to see animations perform as expected, which indicates a situation similar to Macromedia's Flash plug-in occasionally encountering sluggish performance on older computers.

Workshop

The Workshop is designed to help you anticipate possible questions, review what you've learned, and begin learning how to put your knowledge into practice.

Quiz

1. True or False: Filter effects and transformations cannot be animated.
2. What causes the "flickering" of typefaces when an SVG loads?
3. Which two style properties render more expediently than `opacity`?
4. True or False: All images exported from Adobe Illustrator as embedded content within an SVG are encoded as JPEG content.

Answers

1. False. Of course filter effects and transformations can be animated! What is true is that certain viewers have a hard time efficiently playing some complex animations. The amount of calculations necessary to display your animating effects or transformations may require more processor muscle than a user's machine has. Be sure to test your animations across several viewers, platforms, and machine specifications to ensure your animation will appear as you desire.

2. Type may flicker in SVG when an external typeface hasn't yet loaded and been applied. Embedding the typeface within your document before your text elements ensures that no flicker will occur.

3. The `fill-opacity` and `stroke-opacity` properties tend to provide better performance when animating their values than does the overall `opacity` property.

4. True. Illustrator converts all image data into JPEG image data upon export if it is selected to be embedded, regardless of the image's original format.

Exercises

1. Compare the `opacity` properties in action. Create a group of simple objects, such as several different colored squares. Place this group inside a `defs` library and put two instances of this artwork in your document with the `use` element. Create two `animate` elements: the first animating the `opacity` of the first instance, and the second animating the `fill-opacity` of the second instance.

2. If the bulk of your audience is not using AOL, you may choose to avoid embedding your images within your SVG to ensure the quality of your images. If so, consider creating a small chunk of artwork/text that explains to AOL users why they are not seeing the SVG as intended. By placing this material behind your image, non-AOL users will not see this explanation, but AOL users will have some idea why the SVG doesn't look right.

Hour **23**

Applying Your Knowledge

This book was created with the intent of providing you, the reader, with a strong set of fundamental knowledge required to create SVG. Along the way, if you've gathered some more advanced knowledge, then the book has been all the more successful.

Throughout the book, many of the examples referenced a news center graphic shown in Figure 1.1. By building many of the components of this master graphic, the author has intended to provide you with some practical applications of each skill set. Also, by producing a final graphic that attractively shows off the technology, you will hopefully: 1) be encouraged to create more impressive examples, and 2) impress your contemporaries enough to explore the technology themselves.

With this in mind, this final hour will review the entire code base of the final news center graphic. This graphic is truly built using the same code you generated in previous examples, with some modifications and additions where necessary. And, though typing this code in by hand will certainly give you an appreciation for how the piece works, the example is available for download in the "Book" section of this book's companion Web site: www.svgnow.com.

The Code

As this code is a culmination of nearly all this book's examples, plus more, there are two components to the news center graphic's code. The first is the style sheet, and the second is the actual content code.

The Style Sheet

You will notice that the style sheet (Listing 23.1) and SVG code (Listing 23.2) have line breaks between certain groups of styles. These line breaks are not mandatory; they serve merely to visually distinguish the types of styles and content. Just as a book with no paragraphs makes reading a chore, so too does code without breaks. By adding breaks between separate groupings, you can find the type of style you are looking for much faster.

The style sheet, following, is thus broken into several sections, based upon the function of the classes. For instance, all classes concerning the fill of an object are separated from the remainder of classes. To help shed light on some of the classes you may not have seen yet, the style sheet's code will be commented after each grouping.

LISTING 23.1 This Book's Final Example, the News Center Graphic, Relies on a Large Style Sheet to Define Its Appearance

```
01: .EnableBackgroundNew{enable-background:new;}
02: .DisplayNone{display:none;}
03: .WeatherMaskBox{clip-path:url(#WeatherMask);}
04: .GradientSun{fill:url(#GradientSunCenter);}
05: .RainFalling{fill:url(#RainDrops);}
06: .AliasedObject{shape-rendering:optimizeSpeed;}
07: .FilterDropShadow{filter:url(#DropShadow);}
08:
```

The classes in the first group of styles, lines 1 through 7, are very loosely related. Rather than having similar functions, they are related due to their very lack of relation to other classes, although these classes largely affect document issues.

Line 1 allows filters to access the background image (all content behind the object with the filter applied), whereas line 2 is used to disable content from appearing. Line 3 creates a clipping path that trims off any content it is applied to that falls outside of WeatherMask's shape.

Lines 4 and 5 fill objects with a gradient and pattern (respectively). (The objects referenced in lines 3, 4, and 5 will be found later, in the SVG code following this style sheet.)

Line 6 disables an object's anti-aliased rendering, thus creating crisp edges on all the object's lines and shapes. Line 7 applies the DropShadow filter effect on its applied object.

```
09: .Fill000000{fill:#000000;}
10: .Fill333333{fill:#333333;}
11: .Fill493D56{fill:#493D56;}
12: .Fill664785{fill:#664785;}
13: .Fill666666{fill:#666666;}
14: .Fill999999{fill:#999999;}
15: .Fill99CCFF{fill:#99CCFF;}
16: .FillCCCCCC{fill:#CCCCCC;}
17: .FillC66A10{fill:#C66A10;}
18: .FillFFFF00{fill:#FFFF00;}
19: .FillFFFFFF{fill:#FFFFFF;}
20: .FillNone{fill:none;}
21:
```

Lines 9 through 20 are rather straightforward. Each class fills an object with the hexadecimal RGB value enclosed. By naming the classes with the hex value, you can create a convention that is easily replicable. This will allow other developers to quickly determine the name of the appropriate fill class simply by knowing the hexadecimal value. Line 20 is used to disable an object from using a fill at all.

```
22: .Stroke000000{stroke:#000000;}
23: .StrokeWidth1{stroke-width:1;}
24: .StrokeWidth1Point5{stroke-width:1.5;}
25: .StrokeDasharray1Space2{stroke-dasharray:1,2;}
26: .StrokeNone{stroke:none;}
27:
```

The definitions for the document's stroke application are held in lines 22 through 26. A black line is defined in line 22, and the two line weights (1 point and 1.5 points) are defined on lines 23 and 24.

Line 25 introduces a new style: the dotted line. The stroke-dasharray property can accept two types of values:

1. A single value designates the user unit length of a dash and the gap between it and the next dash. In other words, stroke-dasharray:5 creates a dotted line consisting of 5–user–unit dashes separated by 5–user-unit spaces. And,

2. A series of values (separated by commas) defines the dash by alternating between dash, gap, dash, and so on. In this case, stroke-dasharray:5,7,5,2 creates a dotted line consisting of a 5–user-unit dash separated by a 7–user-unit space, followed by a 5–user-unit dash trailed by a 2–user-unit space. After this 2–user-unit space, the process repeats.

Thus, line 25 converts a solid line into a dashed line with 1–user-unit dashes separated with 2–user-unit spaces. Line 26 ends this grouping of stroke information with a class to prevent a stroke from being applied.

```
28: .FillOpacityPoint25{fill-opacity:0.25;}
29: .FillOpacityPoint75{fill-opacity:0.75;}
30: .OpacityPoint5{opacity:0.5;}
31:
```

Lines 28 and 29 coordinate the transparency of an object using the fill-opacity property. Line 30, instead of using the specific fill-opacity property, uses the opacity property, as images (such as external JPEGs) technically have no fill or stroke to modify. As such, opacity is the only property available to change the transparency of an image.

```
32: .FontFamilyArialNarrow{font-family:'ArialNarrow', 'Arial Narrow', 'Arial',
        sans-serif;}
33: .FontFamilyArialMT{font-family:'ArialMT', 'Arial', sans-serif;}
34: .FontFamilyArialBlack{font-family:'Arial-Black', 'Arial Black', 'Arial',
        sans-serif;}
35:
```

Typefaces are applied to objects using the classes on lines 32 through 34. Each class offers substitute fonts in the likely chance that an end-user may not have the first specified font. In the more unlikely scenario that a user has none of the specified fonts, the font classification description (sans-serif) will ensure that the typeface used will roughly stay within the same typeface as the original.

```
36: .FontSize8{font-size:8;}
37: .FontSize10{font-size:10;}
38: .FontSize12{font-size:12;}
39: .FontSize14{font-size:14;}
40: .FontSize18{font-size:18;}
41: .FontSize36{font-size:36;}
42:
```

Lines 36 through 41 define various type sizes to be used throughout the document. The simple naming convention allows a developer to correctly guess the name of a class if they know the type size to be used.

```
43: .TextAnchorMiddle{text-anchor:middle;}
```

Line 43 finalizes the style sheet. It contains a class to align its applied text to a center point.

The Document

The meat of the graphic, the SVG code, is 241 lines long. Rather than comment all the code beforehand, comments will directly follow a chunk of code, describing the previous work. (Hopefully this will help give you a mental break every couple lines if you are hand-coding this entire document.)

LISTING 23.2   This Book's Final Example, the News Center Graphic, Relies on 241 Lines of Code to Define Its Artwork

```
01: <?xml version="1.0" standalone="no"?>
02: <?xml-stylesheet href="listing2301.css" type="text/css"?>
03: <!DOCTYPE svg PUBLIC "-//W3C//DTD SVG 1.0//EN"
            "http://www.w3.org/TR/2001/REC-SVG-20010904/DTD/svg10.dtd">
04:
```

Lines 1 through 4 are the standard document data code you've seen throughout this book. Line 1 declares that this is XML code and then declares its version number and its dependence on outside elements. Line 2 points the document to the outside style sheet you just completed in Listing 23.1. Line 3 declares that this is an SVG document and points to the W3C's SVG 1.0 DTD (Document Type Definition) so the file can be validated. Remember, without a DTD, your document cannot be checked for validity!

```
05: <svg  width="500pt" height="300pt" viewBox="0 0 500 300">
06:
07:        <defs>
08:                <filter id="DropShadow" filterUnits="userSpaceOnUse">
09:                        <feGaussianBlur in="SourceAlpha" stdDeviation="10"
                                   result="shadow"/>
10:                        <feOffset dx="10" dy="10" in="shadow"
                                   result="shadow"/>
11:                        <feMerge>
12:                                <feMergeNode in="shadow"/>
13:                                <feMergeNode in="SourceGraphic"/>
14:                        </feMerge>
15:                </filter>
16:
```

Line 8 defines the first symbol stored within the `defs` element (beginning on line 7)—the `DropShadow` filter. This filter is the same used in listing 10.5, where you added a shadow to the sun. It first applies a blur to the alpha channel of its applied object (line 9), offsets the shadow 10–user-unit to the right and down (line 10), and then places the offset shadow below a copy of the original artwork (line 11).

```
17:                <rect id="WeatherBox" x="10" y="45" width="200"
                          height="245"/>
18:                <rect id="RainBox" x="10" y="45" width="200" height="220"/>
19:                <clipPath id="WeatherMask">
20:                        <use xlink:href="#WeatherBox" class="FillNone
                                   StrokeNone"/>
21:                </clipPath>
22:
```

23

Line 17 defines the shape of the rectangle that the weather animation will occur within. Line 18 is a similarly shaped box that will later be used to contain the raindrop pattern in the thunderstorm illustration within a smaller confine so the drops do not clutter the temperature display area. The clipping path used to ensure neither of the weather illustration's clouds bleed into the remainder of the news center graphic is defined on line 19 and references (line 20) the shape of the already-made WeatherBox (just created in line 17).

```
23:                <g id="IconPaper"
24:                    class="FillFFFFFF Stroke000000 StrokeWidth1
                             AliasedObject">
25:                    <rect id="PaperOutline" x="0" y="0" width="13"
                             height="10"/>
26:                    <rect id="PaperPhoto" x="7.5" y="5" width="3"
                             height="5"/>
27:                    <line id="PaperHeadline" x1="2" y1="2.5" x2="11"
                             y2="2.5"
28:                          class="StrokeWidth1Point5"/>
29:                    <line id="PaperLine1" x1="2" y1="5" x2="5.5" y2="5"/>
30:                    <line id="PaperLine2" x1="2" y1="7" x2="5.5" y2="7"/>
31:                </g>
32:
```

Line 23 creates a group of artwork to define the newspaper icons. These icons were first seen in Listing 13.1 when you learned how to link objects to external files. As some of this artwork consists of overlapping lineweights that double with odd results when anti-aliased, the AliasedObject class is applied.

```
33:                <path id="RainDrop" class="Fill99CCFF StrokeNone"
                        d="M16,0
                        C 16,0 0,24 0,33
                        C 0,42 7,49 16,49
                        C 25,49 32,42 32,33
                        C 32,24 16,0 16,0"
                        transform="scale(0.25)"/>
34:                <pattern id="RainDrops" x="10" y="15" width="50" height="50"
                        patternUnits="userSpaceOnUse">
35:                    <use xlink:href="#RainDrop" x="10" y="10"/>
36:                    <use xlink:href="#RainDrop" x="10" y="10"
                             transform="translate(25,20)"/>
37:                </pattern>
38:
```

Line 33 creates the raindrop illustration to be used as a pattern in line 34. This object was first seen in Hour 5's path lesson as Listing 5.10. To easily decrease the size of the drop without replotting every coordinate, a scale transformation has been applied to reduce it to one quarter of its original size.

The pattern, RainDrops, is used to repeat the raindrops in the thunderstorm illustration. By containing two versions of the raindrop, one offset in line 36, the pattern creates a staggered display.

```
39:              <polygon id="SunRay" points="7.5,0 0,15 15,15"/>
40:              <g id="SunRay1" transform="translate(-7.5,-69)">
41:                     <use xlink:href="#SunRay"/>
42:                     <use xlink:href="#SunRay" x="-15" y="-138"
                              transform="rotate(180)"/>
43:              </g>
44:
```

The triangle that defines the sunray is created in line 39. Line 40 creates the grouping of opposing sunrays, first shown in Listing 14.6. By applying a transform to the group, the coordinates of the group shift from the top left corner to the very center of the two objects, simplifying the series of transformations necessary to create the sun's multiple rays (shown in line 88).

```
45:              <g id="Cloud1">
46:                 <circle cx="24" cy="36" r="15"/>
47:                 <circle cx="41" cy="26" r="17"/>
48:                 <circle cx="90" cy="40" r="13"/>
49:                 <circle cx="105" cy="31" r="13"/>
50:                 <ellipse cx="75" cy="20" rx="27" ry="20"/>
51:                 <ellipse cx="56" cy="50" rx="25" ry="18"/>
52:              </g>
53:              <g id="Cloud2">
54:                 <circle cx="18" cy="37" r="18"/>
55:                 <circle cx="39" cy="26" r="20"/>
56:                 <circle cx="75" cy="43" r="15"/>
57:                 <circle cx="93" cy="31" r="15"/>
58:                 <ellipse cx="65" cy="21" rx="23" ry="22"/>
59:                 <ellipse cx="48" cy="47" rx="21" ry="13"/>
60:              </g>
61:
```

Lines 45 and 53 create groupings of the two clouds used in both weather illustrations. These clouds, first shown assembled in Listing 8.1, are composed of no more than a series of basic shapes (the circle and ellipse elements).

```
62:              <polygon id="LightningBolt" class="FillFFFF00"
                        points="13,0 4,25 8,25 2,48 6,48 0,72 18,44 14,44
                        25,21 20,21 32,0"/>
63:        </defs>
64:
```

The lightning bolt used for the thunderstorm illustration is defined on line 62. This image was first created in Listing 5.8, where you learned to use the polygon and polyline elements. Line 63 ends the defs section; now you'll be moving into the actual displayed content.

```
65:            <g id="NewsCenter" class="Stroke000000 EnableBackgroundNew
                  FontFamilyArialMT FontSize10">
66:
67:            <rect id="Background" x="-10" y="-10" width="520" height="320"
                  class="FillFFFFFF StrokeNone"/>
68:
```

Line 65 groups all the graphic content to come. By applying to this group a series of
style classes common to the most objects in the document, you can reduce the amount of
style application necessary. This saves clutter and file size. Also, by applying the
EnableBackgroundNew class, the DropShadow filter (created back on line 8) can access
the artwork behind the object to which it is applied.

The white background of the document is created with a rect element on line 67.
Although some SVG viewer/browser combinations fill the background of an SVG object
with white, some do not. As such, you should always place a rectangle behind all of your
artwork. Otherwise, your document's background may occasionally appear transparent,
allowing the HTML document's background image or color to bleed through.

```
69:            <g id="Rainy" class="StrokeNone WeatherMaskBox">
70:              <use id="RainBkgd" xlink:href="#WeatherBox"
                    class="Fill664785"/>
71:              <use id="RainDropsFalling" xlink:href="#RainBox"
                    class="RainFalling"/>
72:              <g id="RainCloudsBackGround" class="Fill493D56"
                    transform="scale(2)">
73:                <use xlink:href="#Cloud1" x="-50" y="-6"/>
74:                <use xlink:href="#Cloud2" x="45" y="-4"/>
75:              </g>
76:              <use id="RainCloudsForeGround2" xlink:href="#Cloud2"
                    x="20" y="40"
                        class="FillCCCCCC" transform="scale(1.5)"/>
77:              <use id="RainCloudsForeGround1" xlink:href="#Cloud1"
                    x="275" y="-220"
                        class="Fill999999" transform="rotate(180)"/>
78:
79:              <use id="Lightning1" xlink:href="#LightningBolt" x="60"
                    y="160"/>
80:              <use id="Lightning2" xlink:href="#LightningBolt" x="10"
                    y="270"
                        transform="skewX(30) scale(0.65)"/>
81:            </g>
82:
```

Lines 69 through 81 define the thunderstorm illustration. Line 70 uses the WeatherBox
symbol to create the dark sky background, and line 71 places a raindrop pattern-filled
RainBox symbol right above.

The Cloud1 and Cloud2 symbols get referenced several times over the next six lines. A
group of two scaled rain clouds are placed with line 72, whereas lines 76 and 77 place
two lighter, rearranged clouds in the foreground of the rain.

The lightning bolt created back on line 62 is referenced once on line 79 and again, scaled down and skewed 30 degrees horizontally, on line 80. This transformation creates a second lightning bolt that looks markedly different from the original, saving the need to plot and draw a second bolt.

```
83:                    <g id="Sunny" class="StrokeNone WeatherMaskBox">
84:                        <use id="SunBkgd" xlink:href="#WeatherBox"
                                class="Fill99CCFF"/>
85:                        <use id="SunCloud1" xlink:href="#Cloud1" x="-120" y="20"
                                class="FillFFFFFF"/>
86:                        <use id="SunCloud2" xlink:href="#Cloud2" x="210" y="210"
                                class="FillFFFFFF"/>
87:                        <g id="Sun" class="FillFFFF00 StrokeNone">
88:                            <g id="SunRays">
89:                                <use xlink:href="#SunRay1"
                                        transform="translate(105,160)"/>
90:                                <use xlink:href="#SunRay1"
                                        transform="translate(105,160)
                                        rotate(15)"/>
91:                                <use xlink:href="#SunRay1"
                                        transform="translate(105,160)
                                        rotate(30)"/>
92:                                <use xlink:href="#SunRay1"
                                        transform="translate(105,160)
                                        rotate(45)"/>
93:                                <use xlink:href="#SunRay1"
                                        transform="translate(105,160)
                                        rotate(60)"/>
94:                                <use xlink:href="#SunRay1"
                                        transform="translate(105,160)
                                        rotate(75)"/>
95:                                <use xlink:href="#SunRay1"
                                        transform="translate(105,160)
                                        rotate(90)"/>
96:                                <use xlink:href="#SunRay1"
                                        transform="translate(105,160)
                                        rotate(-75)"/>
97:                                <use xlink:href="#SunRay1"
                                        transform="translate(105,160)
                                        rotate(-60)"/>
98:                                <use xlink:href="#SunRay1"
                                        transform="translate(105,160)
                                        rotate(-45)"/>
99:                                <use xlink:href="#SunRay1"
                                        transform="translate(105,160)
                                        rotate(-30)"/>
100:                               <use xlink:href="#SunRay1"
                                        transform="translate(105,160)
                                        rotate(-15)"/>
101:                           </g>
102:                           <circle id="RingOuter" cx="105" cy="160" r="56"
                                    class="GradientSun"/>
```

23

```
103:                          <radialGradient id="GradientSunCenter">
104:                              <stop offset="50%" style="stop-color:#FFFFCC"/>
105:                              <stop offset="85%" style="stop-color:#FFFF00"/>
106:                          </radialGradient>
107:                      </g>
108:          </g>
109:
```

The sunny-skied illustration is defined on lines 83 through 108. Line 83 groups the artwork and applies the WeatherMask clipping path created on line 19. The blue sky is created on line 84 using the WeatherBox symbol, and the two white clouds are placed on lines 85 and 86.

The sun itself (grouped and filled on line 87) is composed of two sections—the rays and the gradated disc. Line 88 opens the group of sunrays, first assembled in Listing 14.8. Each instance of the pair of rays symbol (SunRay1) is subsequently moved to the center of the sun and then rotated by a factor of 15 degrees until the sun is completely encompassed with rays. The sun disc is created on line 102, and is filled with the gradient created on line 103.

```
110:          <g id="TempBar" class="Fill000000 FillOpacityPoint75
                  StrokeNone">
111:              <rect id="BarStatistics" x="10" y="245" width="200"
                      height="45" class="Fill333333 FillOpacityPoint25
                      StrokeNone"/>
112:              <text class="FontFamilyArialNarrow FontSize14">
113:                  <tspan x="16" y="280">HIGH:</tspan>
114:                  <tspan x="110" y="280">LOW:</tspan>
115:              </text>
116:              <text class="FontFamilyArialBlack FontSize36">
117:                  <tspan x="50" y="280"
                          id="high_text">74&#xB0;</tspan>
118:                  <tspan x="142" y="280" id="low_text"
                          class="FillFFFFFF">61&#xB0;</tspan>
119:              </text>
120:          </g>
121:
```

The temperature bar first shown in Listing 19.1's dynamic text entry example is defined in lines 110 through 120. Line 111 creates the semi-transparent box the statistics will be housed within. The "High" and "Low" labels are created with line 112, and the actual temperature values are created with line 116's text element.

```
122:          <g id="DottedLines"
                  class="StrokeDasharray1Space2 FillNone
                  AliasedObject">
123:              <line id="DividingLine1" x1="225" y1="132" x2="474"
                      y2="132"/>
124:              <line id="DividingLine2" x1="380" y1="243" x2="474"
                      y2="243"/>
125:          </g>
```

The lines created in the DottedLines group, ranging from lines 122 to 125, are used
to separate the news center's lead paragraph ("Vendors Support SVG") from the lower
content, as well as the advertisement from the credit line. The group has a
StrokeDasharray1Space2 class applied, which makes the lines appear dotted, thus visually
reducing their weight.

```
126:            <g id="TopStory" class="Fill000000 StrokeNone FontSize12">
127:                <text class="FontFamilyArialBlack FontSize14">
128:                    <tspan x="225" y="66">VENDORS SUPPORT SVG</tspan>
129:                </text>
130:                <text>
131:                    <tspan x="225" y="84">Software companies Adobe,
                            Corel, and Quark </tspan>
132:                    <tspan x="225" y="98">have all announced support for
                            Scalable </tspan>
133:                    <tspan x="225" y="112">Vector Graphics (SVG) in their
                            product lines.</tspan>
134:                </text>
135:            </g>
136:
```

The news center's lead paragraph and headline are defined in lines 126 through 135. The
headline, needing a bolder typeface than the body text, is defined separately on line 127,
while the body copy is begun on line 130.

```
137:            <g id="TopHeadlines">
138:                <text class="Fill000000 StrokeNone FontFamilyArialBlack">
139:                    <tspan x="225" y="154">TOP HEADLINES</tspan>
140:                </text>
141:                <a id="StoryLink1" xlink:href="http://www.nytimes.com/">
142:                    <use id="StoryLink1Icon" xlink:href="#IconPaper"
                            x="225" y="168"/>
143:                        <text id="StoryLink1Headline"
                                class="Fill000000 StrokeNone">
144:                            <tspan x="244" y="174">World leaders
                                    unite for </tspan>
145:                            <tspan x="244" y="186">population
                                    crisis</tspan>
146:                        </text>
147:                </a>
148:                <a id="StoryLink2"
                        xlink:href="http://www.adbusters.com/">
149:                    <use id="StoryLink2Icon"
                            xlink:href="#IconPaper" x="225"
                                y="198"/>
150:                        <text id="StoryLink2Headline"
                                class="Fill000000 StrokeNone">
151:                            <tspan x="244" y="204">Congress
                                    passes ban on </tspan>
152:                            <tspan x="244" y="216">gas-guzzling
                                    SUVs</tspan>
```

23

```
153:                                      </text>
154:                    </a>
155:                    <a id="StoryLink3"
                              xlink:href="http://www.justgive.org/">
156:                          <use id="StoryLink3Icon"
                                  xlink:href="#IconPaper" x="225"
                                  y="228"/>
157:                          <text id="StoryLink3Headline"
                                  class="Fill000000 StrokeNone">
158:                                  <tspan x="244" y="234">Charities
                                          report all-time </tspan>
159:                                  <tspan x="244" y="246">highs in
                                          gifts</tspan>
160:                          </text>
161:                    </a>
162:                    <a id="StoryLink4"
                              xlink:href="http://www.apple.com/hotnews/">
163:                          <use id="StoryLink4Icon"
                                  xlink:href="#IconPaper" x="225"
                                  y="257"/>
164:                          <text id="StoryLink4Headline"
                                  class="Fill000000 StrokeNone">
165:                                  <tspan x="244" y="264">Apple reclaims
                                          </tspan>
166:                                  <tspan x="244" y="276">education
                                          market</tspan>
167:                          </text>
168:                    </a>
169:              </g>
170:
```

Lines 137 through 169 define the news headlines with mini-newspaper icons in the middle of the graphic. These icons and headlines were first defined in Listing 13.1, where you learned how to hotlink objects similar to HTML's method.

```
171:              <g id="Advertisement">
172:                    <text class="Fill000000 StrokeNone
                              FontFamilyArialBlack">
173:                          <tspan x="380" y="154" >ADVERTISEMENT</tspan>
174:                    </text>
175:                    <a xlink:href="http://www.svgnow.com/">
176:                          <image id="AdImage" x="380" y="165"
                                  width="88" height="60"
                                  class="OpacityPoint5"
                                  xlink:href="http://www.micahlaaker.com
                                  /images/tysvg24hrs/tysvg24hrs-ad.gif"/>
177:                    </a>
178:              </g>
```

The advertisement, first shown in Hour 11's Listing 11.1, places an external image (line 176), sets it to be semi-transparent with an opacity class, and links it to this book's companion site (line 175). The "Advertisement" title is placed with line 172's text element.

```
180:                    <a id="CreditLine">
181:                         <text class="Fill666666 StrokeNone">
182:                              <tspan x="380" y="262"
                                        class="FontSize8">CREATED BY:</tspan>
183:                              <tspan x="380" y="274">Micah Laaker</tspan>
184:                         </text>
185:                    </a>
186:
```

Lines 180 through 185 create the credit line for the graphic. You created a placeholder
for this credit when creating the event action in Listing 13.6; in this case, you've
replaced the rectangle with two lines of text created with line 181's text element. To let
users know the credit line acts as a button (by changing the cursor to a pointing finger
when over the object), you can use an empty a element (meaning it has no destination
described via an xlink:href attribute value). As the element doesn't point to any location, it serves only a cursor-changing device. (You can also change the name of the creator to your name here. Go ahead; you deserve it after these past 22 hours.)

```
187:                    <g id="GraphicFramework" class="StrokeWidth1 Stroke000000
                            FillNone AliasedObject">
188:                         <rect id="Outline" x="10" y="10" width="480"
                                   height="280"/>
189:                         <rect id="BarTitle" x="10" y="10" width="480"
                                   height="35" class="FillC66A10"/>
190:                         <text class="FillFFFFFF StrokeNone
                                   FontFamilyArialBlack FontSize18">
191:                              <tspan x="22" y="33">SVG-Powered News
                                        Center</tspan>
192:                         </text>
193:                         <text id="WeatherText" x="22" y="66"
                                   class="Fill000000 StrokeNone
                                   FontFamilyArialBlack">WEATHER</text>
194:                    </g>
195:
```

The graphic's framework, such as the one-point box around the graphic (line 188), the
brown box and headline at the top of the graphic (lines 189 and 190), and the "Weather"
text title (line 193), is created in lines 187 through 194.

```
196:          <g id="PopupCredits" class="DisplayNone">
197:                    <rect id="PopupBackground" x="125" y="75" width="250"
                            height="150" class="FillFFFFFF StrokeWidth1
                            StrokeDasharray1Space2 FilterDropShadow"/>
198:                    <text class="Fill000000 StrokeNone FontFamilyArialBlack
                            FontSize12">
199:                         <tspan x="137" y="95">SVG-Powered News Center</tspan>
200:                    </text>
201:                    <text class="Fill000000 StrokeNone FontSize12">
202:                         <tspan x="137" y="115">A textbook example of the
                                   versatility of </tspan>
203:                         <tspan x="137" y="129">Scalable Vector Graphics
                                   (SVG). </tspan>
```

```
204:                    </text>
205:                    <text class="Fill333333 StrokeNone FontSize12
                            FontFamilyArialNarrow">
206:                        <tspan x="137" y="155">Created by Micah Laaker,
                                author of </tspan>
207:                        <tspan x="137" y="169">"Teach Yourself SVG in 24
                                Hours," </tspan>
208:                        <tspan x="137" y="183">available at bookstores
                                everywhere. </tspan>
209:                    </text>
210:                    <a id="PopupCloseBox" xlink:href="Javascript:;">
211:                        <rect id="CloseBox" x="225" y="195" width="50"
                                height="15"
                                class="Fill666666 StrokeWidth1
                                StrokeDasharray1Space2"/>
212:                        <text class="FillFFFFFF StrokeNone FontSize10
                                TextAnchorMiddle">
213:                            <tspan x="250" y="206">CLOSE</tspan>
214:                        </text>
215:                    </a>
216:            </g>
217: </g>
218:
```

Lines 196 through 216 create the pop-up credit box first shown in Listing 13.6. Line 196 creates the group containing the pop-up box and is set to remain hidden (as the box shouldn't appear until activated later). The box's background is defined on line 197; it is placed in the center of the graphic and has the DropShadow filter applied to visually place this object above the background.

Line 198 creates the box's headline, whereas line 201's text element creates the descriptive copy in the middle of the box. Lines 205 through 209 create a longer credit line. (Again, you're welcome to change this text.) Lines 210 through 215 create the button to close the pop-up box. Again, the null JavaScript link is used to make this button appear clickable (line 210).

Finally, line 217 completes the document's artwork group, which started on line 65. The document concludes with the animation and interaction elements following.

```
219:      <set id="ShowAd" xlink:href="#AdImage"
                attributeName="opacity"
                to="1"
                begin="AdImage.mouseover"
                end="AdImage.mouseout"/>
220:
```

Line 219 shows the set element that changes the opacity of the advertisement (the image labeled AdImage on line 176) when the cursor passes over it. The opacity reverts to its original state (0.5) when the mouse is no longer over the image (courtesy of the end attribute's value).

```
221:        <animateTransform id="SunRayScale" xlink:href="#SunRay"
                attributeName="transform"
                type="scale"
                dur="5s"
                repeatCount="indefinite"
                values="1;2;1"/>
222:        <animateTransform id="SunRayRotate" xlink:href="#SunRay"
                attributeName="transform"
                type="rotate"
                dur="9s"
                repeatCount="indefinite"
                values="0;25;0"/>
223:
```

Lines 221 and 222 animate the sunray illustration stored in the defs element. This causes every instance of this ray to rotate and scale, making the sun appear to be pulsating heat from its edges.

In line 221, the illustration is scaled (via the type attribute's value) up to twice its size and then back to its original size (courtesy of the values attributes' values) over 5 seconds (the dur value) and loops infinitely (thanks to the repeatCount attribute's value). Line 222's animateTransform element acts just like line 221's, except that it rotates the illustration 25 degrees and back again over a nine-second stretch.

```
224:        <animateMotion id="Cloud1MoveRight" xlink:href="#SunCloud1"
                path="M-90 20 L320 20"
                dur="11s"
                repeatCount="indefinite"/>
225:        <animateMotion id="Cloud1MoveLeft" xlink:href="#SunCloud2"
                path="M150 10 L-320 10"
                dur="18s"
                repeatCount="indefinite"/>
226:
```

The clouds that move across the sunny sky are animated via lines 224 and 225's animateMotion elements. Each defines its start and stop coordinates with its path values, its varying time with the dur value, and its infinite loop with the repeatCount value.

```
227:        <set id="PopupCloseBoxOpen" xlink:href="#PopupCredits"
                attributeName="display"
                from="none" to="inline"
                begin="CreditLine.click"
                end="PopupCloseBox.click"/>
228:
```

Line 227's set element displays the PopupCredits object (line 196) once the CreditLine object is clicked. The object disappears again once the PopupcloseBox object (line 210) is clicked. This interaction was first shown in Listing 13.6.

23

```
229:       <set id="Lightning1AnimateOff" xlink:href="#Lightning1"
              attributeName="display"
              from="inline" to="none"
              begin="0s;Lightning1AnimateOn2.end"
              dur="0.5s" />
230:       <set id="Lightning1AnimateOn" xlink:href="#Lightning1"
              attributeName="display"
              from="none" to="inline"
              begin="Lightning1AnimateOff.end"
              dur="0.5s" />
231:       <set id="Lightning1AnimateOff2" xlink:href="#Lightning1"
              attributeName="display"
              from="inline" to="none"
              begin="Lightning1AnimateOn.end"
              dur="0.25s" />
232:       <set id="Lightning1AnimateOn2" xlink:href="#Lightning1"
              attributeName="display"
              from="none" to="inline"
              begin="Lightning1AnimateOff2.end"
              dur="4s" />
233:
```

Lines 229 through 232 contain a series of set elements that turn off and on the display of the Lightning1 object (line 79), making the lightning bolt appear to flash in the sky. This animation was created and described in Hour 15's Listing 15.10, where you learned about frame-based animation.

```
234:       <set id="Lightning2AnimateOff" xlink:href="#Lightning2"
              attributeName="display"
              from="inline" to="none"
              begin="0.5s;Lightning2AnimateOn2.end"
              dur="0.4s" />
235:       <set id="Lightning2AnimateOn" xlink:href="#Lightning2"
              attributeName="display"
              from="none" to="inline"
              begin="Lightning2AnimateOff.end"
              dur="0.6s" />
236:       <set id="Lightning2AnimateOff2" xlink:href="#Lightning2"
              attributeName="display"
              from="inline" to="none"
              begin="Lightning2AnimateOn.end"
              dur="0.3s" />
237:       <set id="Lightning2AnimateOn2" xlink:href="#Lightning2"
              attributeName="display"
              from="none" to="inline"
              begin="Lightning2AnimateOff.end"
              dur="3s" />
238:
```

The set elements in lines 234 through 237 mimic the function of the previous animation grouping (lines 229 through 232), performing the same function for the second lightning bolt (Lightning2, defined on line 80).

```
239:        <set id="DisplayRain" xlink:href="#Sunny"
                attributeName="display"
                to="none"
                begin="WeatherText.mouseover"
                end="WeatherText.mouseout" />
240:
```

The sunshine illustration (Sunny) disappears, revealing the thunderstorm illustration (Rainy) whenever a user's cursor is over the "Weather" headline (WeatherText) thanks to line 239's set element. This function allows you to show your colleagues the cool thunderstorm illustration without embedding the graphic within the dynamic HTML/JavaScript framework developed in Listing 19.2.

(However, you can certainly do just that; just be sure to change the name of the target SVG to this new document's filename, as well as deleting line 239's set element. The thunderstorm won't be revealed, as the JavaScript disables its display after the first pressing of the "set svg" link, thus resulting in a blank display.)

```
241: </svg>
```

You did it! Line 241 completes this graphic. With this closing of the svg element, you're ready to load and view the final graphic.

Stepping Stones

This book's final example, now complete, serves as a strong reference point in your future coding endeavors. It contains, on one level or another, all the fundamental lessons of this book. Although not every style class, basic shape element, filter, typeface, and animation element are in this news center graphic, it contains a wealth of different examples and methods for achieving your desired visual results.

So, where can you go from here? Surely there is more to SVG …

Of course there is. Despite the fact that Scalable Vector Graphics is in its first two years of existence, its acceptance within the developer community is tremendous. The amount of material being published on the topic is increasing monthly, not to mention the amazing examples of the technology that are being released.

As XML has become more and more the de facto standard for content markup, so too have its technologies seen an increasing prominence. As you read this paragraph, Adobe, Corel, Jasc, and other big-name software vendors have products sitting on the shelves of your local computer store able to export (if not import) SVG content.

Aside from running out and supporting these developers (and thereby encouraging others) for their inclusion of SVG capabilities, the first step you will need to take after completing this book is to begin coding your own SVG. No instructional knowledge can be easily retained if it is not put into practice. Though this book's examples surely can provide you with a great foundation for the technology, only through your experiments, missteps, and corrections will the knowledge take hold.

Further, if you haven't already, download the final W3C SVG 1.0 Recommendation. This document is the definitive document on SVG. It contains all possible elements, attributes, and properties, as well as rules on how they can be applied and working examples. Though not always the easiest read, this document can almost always answer any question you may have regarding the technology.

Next, not only should you write code, but you should also write letters to vendors. Although several big names have tossed their hat into the SVG arena, several browser vendors have not (namely Microsoft). If you see the value in this technology, it truly is incumbent upon you to write a letter to them, explaining your need for support today (not three version numbers away). If you are like most people, writing letters is neither your forte, nor your enjoyment. Therefore, to ensure you don't just brush this aside, several letters are available for your use on this book's companion Web site (see next paragraph). Truly, every letter helps make a difference. If saying "no" takes more time than actually implementing the technology, you may see support in the very near future.

Last, visit this book's companion site: `www.svgnow.com`. The site not only contains the examples from this book, but it also has a tremendous list of updated resources. You can find examples listed by topic, links to developer groups, and more. If you are serious about wanting to develop SVG beyond the lessons in this book, you will want to check this site, as it serves as a stepping-stone to more information.

Summary

Well, you actually made it. You are now wise in the ways of SVG. When you set this book down, you should be confident in the following:

- You are fully able to write an SVG document by hand without needing a fancy WYSIWYG editor.
- You have a basic knowledge of the many components of an SVG document.
- You understand the common drawing elements and their assorted properties and are able to use them to create basic artwork.
- You have an ability to use filter effects, animation, and interaction with your documents.
- You not only know how to apply fonts to SVG content, but you also have the ability (but not necessarily the time) to create SVG Fonts.
- You have a sense of how SVG can be manipulated and enriched by other technologies, such as JavaScript.

- You have a series of examples of practical experience to guide your future SVG development.

- Last, you are able to evangelize the practical uses of SVG as a technology that can be used today (not some distant point in time).

Though you haven't learned every aspect of the technology, you can rest assured that you are well versed in the fundamentals of SVG creation. As mentioned in the previous section, however, you will need to start creating your own SVG content for this knowledge to stay with you.

As a last note, if you find the examples in this book helpful (or the contrary), please feel free to drop the author a line. This book was truly written in the hopes that others would become enamored with the technology after experiencing its possible uses. Your feedback becomes a tremendous measure of the success of this goal.

With that said, you're ready to go create some amazing SVG! Before you do, you'll want to finish the final hour of this book, "Resources." Now that you've learned the ins and outs of creating your own SVG documents, the next hour will help point you to see what others have created with SVG. There is also a series of links and information to amazing new products and viewers that take advantage of the technology, as well as a comparison chart to show how SVG stacks up to the competition. Last, the hour finishes off with a giant Q&A section to address any questions you may still have about SVG.

If you're excited about developing SVG, the next and final hour should only further drive your enthusiasm by showing but a few of the opportunities available to SVG developers.

Q&A

Q Can I post this book's final example on my Web site?

A You are allowed to recreate this book's examples for your learning purposes. Legally, you are not allowed to reproduce these graphics for distribution. If you would like others to see them, however, you can find all the examples up at the book's companion Web site: www.svgnow.com.

Q I have a specific question that this book did not address. Where can I find an answer to it?

A Hour 22 covers some basic troubleshooting for your SVG code. Also, the appendix has some Frequently Asked Questions. If neither of these answers your question, be sure to check the W3C SVG Recommendation, and then an SVG developers group.

Workshop

The Workshop is designed to help you anticipate possible questions, review what you've learned, and begin learning how to put your knowledge into practice.

Quiz

1. Why is the style sheet for this book's final example referenced as an external file?

2. Where can you find a definitive list of all the elements, attributes, and properties available in SVG?

Answers

1. The style sheet used in this final example is rather large. Rather than further adding to the file's complexity, the author chose to keep it separate. However, you can add the style sheet information to the SVG document as you have for nearly all this book's examples.

2. The W3C's SVG 1.0 Recommendation, available at www.w3.org/tr/svg/, contains appendices that list all possible elements, attributes, and properties, as well as various other resources.

Exercises

1. Place this hour's examples within the HTML file you created in Hour 19 to see how the dynamic JavaScript form can populate your final graphic. Be sure to remove the final set element in Listing 23.2 (line 239) to avoid bizarre display results.

2. Visit this book's companion Web site: www.svgnow.com. After checking out some more examples of great SVG content in action, be sure to use one of the letters available to contact vendors not yet supporting SVG.

3. Start creating your own SVG content!

Hour 24

References

If you've been following this book's lessons in order, you should have just completed your 23rd hour of SVG "basic training." Last hour saw the culmination of all the book's examples, and now you're ready to begin coding SVG documents of your own design.

Now that you are about to be developing SVG on your own, the resources in this chapter can be used to help you along the way. This last hour will feature

- A graphics technology comparison chart, showing how SVG stacks up against other formats

- A list of the available SVG viewers as of press time

- Links to outside Web sites that feature SVG instruction and examples

- A list of products you can use to create SVG

- A jumbo-sized Question & Answers section to answer many often-asked questions you may be faced with

These various resources will serve as launching points for your future development efforts. By familiarizing yourself with each of these, you can be confident that your future questions will not go long unanswered.

Technology Comparison

After finishing the previous 23 hours, you should have a good idea of what SVG offers. To help clarify SVG's feature set in comparison to other popular graphics technologies, Table 24.1 stacks SVG against them in a side-by-side evaluation.

Keep in mind that some of the features are not replicated in the same fashion across the technologies. For instance, though both Flash and SVG accommodate typeface embedding, the technologies use very different methods to accomplish this task. Nonetheless, a comparison table such as this can help you evaluate which technology is appropriate for your graphics. It just may be that SVG is the right choice for your next project.

TABLE 24.1 Technology Comparison Table

Feature	SVG	Flash	GIF	JPEG	PNG	EPS	PDF	XHTML
Vector artwork	•	•				•	•	
Alpha Channel transparency	•	•			•	•	•	
Pixel-precision	•	•	•	•	•	•	•	
Typeface selection	•	•				•	•	•
Typeface embedding	•	•				•	•	
Gradients	•	•	•	•	•	•	•	
Masking	•	•				•	•	
Shared resources (symbols, fonts, text) across multiple files	•							•
Open-standard	•				•			•
Live filter effects	•							
Pinpoint invalid code	•							
Extensible	•							•
Animation	•	•	•					
Interaction	•	•					•	•
Filesize compression	•	•	•	•	•		•	
Editable executable	•		•	•	•	•	•	•

Viewer Compatibility

This book has assumed usage of the Adobe SVG Viewer as the SVG viewer used to display your working examples. There are, however, a variety of viewers available to the public beyond the Adobe product.

Table 24.2 lists several of the viewers available to the public, free-of-charge, their supported platforms, and a Web site where they can be downloaded. (In all likelihood, by the time this book is on the shelves, yet another viewer may be released. Therefore, always refer to this book's companion Web site, www.svgnow.com, for an up-to-date list of available viewers.)

If you are brave of heart, you should consider downloading and installing all the viewers possible for your platform. As each viewer is at a different level of support, knowing how different viewers will interpret your documents can help you prepare for the varying output.

24

TABLE 24.2 Viewer Compatibility Table

Product Name: SVG Viewer
Vendor: Adobe
Platform: Mac/PC/Linux(Beta)
http://www.adobe.com/svg/viewer/install/main.html

Product Name: SVGView
Vendor: IBM
Platform: PC
http://www.alphaworks.ibm.com/tech/svgview

Product Name: SVG Toolkit
Vendor: CSIRO
Platform: Java
http://sis.cmis.csiro.au/svg/

Product Name: PocketViewer
Vendor: CSIRO
Platform: PocketPC
http://www.cmis.csiro.au/sis/SVGpocket.htm

Product Name: X-Smiles
Vendor: Helisinki University of Technology's Telecommunications Software and Multimedia Laboratory
Platform: Java
http://www.x-smiles.org

continues

TABLE 24.2 Continued

Product Name: Amaya
Vendor: W3C
Platform: PC/Linux/Solaris/Unix
`http://www.w3.org/Amaya/Amaya.html`

Product Name: BitFlash VIS Viewer
Vendor: BitFlash
Platform: PalmOS, Blackberry Rim, PocketPC, Agenda VR3
   (via the BitFlash Mobile Messaging Suite/BitFlash Mobility Suite)
`http://www.bitflash.com/`

Product Name: Batik
Vendor: Apache XML Project
Platform: Java
`http://xml.apache.org/batik/`

For a complete list of other SVG viewers, visit:
`http://www.w3.org/Graphics/SVG/SVG-Implementations.htm8#viewer.`

Tools to Create SVG

As mentioned earlier, you can use a number of WYSIWYG programs to export their documents as SVG code. Rather than working in a code environment, these applications let you author your documents in a manner true to their final display.

The cost of these programs varies from free to hundreds of American dollars. Keep in mind that you do not need these programs to create SVG content. Rather, they facilitate the easy translation of their documents' contents into SVG code. Table 24.3 details several products (and their price, supported platforms, and feature set) available to the consumer at press time.

TABLE 24.3 Tools to Create SVG

Product Name: Adobe Illustrator 10, $399
Platform: Macintosh/Windows
SVG Support: Import; Export; CEF Fonts; Live filter effects; Embedding images
`http://www.adobe.com/products/illustrator/`

continues

TABLE 24.3   Continued

Product Name: InDesign 2.0, N/A
Platform: Macintosh/Windows
SVG Support: Export; CEF Fonts; Embedding images
`http://www.adobe.com/products/indesign/`

Product Name: Adobe GoLive 5.0, $248
Platform: Macintosh/Windows
SVG Support: Export
`http://www.adobe.com/products/golive/`

Product Name: CorelDraw 10, $550
Platform: Macintosh/Windows
SVG Support: Export; SVG Fonts
`http://www.corel.com/`

Product Name: JASC WebDraw 1.0, N/A
Platform: Windows
SVG Support: Import; Export; Create filter effects
`http://www.jasc.com/products/webdraw/`

Product Name: DBx Geomatics SVG MapMaker 1.0, $549
Platform: Windows
SVG Support: Export code from MapInfo Pro
`http://www.dbxgeomatics.com/SVGMapMaker.asp?Language=EN`

Product Name: Integriente informationssysteme Sphinx SVG 1.1, $160
Platform: Windows
SVG Support: Export
`http://www.ingmbh.de/en/Products/ingmbh/sphinxsvg/sphinxsvg.htm`

Product Name: Quark Xpress 5.0, N/A
Platform: Macintosh/Windows
SVG Support: Export
`http://www.quark.com/`

Product Name: Software Mechanics SVGMaker 1.0, $24.95
Platform: Windows
SVG Support: Export
`http://www.svgmaker.com/`

24

For a complete list of other SVG authoring applications, visit:
`http://www.w3.org/Graphics/SVG/SVG-Implementations.htm8#edit.`

SVG References

After completing all the examples in this book, you will likely be anxious to begin creating your own SVG content. Luckily, there are other resources to help guide you along your way as you move beyond the initial concepts introduced here.

The foremost authority on SVG is obviously the W3C (the technology's author). Their site will always contain the most up-to-date information on the technology, its specifications, and links to exciting new developments in the SVG space.

- W3C SVG News: `http://www.w3.org/Graphics/SVG`
- W3C SVG 1.0 Recommendation: `http://www.w3.org/tr/svg/`

The second most useful resource for SVG information is the SVG Developers Group, available through Yahoo! Groups (Figure 24.1). Mentioned repeatedly throughout the book, this forum allows any developer to read, post, and search messages related to SVG development. Access to this group requires a free Yahoo! Account.

- Yahoo! Groups' SVG Developers Group:
  `http://groups.yahoo.com/group/svg-developers`

FIGURE 24.1

Though not the most attractive experience online, the SVG-Developers group on Yahoo! Groups is certainly one of the most useful SVG resources.

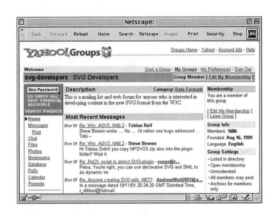

Several software vendors, such as Adobe (Figure 24.2), have created content discussing, displaying, and promoting SVG. In many cases, they will provide links to outstanding examples of SVG technology in practical use.

- Adobe SVG Zone: `http://www.adobe.com/svg/`
- Sun: `http://www.sun.com/software/xml/developers/svg/`
- IBM AlphaWorks: `http://www.alphaworks.ibm.com/tech/svgview`
- Web Developers Virtual Library:
  `http://www.wdvl.com/Authoring/Languages/XML/SVG/`

FIGURE 24.2

Adobe's SVG Zone provides a wealth of tutorials, links, examples, and downloads to encourage developers to adopt SVG.

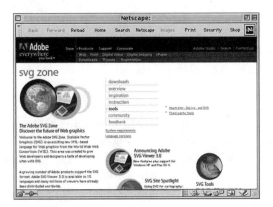

Beyond commercial support, many developers have begun creating their own sites highlighting the possibilities of SVG technology. Some serve as showcases for impressive visual effects and construction (such as PinkJuice, shown in Figure 24.3), whereas others serve as a trove of technical solutions to issues arising from the technology's recent arrival (Kevin Lindsey Development).

- PinkJuice: `http://www.pinkjuice.com/SVG/`
- SVG Magic: `http://www.svgmagic.com/`
- SVG-Spot: `http://www.svg-spot.com/`
- Kevin Lindsey Development: `http://www.kevlindev.com/tutorials/index.htm`
- Nokiko SVG Project: `http://www.nokiko.com/svg/`

FIGURE 24.3

Tobias Reif, one of the technical editors of this book, operates PinkJuice, a site containing a series of attractive SVG examples as well as some informative articles on extending SVG.

Lastly, the author has created, and continues to update, a site devoted to SVG technology. You will be able to find an up-to-date list of resources (and much more) beyond what is possible in a printed publication.

- SVGnow:`http://www.svgnow.com/`

24

As the technology becomes more prevalent, new resources will become available beyond what is known at press time. If you encounter a wonderful resource for or an example of SVG technology, be sure to submit the information to the author at SVGnow.com.

Summary

With this hour's many tables and lists, you will now have a starting point from which you can continue learning about SVG development. Though the previous hours will have provided you with a strong foundation in the technology, you will invariably encounter a stumbling block; such is the joy of working with any technology. The informational resources here, however, can direct you in an appropriate direction to either finding answers or seeking inspiration.

Remember that SVG, being an open standard interactive technology, will continue developing. As of press time, the version 1.1 recommendation is being developed, expanding the features and use of the technology. Such improvements will continue as long as developers actively use and promote the technology.

Keep in mind that, after reading this book, you are fully capable of creating your own SVG content. With determination and a skill at presenting ideas visually, the content you begin creating may be the very work that inspires someone else to begin investigating SVG.

With the American economy and technology sector at such low points at the end of 2001, the speed of SVG's adoption rate will certainly depend on a strong and growing developer community. Now that you're a part of this community, it's time to get started creating awesome uses of SVG technology. Good luck!

Q&A

Q Why would I use SVG instead of Flash?

A SVG and Flash are really not the comparable technologies that most people think they are. Flash was designed for vector animation, whereas SVG was designed to present XML content in a vector format. As such, if you have a data-intensive project, SVG is likely the choice for you. If you are trying to create a Simpsons-like animation for the Web, then Flash is most likely your choice for the time being. As SVG viewers mature in the future, SVG may become a more suitable contender to Flash's animation prowess.

Q When will SVG ship with a browser?

A SVG is already part of some browsers. Both Amaya and X-Smiles are SVG-capable browsers available to the market. As far as mass-market popular browser vendors, such as Netscape and Microsoft, support is still a ways off. Netscape's Mozilla project has a team working on SVG support (code-named "Croczilla") for the Mac, PC, and Linux. Microsoft has yet to announce support for SVG in its Internet Explorer browser.

Q Why won't JavaScript animate my SVG file on the Macintosh in Internet Explorer?

A The Macintosh version of Internet Explorer is plagued with an inability for plug-ins to communicate with the browser, and vice versa, via JavaScript. Due to this, many complex functions and animations that are actually handled via JavaScript functions are unable to play back in this browser. Macintosh users should use Netscape 4.78 to see such SVG content.

Q Do I have to know XML to use SVG?

A Technically, you do not need to know XML to author SVG. Because SVG is an XML grammar, as you learn SVG you will be learning rules inherent to XML itself. However, because SVG is required to conform to XML's syntax, it is in your best interest to at least get a cursory knowledge of the technology.

Q What software do I need to run SVG?

A SVG doesn't actually "run" like an application on your computer. Rather, it is a markup language that can be interpreted (read) and parsed (displayed) by a viewer mechanism. A viewer can be either a standalone application or a component of another application. Currently, the most widely used viewer is the Adobe SVG Viewer, a plug-in available for Mac and PC Web browsers.

Q Who created SVG?

A SVG was developed by the W3C, the standards body responsible for delivering recommendations for a variety of Web technologies. Dr. Chris Lilley of the W3C heads the group responsible for SVG. The group is composed of experts from a variety of fields and from companies that have an interest in successful deployment of graphics technology on the Web. Companies such as Adobe, Kodak, IBM, Macromedia, and more have active members participating in the group.

Q Is it illegal to publish a typeface as an SVG font?

A This is a rather murky area. SVG fonts are designed for display only within SVG viewers and, according to the recommendation, are not to be interpreted by a code editor.

24

As each type foundry defines its own release terms, you should check to make sure you are allowed to export their fonts as either SVG or CEF fonts before you publish them with your documents. Though most foundries (including Adobe's large collection) allow the encapsulization of their typefaces for Web publishing, you should consider contacting them (through either email or letter to their customer service department).

Q How secure is SVG data?

A As you've seen, SVG code is markup text, similar to HTML, and is thus visible to anyone who can view your document. At present, there is no reliable way to secure your SVG data so that no one is able to see the code across all viewers.

Open access to code is not unique to SVG, however. The code of nearly all open-standard markup languages, such as XML and HTML, is accessible through their respective viewers (such as a Web browser). By allowing code to be viewable, other developers (such as yourself) are able to understand how the author achieved the results.

Even more, you can copy code from another SVG file and paste it into your own. By opening the access to this code, you can manipulate others' code to better understand its function.

Q Do I need a plug-in to view SVG?

A SVG requires a rendering engine, referred to as a "viewer," to interpret code and display its intended results. Viewers can take a variety of forms, such as a stand-alone application, a browser plug-in, or a Java class. The W3C recommendation does not confine software vendors to a particular form for a viewer; rather, it specifies what functions a viewer must be able to perform.

Some applications (such as Amaya and Batik) have SVG rendering functionality within their frameworks and thus do not need a plug-in. Presently, though, a plug-in is required to view SVG within the most popular Web browsers and is the most common method people currently use to experience SVG.

Q What are SVG's compatability issues?

A SVG is an open standard, and as such, anyone can create a viewer or editor for SVG documents without paying the W3C royalties or requiring permission. As such, the only thing preventing widespread use of the technology is a lack of developers interested in making applications for the technology. Currently, there are solutions available on Macintosh, Windows, and Linux platforms, as well as PalmOS, PocketPC, RIM, and Agenda. Not every platform has the same support; for instance, the handheld platforms have an ability to *view* SVG, but not *create* it.

Q Can I use SVG on a wireless device?

A BitFlash, a software vendor working to bring advanced graphics technology to handheld devices, has successfully demonstrated rendering SVG content on wireless devices. Their software serves as a SVG viewer for these units, allowing more advanced graphics to be displayed. Widespread use of SVG in such applications has yet to materialize, but the technology is feasible. To read more about BitFlash and their products, you can visit `www.bitflash.com`.

Q Do I always have to write my SVG code by hand?

A Though having a firm knowledge of SVG's markup language will better equip you to manipulate SVG code to your desire, you can use WYSIWYG editors to create your SVG content. Programs such as Adobe Illustrator (versions 9 and 10) and InDesign 2, CorelDraw 10, and JASC WebDraw all allow visual interfaces to SVG authoring.

Workshop

The Workshop is designed to help you anticipate possible questions, review what you've learned, and begin learning how to put your knowledge into practice.

Quiz

1. True or False: SVG content can be viewed on handheld devices.

2. True or False: All WYSIWYG design tools that export SVG are free.

3. Where is the SVG 1.0 Recommendation located?

4. True or false: SVG is the only Web graphics technology available that offers live filter effects.

Answers

1. True. BitFlash, a software vendor, has created a viewer that works on a variety of handheld devices. This allows handheld units to view SVG content on the very small screens people keep close to their sides.

2. False. Though SVG is an open standard, software vendors are welcome to (and do) charge for their products that work with SVG. You can always code SVG content by hand, but software packages with SVG support may ease some of your development efforts.

3. The SVG 1.0 Recommendation is located at the W3C Web site: `http://www.w3.org/tr/svg/`.

4. True. Though filter effects can be applied and stored to static raster images, such as GIFs and JPEGs, they are not applied in real-time. The benefit of such an application is that the filter effects need not be hard-coded to your content; if your content is dynamic (coming from an outside source upon the document's loading), SVG can still apply filter effects to it.

Exercises

1. After installing some of the other SVG viewers available, open some of the more complex documents you've created in this book (such as any style sheet, animation, or typeface examples) within these viewers. Take note of any discrepancies in the files' display.

2. Compile a list of questions you may have about SVG functionality or use and submit these questions to the author at SVGnow.com. Although you can't be guaranteed an answer to each question, the most common questions will be answered and posted online at the site. Your question also may make it into the next edition of this book.

3. Most importantly, go forth and begin creating SVG content of your own! You can submit examples of your best content online at SVGnow.com as well. The most impressive examples will be highlighted in the Gallery section of the site.

APPENDIX

Color Name and Hex Value Reference Table

As mentioned in Hour 6, "Styling SVG," color can be defined using color keywords. The following relational table matches color keywords to their RGB values and hexadecimal notation. These values are all taken from Chapter 4.2 of the W3C SVG Recommendation, "Recognized color keyword names." For a visual display of these colors alongside their values, be sure to visit this book's companion site: www.svgnow.com.

Color Name	RGB Value	Hex Value
aliceblue	240, 248, 255	F0F8FF
antiquewhite	250, 235, 215	FAEBD7
aqua	0, 255, 255	00FFFF
aquamarine	127, 255, 212	7FFFD4
azure	240, 255, 255	F0FFFF
beige	245, 245, 220	F5F5DC
bisque	255, 228, 196	FFE4C4

continues

Color Name	RGB Value	Hex Value
black	0, 0, 0	000000
blanchedalmond	255, 235, 205	FFEBCD
blue	0, 0, 255	0000FF
blueviolet	138, 43, 226	8A2BE2
brown	165, 42, 42	A52A2A
burlywood	222, 184, 135	DEB887
cadetblue	95, 158, 160	5F9EA0
chartreuse	127, 255, 0	7FFF00
chocolate	210, 105, 30	D2691E
coral	255, 127, 80	FF7F50
cornflowerblue	100, 149, 237	6495ED
cornsilk	255, 248, 220	FFF8DC
crimson	220, 20, 60	DC143C
cyan	0, 255, 255	00FFFF
darkblue	0, 0, 139	00008B
darkcyan	0, 139, 139	008B8B
darkgoldenrod	184, 134, 11	B8860B
darkgray	169, 169, 169	A9A9A9
darkgreen	0, 100, 0	006400
darkgrey	169, 169, 169	A9A9A9
darkkhaki	189, 183, 107	BDB76B
darkmagenta	139, 0, 139	8B008B
darkolivegreen	85, 107, 47	556B2F
darkorange	255, 140, 0	FF8C00
darkorchid	153, 50, 204	9932CC
darkred	139, 0, 0	8B0000
darksalmon	233, 150, 122	E9967A
darkseagreen	143, 188, 143	8FBC8F
darkslateblue	72, 61, 139	483D8B
darkslategray	47, 79, 79	2F4F4F
darkslategrey	47, 79, 79	2F4F4F
darkturquoise	0, 206, 209	00CED1
darkviolet	148, 0, 211	9400D3

continues

Color Name	RGB Value	Hex Value
deeppink	255, 20, 147	FF1493
deepskyblue	0, 191, 255	00BFFF
dimgray	105, 105, 105	696969
dimgrey	105, 105, 105	696969
dodgerblue	30, 144, 255	1E90FF
firebrick	178, 34, 34	B22222
floralwhite	255, 250, 240	FFFAF0
forestgreen	34, 139, 34	228B22
fuchsia	255, 0, 255	FF00FF
gainsboro	220, 220, 220	DCDCDC
ghostwhite	248, 248, 255	F8F8FF
gold	255, 215, 0	FFD700
goldenrod	218, 165, 32	DAA520
gray	128, 128, 128	808080
grey	128, 128, 128	808080
green	0, 128, 0	008000
greenyellow	173, 255, 47	ADFF2F
honeydew	240, 255, 240	F0FFF0
hotpink	255, 105, 180	FF69B4
indianred	205, 92, 92	CD5C5C
indigo	75, 0, 130	4B0082
ivory	255, 255, 240	FFFFF0
khaki	240, 230, 140	F0E68C
lavender	230, 230, 250	E6E6FA
lavenderblush	255, 240, 245	FFF0F5
lawngreen	124, 252, 0	7CFC00
lemonchiffon	255, 250, 205	FFFACD
lightblue	173, 216, 230	ADD8E6
lightcoral	240, 128, 128	F08080
lightcyan	224, 255, 255	E0FFFF
lightgoldenrodyellow	250, 250, 210	FAFAD2
lightgray	211, 211, 211	D3D3D3
lightgreen	144, 238, 144	90EE90

A

continues

Color Name	RGB Value	Hex Value
lightgrey	211, 211, 211	D3D3D3
lightpink	255, 182, 193	FFB6C1
lightsalmon	255, 160, 122	FFA07A
lightseagreen	32, 178, 170	20B2AA
lightskyblue	135, 206, 250	87CEFA
lightslate	119, 136, 153	778899
lightslategray	119, 136, 153	778899
lightslategrey	119, 136, 153	778899
lightsteelblue	176, 196, 222	B0C4DE
lightyellow	255, 255, 224	FFFFE0
lime	0, 255, 0	00FF00
limegreen	50, 205, 50	32CD32
linen	250, 240, 230	FAF0E6
magenta	255, 0, 255	FF00FF
maroon	128, 0, 0	800000
mediumaquamarine	102, 205, 170	66CDAA
mediumblue	0, 0, 205	0000CD
mediumorchid	186, 85, 211	BA55D3
mediumpurple	147, 112, 219	9370DB
mediumseagreen	60, 179, 113	3CB371
mediumslateblue	123, 104, 238	7B68EE
mediumspringgreen	0, 250, 154	00FA9A
mediumturquoise	72, 209, 204	48D1CC
mediumvioletred	199, 21, 133	C71585
midnightblue	25, 25, 112	191970
mintcream	245, 255, 250	F5FFFA
mistyrose	255, 228, 225	FFE4E1
moccasin	255, 228, 181	FFE4B5
navajowhite	255, 222, 173	FFDEAD
navy	0, 0, 128	000080
oldlace	253, 245, 230	FDF5E6
olive	128, 128, 0	808000
olivedrab	107, 142, 35	6B8E23

continues

Color Name	RGB Value	Hex Value
orange	255, 165, 0	FFA500
orangered	255, 69, 0	FF4500
orchid	218, 112, 214	DA70D6
palegoldenrod	238, 232, 170	EEE8AA
palegreen	152, 251, 152	98FB98
paleturquoise	175, 238, 238	AFEEEE
palevioletred	219, 112, 147	DB7093
papayawhip	255, 239, 213	FFEFD5
peachpuff	255, 218, 185	FFDAB9
peru	205, 133, 63	CD853F
pink	255, 192, 203	FFC0CB
plum	221, 160, 221	DDA0DD
powderblue	176, 224, 230	B0E0E6
purple	128, 0, 128	800080
red	255, 0, 0	FF0000
rosybrown	188, 143, 143	BC8F8F
royalblue	65, 105, 225	4169E1
saddlebrown	139, 69, 19	8B4513
salmon	250, 128, 114	FA8072
sandybrown	244, 164, 96	F4A460
seagreen	46, 139, 87	2E8B57
seashell	255, 245, 238	FFF5EE
sienna	160, 82, 45	A0522D
silver	192, 192, 192	C0C0C0
skyblue	135, 206, 235	87CEEB
slateblue	106, 90, 205	6A5ACD
slategray	112, 128, 144	708090
slategrey	112, 128, 144	708090
snow	255, 250, 250	FFFAFA
springgreen	0, 255, 127	00FF7F
steelblue	70, 130, 180	4682B4
tan	210, 180, 140	D2B48C
teal	0, 128, 128	008080

A

continues

Color Name	RGB Value	Hex Value
thistle	216, 191, 216	D8BFD8
tomato	255, 99, 71	FF6347
turquoise	64, 224, 208	40E0D0
violet	238, 130, 238	EE82EE
wheat	245, 222, 179	F5DEB3
white	255, 255, 255	FFFFFF
whitesmoke	245, 245, 245	F5F5F5
yellow	255, 255, 0	FFFF00
yellowgreen	154, 205, 50	9ACD32

INDEX

Hey, you've got enough worries.

Don't let IT training be one of them.

Get on the fast track to IT training at InformIT,
your total Information Technology training network.

 | **www.informit.com** | **SAMS**